FROM ANCIENT ISRAEL TO MODERN JUDAISM

INTELLECT IN QUEST OF UNDERSTANDING

Program in Judaic Studies
Brown University
BROWN JUDAIC STUDIES

Edited by
Jacob Neusner
Wendell S. Dietrich, Ernest S. Frerichs, William Scott Green,
Calvin Goldscheider, David Hirsch, Alan Zuckerman

Project Editors (Projects)

David Blumenthal, Emory University (Approaches to Medieval Judaism)
William Brinner (Studies in Judaism and Islam)
Ernest S. Frerichs, Brown University (Dissertations and Monographs)
Lenn Evan Goodman, University of Hawaii (Studies in Medieval Judaism)
William Scott Green, University of Rochester (Approaches to Ancient Judaism)
Norbert Samuelson, Temple University (Jewish Philosophy)
Jonathan Z. Smith, University of Chicago (Studia Philonica)

Number 173

FROM ANCIENT ISRAEL TO MODERN JUDAISM

Intellect in Quest of Understanding

Edited by
Jacob Neusner
Ernest S. Frerichs
Nahum M. Sarna

FROM ANCIENT ISRAEL TO MODERN JUDAISM

Intellect in Quest of Understanding

Essays in Honor of Marvin Fox

Volume Two

**Judaism in the Formative Age:
Theology and Literature**

**Judaism in the Middle Ages:
The Encounter With Christianity
The Encounter With Scripture
Philosophy and Theology**

Edited by
Jacob Neusner
Ernest S. Frerichs
Nahum M. Sarna

Managing Editor
Joshua Bell

Scholars Press
Atlanta, Georgia

FROM ANCIENT ISRAEL TO MODERN JUDAISM
INTELLECT IN QUEST OF UNDERSTANDING

The editors acknowledge with thanks the support of the
Tisch Family Foundation in the publication of this volume.

Library of Congress Cataloging in Publication Data

From ancient Israel to modern Judaism : intellect in quest of understanding : essays in honor of Marvin Fox / edited by Jacob Neusner, Ernest S. Frerichs, Nahum M. Sarna.
p. cm. -- (Brown Judaic studies ; no. 159, 173-175)
Contents: v. 1. What is at stake in the Judaic quest for understanding. Judaic learning and the locus of education. Ancient Israel. Formative Christianity. Judaism in the formative age: religion -- v. 2. Judaism in the formative age: theology and literature. Judaism in the Middle Ages: the encounter with Christianity, the encounter with Scripture, philosophy, and theology -- v. 3. Judaism in the Middle Ages: philosophers. Hasidism, Messianism in modern times. The modern age: philosophy -- v. 4. The modern age: theology, literature, history.
ISBN 1-55540-341-7 (v. 2 : alk. paper)
1. Judaism--History. 2. Philosophy, Jewish. 3. Fox, Marvin. I. Fox, Marvin. II. Neusner, Jacob, 1932- . III. Frerichs, Ernest S. IV. Sarna, Nahum M. V. Series: Brown Judaic studies ; no. 159, etc.
BM157.F76 1989
296'.09--dc20 89-61111

Printed in the United States of America
on acid-free paper

TABLE OF CONTENTS

Part Six
FORMATIVE JUDAISM: THEOLOGY

Part Seven
FORMATIVE JUDAISM: LITERATURE

Part Eight
JUDAISM IN THE MIDDLE AGES: THE ENCOUNTER WITH CHRISTIANITY

Part Nine
JUDAISM IN THE MIDDLE AGES: THE ENCOUNTER WITH SCRIPTURE

Part Ten
JUDAISM IN THE MIDDLE AGES: PHILOSOPHY AND THEOLOGY

VOLUME ONE

PART ONE:
WHAT IS AT STAKE IN THE JUDAIC QUEST FOR UNDERSTANDING

PART TWO:
JUDAIC LEARNING AND THE LOCUS OF EDUCATION

PART THREE:
ANCIENT ISRAEL AND THE ANCIENT NEAR EAST

PART FOUR:
FORMATIVE CHRISTIANITY

PART FIVE:
FORMATIVE JUDAISM: RELIGION

VOLUME THREE

PART ELEVEN:
JUDAISM IN THE MIDDLE AGES:
PHILOSOPHERS: MAIMONIDES AND HIS HEIRS

PART TWELVE:
JUDAISM IN THE MIDDLE AGES:
PHILOSOPHERS: JUDAH HALEVI

PART THIRTEEN:
HASIDISM. MESSIANISM IN MODERN TIMES

PART FOURTEEN:
THE MODERN AGE: PHILOSOPHY

VOLUME FOUR

PART FIFTEEN:
THE MODERN AGE: THEOLOGY AND IDEOLOGY

PART SIXTEEN:
THE MODERN AGE: LITERATURE

PART SEVENTEEN:
THE MODERN AGE: HISTORY

Preface

In these essays, collected in four volumes, we honor as principal and leader of Judaic Studies in our generation Professor Marvin Fox, Philip W. Lown Professor of Jewish Philosophy and Director of the Lown School of Near Eastern and Judaic Studies at Brandeis University, because in our generation, Professor Fox has occupied the position of *doyen* of Judaic Studies in the academy. This position has come to him through force of character and conscience and is one that expresses the man's moral authority, as much as his acknowledged excellence as scholar and teacher. His scholarship is attested by the bibliography that follows, his teaching by the excellent contributions to this volume of many of his doctoral students. But while in learning and teaching he competes on equal terms with many, in stature and universal respect there is none anywhere in the world of Judaic Studies, at home or in the State of Israel, who compares. It is a simple fact that the scholars who contributed to these volumes, have nothing whatsoever in common save that they concur in expressing esteem for this remarkable colleague. This is a scholars' tribute to a great man; in paying this honor to Marvin Fox, we identify the kind of person we want as our representative and academic avatar. In our generation, this is the sort of scholar we have cherished.

The facts of his career do not account for the honor in which he is held, even though he has pursued, and now pursues, a splendid career in higher education. But the facts do explain something about the man. Professor Marvin Fox received his B.A. in philosophy in 1942 from Northwestern University, the M.A. in the same field in 1946, and the Ph.D. from the University of Chicago in 1950 in that field as well. His education in Judaic texts was certified by rabbinical ordination as Rabbi by the Hebrew Theological College of Chicago in 1942. He taught at Ohio State University from 1948 through 1974, rising from Instructor to Professor of Philosophy. During those years he served also as Visiting Professor of Philosophy at the Hebrew Theological College of Chicago (1955) and also at the Hebrew University of Jerusalem and Bar Ilan

University (1970-1971). In 1974 he came to Brandeis University as Appleman Professor of Jewish Thought, and from 1976 onward he has held the Lown Professorship. From 1975 through 1982 and from 1984 through 1987 he was Chairman of the Department of Near Eastern and Judaic Studies at Brandeis. From 1976 he has also served as Director of the Lown School of Near Eastern and Judaic Studies. In 1980-1981 he was Visiting Scholar in Jewish Philosophy at the Center for Jewish Studies of nearby Harvard University.

He has received numerous academic awards, a selected list of which includes the following: 1956-1957: Elizabeth Clay Howald Post-Doctoral Scholarship; 1962-1963, Fellow of the American Council of Learned Societies; 1975-1978, Director of the Association for Jewish Studies regional conferences, funded by the National Endowment for the Humanities; 1977-1980, Director of the project, "For the Strengthening of Judaic Studies at Brandeis and their Links to the General Humanities," also funded by the National Endowment for the Humanities. From 1979 he has been Fellow of the Academy of Jewish Philosophy; 1980-1981, Senior Faculty Fellow, National Endowment for the Humanities. He has served on the editorial boards of the *AJS Review, Daat, Judaism, Tradition, Journal for the History of Philosophy*, and other journals. He has lectured widely at universities and at national and international academic conferences and served as Member of the National Endowment for the Humanities National Board of Consultants for new programs at colleges and universities. Over the years he has counseled various universities and academic publishers as well.

His ties to institutions of Jewish learning under Jewish sponsorship are strong. He has served on the Advisory Committee of the Jewish Studies Adaptation Program of the International Center for University Teaching of Jewish Civilization (Israel), since 1982; International Planning Committee of the Institute for Contemporary Jewry of the Hebrew University since that same year; member of the governing council of the World Union of Jewish Studies since 1975; secretary, 1971-1972, vice president, from 1973-1975, and then president, from 1975-1978, of the Association for Jewish Studies; and he has been on the board of directors of that organization since 1970. From 1964 through 1968 he served on the Executive Committee of the Conference on Jewish Philosophy; from 1970 to the present on the Executive Committee of the Institute of Judaism and Contemporary Thought of Bar Ilan University; from 1972 as member of the Academic Board of the Melton Research Center of the Jewish Theological Seminary of America; member of the board of directors of the Institute for Jewish Life from 1972 through 1975; member of the board of directors of the Library of Living

Philosophers, from 1948; Associate of the Columbia University Seminar on Israel and Jewish Studies from 1968 through 1974; and many other organizations.

His committee service at Brandeis University has covered these committees: Graduate School Council; Philosophy Department Advisory Committee and Reappointment and Promotions Committee; University Tenure Panels; Academic Planning Committee (Chairman, 1982-1984); Faculty Committee for the Hiatt Institute; Tauber Institute Faculty Advisory Committee and its academic policy subcommittee; Committee on University Studies in the Humanities; Faculty representative on the Brandeis University Board of Trustees (1978-1980). His professional memberships include the American Philosophical Association, the Metaphysical Society of America, the Medieval Academy of America, as well as the Association for Jewish Studies, Conference on Jewish Philosophy, and American Academy for Jewish Research.

The editors of this volume bear special ties of collegiality and friendship with Professor Fox. In this project Professor Sarna represents Brandeis University and also has been a close and intimate colleague and friend for many years. Professors Frerichs and Neusner have called upon Professor Fox for counsel in the fifteen years since Professor Fox came to Brandeis University. And Professor Fox has responded, always giving his best judgment and his wisest counsel. Professor Fox has been a good neighbor, a constant counsellor, and valued friend. In the sequence of eight academic conferences, run annually at Brown University in the 1970s, Professor Fox played a leading role in the planning of the programs and in scholarly interchange. Through him and the editors of this volume Brown and Brandeis Universities held a conference at which graduate students in the respective graduate programs met and engaged in shared discussion of common interests. Professor Fox moreover has taken a position on numerous dissertation committees in Brown's graduate program in the History of Judaism. His conscientious and careful reading of these dissertations give to the students the benefit not only of his learning but also of his distinct and rich perspective on the problem of the dissertation. Consequently, among the many other universities besides Ohio State and Brandeis at which Professor Fox has made his contribution, Brown University stands out as particularly indebted to him for wisdom and learning.

The editors express their thanks to President Evelyn Handler of Brandeis University for sponsoring the public event at which the contributors to these volumes presented the books to Professor Fox and enjoyed the opportunity of expressing in person their esteem and affection for him; and to the Max Richter Foundation of Rhode Island

and the Program in Judaic Studies at Brown University for financial and other support in organizing and carrying out this project. Mr. Joshua Bell, Verbatim, of Providence, Rhode Island, produced the camera ready copy with the usual attention to aesthetic excellence and also accuracy of detail that have characterized all of his work for Brown Judaic Studies, Brown Studies in Jews and their Societies, Brown Studies in Religion (Scholars Press), and also Studies in Judaism (University Press of America). The staff of Scholars Press, particularly Dr. Dennis Ford, gave to this project their conscientious attention. Professors Frerichs and Neusner therefore express thanks to Verbatim, Scholars Press, and University Press of America, which in the past ten years have made Brown University's Judaic Studies Program the world's largest publisher of scholarly books and monographs in the field of Judaic Studies. All three editors thank the contributors to these volumes for their willingness to collaborate in what we believe is an important tribute to greatness in our field and in our time.

Jacob Neusner
Ernest S. Frerichs
Program in Judaic Studies
Brown University
Providence, Rhode Island

Nahum M. Sarna
Department of Near Eastern
and Judaic Studies
Brandeis University
Waltham, Massachusetts

Bibliography of Marvin Fox 1946-1989

1. "Three Approaches to the Jewish Problem," *Antioch Review*, 6(1), Spring 1946, pp. 54-68.

2. "Towards a Life of Joy: A Theological Critique," *Menorah Journal*, 36(2), Spring 1948, pp. 248-251.

3. "On Calling Women to the Reading of the Torah," *The Reconstructionist*, 13(19), January 1948. An exchange of letters with Robert Gordis. For Gordis' reply see *idem.*, 14(7), May 1948.

4. *Kant's Fundamental Principles of the Metaphysic of Morals*, edited with an introduction (Liberal Arts Press, 1949). Reprinted in numerous editions by the original publisher, then acquired by Bobbs-Merrill, and most recently by Macmillan.

5. Review of Chaim Weizmann, *Trial and Error*, in *Heritage*, Spring 1949, pp. 16-18.

6. Review of Morris R. Cohen, *Reason and Law*, in *Illinois Law Review*, 45(2), May 1950, pp. 305 -307.

7. *Moral Fact and Moral Theory: A Study of Some Methodological Problems in Contemporary Ethics*. Unpublished doctoral dissertation, University of Chicago, 1950.

8. Review of John A. Nicholson, *Philosophy of Religion*, in *Philosophy and Phenomenological Research*, 11(3), March 1951.

9. Review of Maxwell Silver, *The Way to God*, in *Philosophy and Phenomenological Research*, 11(4), June 1951.

10. "On the Diversity of Methods in Dewey's Ethical Theory," *Philosophy and Phenomenological Research*, 12(1), September 1951.

11. Review of Abraham Joshua Heschel, *Man is Not Alone*, in *Commentary*, 12(2), August 1951, pp. 193-195.

12. "Kierkegaard and Rabbinic Judaism," *Judaism*, 2(2), April 1953, pp. 160-169.

13. "Day Schools and the American Educational Pattern," *The Jewish Parent,* September 1953.
14. Review of J. Guttmann, *Maimonides' Guide of the Perplexed,* in *Judaism,* 2(4), October 1953, pp. 363-367.
15. "Moral Facts and Moral Theory," in *Perspectives* (Ohio State University Press, 1953), pp. 111-127.
16. Review of Martin Buber, *At the Turning, New Mexico Quarterly,* 24(2), Summer 1954, pp. 217-220.
17. "What Can the Modern Jew Believe?" Alfred Jospe, ed., *Judaism for the Modern Age* (B'nai B'rith Hillel Foundations, 1955).
18. "Our Missing Intellectuals: Another View," *National Jewish Monthly,* December 1954, pp. 10-13.
19. Review of Abraham Cronbach, *Judaism for Today,* in *Judaism,* 4(1), Winter 1955, pp. 82-84.
20. "Amicus Jacobus, sed Magis Amica Veritas," *Conservative Judaism,* 10(3), Spring 1956, pp. 9-17.
21. "The Trials of Socrates: An Analysis of the First Tetralogy," *Archiv fuer Philosophie,* 6(3/4), 1956, pp. 226-261.
22. "What's Wrong – and Right – with Deweyism," *The Jewish Parent,* December 1956.
23. Review of Abraham Joshua Heschel, *God in Search of Man: A Philosophy of Judaism,* in *Judaism,* 6(1), Winter 1957, pp. 77-81.
24. "Can Modern Man Believe in God," in Alfred Jospe, ed., *The Jewish Heritage and the Jewish Student* (New York, 1959), pp. 40-50.
25. "Who is Competent to Teach Religion," *Religious Education,* 54(2), March-April 1959, pp. 112-114.
26. "Torah Jews in the Making," *The Jewish Parent,* April 1960, pp. 4-5, 22.
27. "Heschel, Intuition, and the Halakhah," *Tradition,* 3(1), Fall 1960, pp. 5-15.
28. "Tillich's Ontology and God," *Anglican Theological Review,* 43(3), July 1961, pp. 260-267.
29. "Ve-al ha-Medinot Bo Ye'amer," *Panim el Panim,* No. 124-125, September 10, 1961, pp. 18-19. A symposium with Professor Salo Baron.
30. Review of Samuel Dresner, *The Zaddik,* in *Conservative Judaism,* 15(4), Summer 1961, pp. 39-42.
31. Review of Robert Gordis, *A Faith for Moderns,* in *Commentary,* 32(4), October 1961.

32. "Modern Faith," *Commentary,* 33(2), February 1962. An exchange of letters with Robert Gordis.

33. Review of Jakob Petuchowski, *Ever Since Sinai, Judaism,* 10(4), Fall 1961.

34. Review of Harry A. Wolfson, *Religious Philosophy: A Group of Essays,* in *The Classical Journal,* 58(2), November 1962.

35. "Einige Probleme in Buber's Moralphilosophie," in Paul A. Schilpp and Maurice Friedman, eds., *Philosophen des 20. Jahrhunderts: Martin Buber* (Kohlhammer, 1963), pp. 135-152. German translation of # 47.

36. "Theistic Bases of Ethics," in Robert Bartels, ed., *Ethics in Business* (Ohio State University Press, 1963).

37. Reviews of Joseph Blau, *The Story of Jewish Philosophy,* and Gerald Abrahams, *The Jewish Mind,* in *Commentary* , 35(1), January 1963.

38. Review of Arthur A. Cohen, *The Natural and the Super-Natural Jew,* in *Commentary,* 35(4), April 1963.

39. Review of Ephraim Shmueli, *Bein Emunah Likfirah,* in *Commentary,* 36(2), August 1963.

40. "Religion and Human Nature in the Philosophy of David Hume," in William L. Reese and Eugene Freeman, eds., *Process and Divinity: Philosophical Essays Presented to Charles Hartshorne* (Open Court, 1964), pp. 561-577.

41. "Character Training and Environmental Pressures," in *The Jewish Parent,* October 1964.

42. Review of W. Gunther Plaut, *The Rise of Reform Judaism,* in *Commentary,* 37(6), June 1964.

43. Review of Max Kadushin, *Worship and Ethics,* in *Commentary,* 38(6), December 1964.

44. Review of Israel Efros, *Ancient Jewish Philosophy,* in *Commentary,* 40(1), July 1965.

45. "Religion and the Public Schools – A Philosopher's Analysis," in *Theory into Practice,* 4(1), February 1965, pp. 40-44.

46. Review Essay on *Maimonides" Guide to the Perplexed,* Shlomo Pines, tr., with introductory essays by Leo Strauss and Shlomo Pines, in *Journal of the History of Philosophy,* 3(2), October 1965, pp. 265-274.

47. "Some Problems in Buber's Moral Philosophy," in Paul A. Schilpp and Maurice Friedman, eds., *The Philosophy of Martin Buber* (Open Court, 1966), pp. 151-170.

48. "The Case for the Jewish Day School," in Judah Pilch and Meir Ben-Horin, eds., *Judaism and the Jewish School* (New York, 1966), pp. 207-213.

49. "The State of Jewish Belief: A Symposium," *Commentary,* 42(2), August 1966, pp. 89-92.

50. "Heschel's Theology of Man," *Tradition,* 8(3), Fall 1966, pp. 79-84.

51. "Jewish Education in a Pluralistic Community," *Proceedings of the Rabbinical Assembly of America,* 30, 1966, pp. 31-40, 47-51.

52. Review of Arnold Jacob Wolf, ed., *Rediscovering Judaism: Reflections on a New Theology, Commentary,* 41(2), February 1966.

53. "Sakkanah Lishelemutah shel ha-Yahadut," *Hadoar,* 47(38), October 1967.

54. Chapter in *The State of Jewish Belief* (Macmillan, 1967), pp. 59-69. Reprint of #49.

55. "Heschel, Intuition, and the Halakhah," in Norman Lamm and Walter S. Wurzburger, eds., *A Treasury of Tradition* (New York, 1967), pp. 426-435. Reprint of #27.

56. Review of *Harry Austryn Wolfson Jubilee Volumes,* in *Judaism,* 16(4), Fall 1967.

57. "Prolegomenon" to A. Cohen, *The Teachings of Maimonides* (New York, 1968), pp. xv-xliv.

58. "The Meaning of Theology Today," *Bulletin of the Central Ohio Academy of Theology,* January 1968.

59. Review Article on Sidney Hook, in *Religion in a Free Society, The Journal of Value Inquiry,* 2(4), Winter 1968, pp. 308-314.

60. "The Function of Religion," *Congress Bi-Weekly,* 36(3), February 1969, pp. 56-63.

61. "La Teologia Dell'uomo Nel Pensiero di Abraham J. Heschel," *La Rassegna Mensile di Israel,* 25(4), April 1969. Italian translation of #50.

62. Review of Zvi Adar, *Humanistic Values in the Bible,* in *Commentary* 47(1), January 1969.

63. Review of Richard L. Rubenstein, *After Auschwitz* and *The Religious Imagination,* in *Commentary,* 47(6), June 1969.

64. "Religion and the Public Schools," Kaoru Jamamotie, ed., *Teaching* (Houghton Mifflin, 1969), pp. 239-248. Reprint of #45.

65. "The 'Commentary' Problem," *Judaism,* 18(1), Winter 1969, pp. 108-110.

66. Review of Nathan Rotenstreich, *Jewish Philosophy in Modern Times,* in *Commentary,* 49(5), May 1970.

67. "Naturalism, Rationalism and Jewish Faith," *Tradition,* 11(3), Fall 1970, pp. 90-96.

68. "Day Schools and the American Educational Pattern," in Joseph Kaminetsky, ed., *Hebrew Day School Education: An Overview* (New York, 1970). Reprint of #13.

69. "Day Schools and the American Educational Pattern," in Lloyd P. Gartner, ed., *Jewish Education in the United States* (Teachers College, Columbia University Press, 1970), Classics in Education Series, No. 41. Reprint of #13.

70. "Continuity and Change in Jewish Theology," *Niv Hamidrashia,* Spring-Summer 1971, pp. 15-23.

71. Review of Mendell Lewittes, *The Light of Redemption,* in *The Jerusalem Post Magazine,* April 9, 1971.

72. "Moral Facts and Moral Theory," in Julius Weinberg and Keith Yandell, eds., *Problems in Philosophical Inquiry* (Holt Rinehart Winston, 1971), pp. 368-381. Reprint of #15.

73. "Freedom and Freedom of Thought," *Encyclopaedia Judaica,* Vol. 7, 119-121.

74. "God, Conceptions of," *Encyclopaedia Judaica,* Vol. 7, 670-673.

75. "God in Medieval Jewish Philosophy," *Encyclopaedia Judaica,* Vol. 7, 658-661.

76. "God in Modern Jewish Philosophy, " *Encyclopaedia Judaica,* Vol. 7, 662-664.

77. "God, Names of in Medieval Jewish Philosophy," *Encyclopaedia Judaica,* Vol. 7, 684-685.

78. "God, Names of in Modern Jewish Philosophy, *Encyclopaedia Judaica,* Vol. 7. 685.

79. "Maimonides and Aquinas on Natural Law," *Dine Israel: An Annual of Jewish Law, Tel-Aviv University,* Vol. 3, 1972, pp. 5-36.

80. "Kierkegaard and Rabbinic Judaism," in Robert Gordis and Ruth B. Waxman, eds., *Faith and Reason* (New York, 1972), pp. 115-124. Reprint of #12.

81. "Tillich's Ontology and God," in Keith Yandell, *God, Man and Religion* (McGraw-Hill, 1972). Reprint of #28.

82. Review of Nathan Rotenstreich, *Tradition and Reality,* in *Commentary,* 55(2), February 1973.

83. "Philosophy and Contemporary Jewish Studies," *American Jewish Historical Quarterly,* 53(4), June 1974, pp. 350-355.

84. "Berkovits on the Problem of Evil," *Tradition,* 14(3), Spring 1974, pp. 116-124.

85. "God in Modern Jewish Philosophy," *Jewish Values* (Keter, Jerusalem, 1974). Reprinted from #76.

86. "Conceptions of God," *Jewish Values* (Keter, Jerusalem, 1974). Reprinted from #74.

87. "The Future of Hillel from the Perspective of the University," in Alfred Jospe, ed., *The Test of Time* (Washington, 1974).

88. "Philosophy and Contemporary Jewish Studies," in Moshe Davis, ed., *Contemporary Jewish Civilization on the American Campus* (Jerusalem, 1974). Reprinted from # 83.

89. *Modern Jewish Ethics: Theory and Practice* (Ohio State University Press, 1975). Edited with introduction.

90. "Judaism, Secularism and Textual Interpretation," in M. Fox, ed., *Modern Jewish Ethics: Theory and Practice,* pp. 3-26.

91. "On the Rational Commandments in Saadia: A Re-examination," in M. Fox, ed., *Modern Jewish Ethics: Theory and Practice,* pp. 174-187.

92. "Philosophy and Religious Values in Modern Jewish Thought," in Jacob Katz, ed., *The Role of Religion in Modern Jewish History* (AJS, 1975), pp. 69-86.

93. Review of *The Code of Maimonides: Book IV, The Book of Women,* in *Journal of the American Academy of Religion,* March 1975.

94. "Maimonides and Aquinas on Natural Law," in Jacob I. Dienstag, ed., *Studies in Maimonides and St. Thomas Aquinas* (New York, 1975), pp. 75-106. Reprint of #79.

95. "Law and Ethics in Modern Jewish Philosophy: The Case of Moses Mendelssohn," *Proceedings of the American Academy for Jewish Research,* Vol. 43, 1976, pp. 1-13.

96. "Translating Jewish Thought into Curriculum," in Seymour Fox and Geraldine Rosenfeld, eds., *From the Scholar to the Classroom* (Jewish Theological Seminary, 1977), pp. 59-85.

97. Discussion on the "Centrality of Israel in the World Jewish Community," in Moshe Davis, ed., *World Jewry and the State of Israel* (New York, 1977).

98. "On the Rational Commandments in Saadia's Philosophy," *Proceedings of the Sixth World Congress of Jewish Studies,* Vol. 3 (Jerusalem, 1977), pp. 34-43. Slight revision of #91.

99. "Ha-Tefillah be-Mishnato shel ha-Rambam," in Gabriel Cohn, ed., *Ha-Tefillah Ha-Yehudit* (Jerusalem, 1978). pp. 142-167.

100. Review of Louis Jacobs, *Theology in the Responsa, AJS Newsletter,* No. 22, March 1978.

101. Review of Frank Talmage, *David Kimhi: The Man and his Commentaries, Speculum,* 53(3), July 1978.

102. "The Doctrine of the Mean in Aristotle and Maimonides: A Comparative Study," in S. Stern and R. Loewe, eds., *Studies in Jewish Intellectual and Religious History. Presented to Alexander Altmann* (Alabama, 1979), pp. 43-70.

103. Foreword to Abraham Chill, *The Minhagim* (New York, 1979).

104. *The Philosophical Foundations of Jewish Ethics: Some Initial Reflections.* The Second Annual Rabbi Louis Feinberg Memorial Lecture in Judaic Studies at the University of Cincinnati, 1979, pp. 1-24.

105. "Reflections on the Foundations of Jewish Ethics and their Relation to Public Policy," in Joseph L. Allen, ed., *The Society of Christian Ethics, 1980 Selected Papers* (Dallas, 1980), pp. 23-62. An expansion of #104.

106. Introduction to the *Collected Papers of Rabbi Harry Kaplan* (Columbus, 1980).

107. Review of Jacob Neusner, *A History of the Mishnaic Law of Women,* 5 Vols., in AJS Newsletter, No. 29, 1981.

108. "Human Suffering and Religious Faith: A Jewish Response to the Holocaust," *Questions of Jewish Survival* (University of Denver, 1980), pp. 8-22.

109. "The Role of Philosophy in Jewish Studies," in Raphael Jospe and Samuel Z. Fishman, eds., *Go and Study: Essays and Studies in Honor of Alfred Jospe* (Washington, D.C., 1980). pp. 125-142.

110. "Conservative Tendencies in the Halakhah," *Judaism,* 29(1), Winter 1980, pp. 12-18.

111. Review of Isadore Twersky, *Introduction to the Code of Maimonides, AJS Newsletter,* No. 31, 1982.

112. "The Moral Philosophy of MaHaRaL," in Bernard Cooperman, ed., *Jewish Thought in the Sixteenth Century* (Cambridge, 1983), pp. 167-185.

113. Review of Michael Wyschogrod, *The Body of Faith: Judaism as Corporeal Election,* in *The Journal of Religion,* 67(1), January 1987.

114. "Change is Not Modern in Jewish Law," *Sh'ma,* 13/257, September 16, 1983.

115. "Graduate Education in Jewish Philosophy," in Jacob Neusner, ed., *New Humanities and Academic Disciplines: The Case of Jewish Studies* (University of Wisconsin Press, 1984), pp. 121-134.

116. "Some Reflections on Jewish Studies in American Universities," *Judaism,* 35(2), Spring 1986, pp. 140-146.

117. "The Holiness of the Holy Land," Jonathan Sacks, ed., *Tradition and Transition: Essays Presented to Chief Rabbi Sir Immanuel Jakobovits* (London, 1986), pp. 155-170.

118. "The Jewish Educator: The Ideology of the Profession in Jewish Tradition and its Contemporary Meaning," in Joseph Reimer, ed., *To Build a Profession: Careers in Jewish Education* (Waltham, 1987).

119. "A New View of Maimonides' Method of Contradictions," in Moshe Hallamish, ed., *Bar-Ilan: Annual of Bar-Ilan University Studies in Judaica and the Humanities: Moshe Schwarcz Memorial Volume,* 22-23 (Ramat-Gan, 1987), pp. 19-43.

120. "Law and Morality in the Thought of Maimonides," in Nahum Rakover, ed., *Maimonides as Codifier of Jewish Law* (Jerusalem, 1987), pp. 105-120.

121. "Maimonides on the Foundations of Morality," *Proceedings of the Institute for Distinguished Community Leaders* (Brandeis University, 1987), pp. 15-19.

122. Foreword to Morris Weitz, *Theories of Concepts* (London & New York, 1988) pp. vii-xi.

123. "The Doctrine of the Mean in Aristotle and Maimonides: A Comparative Study," in Joseph A. Buijs, ed., *Maimonides: A Collection of Critical Essays* (University of Notre Dame Press, 1988), pp. 234-263. Reprint of #102.

124. "Nahmanides on the Status of Aggadot: Perspectives on the Disputation at Barcelona, 1263," *Journal of Jewish Studies,* 40(1), Spring 1989.

125. "The Holiness of the Holy Land," in Shubert Spero, ed., *Studies in Religious Zionism* (Jerusalem, 1989). Reprint of #117.

126. *Interpreting Maimonides: Studies in Methodology, Metaphysics and Moral Philosophy* (Jewish Publication Society, 1989).

127. "The Unity and Structure of Rav Joseph B. Soloveitchik's Thought," *Tradition,* 24(3), Fall 1989.

128. "Rav Kook: Neither Philosopher nor Kabbalist," in David Shatz and Lawrence Kaplan, eds., *Studies in the Thought of Rav Kook* (New York, 1989).

Part Six
FORMATIVE JUDAISM: THEOLOGY

16

Judaism in Crisis? Institutions and Systematic Theology in Rabbinism

Roger Brooks
University of Notre Dame

The rabbinic movement seems to grow younger and younger with each new scholarly treatment of Judaism. The academy skeptically regards the historical veracity of miraculous accounts, the accuracy of names and dates provided by rabbinic literature, and the status of rabbinic teaching as revealed truth. Each bit of scholarly incredulity in turn has eroded a portion of the reconstruction of Jewish history that was standard one century ago, and so has led to Judaism itself being a more and more recent phenomenon.

So it is that the scholars of the *Wissenschaft des Judentums* movement emphasized the human role in creating rabbinic literature,[1] and decisively laid to rest the traditional notion – propounded first in the Mishnah Tractate Avot, then in virtually all rabbinic literature – that the content of Rabbinism hailed from Sinaitic revelation. In parallel work regarding the Hebrew Bible and the history of ancient Israel, Julius Wellhausen placed the definitive moment at the end of Israelite development – during the centuries after the return from Babylonian exile – at which time were formed attitudes toward law

[1]See for example Leopold Zunz, "Etwas über die rabbinischen Literatur," in *Gesammelte Schriften. Herausgegeben vom Curatorium der "Zunzstiftung"* (Hildesheim and New York: Georg Olms Verlag, 1976), pp. 1-31, which calls for application of scientific methods of study so as to uncover the valuable contributions to humanity made by the authors of rabbinic literature, both early and late.

and meticulous praxis that characterized his "*Spätjudentum*" and the rabbinic movement.[2] Or, in a more sympathetic treatment of Judaism's development, as found in traditional Jewish scholars' accounts, some might have portrayed the late-first century B.C.E. Pharisees Hillel and Shammai as two great legal innovators who revised and handed on older legal materials.[3]

Twentieth century work in our field has set the formulation of the Mishnah (compiled in the first two centuries of the Common Era) as the crucial moment in Jewish history.[4] According to this view, represented at least partially by Moore and Urbach, Rabbi Judah the Patriarch responded to the gradual loss of tradition and learning by putting into written form previously oral materials to be preserved for posterity. Jacob Neusner has sketched a different scenario, in which Judah the Patriarch responded to the destruction of the Temple in 70 C.E. and the Jews' defeat at the hands of Rome in 135 by editing and formulating the Mishnah as the first document of the rabbinic corpus. And in his recent studies, Neusner has shown how the fourth century encounter with nascent Christianity in fact gave the impetus for construction of the fully-articulated system that we call Judaism (that is *rabbinic* Judaism).[5]

So the rabbinic movement becomes younger and younger – first Sinaitic (*ca.* 1400-1250 B.C.E.), then post-exilic (*ca.* 450 B.C.E.), then early Pharisaic (*ca.* 50 B.C.E.-50 C.E.), then Ushan (*ca.* 185-200 C.E.), and finally Talmudic (*ca.* 450 C.E.). Each shift has been accompanied by

---

[2]Julius Wellhausen, *Prolegomenon to the History of Ancient Israel,* Preface by W. Robertson Smith (Gloucester, MA: Peter Smith Publishers, 1973; originally published, 1882).

[3]See for example Naḥum Norbert Glatzer, *Hillel the Elder,* Revised Edition (New York: Schocken Books, 1966); or Adolf Buchler, *Types of Jewish-Palestinian Piety from 70 B.C.E. to 70 C.E. The Ancient Pious Men* (New York: KTAV Publishers, 1968; originally published, 1922).

[4]See G.F. Moore, *Judaism in the First Centuries of the Christian Era* (Cambridge: Harvard University Press, 1927-30); Ephraim Elimelech Urbach, *The Sages: Their Concepts and Beliefs,* second English edition (Jerusalem: Magnes Press, 1979); Jacob Naḥum Epstein, *Introduction to Tannaitic Literature. Mishnah, Tosefta, and Halakhic Midrashim,* Edited by Ezra Tzion Melamed (Jerusalem: Magnes Press, 1957).

[5]See Jacob Neusner, *Judaism: The Evidence of the Mishnah* (Chicago: University of Chicago Press, 1981), pp. 25-28, 119-121, 281-283; and *Judaism in Society: The Evidence of the Yerushalmi* (Chicago: University of Chicago Press, 1983), pp. 16-17. See also Gilles Quispel, "Review of Gedaliahu A. G. Stroumsa, *Another Seed: Studies in Gnostic Mythology,*" in *Vigiliae Christianae* 40 (1986), pp. 96-101, and "Anthropos and Sophia," delivered in 1986 at the University of Notre Dame, for the claim that Judaism as we know it arose after, and, at least partially, in response to the development of Christianity.

a perduring question: "Why does the movement that results in Judaism as we think of it happen at just this time?" And scholars across a wide range of interests answer in a more or less uniform voice: "A crisis in the Jewish world prompted great leaders to create – or at least to revitalize – Judaism, so as to cope with pressures from inside or out."

A Typology of Crisis

Traditional rabbinic accounts present this as a *crisis of ignorance*.[6] The Jews, so the story goes, had received the substance of rabbinic Judaism in oral form at Sinai. The rules that we consider to be of rabbinic origin in fact guided the life of Jews throughout their entire history, from the biblical period onward. But near the end of the second century C.E., people became forgetful. And rather than see the treasury of Jewish values and practices lost to Judaism forever, Judah the Patriarch embarked on a plan to write down the oral law. So out of a crisis of ignorance and forgetfulness, rabbinic literature as we know it was born.

Recent scholars have taken a decidedly more skeptical view of this account. In place of a revealed truth simply coming to literary expression, we find sophisticated accounts of Judaism in crisis, based upon considerations of historical, political, economic, and social factors.

Daniel Sperber has shown the role of a *crisis of economy* in the formulation of portions of the rabbinic legal corpus.[7] Rabbinic legislation attempted to cope with the rising inflation, declining crop yields, increasing taxation, and the overall Greco-Roman depression of the third and fourth centuries. The rabbis promulgated laws that might lead the Jewish people in the face of this crisis. They sought to soften its impact, and reflect the various options that lay before their constituency.

The seminal work of Jacob Neusner assigns the critical position to a *crisis of history and theology*.[8] He employs a tripartite historical framework reminiscent of the Hegelian dialectic to understand the creation of the early rabbinic movement. Both the Mishnah and the Talmud of the Land of Israel were formulated and redacted at the end

---

[6]See Benjamin Menasseh Lewin, ed., *Iggeret Rav Sherirah Gaon in der französchen und spanischen Version* (Haifa, 1921), pp. 4-35.

[7]See Daniel Sperber, *Roman Palestine: 200-400. I. Money and Prices* (Ramat Gan: Bar Ilan University Press, 1974); *II. The Land: Crisis and Change in Agrarian Society as Reflected in Rabbinic Sources* (Ramat Gan: Bar Ilan University Press, 1978).

[8]Neusner's own formulation of these crises is found, e.g., in Neusner, *Judaism in Society*, pp. 19-25.

of a three-stage process of (1) Messianic hope, (2) disappointment, and (3) the production of a holy book. The Messianic hope constituted the *Thesis*: Return to Judaic life centered around Jerusalem and the Temple cult, in its regularity and ordered daily schedule, to be brought about either by Bar Kokhba (*ca.* 132 C.E.) or by Julian the Righteous (*ca.* 363 C.E.). The *Antithesis* is found in bitter defeats, which saw the failure of the Messianic Bar Kokhba Revolt against Roman domination (*ca.* 135 C.E.), or the suspension of plans to rebuild the Temple following the earthquake in Julian's reign (*ca.* 362 C.E.). Finally, the Mishnah (*ca.* 200 C.E.) and the Talmud of the Land of Israel (*ca.* 450 C.E.) represent the *Synthesis* created by rabbis in response to these two crises.

So the formation of the rabbinic movement – that is, the formation of Judaism in the mode we know it – is thought to result from crises between 200 and 450 C.E. The great events of history – whether war and destruction, economic depression, or religious decline – were successfully repressed by the formation of books and law codes determined to lead Jews to a holier and better way of life.

But we must note that the literature created as a response to these crises itself remains nearly silent about them. The Mishnah mentions Rome only a few times; its utopian depiction of a world perfectly ordered around the Temple, Sanhedrin, and rabbinic authorities simply had no place for the Empire and its meddling officials. And the closing of the Mishnah as a literary piece heralded not radical discontinuity with all that followed, but great continuity as Judaism moved from one period to another. *The crisis of the first century? It had little literary impact.*

What about all those sources from the Talmud of the Land of Israel that Sperber uses to document declining crop yields and monetary values? These occur primarily in contexts intended to say quite other things about entirely other issues.[9] Of concern to the Talmud's formulators seemed to be not so much reflection *of* reality – one measure of wheat does not return as much flour as it used to – but reflection *upon* reality, at least as faced by the Israelites – the decreased fecundity of the Land of Israel stems from the Jews' sinfulness, just as was the case for the earlier destruction of the Temple. *The economic crisis of the fourth century? It had little literary impact.*

---

[9]Cf. Y. Peah 7:1-3, a text that Sperber mines for information about crop yields, but which has its own point to make about the Land's miraculous fertility while the Temple stood. See Roger Brooks, *The Talmud of the Land of Israel. A Preliminary Translation and Explanation. Volume 2. Tractate Peah* (Chicago: University of Chicago Press, forthcoming 1990), Introduction and *ad loc.* Compare Sperber, *Roman Palestine. II*, pp. 16-24.

Now I do not wish to imply that there were no crises facing the nascent rabbinic movement. Surely there were crises of many kinds. Combining rabbinic and pagan sources, Sperber shows a land, economy, and society in trouble through years of Roman crisis under the Severan Emperors up to 285. More convincingly, Neusner, working out of the framework of a few critical and well established facts, shows the theological crises surrounding the failure of Bar Kokhba's Revolt and of Julian's attempt to rebuild the Temple in the face of the Christianization of the Empire.

But if "crisis" is a *necessary* category, it is not *sufficient* for study and explanation of the early rabbinic movement. We find too little information in our sources, not enough self-conscious reflection, and too many arguments from silence. If we couple all of this with other possible readings of the historical situation, according to which the Jews and Judaism *flourished* during this period, the result is that the crises do not tell the whole story.

Stability and Latent History

Given sources that speak so rarely of events and crisis, and given times in which the critical events are not year-by-year political successions or even decade-by-decade happenings, but rather few and far between (note that 70, 135, 285, and 335 C.E. are the crucial dates), we must look for an additional interpretive crux. One way forward is to eschew narrative frameworks built upon the acts of a few famous leaders and the great events in which they were the major actors.

Instead I propose to look more toward the latent history of Jewish culture and society during the period from 200 to 400 C.E.[10] In particular, I want to ask how a few crucial institutions of corporate Jewish life fared during this broad period of supposed crisis. In so doing, I hope to gain the vantage point of

> one of the most important developments in current historiography,...[namely] the emerging integration of latent and manifest events....The resulting conflation is beginning to produce the outline of a general history different from what we have known before. Major public events will, of course, remain in their key locations, but when

---

[10]See Bernard Bailyn, "The Challenge of Modern Historiography," in *American Historical Review*, 87:1 (1982), esp. pp. 9-10, who coins the term "latent history" to refer to the study of "events that contemporaries were not fully aware of, at times were not aware of at all, events that they did not consciously struggle over, however much they might have been forced to grapple with their consequences."

seen in connection with the clarifying latent landscape, they appear to occupy different positions than heretofore.[11]

As we shall see, several key institutions of Jewish life exhibit a rather evolutionary development during the period at hand, not a discontinuous or halting progression. It follows that economic and theological crises hardly repressed Jewish life *in the long run*. Rather, rabbinic leaders adopted a conservative response to such crises, strengthening and reformulating already established structures of society. The networks and institutions they fortified provided shelter against any onslaught from the outside, and prepared Judaism for the long life it has led from their day to ours.

Four aspects of Jewish life under Roman rule form the core of this investigation. These constitute some (by no means all) of the institutions that guided the formative rabbinic movement. They are the Patriarchate, the Academy, the Synagogue, and the intellectual and theological agenda of the rabbinic world as exhibited in Mishnaic and Talmudic literature.

Institutions: the Patriarchate

During the rabbinic era, the provincial Roman government appointed (or issued its approval of) a Patriarch who would serve as local leader of the Jewish people in Syria-Palestina. This Roman political office initially was concentrated within a single family, that of Rabban Gamaliel II, which ruled with a more or less dynastic character.[12] Of course, the Patriarch also was Rome's local representative, who, despite the fact that he wielded some independent power, was nonetheless a sign of Roman dominance over the Jews. The Roman-backed Patriarchate endured until the mid-fifth century as one of the foundational institutions of rabbinic society.

In order to understand this institution we need to see beyond the Romans' first recognition of a Patriarch, shortly after 70 C.E.[13] Rather, the Patriarchate exhibits continuity with, and stands at the end of, a chain of earlier officials and leaders of the Jewish community, most of whom served under the approval of foreign rulers. So pervasive was

---

[11]Bailyn, "Modern Historiography," p. 11.

[12]See M. Ed. 7:7, which describes Rabban Gamaliel as an ambassador consulting with governmental authorities in Syria regarding changes in the calendar. His son Simeon III served as Patriarch from 135 and his grandson, Judah the Patriarch, served at the time of the Mishnah's redaction, ca. 200.

[13]Some would place this recognition after the abolition of Hadrian's decree under the reign of Antonius Pius in 150 C.E. Cf. Shaye J.D. Cohen, *From the Maccabees to the Mishnah* (Library of Early Christianity; Philadelphia: Westminster Press, 1987), p. 108.

the figure of a self-governing Jewish leader that entire histories of Judaism in antiquity can be forged around the transfer of power from one such leader to another.[14] Such studies trace power over Palestine from High Priests in rough relationship to Ptolemaic (300-200 B.C.E.) or Seleucid (200-135) rulers, to the independent Hasmonean dynasty (135-63), with its own priestly family. After the creation of the Roman province of Syria-Palestina in 63 B.C.E., power was centralized in King Herod (37-4) and increasingly under Roman procurators and provincial governors (6-66 C.E.).[15] During this age, the *Nasi*, or head of the rabbinic Sanhedrin, emerged as some fashion of social leader. The Roman officials recognized that rabbinic leadership, and their recognition marked the inception of the official Patriarchate (from between 70 and 150, to *ca.* 430). At the same time, an independent anti-Roman leader, Bar Kokhba, also claimed the title of *Nasi* (132-135).

A political history that traces such transfers of power tends to focus on manifest events – the two wars against Rome, for example – and individual leaders, whether High Priest, *Nasi*, or Patriarch. But the overall organization of a Palestinian political history along such lines shows some of the continuity, if not genetic connections, in local leadership (imposed or recognized by the ruling empire).

So when the Roman-appointed Patriarch emerged on the scene after the destruction of the Temple in 70 C.E., he did not represent an altogether new institution, but inherited his function from some of these earlier models, even while adding nuance.[16] Non-Jewish sources bear out the notion that soon after imposition of direct Roman rule over the province of Syria-Palestina in 6 C.E. the Romans probably would have established something akin to this office. The Patriarchate represented the common Roman practice of utilizing a conquered people's own pre-existing leaders to institute some level of rule.[17]

By the third and fourth centuries, the Patriarch seems to have acquired a great deal of power. Robert Wilken shows imperial references to the Patriarch as *vir clarissimus et illustris*, a title usually

---

[14]See, e.g., the structure of Peter Schäfer, *Geschichte der Juden in der Antike. Die juden Palästinas von Alexander dem Großen bis zur arabischen Eroberung* (Stuttgart: Katholisches Bibelwerk, Neukirchener Verlag, 1983), pp. 7-9.

[15]See Fergus Millar, *The Emperor in the Roman World. 31 B.C. to A.D. 337* (Ithica, NY: Cornell University Press, 1977), pp. 376-7.

[16]See Hugo Mantel, *Studies in the History of the Sanhedrin* (Cambridge, Mass.: Harvard University Press, 1961), pp. 1-53, 175-253. And compare Cohen, *Maccabees to Mishnah*, p. 108.

[17]See Luttwak, *The Grand Strategy of the Roman Empire from the First Century A.D. to the Third* (Baltimore: Johns Hopkins University Press, 1976), pp. 21-24, 111-112.

reserved for a praetorian prefect.[18] In the case at hand, the Patriarch and his *apostoli* had responsibility for tax gathering, e.g., the *annona*, a tax-in-kind for military, then government use, as well as regular imperial taxes. In the Diaspora, these officials gathered voluntary taxes known as the *apostole* or *aurum coronarium*.[19] The Patriarch also served local judicial functions, fixed holiday dates, and influenced Roman leaders in court sentencing.[20]

So if the appointment of a Patriarch represents Roman domination over the Jews (the crisis), the Patriarch's growing power and sphere of authority also indicate the Jews' gaining a measure of autonomy with their own local leader. Furthermore, the long lasting nature of the Patriarchate as an institution and the long-standing foundations on which it was modeled argue principally for continuity with the Judaic past.

Institutions: The Academy

Academies and schools were founded in the Land of Israel, especially in Galilee, throughout much of the rabbinic era. The school that epitomizes this rabbinic institution, that of Rabban Yoḥanan ben Zakkai, has occupied a central location within historical accounts of the period. More than any other, Yoḥanan's academy at Yavneh (= Jamnia), site of a supposed rabbinic "Council" in 90, is held up as a refuge from political oppression. According to the rabbinic version of this story (*Avot deRabbi Natan*, 4), during the First Jewish War, just prior to the destruction of the Temple, Yoḥanan ben Zakkai met with the Emperor Vespasian, and extracted a minor concession: the gift of a school at Yavneh, in which to carry forward study of Torah, and to institute new laws for the post-Temple situation.

Recently scholars have taken a less gullible approach to the story of the founding of the Yavnean academy. Some have seen it as a place of internal exile for the rabbinic leader and a small group of student

---

[18]See Robert Louis Wilken, *John Chrysostom and the Jews. Rhetoric and Reality in the Late Fourth Century* (Berkeley, CA: University of California Press, 1983), pp. 58-62.

[19]See Werner Stenger, *"Gebt dem Kaiser was des Kaisers ist!" Eine sozialgeschichtliche Untersuchung zur Besteuerung Palästinas in neutestamentlicher Zeit*, (Bonner Biblische Beitrage, Band 68; Frankfurt am Main: Athenäum, 1988), pp. 19-29.

[20]For the Patriarch's range of activities, see E. Mary Smallwood, *The Jews Under Roman Rule: From Pompey to Diocletian. A Study in Political Relations* (Studies in Judaism in Late Antiquity; Leiden: E.J. Brill, 1981; originally published 1976), pp. 476 and 512; Mantel, *Sanhedrin*, pp. 175-253. See also Cohen, *Maccabees to Mishnah*, pp. 221-223.

rebels;[21] others imply that the story is a late rabbinic reinterpretation of a meeting Vespasian might have had with Josephus.[22] On either reading, the main point is the same: this "academy" was in fact an institution created out of crisis. As an institution, it constituted the core of the rabbinic attempt to negotiate that difficult period of time under Roman rule.

Yet Jewish academies had a long history by the time of the crises under discussion. We may trace the academy back to Alexandrian schools of thought and exegesis, about which we know from Philo; to the Bet Midrash mentioned at Ben Sira 51:23; to the Schools of Shammai and Hillel; and of course to other groups of Jews within the Land itself who participated in the intellectual endeavor of reading Jewish Scripture, reflecting upon it, and producing new texts of exegesis and interpretation (e.g., those at Qumran who produced or studied the *pesharim*). So schools were nothing new to Judaism at the creation of rabbinic academies.

The particularly *rabbinic* academies apparently flourished from the second through the fourth centuries. We can establish the presence of schools in Beror Ḥayil, Yavneh, Lydda, Peki^{c}in, Benei Beraq, Sikhnin, Sepphoris, Bet She^{c}arim, Tiberias, and Caesarea. Well into the fourth century, we still find ample evidence of schools becoming more and more well established.[23]

This broader look indicates that the rabbinic academies were created in a sense of conservativism and retrenchment. The rabbis took an existing institution and developed it so as to strengthen Judaism against – or beyond – crisis. They succeeded in taking the institution from more or less peripatetic study circles, in which any rabbi and his students constituted an academy, to comprehensive schools with regular patterns of study, fixed locations, and noted approaches to the law.

Briefly, I should touch upon a phenomenon entirely parallel to the academy, namely evidence of other types of education within the province. Robert Wilken has shown, through his study of an exchange of letters between a Patriarch and a certain Libanius, that the Patriarch probably had the same kind of education and access to Greco-Roman society as those appointed from other ethnic groups to rule their

---

[21]See Jack P. Lewis, "Jamnia Revisited," presented to the Society of Biblical Literature, Early Rabbinic Studies Section in 1988 (cf. *Abstracts. American Academy of Religion, Society of Biblical Literature. 1988*, p. 340).

[22] See Jacob Neusner, "Story and Tradition in Judaism," in *Judaism: Mishnah*, pp. 307-328 and cf. Schäfer, *Geschichte der Juden*, pp. 152-153.

[23]See Martin Goodman, *State and Society in Roman Galilee.* A.D. *132 to 212* (Totawa, NJ: Rowman and Allenheld, 1983), pp. 32-33, 75-81.

own peoples.[24] These sources detail a gymnasium education, at least for the children of local leaders. So we find in Palestine, as in Alexandria and Caesarea, the full participation of some Jews in a Greco-Roman education and culture. Inscriptions throughout the Land of Israel – which exist in Greek, Latin, Aramaic and Hebrew, from the first century on[25] – together with the pervasive quality of Greek and Latin terminology and philosophic concepts in the Talmud itself,[26] likewise reflect this infusion of Greco-Roman culture into the province. And under the Severan dynasty, in particular during the reign of Caracala (198-217), Jews were granted the status of Roman citizens, together with most people in occupied territories. None of this penetration of Greco-Roman culture and literature seems to have been sharply affected by the crises of the second, third, and fourth centuries. Just as rabbinic academies evolved into more and more structured institutions, so too social and educational patterns seem to have been remarkably stable *vis à vis* Greco-Roman culture.

A well known rabbinic episode illustrates the continuity of institution of which I speak and melds together these first two institutions, that of the Patriarchate and the Academy. I refer to the famous deposition of Rabban Gamaliel as Patriarch and head of the local academy, all of which took place in the outdoor school with the full rabbinic consistory as onlookers.[27] I fully recognize that the details of such a story may well have been fabricated in order to make some point about intolerable abuses of power by the Patriarchate. Still, the image of the school, with its assigned semi-circular seats, scribes taking notes, and regular curriculum, makes a quite separate statement about the institution itself.

What happened to the academies during the third century crisis? Did they fold up or lose their constituency? Quite the contrary, over the succeeding century and one half, the academies produced the Talmud of

[24]Wilken, *John Chrysostom and the Jews*, pp. 55-65.

[25]See Eric M. Meyers and James F. Strange, *Archeology, the Rabbis, and Early Christianity. The Social and Historical Setting of Palestinian Judaism and Christianity* (Nashville: Abingdon, 1981), pp. 62-91.

[26]See Saul Lieberman, *Greek in Jewish Palestine. Studies in the Life and Manners of Jewish Palestine in the II-IV Centuries* C.E. (New York: Jewish Theological Seminary of America, 1942), *passim*, and *Hellenism in Jewish Palestine. Studies in the Literary Transmission, Beliefs, and Manners of Palestine in the I Century* B.C.E. *- IV Century* C.E. (New York: Jewish Theological Seminary of America, 1950), *passim*, but especially pp. 1-19.

[27]For a presentation of this story in its various forms, see Robert Goldenberg, "The Deposition of Rabban Gamaliel II: An Examination of the Sources," in William Scott Green, ed., *Persons and Institutions in Early Rabbinic Judaism* (Brown Judaic Studies 3; Missoula, Montana: Scholars Press, 1977), pp. 9-47.

the Land of Israel! Rather than retreating in the face of crisis, the academy's creation of this literature speaks for a position of power and confidence: a triumphant Judaism, not one in crisis.

Even at this level of background culture, in terms of both language and education, the Jews stood *above* crisis. They were not only the people whose Messianic hopes were dashed, but also a people fully at home in the Roman world that dominated the Palestinian province.

Institutions: The Synagogue

More than any other, this institution seems to have weathered the crises of the third through fifth centuries and to have prospered. Of course, we find evidence of synagogues as central social structures in the Land of Israel as early as the first century:[28] the fortress at Masada has its famous synagogue,[29] and the town of Gamala had what archaeologists describe as a rather grand structure, destroyed by the Romans in the First Jewish War.[30] Many of our sources – Philo, Josephus, the New Testament, the Mishnah, and the Talmuds – testify to synagogues in the diaspora and in the Land itself serving a function in tandem with the Temple in Jerusalem. Some rabbinic sources indicate that within the Land of Israel synagogues were as numerous as 400 at the time of the Temple's destruction in 70.[31]

In terms of the development of the synagogue as a communal structure, the Mishnah details certain aspects of synagogue practice and rite, confirming the growing role of the synagogue in the Land of Israel after the destruction of the Temple. Use of Temple motifs in synagogue art shows a steady shift from cultic images to Torah shrines.[32] As Judaism moved through the crisis of the Temple's destruction, in other words, the role played by the Temple as an institution – the cultic center of Judaism – simply was transferred to a

---

[28]See Cohen, *Maccabees to Mishnah*, pp. 112-113.

[29]See G. Foerster, "The Synagogues at Masada and Herodium," and Yigal Yadin, "The Synagogue at Masada," in Lee I. Levine, ed., *Ancient Synagogues Revealed* (Jerusalem: The Israel Exploration Society, 1981), pp. 25-29 and 19-23, respectively.

[30]See Marilyn Chiat, "First Century Synagogue Architecture: Methodological Problems," in Joseph Guttmann, ed., *Ancient Synagogues. The State of Research* (Brown Judaic Studies 22. Chico, CA: Scholars Press, 1981), pp. 49-60, for an appraisal of this sometimes difficult material.

[31]See Y. Meg. 3:1, which mentions 480 synagogues; B. Ket. 105a, which mentions 394.

[32]See Bernard Goldman, *The Sacred Portal. A Primary Symbol in Ancient Judaic Art* (Brown Classics in Judaica; Lanham, MD: University Press of America, 1986; originally published 1966), *passim*, and esp. pp. 68, 125-6.

new institution and focus – the synagogue and Torah.[33] Such institutions coped with crisis by migrating away from it.

The economic crisis similarly had little impact upon the building and maintenance of synagogues. A first major wave of building occupied the third and fourth centuries, resulting in some truly monumental synagogues, followed by a second wave in the fifth and sixth centuries. During the entire period (including the decline under the Severan dynasty), we find constant rebuilding after earthquakes or other disasters, as well as routine maintenance and additions.[34]

A single example deserves special note, namely, the synagogue excavated at Capernaum (=*Kfar Naḥum*).[35] Dating for this structure remains somewhat a matter of dispute, with a few authorities leaning toward a date in the late second century. A growing consensus,[36] however, sees the Capernaum synagogue as a construction project more likely undertaken at the end of the fourth century, perhaps between 375 and 425. In the very moment of crisis – that is, during the triumph of Christianity as state religion – Jews built a synagogue of mammoth proportion, some 482 square yards – about 60 x 64 feet! And they built that synagogue scarcely one block away from the local church, which is quite a bit smaller than the combined study house and synagogue proper. This suggests that as a cultural institution, the synagogue fared quite well during the period at hand.

Institutions: Systematic Theology

The last institution I wish to describe is in fact an intellectual program rather than a social structure. Here I refer to the rabbinic agenda, set by the Mishnah. Leaning heavily upon the Priestly Writer of the Pentateuch, the Mishnah laid out the issues that would occupy Jewish legal thought for centuries.

---

[33]For an early statement of this shift, see Samuel Krauss, *Synagogale Altertümer* (Hildesheim: Georg Olms Verlagsbuchhandlung, 1966; originally published 1922), pp. 93-102.

[34]See, e.g., Marilyn Joyce Segal Chiat, *Handbook of Synagogue Architecture*, Brown Judaic Studies 29 (Chico, CA: Scholars Press, 1982), pp. 26, 36, 44, 95-96, 101, 105, 110, 138, 143, and many others.

[35]See Virgilio C. Corbo O.F.M., *Cafarnao: I. Gli edifici della Città* (Pubblicazioni dello Studium Biblicum Franciscanum 19; Jerusalem: Franciscan Printing Press, 1975), pp. 113-169.

[36]This controversy is drawn together in three articles in Levine, *Ancient Synagogues*. See Stanislao Loffreda O.F.M., "The Late Chronology of the Synagogue of Capernaum" (pp. 52-56); G. Foerster, "Notes on Recent Excavations at Capernaum" (pp. 57-59); and Michael Avi-Yonah, "Some Comments on the Capernaum Excavations" (pp. 60-62).

The Talmud of the Land of Israel, for example, in the main addressed not the crisis of economy or of theology, but the Mishnah itself and the legal agenda it laid forth. Jacob Neusner has estimated that two thirds of the Talmud's materials constitute straightforward, rather low-level analysis of the Mishnah passage at hand (defining words, identifying speakers, illuminating realia, etc.).[37] And Neusner estimates that less than 15% of the whole is devoted to units of discourse that stand independent of the Mishnah and its agenda. My own work on Tractate Peah confirms Neusner's figures: 67% of Tractate Peah's units aim solely at the Mishnah; only 9% stand independent of Mishnah in any meaningful way.[38]

The Hebrew Bible, the Mishnah, and the Tosefta, in other words, set the overall limits within which rabbinic innovation was carried out. I propose the image of Systematic Theology to help us think of this agenda as an institution that fixes and secures part of Judaism, allowing it to transcend whatever crises we may note. In particular, the Mishnah divided life into its component parts as the rabbis themselves saw things. These parts constitute a theological network representing three major interests: *priestly* attention to holiness, *scribal* concerns for the correspondence of word and act, and ordinary *householders'* regard for daily conduct.[39]

The Mishnaic system built of these parts is comprehensive, in that virtually any part of early rabbinism fits within; the system is thoroughly interconnected, for to understand any single paragraph or chapter, one needs to know a myriad of others; and the system is elegantly rigorous, because the Mishnah carefully combines formulaic patterns and themes to emphasize the detailed rules under discussion. So the Mishnah constituted Judaism's primary first-order systematics, in that it provides a sustained, rational discourse on a set of intellectual categories and problems, which establishes a comprehensive framework for the religion.

It should now be clear that the Mishnah's topics do not merely represent everything in Scripture; the Mishnah often reads the Hebrew Bible in quite unpredictable ways, sometimes even ignoring basic scriptural conceptions.[40] For example, one of the Mishnah's crucial concerns is to establish the correspondence of a householder's actions and intentions. Earlier biblical materials ruled that anything placed

---

[37]Jacob Neusner, *The Talmud of the Land of Israel. A Preliminary Translation and Explanation. Volume 35. Introduction: Taxonomy* (Chicago: University of Chicago Press, 1983), pp. 49-51, 85-90.
[38]Brooks, *Tractate Peah*, Introduction.
[39]See Neusner, *Judaism: Mishnah*, pp. 230-256.
[40]See Neusner, *Judaism: Mishnah*, pp. 167-172, 217-229.

upon the altar immediately became sanctified (e.g., Exod 29:37). The Mishnah, for its part, held that only items offered with the priest's proper intention take on consecrated status.[41] In like fashion throughout the Mishnah, the major ideas expressed, building upon but not limited to the scriptural account, are those of the rabbinic movement. So too the Mishnah's interests do not reflect real legislative settings alone. At least two-thirds of the Mishnaic law addressed the Temple and its regular maintenance, a full 130 years after the Temple had been destroyed.[42]

So the rabbis' theological program was neither wholly fundamentalistic nor solely determined by legislative needs. On the contrary, although compiled after the Temple's destruction, the Mishnah's clear aim was to establish continuity with that institution and its rite (especially in the Divisions of Agriculture, Appointed Times, Holy Things, and Purities). The rabbinic insistence upon holiness (expressed within each division) stems from the particularity of God's relationship with Israel. The rabbis might well have summarized this relationship in the following paragraph, which lays bare the basic assumptions of the Mishnaic system, both as a cultural artifact and as the beginning of rabbinic theology as a whole.

> (1) God owns the Holy Land [*Division of Agriculture*], and (2) gives it to the people with whom he has had a long-standing historical relationship [*Division of Appointed Times*], namely Israel (hence the appropriate Judaic idiom, the Land of Israel). (3) The Israelites owe God and his appointed representatives payment for their use of the Land [*Divisions of Agriculture and Holy Things*], in addition to (4) special actions in response to history [*Division of Appointed Times*]. (5) The holiness required in God's worship must also inform mundane activity [*Division of Purities*], extending to both levels of the Israelite clan – (6) one's own immediate family [*Division of Women*] and (7) the larger family of the Children of Israel [*Division of Damages*].

In many ways, then, the Mishnah's authorship *did* attend to recent history by systematizing and organizing Jewish thought. Three centuries of Roman domination over the Land of Israel (the crisis, once again) helped to determine the content and message of the Mishnah,

---

[41]See Howard Eilberg-Schwartz, *The Human Will in Judaism. The Mishnah's Philosophy of Intention* (Brown Judaic Studies 103; Atlanta: Scholars Press, 1986), pp. 149-163.

[42]Compare Cohen, *Maccabees to Mishnah*, pp 215-219.

with its assertion that God alone ruled sovereign over the Land. Later rabbinic literature – the early Midrash compilations and the Talmuds – endorsed this statement. Such books, that is, took the Mishnah as the constitution of the Jewish nation (however removed from autonomy that nation might have been). The Jews' situation as a defeated people forced them to retreat into a systematic never-never land, in which Rome played little or no part whatsoever. This reaction – in fact a response to the manifest crisis of Roman rule – tends to dominate accounts of early rabbinic culture.

But the difficult circumstances facing the Jewish people also led the rabbis to create real and lasting social structures, within which they could live under Rome, yet apart from the Empire. Rabbis emerged as leaders, if not quite "political," in our sense of the word. Through their books, they purported to guide all aspects of the daily routine of the Jews (hence their focus on both "secular" and "religious" topics). By the beginning of the third century, these same rabbis had established institutions in which to teach their system of thought, the rabbinic academies. Set throughout lower Galilee, these schools had strongly defined networks of authority, teachers and students sitting in assigned seats that indicated their merits within the emerging Rabbinate, studying a common curriculum, working out an ordered, ordained livelihood.

Conclusions

If we draw together the four areas surveyed above, we find a singular pattern. Each institution *does* respond in some measure to overt and manifest history, often a tragic history at that. The Patriarch was, as I said, a symbol of Roman domination; the academies were a retreat from politics, an alternative of sorts to open confrontation; the synagogue was merely a replacement and a shadow of the holy Temple destroyed by Rome; and the Mishnah simply ignored the real world, mounting an argument from silence in response to political and human defeat.

Scholars have noted carefully the important role of such manifest crises in their historical reconstruction of the early rabbinic period. It follows that a specific type of watershed event becomes their focus: the Temple's destruction, the imposition of Roman rule, the Christianization of the Empire – all these figure as the events of the day that really matter; all these are reckoned as the decisive and formative events in determining Judaic history.

But to stop our reconstructions at this point is to miss the conclusion of the story. For Judaism did not find itself in crisis at the latent level, even if embroiled at the manifest level. The rabbinic system we know as Judaism evolved out of the strength and enduring character of long-standing institutions nurtured and carefully reshaped in the face of transitory disarray.

Despite the political turmoil of manifest history, and despite the depression rampant in economic history, the Jews of the second through fifth centuries, under the tutelage of the rabbis, prospered and produced literary monuments that remain formative for Jews into our own day – the Mishnah and the Talmud. These Jews created the social institutions – the Patriarchate and Rabbinate, the Academy, and the Synagogue – that sustained their nation then and now. In place of the Temple as the locus of worldly power and authority, they created a system of thought, in which the paramount virtue was found in study of the Mishnah's various rules regarding the Temple cult and proper maintenance of its purity.

If our goal is a deeper understanding of the history of Jews and Judaism in the early centuries of the Common Era, therefore, we need to move between two analytic poles. First, the *crises* of military, economic, political, and religious experience must take their places. Such events locate landmarks upon the historian's terrain, marking out the map constructing the past as best we can. But second – and although often ignored, just as important – the *continuity* of institutions and thought requires attention. Only a view toward the incremental aspect of culture can help to fill blank areas on the scholarly chart of the past.

This continuity alone explains why Judaism remained Judaism, despite all the vicissitudes of fortune and history. For radical shifts occurred in the centuries at hand. The established Judaic culture at the turn of the era was a Temple-centered community, run by priests with a theological elitism, both for their holy city – Jerusalem – and their own holy caste – the Levites and priests. Yet by the fourth century, the Jews in the Land of Israel were ruled by a Patriarchal class and by rabbis qualified because of their theological attainments; Jews constituted a community based in synagogues spread throughout the entire Land. For all these changes, however, great continuity linked Patriarch with High Priest, Synagogue with Temple, and Mishnaic theology with Levitical rite.

This historical perspective, mixing both crisis and continuity, permits us to sort through the adjustments and permutations in the course of Judaic history, but also to show that historical current as a single continuum. And *that* allows us to make sense of the larger whole known as Judaism.

17

The Problem of Originality in Talmudic Thought

Robert Goldenberg
State University of New York at Stony Brook

When Rabbi Moses Schreiber, the *Hatam Sofer,* early in the last century announced with elegant simplicity that the Torah forbids all innovation,[1] he invoked an idea with deep and ancient roots in the rabbinic tradition. Rabbinic sources, from the earliest on, repeatedly assert – often in connection with the last verse in the Book of Leviticus – that once the Torah had been revealed to an earlier Moses at Mount Sinai no prophet had the right to initiate any further innovation in Jewish religious life.[2] Of R. Yohanan b. Zakkai and his disciple R. Eliezer it was reported that they took pride in never teaching their disciples anything they had not learned from their own masters,[3] and at M. `Eduyyot 1:3[4] an anonymous glossator accounts for the apparently odd formulation of one of Hillel's dicta by saying that "a man must always speak in the language of his teacher." In short, the classical

---

[1]Responsa, *Yoreh De`ah,* 19 (1818/9); *Orah Hayyim,* 28 (1829/30); *Even ha-`Ezer,* 2:29 (1830/1). I owe these references to Prof. Jay Harris of Columbia University, to whom I am happy to express my warm thanks. Schreiber drew the aphorism from the last sentence of M. `Orlah, where it has an entirely different meaning.

[2]Sifra, end; B. Shabbat 104a, Yoma 80a, Megillah 2b, Temurah 16a; J. Megillah 1:5 70d.

[3]B. Sukkah 28a, T. Yevamot 3 end; see Jacob Neusner, *Development of a Legend* (Leiden: Brill, 1970), 144, 219; *idem, Eliezer ben Hyrcanus* (Leiden: Brill, 1973), 1:115, 142.

[4]Also at B. Shabbat 15a. See Neusner, *The Rabbinic Traditions about the Pharisees before 70* (Leiden: Brill, 1991), 1:143, 305; 3:168, 263.

texts of the rabbinic tradition exhibit powerful dedication to the idea that the proper reaction to all voluntary change is resistance; a proper disciple of the Sages teaches what he has learned from his masters, unexpanded and unchanged.[5] When this loyalty to received lore was violated, the matter could become an embarrassment to those who came after. R. Joshua is reported to have despaired of ever explaining a certain rule: "the Soferim invented something new," he purportedly said, "and I cannot answer [for them]."[6]

There is, however, another side to the story. When R. Judah the Patriarch (Rabbi) declared the region of Bet Shean free of the obligation to tithe, his ruling provoked a storm of protest; his ancestors had forbidden untithed produce from Bet Shean, and now he would undo the prohibition! Rabbi's answer, that "his ancestors had left him an area in which he might distinguish himself,"[7] directly contradicts the tendency of the passages just reviewed. Instead, it posits as one of the fundamental principles of the Oral Torah a wide-ranging right – indeed possibly an obligation – on the part of each generation to alter or at least enlarge the received tradition. Unlike the position of those who felt their teachers expected the tradition to be handed on unchanged, Judah's stance demands of each generation that it intend for its heritage to be altered by those who receive it. On similar grounds, the same R. Joshua who reportedly expressed such embarrassment about scribal innovation is said to have reminded his students that the House of Study could not have met without something new being taught.[8]

There are several different ways in which one might try to resolve the apparent conflict between these two points of view. Various rabbinic authorities of late antiquity were known as specialists in some particular field of Oral Torah, or some particular approach to Oral Torah, and one could try to correlate such lines of individual preference or professional specialization with possible attitudes toward originality or innovation. Just as one rabbi might be known for his

---

[5]See the remarks of M. Aberbach in his essay "The Relations between Master and Disciple in the Talmudic Age," *Essays presented to Chief Rabbi Israel Brodie on the occasion of his seventieth birthday*, H. J. Zimmels, J. Rabbinowitz, and I. Finestein, eds., (London: Soncino Press, 1967), 18-19.
[6]M. Kelim 13:7, Tevul Yom 4:6 (=T. Tevul Yom 2:14); see Neusner, *A History of the Mishnaic Law of Purities* (Leiden: Brill, 1974), 2:27.
[7]B. Hullin 7a. See also J. Demai 2:1 22c, where a similar claim, again attributed to Judah the Patriarch, is couched in different language.
[8]B. Hagigah 3a; Mekhilta de-R. Ishmael, Pisha 16; T. Sotah 7:9; J. Hagigah 1:1 75d.

erudition while another was respected for the acuity of his reasoning,[9] just as one might be famous as an expert in exotic legal rubrics[10] while another excelled in homiletics or religious polemics,[11] so it may have been that some authorities sought every opportunity to stress the weight of tradition in rabbinic teaching while others preferred to emphasize every scholar's independence of his teachers and predecessors.

Alternatively, one might hypothesize that different authorities were led to adopt conflicting points of view on the present question because they found themselves in different situations. In particular, Judah the Patriarch might have been led to emphasize his relative freedom from restraint because he was the *Nasi*, the heir to his family's long struggle to retain its prerogatives in the face of efforts by the rabbinic collective to overcome them.[12]

Any such efforts, however, would be more convincing if the evidence revealed a collegial willingness among ancient rabbis to differ on this question as they differed with respect to the other matters mentioned above. In fact, however, there seems to have been no such agreement to disagree; instead, anxiety and ambivalence toward innovation in the realm of Torah pervade the early rabbinic tradition. Rabbinic authorities in late antiquity made two claims that cannot easily be reconciled with one another: they asserted the utter reliability of the teachings they sought to transmit and at the same time presumed the right to interpret (which sometimes meant alter) those very teachings as they saw fit, without any undue restraint on their autonomy.[13]

---

[9]The Amora R. Joseph was known as "Sinai" while his contemporary Rabbah was called "uprooter of mountains." See B. Berakhot 64a, Horayot 14a.

[10]According to later reports, even the famous `Aqiva was instructed by his peers to stop toying with *aggadah* and stick with the laws of leprosy and corpse-defilement. See B. Hagigah 14a, Sanhedrin 38b, 67b.

[11]See the comments by Lee Levine on R. Abbahu of Caesarea, *Christianity, Judaism, and Other Greco-Roman Cults* (Leiden: Brill, 1975), 4:59-62.

[12]On other occasions as well, Rabbi's willingness to make changes in the tradition aroused confused horror in his successors; see the report (B. Megillah 5b and Tosafot *ad loc.*) on his attempt to abolish the observance of Tisha B'Av. On previous stages in the struggle between the Patriarchate and the rabbinic collective see my earlier studies "The Deposition of Rabban Gamaliel II: An Examination of the Sources," *Journal of Jewish Studies* 23 (1972), 167-190 and "History and Ideology in Talmudic Narrative," *Approaches to Ancient Judaism* IV (Chico: Scholars Press, 1983), 159-173.

[13]Jacob Neusner has shown that different accounts of Hillel's institution of the *prozbul* reflect this difference; some emphasize the exegetical basis of the innovation, as though it would have been unacceptable without some such

Rabbinic dicta on the subject at hand reveal this anxiety through their exaggerated claims. The statement that anything a student may someday say to his teacher was already spoken to Moses[14] seems to acknowledge the familiar reality that students say new things all the time, and expresses deep unease in the face of such originality. A talmudic *aggadah* insists that the numerous laws forgotten in the turmoil following Moses' death had to be restored through the dialectic of Othniel ben Kenaz because no new revelation – not even the simple reiteration of a previously revealed law – was possible;[15] this too bespeaks a desperate refusal to admit that anything new can have legitimate standing in the religion of Torah. And yet those who transmitted Joshua's reminder to his students acknowledged each time they repeated it that rabbis were innovating all the time.

What is signified by this deep ambivalence in the face of originality? Why would any group of religious leaders as busily engaged as the ancient rabbis in audacious and constant innovation work so hard to pretend there was nothing new in what they were saying? Previous scholars have already responded to these or related questions. E. E. Urbach addresses these matters in connection with the report that all prophecy was already revealed to Moses at Sinai,[16] and finds implied in this motif both of the fundamental dogmas that underlie the rabbinic conception of Torah: post-Mosaic revelation is in principle impossible, while Oral Torah must be accepted as equal to the Written.[17] This apparently mystical and obscurantist notion thus actually functioned in Urbach's view as a powerful tool for resisting charismatic authority. Holy men claiming to have new, direct revelations from the Creator might now be disregarded, while rabbinic teaching might now be offered as the only available source of divinely-sanctioned guidance for a community thirsting for such instruction and surrounded by all sorts of people eager to supply it.

From an entirely different angle, Jacob Neusner's studies of the early Babylonian rabbinate made much of the extremely rigorous

---

grounding, while others simply report it as a desirable legislative improvement *(tiqqun `olam)*. See his *Pharisees*, 1:219, 262-3, 284.

[14]Leviticus R. 22:1; J. Peah 2:4 17a. A related statement appears at B. Megillah 19b.

[15]B. Temurah 16a.

[16]See above note 2, and Urbach, *The Sages* (in Hebrew; Jerusalem: Magnes, 1969), p. 364. At Exodus R. 28:4 this idea is expanded to include the claim that even rabbinic teachings were revealed in this way.

[17]The second of these principles follows from the first: how can later prophets have learned their prophecies if not *via* oral transmission?

apprenticeship that every rabbinic disciple was expected to undergo.[18] Disciples, he writes, "had to watch every movement to conform to the ritualistic patterns expected of a student of the sages." Neusner subsumes these considerations under the general category of "academic etiquette," and makes no particular reference in this connection to the substance or formulation of disciples' learning, but it is clear that a general tendency of the sort he describes would produce extreme conservative attitudes even toward the wording of memorized lore. Disciples who had successfully undergone such a training would then wish, however, to enjoy the same freedom of interpretation with respect to the sources and the same power over their students they imagined their own teachers had possessed over them: "men who were carefully trained to emulate, even to imitate, their master's gestures, would, when they rose to eminence, exact the same kind of consistent standards of behavior." In other words, senior masters' insistence on their own autonomy follows from the same logic as their demand for disciples' complete submission to their authority.

Neither of these approaches, however, directly addresses the relation between originality and traditionalism that is under discussion here; in that connection, it seems more to the point to suggest that the mixed attitude toward innovation displayed by rabbis in late antiquity reflected their mixed role in society. On the one hand, the rabbinic insistence on fidelity to the received text is one of the signs that Torah-study was being converted into a religious ritual, a development that constitutes another of the focal themes of Neusner's work.[19] Akin to kabbalistic attempts to make sure that the obligatory prayers contain exactly the right number of words and letters, the early rabbis' demand that traditions of oral Torah be transmitted exactly as they had been learned is clear evidence that the recitation of such traditions was a religious performance, and not merely an aspect of academic training or judicial function.

Nevertheless, the religious virtuosi who carried out such performances were in fact trained experts and functioning judges as well. They could not carry out their official tasks (especially in the latter capacity) without fairly wide discretion; a judge or decisor might feel

---

[18]Neusner, *A History of the Jews in Babylonia* (Leiden: Brill, 1964-70), 3:130, 140-1, 145-7; 4:304-7; 5:157-8, 162-8. Quotations in the following sentences are from 3:146-7. See also the materials assembled by David Goodblatt, *Rabbinic Instruction in Sasanian Babylonia* (Leiden: Brill, 1975), 147, 181, 208.

[19]For discussion of very similar developments in an entirely different religious environment, see Brian K. Smith, "Ritual, Knowledge, and Being: Initiation and Veda Study in Ancient India," *Numen* 33 (1986), 65-89, especially 73-79.

obliged to cite existing law exactly as he had learned it, but in the nature of things he had to apply that law to situations of which his teachers had not spoken. The rabbis' insistence on both absolute fidelity to the received tradition and also on the untrammeled freedom of each Sage to interpret that tradition as he saw fit was not, then, merely a case of theological confusion or of wanting to have their cake and eat it too; it reflects an inner tension between two different aspects – each quite central – of their role in the Jewish community. Rabbis were both civil servants of the Jewish community[20] but also the priesthood of its new central rite, and the two roles did not always fit together very well.

Historical fluctuations in rabbinic tolerance of novelty can be charted in terms of this duality of role. When the public authority of the rabbinate seemed relatively safe from challenge then judges and halakhic authorities seem to have been open to considerable innovation: witness the appearance and rapid acceptance of the *heter `iska* toward the end of the Middle Ages, or the third paragraph of *tosafot* to `Avodah Zarah and its removal of Christendom from the world of so-called "alien worship," or – though here, to be sure, one stands on shakier historical ground – Hillel and his famous *prozbul*.[21] On the other hand, when rabbinic authority was in question a standard reaction was to invoke the purity of the tradition by insisting that nothing of substance has been changed in the Torah since it was first revealed. On these grounds one can understand why the assertion that they had never changed their teachers' formulations was put into the mouths of two Yavnean sages, men who lived at a time when rabbinic claims for leadership were first being asserted,[22] and one begins to see

---

[20]See the comments by Goodblatt about "apprentice lawyers," *op. cit.*, 272-3.

[21]See above, note 13.

[22]At J. Niddah 2:7 50b, the third-century authority R. Hanina, a man who flourished at a time when rabbinic authority was apparently quite well established, is reported to have claimed he never judged a case single-handedly when it concerned a matter on which he had not already learned the law from his teachers. At two other locations (J. Shevi`it 6:1 36d, J. `Avodah Zarah 1:4 39d), an anonymous report claims on Hanina's behalf that he never said anything he had not heard from his teachers – the same claim that Yohanan b. Zakkai and Eliezer b. Hyrcanus are reported to have voiced with respect to themselves. If Hanina himself claimed this, then the suggestion made here that such an assertion reflects conditions in which rabbinic authority was not widely accepted requires further thought. If, however, Hanina only expressed the principle quoted in J. Niddah, and other tradents, influenced by the reports concerning the first-century authorities, expanded this principle into the version found in Shevi`it and `Avodah Zarah, then we are

why the greatest crisis in the history of rabbinic authority – the Emancipation and its aftermath – should have elicited from the Hatam Sofer the pronouncement already cited.

* * * * *

The early rabbis' ambivalence toward innovation in the transmission of Torah was part of a more pervasive ambivalence toward their own inventiveness. Rabbinic Judaism is in significant measure the outcome of the destruction of Jerusalem and the readjustments that disaster made necessary.[23] One need not lapse into the "lachrymose" view of Jewish history to accept as self-evident that so stupendous a catastrophe as the *hurban* imposed vast changes on all aspects of Jewish life, intellectual and religious, political and administrative alike. As stated above, a cardinal tenet of rabbinic traditionalism was that "the proper reaction to all voluntary change is resistance," but much involuntary change had recently been imposed on Jewry, and the rabbinic movement found itself trying to direct that change toward goals of its own choosing.

The task assumed by the early rabbis produced in them an intense awareness that they were indeed innovating,[24] but innovating in order to save a threatened heritage. Rabbis believed that those who remained loyal to God's law could never really abandon God, but they also knew, or at least asserted, that from time to time one could "act for God" only by violating God's law.[25] They no doubt understood their whole program of making Torah, not Temple, the central institution of Judaism as fitting that latter rubric, but just the same the consciousness

---

dealing here with a much more limited expression of judicial humility, which is not the same thing. The general argument of this paper suggests that the second hypothesis is the more likely, but in order to avoid circular reasoning I prefer to leave this question open for additional investigation.

[23]See my article "The Broken Axis: Rabbinic Judaism and the Fall of Jerusalem," *Journal of the American Academy of Religion,* Supplement, XLV/3 (1977), F:869-882.

[24]M. Rosh Hashanah 4:1,3-4 gives a list of enactments supposedly issued by Yohanan b. Zakkai after the destruction of the Temple. The tentative and ambivalent character of all such enactments is captured in a remark attributed in most manuscripts to his younger contemporary Joshua b. Qorhah: "R. Yohanan b. Zakkai ordained these things after the Temple was destroyed; when it is rebuilt soon, these matters will return to their original state" (T. Rosh Hashanah 2:9). See also M. Ma`aser Sheni 5:2.

[25]See the *midrash* on Jeremiah 16:11 at J. Hagigah 1:7 76c, and Rava's counterpart *midrash* on Psalm 119:126 at B. Berakhot 63a.

that at every step they were departing from traditional religious conceptions and norms cannot have failed to provoke deep anxiety, and this anxiety is reflected in the extraordinary exaggerations contained in the rabbinic *aggadot* already cited.

The *aggadot* reflect the anxiety, but no recorded statement acknowledges it; just as rabbinic discourse would often answer a question without stopping first to ask it, so too here it tried to allay unease without first bringing it to consciousness. The combination of devotion to tradition and constant need for originality (both imposed necessity and scholarly inner need are meant here)[26] remained fructifying so long as rabbis were able to sustain both sides of it without excessive tension or sense of conflict. That combination became crippling, however, when this ability grew weaker.

In recent times, rabbis' capacity to sustain this tension has dramatically declined; on one side of the battle now stand those who consider resistance to innovation the only true sign of reverence for the tradition, on the other those who justify their advocacy of innovation by turning the concept of tradition into something halfway between nostalgia and folklore. The most spectacular achievements of rabbinic creativity – the initial creation of a post-*hurban* framework for Jewish life and then the successful transfer of this framework from the world of pagan antiquity into the Christian and Muslim worlds of the Middle Ages – were brought about by leaders who could affirm as the situation required either or both of the beliefs under discussion here. Both were necessary if rabbinic leadership was to succeed, one because it validated rabbinic authority and the other because it freed rabbis to use their authority as the times required, but it was possible to sustain them both only so long as Jews in general and rabbis in particular genuinely believed in the sacred character of their community and also in the competence of rabbinic leadership to guide that community and its members through any situation that might arise. Once such belief began to fail – it hardly matters which tenet was the first to lose its hold or in which circles the failure began – the unity of the tradition began to crumble, and there appeared the first signs of the polarization just described. The inability of contemporary rabbinic leadership to regain the confidence needed to sustain this paradoxical set of beliefs is

---

[26]See the illuminating remarks about this combination in Isadore Twersky, *Rabad of Posquières* (rev. ed.; Philadelphia, Jewish Publication Society, 1980), xx-xxiv.

just one more sign that the long age of rabbinic dominance over Jewish religious life may finally be nearing its end.[27]

[27]An earlier version of this essay was read by Professor Baruch M. Bokser of the Jewish Theological Seminary of America, and the present version is much improved thanks to his numerous helpful suggestions. I wish to express my gratitude to Prof. Bokser for his kind assistance, and to absolve him for deficiencies that remain.

18

On Man's Role in Revelation

David Weiss Halivni
Columbia University

In a forthcoming book[1] we argue that there exist three rabbinic positions on the nature of the revelation of the Oral Torah. Authors dealing with this subject have tended to blur the distinctions between the different positions by juxtaposing the relevant quotations from the Talmud without noting their mutually exclusive character. There seems to be a reluctance on the part of post-Talmudic scholars to admit to divided and varied opinion on such a sensitive issue as the nature of revelation. For understandable reasons they prefer a monolithic, uniform position which more and more has come to be defined by the extreme maximalist stance. In fact, however, no such rigid uniformity of opinion on the nature of revelation exists in rabbinic literature.

The three rabbinic positions vis-a-vis revelation may be classified as maximalistic, intermediary and minimalistic. The maximalistic position claims that God revealed to Moses on Mount Sinai the entire Oral Torah consisting of all the legitimate arguments of, and all the legitimate solutions to, every issue that may arise, including "the comments that an astute student will someday make in the presence of his teacher."[2] Man merely needs to uncover them. True learning is rediscovering the given and the revealed.

The intermediary position claims that God revealed to Moses on Mount Sinai all the legitimate arguments of every issue that may arise but not their solutions. The solutions were left for man to offer, and whatever he offers becomes a part of "the words of the living God."

---

[1]Tentatively titled *Peshat and Derash: Plain and Applied Meaning in Rabbinic Exegesis* (Oxford University Press, 1990).
[2]P.T. Peah 17a.

This intermediary position is expressed quite forcefully in the following rabbinic midrash: "R. Yannai said: The words of the Torah were not given as clear-cut decisions. For with every word which the Holy One, blessed be He, spoke to Moses, He offered him forty-nine arguments by which a thing may be proved clean, and forty-nine other arguments by which it may be proved unclean. When Moses asked, 'Master of the universe, in what way shall we know the true sense of a law?' God replied, 'The majority is to be followed – when a majority says it is unclean, it is unclean; when a majority says it is clean, it is clean.'"[3] Contradictions are thus built into revelation. Revelation was formulated within the framework of contradiction in the form of argumentation pro and con. No legitimate argument or solution can be in conflict with the divine opinion, for all such arguments and solutions constitute a part of God's opinion.

The minimalistic position claims that God revealed to Moses on Mount Sinai directions for man to follow, principles for man to implement, but not detailed stipulations. This minimalistic approach to revelation is advanced in Midrash Tanchuma.[4] Employing a derash on the word, "kechaloto," the midrash states that only principles, "kellalim," and not all the details of the Oral Law, were revealed to Moses at Sinai. In contrast to the intermediary conception of revelation, in which only ultimate halachic rulings were left for man to determine, the minimalistic position presents man with the opportunity, and authority, for the fleshing out of halachic arguments and details from directional principles.

Though the minimalistic position posits a more limited revelation in terms of specific, concrete content than does the intermediary, it proposes that the principles revealed embodied, *in potentia,* all the legal details yet to be decided by generations of scholars. This minimalistic conception of the organic relationship between divinely-revealed principles and humanly-determined details is best reflected in the following frequently quoted, but often misunderstood, rabbinic story: "...Moses went [into the academy of Rabbi Akiba] and sat down behind eight rows [of R. Akiba's disciples]. Not being able to follow their arguments he was ill at ease, but when they came to a certain subject and the disciples said to the master, 'Whence do you know it?' and the latter [R. Akiba] replied, 'It is a law given to Moses at Sinai,'

---

[3]Midrash Tehillim, 12:4.

[4]*Midrash Tanchuma* Tisah: 16. Variations within rabbinic literature on this minimalistic theme of the revelation of principles only – and not of a plethora of details – will be discussed further on.

Moses was comforted."[5] Though this story is sometimes interpreted to support the claim that each succeeding generation has an equal share in revelation, and that contemporary exegesis is not beholden to the past, it actually expresses the contrary notion that the arguments and details worked out by scholars like R. Akiba were grounded upon principles that had been revealed to Moses at Sinai.[6] Though Moses could not follow the argumentation in R. Akiba's academy, because these specific legal details had not been revealed to him, he was relieved to discover that the divinely-revealed principles were still being utilized as the wellspring of the legal system. The continuity and integrity of the revelatory process is affirmed, in this aggadah, within the conceptual framework of the minimalistic position. The halachic arguments of R. Akiba, though unfamiliar to Moses, are the legitimate offspring of the original, foundational principles of revelation.

The diversity of views regarding the nature and scope of revelation underlies many statements throughout the Talmud. A prominent example is that of R. Zera in the name of Rava bar Zimuna: "If the earlier [scholars] (rishonim) were sons of angels, we are sons of man; and if the earlier [scholars] were sons of man, we are like asses."[7] The statement of R. Zera indicates an uncertainty as to how later generations should look upon earlier generations and, consequently, how later generations should self-consciously view themselves. R. Zera's reference to "rishonim" is, of course, to earlier scholars who constituted the links of the chain of tradition, who conveyed God's word to succeeding generations. These "rishonim" were the expositors of tradition and therefore the carriers and bearers of revelation.

R. Zera's statement posits the necessary inferiority of later generations to earlier ones. His saying constitutes the classical exposition of "nitkatnu ha-dorot," the concept of the inevitable decline of generations. An historical hierarchy is therefore established, but the parameters of that hierarchy are left imprecise. R. Zera is apparently sure of the superior status of his ancestors, but unsure of the standing due them. Is the gap between generations reflective of the

---

[5]B.T. Menachot 29b.

[6]That this story reflects a minimalistic, and not a maximalistic, conception of revelation, has already been noted by R. Zev Einhorn in his commentary on *Midrash Rabbah*, Chukat (Numbers 19:6). It is not surprising that in his commentary on this aggadah, the Maharal of Prague, an arch-maximalist, rejects the theoretical possibility, implied by this story, that R. Akiba could have known more than did Moses. We will address the Maharal's maximalism, in a different context, further on in the essay.

[7]B.T. Shabbath 112b; P.T. Demai 1:3.

difference between angels and human beings or between human beings and animals?[8] In either case, the reality of the "generational gap" is indisputable.

Although it most basically pertains to the notion of the decline of generations, R. Zera's statement can also be understood to underscore the range of rabbinic perspectives of the character of revelation. The uncertainty involving the precise characterization of earlier generations reflects a concomitant uncertainty on the part of R. Zera regarding the role of earlier generations in the process of revelation. Although the gist of R. Zera's statement is not to convey alternative conceptions of revelation, his choice of metaphors is not accidental, nor incidental to a nuanced understanding of his message. His use of these metaphors intimates that he entertained the theoretical legitimacy of two divergent conceptions of man's part in revelation.

The subtext of R. Zera's statement thus involves the issue of the stance of earlier generations toward the "receiving" of the Torah. Were they active participants in the "process" of revelation or merely bystanders, onlookers to an event which they only passively witnessed? If their role was that of active participants in revelation, then they must be accorded a status elevated above that of later generations, indeed, above that of average human beings, to the status of "sons of angels." The rishonim would then be, on a mortal scale, superhuman. Such a classification would be warranted because of their autonomy and license to contribute creatively to the process of revelation. If, alternatively, the role of earlier generations was merely passive, if they acted not as participants in but only as recipients of God's revelation, then their deserved title is "sons of man," befitting the typical station of human beings. This image of the rishonim depicts them as credible and faithful transmitters of revelation, as mouthpieces of the divine word, but not as active collaborators with God in the revelatory process.

This uncertainty as to man's role in revelation is a prevalent motif in rabbinic literature. Rabbinic attitudes vacillate between two extreme views which highlight, respectively, man's passivity or activity in the revelatory process. These views are suggested by R. Zera's metaphorical alternatives. One view (the maximalistic) claims that Moses received from God the Oral Torah in its entirety. The

---

[8]The B.T. appends mention of the famous ass of R. Chanina ben Dosa and of Pinchas ben Yair to the statement of R. Zera to clarify that, in the latter scenario, later generations cannot even attain the stature of this extraordinary ass, but must settle for the status of ordinary asses. The qualitative gap between the generations is yet wider.

compass of man's creative role in revelation is, upon this view, severely restricted. The other end of the conceptual spectrum (the mimimalistic) asserts that God gave man "a kab of wheat (from which to produce fine flour) and a bundle of flax (from which to produce cloth)."[9] Man must, allegorically, strive to complete the process of baking and weaving, or in real terms, contribute to and complete the process of revelation. Not every law was transmitted to man through God's revelation of the Torah. Halachic questions and their resolutions are not always pre-determined. Revelation is, upon this conception, a process in which man is a worthy and valuable partner to God. Man's interpretive efforts are therefore imperative and indispensable to the continual revelation of God's will and to the fulfillment of His dictates. As man is partner to God in the act of creation, so is he God's associate in the task of revelation.

The disparate conceptions of man's role in revelation are again expressed in the well-known Talmudic discussion of the biblical sanction of the blessing said over the lighting of the Chanukkah lamp: "What blessing is said? It is 'who sanctified us by His commandments and commanded us to kindle the light of Chanukkah.' And where did He command us? R. Avia said, [it follows] from 'you must not deviate.' R. Nehemiah said, [from] 'Ask your father, he will inform you; your elders, they will tell you.'"[10] Of course, the rabbis are here compelled to furnish a biblical prooftext in order to justify the use of the de-oraita language of the blessing for a precept which is obviously not biblical. Both verses offered serve a common purpose of justification by grounding rabbinic authority in a biblical foundation.

Though they appear functionally equivalent, however, these biblical prooftexts are not simply interchangeable. Their shared utility in this context must not obscure the fact they are different in subtle, but significant, ways. Indeed, these verses help elucidate the subtleties of the varied conceptions of revelation and of man's role in it. R. Avai's prooftext of "You must not deviate [from the verdict that they announce to you either to the right or to the left]" (Deut. 17:11) corresponds to a maximalistic conception of revelation, one which views the body of revelatory truth as comprehensive. The slightest deviation from the ordinances and truth claims of such a revelation, one which encompasses an infinite array of particular instructions and detailed information, cannot be tolerated. Because all details of the law have already been revealed, there exists no potential for interpretive latitude, for swerving from the straight and narrow path

---

[9]Tana Debei Eliyahu Zuta, ch. 2.
[10]B.T. Shabbath 23a.

of divine truth. R. Nehemiah's prooftext (Deut. 32:7) also maintains the divine sanction and pedigree of rabbinic statutes, but it conveys the impression of a more minimalistic underlying conception of the scope of revelation. The verse that R. Nehemiah brings implies an orientation towards revelation that is less rigid and uncompromising. Revelation is not fully comprehensive and not all-inclusively prescriptive. Such revelation is inherently more pliable and fluid, its decrees less absolute and pre-ordained. The shaping of the contours of the halachic path demands the creative contributions of sons as well as of their fathers.

This notion that God's revelation permits of, and requires, human augmentation and adaptation, that it is not yet exhaustive, is captured in the rabbinic midrash quoted earlier: "R. Yannai said: The words of the Torah were not given as clear-cut decisions...When Moses asked, 'Master of the universe, in what way shall we know the true sense of a law?' God replied, 'The majority is to be followed – when a majority says it is unclean, it is unclean; when a majority says it is clean, it is clean.'" This midrash embodies a vivid portrayal of man's decisive input into the process of implementing God's word. The Torah is not absolutely self-sufficient. Man's participation not only is permissible and legitimate but is compulsory. Human autonomy in the halachic process itself falls under the rubric of the divine mandate. Man must rely upon himself, and not upon God, to fashion a system that is conclusive and categorical from a revelation that was purposefully inconclusive and indeterminate.

The governing systemic principle of "acharei rabim le-hatot," of following majority opinion in matters of dispute, reflects the divinely-sanctioned human factor in halachic decision-making. Man is thereby empowered and commissioned by God to consummate the process of revelation, to make tangible and exact what had been revealed only in outline. The issue of the status and serviceability of minority opinion within a system that is governed by majority rule becomes a thorny one, and is addressed explicitly in the Mishnah itself.[11] The rationale behind the preservation and continued teaching of dissenting opinions is questioned. If revelation is concretized and realized in accordance with majority opinion, why then should minority positions ever be recorded rather than simply discarded and forgotten? Why maintain for posterity a textual record of rejected opinions?

The Mishnah in *Eduyoth* offers two answers, the first anonymously and the second in the name of R. Judah. The first answer explains that the preservation of minority opinion justifies and legitimates the reversal of past decisions by future courts. An uncontested opinion could

---

[11]Mishnah Eduyoth, 1:5-6.

never be reversed. Therefore, the presence of a dissenting opinion creates an avenue of reopening the case and repealing a previous decision. A recorded minority position, though currently rejected, is thus not consigned permanently to halachic oblivion. R. Judah assesses the value of the recording of minority opinion quite differently. His proposed rationale curtails the potential future usefulness of dissenting opinions. R. Judah explains that minority opinions are registered so that if a man shall say, 'I hold such a tradition' (in opposition to the majority tradition), another may reply to him, 'You have but heard it as the view of so-and-so.' The "tradition" in question can thus immediately and unambiguously be labeled a minority opinion, nullifying its claim to halachic legitimacy. According to R. Judah, the recording of minority views is motivated not by a desire to maintain avenues of judicial discretion, but by a need to close them off. For R. Judah, the label of "minority opinion" renders a dissenting opinion not potentially halachically viable, but halachically disabled and disqualified.

In analyzing these mishnayot, R. Samson ben Abraham of Sens (late 12th-early 13th century), one of the great French Tosafists, understood these two answers to correspond to contrasting implicit conceptions of revelation.[12] The first answer correlates to what we may call a non-maximalistic (this term henceforth encompasses both the intermediary and minimalistic rabbinic positions) conception of revelation. R. Samson of Sens explains that even though the minority opinion was not accepted previously, a later court may arise whose majority agrees with the minority position, and the dissenting opinion would then become legally binding. This halachic reversal is systemically legitimate and viable because of the underlying notion of revelation encapsulated within the midrash in the name of R. Yannai discussed earlier: "The majority is to be followed – when a majority says it is unclean, it is unclean; when a majority says it is clean, it is clean." The avenues of judicial discretion must remain open because man's participation in the process of revelation is a continual one. The halachic system was not revealed at Sinai *in toto,* and the legal process must therefore remain vibrant and active. Judicial recourse even to minority opinion must not be impeded.

According to R. Samson of Sens, the second answer offered in *Eduyoth,* that of R. Judah, corresponds to a maximalistic conception of revelation, which cannot tolerate the systemic viability of judicial reversal. Once the divine will has been clearly determined according to majority opinion, all divergent positions are rendered null and void.

---

[12]Tosafot Shanz, *ad. loc.*

Minority opinions are preserved precisely so that they will be recognized as halachically invalid, as non-revelatory, and thus incapable of being legally resuscitated. Upon this conception of revelation as all-encompassing, and as reflective purely of the divine will, man's role in the judicial process is merely *pro forma.* Because revelation is comprehensive, judicial discretion – the human component – must necessarily be circumscribed.

The issue of the status of minority opinion is thus linked to, and governed by, varying notions of revelation. A maximalistic conception of revelation is allied to the proclivity to diminish the stature of minority opinion, to curb judicial discretion, in an effort to maintain absolute halachic consistency and uniformity over time. A minority opinion must be branded an illegitimate halachic alternative because it runs counter to the directives of revelation. But the very existence of dissenting opinion – and of *machloketh* in general – in a system governed by a maximalistic conception of revelation is troublesome and unsettling. The reality of controversy in the midst of a relevation that is supposedly comprehensive and enveloping in scope is obviously problematic. Theoretically, that which is determined to be the minority position should not be invested with any halachic stature at all. In the introduction to his *Commentary to the Mishnah,* Maimonides states that nobody can disagree with a law claimed to be a "halacha le-Moshe mi-Sinai" (law given to Moses at Sinai). Based upon the logic of the maximalistic perspective, all the halachic determinations of the Oral Torah should be accorded the same treatment that Maimonides claims for a "halacha le-Moshe mi-Sinai," for all these, too, are of Sinaitic origin. The halachic preeminence and sanctity of majority opinions would then become inviolate, and minority opinions would become halachic non-entities. Yet, if minority opinion within a *machloketh* **is** granted any halachic legitimacy, then a maximalistic conception of revelation can account for controversies which entail deviation from the revealed on the part of the minority position only through mystical transcendence of the law of contradiction. Somehow, though the majority position represents and reflects absolute divine truth, the minority opinion is yet partially true. A maximalistic conception of revelation is forced to admit, in practice, the reality of *machloketh* and the continued record of minority views, even though, in theory, it cannot tolerate the persistence of dissenting opinion.

A non-maximalistic conception of revelation can more smoothly account for the reality of controversy and accommodate the halachic status of minority opinion. A recognition of the human component of the process of revelation can easily explain the reality of disagreement regarding the proper implementation of divinely-revealed principles. No human judgment, even if it follows the dictates of majority opinion, can be unequivocally true or certain. Both sides to a *machloketh* can retain a claim to truth if God offered Moses "forty-nine arguments by which a thing may be proved clean, and forty-nine other arguments by which it may be proved unclean." Even dissenting views can be subsumed under the legitimizing canopy of revelation.

The rabbinic principle of "Kedai hu R. Peloni lismokh alav bi-she'at ha-dechak"[13] (Rabbi X is sufficiently worthy to be relied upon in time of great need) supports the notion of revelation as supple and adaptable, able to accommodate the halachic merit of minority views. According to a maximalistic perspective of revelation, majority opinion is equivalent to absolute truth and minority opinion to absolute falsity – and an absolutely false position could never be justifiably relied upon.[14] The inclusion of the views of Beit Shammai in the Mishnah also constitutes evidence for an implicit non-maximalistic conception of revelation. Despite the fact that by the time of R. Judah the Prince the supremacy of Beit Hillel was already well-established and entrenched, the views of Beit Shammai, representative of the "losing" side of the halachic competition, are nevertheless recorded. The language of the Mishnah itself gives no indication that the views of Beit Shammai are absolutely false, which would not be the case were the maximalistic conception of revelation regnant. Although the statement "Beit Shammai be-makom Beit Hillel eino mishnah" (the view of Beit Shammai, when found side-by-side with that of Beit Hillel, is not even considered a legitimate teaching) can be found in the Gemara,[15] the evidence of the Mishnah does not favor the image of Beit Shammai as lacking all halachic value. Indeed, the purposeful inclusion of the views of Beit Shammai in the Mishnah argues not for their halachic triviality, but rather for their theoretical halachic validity.

Although a non-maximalistic conception of revelation can more easily tolerate the dissemination of minority opinion than can the maximalistic position, because of its acknowledgment of the human, and thus fallible, aspect of revelation, there still exist systemic halachic boundaries that limit the abrogation of majority views. The adoption of a non-maximalistic perspective of revelation does not

---

[13]B.T. Berakhoth 9a and parallels.

[14]"Maximalists" later tried to curtail the applicability of this principle by limiting it to cases in which the entire *issur* is *de-rabbanan,* and to cases in which the relevant law has not yet been codified.

[15]B.T. Berakhoth 36b and parallels.

necessitate an adjunct approach to halacha that is anarchic or unrestrained. The realization that human reason, judgment and interpretation are integral elements of the implementation of divine revelation does not mandate a legal system that is unbounded and unbridled in its creative license. Though it may more naturally and successfully carve a legal niche for minority opinion within the halachic system, the non-maximalistic conception of revelation is still committed to the overarching principle of "acharei rabim le-hatot," of following consensus in matters of dispute.

Recourse to an existent minority opinion is always a halachic alternative, but the reversal of consensus practice in the absence of a minority option is unsanctioned by systemic guidelines. Even the non-maximalistic position does not warrant the unchecked annulment of unanimous opinions. A consensus view on a legal issue, which had not been challenged by dissenting views when the issue originally arose, cannot validly be declared inoperative by a later generation. Unanimous positions of a previous generation cannot simply be abolished. Only when a new legal issue arises, one that has not been addressed in previous halachic discourse, does the requirement of recourse only to extant minority opinion become irrelevant.[16] The non-maximalistic conception of revelation does support the reopening of halachic avenues in the face of changing historical or social circumstances, but the range of legitimate halachic alternatives is bounded. The parameters of the original revelation, or in the formulation of the intermediary position, the "forty-nine arguments by which a thing may be proved clean, and forty-nine other arguments by

---

[16]The divergence between the maximalistic and non-maximalistic conceptions of revelation, as refracted through the prism of practical halacha, is prominent in the halachic decision-making process concerning a new legal issue. For the posek (jurist) who espouses a maximalistic position, the solution to a new halachic issue must already have been revealed, that is, can be found within the compass of previous halachic discourse. A posek who maintains a non-maximalistic position approaches a new halachic question with the realization that advances in science and factual information may be highly relevant, indeed, crucial to the determination of a solution. While the personal piety of the posek may be deemed of equal importance to cognitive knowledge for the maximalist, a non-maximalist posek applies with less hesitation his own cognitive resources, the fruits of his historical present, to the halachic issue at hand. The non-maximalist posek is more readily disposed to disagree with his predecessors than would the maximalist posek. He is also more inclined towards leniency to be a "meikel" where there is a dispute. For the non-maximalist, the solution to a new halachic issue had not been revealed at Sinai and is thus not pre-determined.

which it may be proved unclean," exercise a systemic restraint on halachic innovativeness. Recourse to a minority opinion already encompassed and embedded within the system ensures that this halachic alternative remains within the parameters of revelation, based on revelatory principles tacitly assumed within rabbinic halachic discourse. Options within the framework of an "old" issue are thus limited to minority positions already ratified by past generations, for this safeguards against interpretive free-for-all and halachic chaos. Therefore, though the non-maximalistic position respects the continued viability of minority opinion, it does not indulge an infinite range of halachic possibilities.

The right of minority opinion is most dramatically expressed in two stories, the first that of R. Eliezer and R. Joshua (wherein the Heavenly Voice sides with R. Eliezer, yet the law is nevertheless decided according to R. Joshua, who declares that the Torah "is not in heaven!")[17] and the second that of the dispute between God and His Heavenly Academy (a lesser known but more dramatic aggadah in which God and His Heavenly Academy are disputing a halachic question and summon Rabbah, a fourth century Amora, to decide the case).[18] There exists an extensive literature which discusses the

---

[17]B.T. Baba Metzia 59b. For readers unfamiliar with these stories, a fuller account follows: "...It has been taught: On that day R. Eliezer brought forward every imaginable argument, but they did not accept them. Said he to them: 'If the halacha agrees with me, let this carob tree prove it!' Thereupon the carob tree was torn a hundred cubits out of its place – others affirm, four hundred cubits. 'No proof can be brought from a carob tree,' they retorted. Again he said to them: 'If the halacha agrees with me, let the stream of water prove it!' Whereupon the stream of water flowed backwards. 'No proof can be brought from a stream of water,' they rejoined. Again he urged: 'If the halacha agrees with me, let the walls of the schoolhouse prove it,' whereupon the walls inclined to fall. But R. Joshua rebuked them, saying: 'When scholars are engaged in a halachic dispute, what concern is it of yours?' Hence the walls did not fall, in honor of R. Joshua, nor did they return to their upright position, in honor of R. Eliezer; and they are still standing thus inclined. Again he said to them: 'If the halacha agrees with me, let it be proved from Heaven!' Whereupon a Heavenly Voice cried out: 'Why do you dispute with R. Eliezer, seeing that in all matters the halacha agrees with him.' But R. Joshua arose and exclaimed: 'It is not in heaven' (Deut. 30:12). What did he mean by this? Said R. Jeremiah: 'That the Torah had already been given at Mount Sinai [and is thus no longer in heaven]. We pay no attention to a Heavenly Voice, because You have long since written in the Torah at Mount Sinai, 'One must incline after the majority' (Exod. 23:2)..."

[18]B.T. Baba Metzia 86a. "...Now, they were disputing in the Heavenly Academy thus: If the bright spot preceded the white hair, he is unclean; if the reverse, he

purpose of the story of R. Eliezer and R. Joshua. Some commentators claim that the purpose of the story was to extol the greatness of R. Eliezer, as a Heavenly Voice intervened in his behalf. Others claim that the purpose was to preserve the independence of the judicial system, including majority rule, by safeguarding it against outside encroachment – even that of divine intervention. Still others see in the story a triumph of the human over the divine, as divine intervention failed to change the decision of the human majority. None of these purposes, however, successfully accounts for the other story concerning the dispute between God and His Heavenly Academy. That story does not explicitly mention that the law was decided according to the majority, a crucial aspect if the latter two purposes are to be maintained. On the contrary, Rabbah, the Babylonian Amora summoned to heaven to decide the case, sides with God against the heavenly majority.

In the forthcoming book, I have therefore suggested a different purpose, namely that the intention of these two stories was to promote the right of the minority to advocate its opinion by endowing the minority opinion with a divine imprimatur even as, practically, it is being rejected. Minority opinion, the stories tell us, may sometimes be expressive of divine opinion and because of that eventuality must never be suppressed. Minority opinion must always be allowed to compete freely for the acceptance of its intellectual worth even as, at the same time, it must be accompanied by an awareness of its consignment to the realm of study only.

In the story of R. Eliezer and R. Joshua, God admitted that "my children (the majority) have defeated me, my children have defeated me." Practically, God's opinion could not prevail. It was the opinion of the minority, and by systemic guidelines minority opinion cannot prevail in the realm of practical law. A similar fate awaited God's opinion in His dispute with the Heavenly Academy. The law was

---

is clean. If [the order is] in doubt – the Holy One, blessed be He, ruled, 'He is clean'; while the entire Heavenly Academy maintained, 'He is unclean.' 'Who shall decide it?' they asked. – Rabbah b. Nachmani; for he said, 'I am pre-eminent in the laws of leprosy and tents.' A messenger was sent for him, but the Angel of Death could not approach him, because he did not interrupt his studies [even for a moment]. In the meantime, a wind blew and caused a rustling in the bushes, when he imagined it to be a troop of soldiers. 'Let me die,' he exclaimed, 'rather than be delivered into the hands of the State.' As he was dying, he exclaimed, 'Clean, clean!' when a Heavenly Voice cried out, 'Happy are you, O Rabbah b. Nachmani, whose body is pure and whose soul had departed in purity!'..."

ultimately to be decided in favor of the majority. Nevertheless, the minority position was the opinion of the Divine, "whose stamp is truth." It is thus in a fundamental sense a true opinion and, as such, must be intellectually tolerated. In the story of the Heavenly Voice, when the majority excommunicated R. Eliezer and prevented him from communicating with his students, God, as it were, became angry and "the world was smitten." R. Eliezer's dissenting opinion, though a minority position by quantitative standards, must be granted intellectual tolerance on account of its qualitative merit. Minority opinion here coincides with divine truth and, as a result, must not be suppressed.

As these stories indicate, the implementation of the revealed principles may not be in consonance with the dictates of the "objective" content of revelation – which in these stories is identical with divine opinion – yet as part of the divine relinquishment to man it becomes the obligatory law for practical purposes. Intellectually, however, it is not binding. A non-maximalistic view of revelation thus leads to a necessary acceptance of "dichotomism," or a dual exegetical mode, one reserved for practical law and one for intellectual endeavor. A dichotomy between matters of the intellect and matters of practical law can maintain halachic uniformity while permitting intellectual multiformity. The notion of "dichotomization" (though too large a topic to be treated fully here, it will be dealt with at greater length in my forthcoming book) can be wedded fruitfully to a non-maximalistic conception of revelation. Halachic homogeneity and intellectual latitude can then be embraced simultaneously.

The fundamental issue of the substantive scope of revelation occupied the attention of prominent Jewish thinkers throughout the middle ages. As the halachic system developed and expanded, the question of man's role in revelation could not be evaded. The perennial tension between revelation and reason was felt by Jewish legal authorities responsible for the continued workability of the halachic system. R. Joseph Albo (1380-1444) tackled the issue of the revelation of the Oral Torah in his *Sefer Ha-Ikkarim:* "Why wasn't the entire Torah given in written form? This is because the law of God cannot be perfect so as to be adequate for all times, because the ever new details of human relations are too numerous to be included within a book. Therefore, Moses was given orally at Sinai only general principles, only briefly alluded to in the Torah, by means of which the wise men in every generation may work out the details as they appear."[19] This statement epitomizes the minimalistic conception of revelation and

---

[19]*Sefer Ha-Ikkarim*, Book Three, section 23.

affirms the indispensability of human participation and contribution. Without the creative efforts of human beings, God's revelation would remain fragmentary and amorphous.

In stark contrast to the minimalist position of R. Joseph Albo stands the extreme maximalist position of R. Avraham Yeshayahu Karelitz, the "Chazon Ish" (1878-1953). Although the stance of the Chazon Ish emerges from a very different milieu from that of R. Joseph Albo, the juxtaposition of their divergent conceptions of revelation is quite illuminating. The Chazon Ish writes that "everything written in the Talmud, whether in the Mishnah or in the Gemara, whether in halacha or *in aggadah,* (emphasis added) were things revealed to us through prophetic powers (i.e., divinely) ...and whoever deviates from this tenet is as one who denies the words of our Rabbis, and his ritual slaughtering is invalid and he is disqualified from testimony."[20] For the Chazon Ish, the revelation of the Oral Torah was all-inclusive, embracing even the non-halachic portions of the Talmud. This stance takes us infinitely beyond the revelation of mere principles.

Another medieval Talmudic commentator who struggled with the parameters of revelation was R. Yom Tov ben Abraham Ishbili (Ritba, ca. 1250-1330). The Ritba was especially engaged with the question of the status of *asmachta,* the exegetical device of a scriptural verse being used as a loose support for a rabbinical enactment. Being of the maximalist school, the Ritba was uncomfortable with the notion of *asmachta* as merely a mnemonic device, a "decorative" technique of exegesis. He had difficulty accepting the nebulous status of *asmachta* ordinances, and felt theologically compelled to elevate their standing. The Ritba writes: "Everything for which we have an *asmachta* from a verse, the Holy One, Blessed Be He, has noted that it is fitting to do so; however, He did not fix it as an obligation, but passed it on to the Sages. And this is a clear and true idea, and it is contrary to the words of those who explain *asmachtot* as merely mnemonic devices which the Sages give and which the Torah itself did not intend. God forbid that this opinion [that an *asmachta* is merely a mnemonic device] should gain permanence and it not be said that, in fact, it is a heretical view...The Sages give in every instance a proof, an allusion, or an *asmachta* to their words from the Torah. That is to say, they never invent things themselves, but rather the whole Oral Law is hinted at in the written Torah, which is perfect, and God forbid that it is lacking anything."[21] The Ritba could not deny that these rabbinic ordinances are not explicitly mentioned in the written Torah, but he attempted

---

[20]*Kovetz Iggerot,* 1:59.
[21]Commentary on B.T. Rosh ha-Shanah 16a.

neverthless to reinforce their quasi de-oraitha status. These *asmachta* ordinances become exegetical hybrids in the Ritba's effort to maximize their status. What emerges is an intermediary conception of revelation, a compromise position which vacillates between the minimalistic and maximalistic stances. Though aware of the rabbinic role in creating and classifying halacha, the Ritba strains to maintain a comprehensive conception of revelation.

A similar, but even more strident, affirmation of the elevated status of *asmachta,* in line with a maximalistic conception of revelation, was made by R. Judah Loew ben Betzalel, the Maharal of Prague (1512-1609). The Maharal censures those who would assess the technique of *asmachta* as merely an artificial exegetical device, designed only to fabricate a textual link where none really exists. The Maharal writes that *asmachta* represents a divine allowance for scriptural supplementaion on the part of the sages, and not a synthetic and deceptive excuse for textual embellishment: "*[asmachta]* is as if the Torah said, 'You sages have the right to add in this place [in the text] and it will be considered your opinion.' ...But now [in contrast to the sages' use of *asmachta*] there are commentators who are explicating the text falsely, in whatever way moves their fancy. I have no doubt that the Torah mourns over those who interpret [the text] as they please, for this is like the non-Jewish exegetes who interpret so capriciously."[22] For the Maharal, the claim that the rabbis of the Talmud simply manipulated the scriptural text through the contrivance of *asmachta* is insupportable and objectionable. *Asmachta,* for the Maharal, is the exegetical product of a joint divine-human effort, legitimately anchored in the divine text. Such interpretation is neither artificial nor whimsical as detractors of rabbinic exegesis may claim, but mandated, and actuated, by the divine text itself. Like the Ritba, the Maharal downplays the creative human role in revelation, diminishing the hermeneutic autonomy of exegetes.

These contrasting theoretical conceptions of man's role in revelation yield divergent practical, that is, halachic, dividends. The theoretical, abstract discussion of whether earlier generations should be properly characterized as angels or as human beings, of whether they were active or passive in the process of revelation, impinges upon concrete halachic issues. The issue of the encounter between halacha and science, for example, is directly affected by one's underlying conception of revelation. One's notion of revelation will have a halachic bearing on the question of what attitude one should assume toward science and other acceptable cultural values. Theoretical

---

[22]Maharal, *Gur Aryeh,* Yithro (Exod. 19:15).

discourse on the matter of the nature of revelation thus cannot be sequestered within the realm of idle and inconsequential speculation, for it may produce weighty ramifications for the sphere of practical halacha. Conceptions of revelation are necessarily tied to notions of truth and its sources and thus will inform and shape the halachic decision-making process.

The maximalistic view of revelation avows that the scope of revelation is all-encompassing. Revelation embodies the totality of truth, and all claims which run counter to revelation are, *ipso facto*, false. Upon this view, there exists no legitimate autonomous source of truth which can potentially furnish truth claims in conflict with those of revelation. To earn the stamp of legitimacy and truth, a claim must thus find its prooftext in revelation. Scientific claims and cultural norms constitute, at best, tentative truths which must be validated and justified through reference to the body of revealed truth. These tentative truths cannot be invested with the same authority and certainty with which the divinely-revealed Law is endowed and thus are, in a fundamental sense, inferior to explicit truths of revelation.

The minimalistic conception of revelation, which shies away from such an all-embracing conception of revelation and asserts that God revealed to man only principles to implement and not a fully-comprehensive catalog of details, leaves room for autonomous sources of truth. Indeed, from this non-maximalistic perspective, revelation *must* be complemented and supplemented by the results of man's rational endeavors. To implement and concretize the principles of revelation, human beings must depend upon their most reliable "mortal" channels of the affirmation of truth, and for modern man, these are science and reason. Uncertainty is an ineluctable factor of such human effort, but the limited scope of the content of revelation demands that man complete the process that God only initiated.

These polar conceptions of revelation, and their corollary attitudes towards the range of legitimate sources of truth, are reflected in the views of two leading medieval rabbinic authorities. The disjunction between their positions will be readily apparent, yet both views can be traced to derivations from rabbinic thought. The first view is embodied within a famous responsum (no. 98) of R. Solomon ben Abraham Adret (Rashba, 1235-1310) which deals with the issue of the life-expectancy of t'refa animals. The Rashba was asked whether the statement found in the Talmud, that claims that t'refa animals do not live more than twelve months, could be relied upon in all instances. The questioner suggested that the Talmudic categorization of t'refa animals was not universally valid, that exceptions to it seemed reasonable. If animals classified as t'refa could survive, despite illness, longer than twelve months, could they be retroactively considered as no longer t'reifa? This question subtly advanced the notion that the veterinary science of the rabbis was neither infallible nor immutable.

The Rashba could not tolerate such a notion, which he considered heretical and subversive. His responsum bristles with displeasure, its tone indignant and acrimonious: "To slander the Rabbis is intolerable. Let people of this sort be put to naught, but let not one iota of what was approved by the holy wise men of Israel, prophets and sons of prophets, their words spoken to Moses on Sinai, be nullified." The Rashba goes on to state that even if such people claim that the rabbis' proposition has been empirically disproved, their claim should be forcefully denied so that the words of the rabbis should be confirmed and not disparaged.

The Rashba is annoyed on both a practical and a theoretical level. First, his concern is that the slightest deviation from the established laws of t'refot can undermine the practical stability and authority of the halachic system.[23] This solicitude for communal halachic uniformity is easily understood. On a more theoretical level, the responsum reveals that the Rashba's conception of the rabbis approximates the "sons of man" category of R. Zera's statement. The words of the rabbis are immutable and unimpeachable, for their derivation is Sinaitic. The rabbis have transmitted a revelation that is comprehensive in scope and divine in all its particulars. Because they have exercised no creative interpretive license, the legacy of revelation that they have imparted to future generations is of an unadulteratedly divine nature. Revelation is the fountainhead of rabbinic thought, and medieval reason can neither challenge nor supersede the sovereignty of revelation in the realm of halacha. For the Rashba, the rabbis must be considered all-knowing even in matters of veterinary science. The divinity of rabbinic claims cannot admit of error. To concede that the scientific knowledge of the rabbis is somehow deficient or flawed is to concede that divine revelation itself is somehow blemished. Such a prospect is, for the Rashba, unthinkable and repugnant.

The Rashba thus assumes a maximalistic stance towards revelation and imbues rabbinic dicta with the status of revealed truth. Revelation is for him all-emcompassing, and the rabbis, as the bearers of its truth, are the greatest of scientists as they are the greatest of jurists. Rav

---

[23]C.f. *Mishnah Torah*, Sechita 10, 11-13. He, however, stops short of saying that all of the rules of *trefa* were given to Moses on Sinai. See also his responsum to R. Jonathan of Lunel, published in Blau's edition, vol. 11, 315. For an interesting comment on this Rambam, see R.N.S. Glausner, *Dor Revii*, Klausenburg, 1921, Introduction, p. 4.

Sherira Gaon (10th century) had adopted a quite different perspective of both revelation and the rabbis. Through his theoretical prism, revelation emerges as circumscribed and the rabbis as quite mortal. His attitude towards the fallibility of rabbinic scientific claims thus contrasts quite dramatically with that of the Rashba. In a responsum of his own, Rav Sherira Gaon states quite straightforwardly: "We have to conclude that our Rabbis, of blessed memory, were not doctors and their claims are based on their observations in their own day of cases of illness and are not matters of religious duty for which one receives reward. Therefore, do not rely on their medical cures and only act on their prescriptions after consulting medical specialists, so that neither harm nor danger will befall you."[24]

This statement clearly depicts the rabbis as fallible mortals, at least in the realm of medical knowledge. But even this minimal allowance for rabbinic imperfection is intolerable for the Rashba. Rav Sherira Gaon unambiguously conceives of Talmudic medical knowledge as provisional, as non-eternal, and thus distinguishable from revealed truth. For Rav Sherira, not all rabbinic claims fall within the province of revelation or are of divine provenance. This conception of revelation leaves room for scientific advances, and the accompanying conception of truth allows leeway for rabbinic fallibility. The divinity of revelation is left untarnished despite Rav Sherira's down-to-earth conception of the rabbis. Though the rabbis are possessed of scientific knowledge that is time-bound and conditional, they are nevertheless "sons of angels," for their interpretive effort has been directed, by divine mandate, towards the explication and amplification of God's revelation.

The responsa of the Rashba and Rav Sherira Gaon recommend two divergent approaches to the issue of the permissibility of new scientific evidence as a legitimate factor in the halachic process. But the theoretical underpinnings of their halachic responsa, though implicit, are actually determinative of their practical recommendations. Their contrasting attitudes towards revelation, reason and the rabbis were culled from the rich diversity of rabbinic perspectives on these issues, all packaged tightly in R. Zera's statement, "If the earlier [scholars] were sons of angels..." If the rabbis were ordinary men upon whom

---

[24]This responsum is referred to in B.M. Levine's *Biography of Rav Sherira Gaon*, p. 15 and *idem.*, *Otzar Ha-Geonim*, Gittin, responsum no. 376. See also R. Azariah de Rossi (1511-1578), *Meor Enayim*, p. 167: "For in these matters they (the Rabbis) did not claim that they had prophetic traditions."

revelation was imposed heteronomously,[25] who introduced no human component into the composition of revelation due to the passivity of their role but rather communicated revelation literally, then their statements even about science must be accepted as eternally valid and binding. As the Rashba maintained, even their scientific claims then carry the aura of divinity. On the other hand, Rav Sherira Gaon, more comfortable with the representation of the rabbis as inventive and autonomous agents of revelation, can less problematically accept the reality of advancing scientific knowledge, without damage to the integrity of the halachic process. The opinions of the rabbis of the Talmud in matters which are not strictly ritual are not necessarily more trustworthy than the general consensus of contemporary experts. This conception of revelation can securely accommodate the progress of reason.

The maximalistic stance of the Rashba has gradually gained ascendancy in the arena of competing conceptions of revelation (partially due to the fact that the Rambam, at the beginning of the *Mishneh Torah,* seems to favor this view of revelation). But the diversity of views expressed within rabbinic literature cannot be denied, and the speculative question of the nature of revelation remains an open one. Shall we view the "rishonim" as "sons of angels" or as "sons of man," as active or passive in the process of revelation? Should we conceive of revelation as a circumscribed or comprehensive body of truth? These questions are not merely theoretical, for they may impinge on decisions of practical halacha and influence attitudes towards science, as we have seen in the cases of the Rashba and Rav Sherira Gaon. If everything was determined at Sinai, interpretive maneuverability and latitude become constricted.[26] Man's creative role in revelation becomes a highly limited and restricted one.

---

[25]We are not unaware of the philosophical innuendo that attends the term "heteronomy" for the reader familiar with the Kantian critique of Judaism. Kant's claim that Judaism is a heteronomous religion, and thus lacking in genuine religiosity, has represented a serious philosophical challenge to many post-Kantian Jewish thinkers.

[26]Judgments about man's role in the process of revelation are directly related to conceptions of the relationship between the written and oral Torahs. As might be expected, the maximalistic position lessens the difference between the "Torah she-bikhetav" (written) and the "Torah she-be'al peh" (oral), for the axiomatic belief of this position is that both were revealed at Sinai, and thus both are divine through and through. The only real distinction made between the written Torah and the oral Torah is to be found in the degree of strictness attached to the observance of the practical halachot of each. Laws of the written Torah are more binding, enforced with greater rigor, than those of the

The non-maximalistic conceptions of revelation provide the advantages of exegetical flexibility and halachic elasticity, as well as theoretical support for the acceptability of intellectual freedom. If God limited the scope of revelation so that man must work to complete it, if man must of necessity draw upon his own resources and faculties, namely science and reason, then imprecision and imperfection must be recognized as constituent, because human, elements of the system. In fact, even human error is divinely-sanctioned, for the systemic principle of "acharei rabim le-hatot" represents a divine mandate for human participation, with all its attendant foibles. Uncertainty about whether our human conclusions accord with objective divine truth is an unavoidable dimension of the process of interpreting and implementing revelation. This uncertainty demands that humility and tolerance go hand in hand with intellectual strivings, for it must be borne in mind, as the story of Rabbi Eliezer teaches us, that minority opinion may actually express the divine will. Smug dogmatism must dissipate, and tolerance proliferate, as we recognize that our human intellectual achievements can never achieve the unequivocal certitude of divine truth.

As we have seen, a non-maximalistic conception of revelation can more satisfactorily accommodate controversy, dissension and disagreement within the halachic system. A tolerance of minority opinion is a necessary corollary of a conception of revelation that can securely grant a measure of truth to dissenting opinion without fear of tarnishing the authority and prestige of the system as a whole. An efficacious balance between reason and revelation promotes tolerance of dissent because it deflates the pretensions of the majority to utter surety. Doubt is injected into the system, but man's role in the process of

---

oral Torah. Acharonim have claimed that the rabbinic principle of "mutav she-yehiyu shogegin ve-al yehiyu mezidin" [better that people violate the law inadvertently, i.e., without intent, than violate it willfully] (B.T. Beitzah 30a and parallels) applies only to halachot of the oral Torah. If a person is about to violate a law of the *written* Torah, and it is judged that he would violate the law even if the details of the law and the severity of the matter were made known to him, it is an obligation nevertheless to tell him of the prohibition he is about to violate (based on Levit. 19:17, "hokheach tokhiach et amitekha. . ."). Such would not be the case were the violation of a law of the oral Torah at stake, for then his continued ignorance of the matter is preferable. According to the non-maximalistic position, in contrast, the qualitative distinction between the written Torah and the oral Torah is highlighted to a greater degree, for the recognition of the human component of the oral Torah carries in its wake a corollary recognition of the superior status of the absolutely divine written Torah.

revelation is thereby recognized and respected while the divinity of revelation is safeguarded.[27]

[27]I would like to thank my teaching assistant, Mr. Marc Ashley, for his stylistic assistance in the preparation of this essay.

Part Seven
FORMATIVE JUDAISM: LITERATURE

19

Did the Talmud's Authorship Utilize Prior "Sources"?: A Response to Halivni's *Sources and Traditions*

Jacob Neusner
Brown University

A master of the rabbinic literature who, in his splendid life of intellectual service to Israel and the Jewish people, has exemplified the highest goals for humanity "in our image, after our likeness," as the Torah portrays that likeness, Marvin Fox has devoted his life to study of Torah. And that, in the nature of things, means study of the Talmud and related writings. Accordingly, a paper on rabbinic hermeneutics composed in his honor finds a suitable place in this volume. Not only so, but the specific topic, the assessment of the exegetical results of David Weiss Halivni, the leading exegete of rabbinic literature in our own generation, is particularly germane, since Halivni, also represented in these pages, and Fox form a single cohort, having framed their careers in precisely the same age and model: masters of Torah who also are professors in universities. Having spent fifteen years in a careful reading of Halivni's work, I therefore choose this occasion to set down my final judgment upon it, knowing that, *sine ira et studio*, the results will honor both the subject, David Weiss Halivni, because of the close and careful attention given to his *ouevre*, and the honoree, Marvin Fox, because of the subject matter and its timeliness.

In his commentary to selected passages of the Talmud of Babylonia (Bavli), David Weiss Halivni has worked out not merely episodic and ad hoc remarks about diverse passages but a sustained hermeneutics, in which a theory of the whole has guided him in his identification, in many parts, of problems demanding solution. In his *Sources and Traditions,*[1] Halivni sets forth the theory that the Bavli is made up of sources, "those sayings which have come down to us in their original form, as they were uttered by their author," and traditions, "those which were changed in the course of transmission." Changing these "traditions" required later generations to deal with the remains of earlier statements, and they did so by a "forced interpretation" (in Halivni's language). Halivni knows how to deal with the problem of the "forced interpretation," distinguishing it from the simple one as follows, in the account of Robert Goldenberg:[2]

> The simple interpretation of a text is defined as "the interpretation which arises from the text itself, without either adding to it or subtracting from it." Sometimes a simple comparison with parallel sources is sufficient to show that a forced explanation has its origin in an incorrect text....In most cases, however, it is necessary to study the sugya in depth, to break it into its parts before the motivation for the forced explanation becomes clear.

Halivni's sense for the self-evidence of his position is expressed as follows: "Any divergence from the simple interpretation is a divergence from the truth."[3] The work is entirely exegetical; there is no historical inquiry whatever. He takes for granted the reliability of all attributions, the historicity of all stories.[4] Literary criticism plays no role in his identification of exegetical problems or in their solution, and everything is either a source or a tradition, so Goldenberg, "The reliability of the tradition and the manner of its formation are to a great extent simply assumed, despite the mass of evidence of a more complicated situation that Weiss's own book reveals."[5]

Part of the problem of studying Halivni's *ouevre* is his failure to deal with competing theories of the literature, on the one side, and his incapacity to compose a null hypothesis for the testing of his hermeneutic, on the other. His unwillingness to read other scholars' treatment of the same literature and problems has now become so

---

[1]*Mekorot umesorot* (Tel Aviv: 1968 *et seq.*)

[2]Robert Goldenberg, "David Weiss Halivni, Meqorot umesorot: Ketuvot," in J. Neusner, ed., *The Formation of the Babylonian Talmud* (Leiden: E. J. Brill 1970), p. 136.

[3]Cited by Goldenberg, p. 137.

[4]See Goldenberg, *op. cit.*, p. 146.

[5]Goldenberg, *op. cit.*, p. 147.

notorious as to elicit the comments of book reviewers.[6] We really do not know, therefore, how Halivni has taken into account other approaches to the same literature, competing theories of its character, origins, and, consequently, correct hermeneutics. That fact, his failure to read and comment on the work of others and its implications for his own work, renders the critical reading of Halivni's ouevre exceedingly parlous.

The omission of a null hypothesis can now be demonstrated to form a fatal flaw in his entire hermeneutical fabrication. In this article, I shall show how one might compose and test a null hypothesis as to the character of the sources subjected to exegesis. On that basis we shall see that Halivni's premise of a composite text, in which materials that preserve original versions are mixed together with materials that exhibit deformations of those original versions, contradicts the character of the Talmud of the Land of Israel or Yerushalmi. Indeed, any exegesis that rests upon Halivni's premises will violate the fundamental literary traits of the Yerushalmi, and, everyone must then recognize, the Bavli as well, which in these traits does not differ in any material way. Having devoted considerable effort to the study of Halivni's ouevre,[7] I am now prepared to address its principal positions

[6]Cf., for example, David Singer in *Commentary*, April 1988, p. XXX, on Halivni's disinterest in views other than his own. He apparently does not even read and take account of competing readings of the same documents.

[7]See the articles by Goldenberg, Shamai Kanter, "David Weiss Halivni, *Meqorot uMesorot. Qiddushin*," in *Formation of the Babylonian Talmud*, pp. 148-1563, and David Goodblatt, "David Weiss Halivni, *Meqorot uMesorot. Gittin*," in *Formation of the Babylonian Talmud*, pp. 164-173; also Jacob Neusner, ed., *The Modern Study of the Mishnah* (Leiden: E. J. Brill, 1973), in particular Joel Gereboff, "David Weiss Halivni on the Mishnah," pp. 180-196; and William Scott Green, ed., *Law as Literature = Semeia. An Experimental Journal for Biblical Criticism* 27 (Chico: Scholars Press for Society of Biblical Literature, 1983), pp. 37-116. Note in particular Louis Newman, "The Work of David Weiss Halivni: A Source Critical Commentary to b. Yebamot 87b," in which Newman compares Halivni's exegetical approach to that of Shamma Friedman, treated at length in the same collection of papers. All of these papers were prepared in my graduate seminar. From 1968 through 1983, I regularly devoted semesters to the comparative study and history of the exegesis of the rabbinic literature and paid close attention to Halivni's work in the context of the modern hermeneutics of the Talmud, broadly construed. In the context of Singer's devastating comments on Halivni, the three monographs that I have brought into being, whole or in part, should be called to mind. My impression is that Halivni has so persuaded himself of the correctness of his views that he found it unnecessary to read competing approaches just as he found it unproductive to compose a null hypothesis and to test it. In his defense, however, it should be said that what outsiders might

and to demonstrate that they contradict the evidence, read from an analytical and critical perspective. They form, therefore, merely another chapter in the dreary story of fundamentalist exegesis of a text not studied but merely recited. Absent a null hypothesis presented and analyzed by Halivni himself, we have no alternative but to judge as a missed opportunity his entire exegetical *ouevre* and the hermeneutical theory on which it rests.

If Halivni were right, then we should identify in the Talmuds a multiplicity of voices. But the opposite characterizes the Yerushalmi. The Talmud Yerushalmi utilizes a single, rather limited repertoire of exegetical initiatives and rhetorical choices for whatever discourse about the Mishnah the framers of the Talmud Yerushalmi propose to undertake. The Yerushalmi identifies no author or collegium of authors. When I say that the Talmud Yerushalmi speaks in a single voice, I mean to say it everywhere speaks uniformly, consistently, and predictably. The voice is the voice of a book. The ubiquitous character of this single and continuous voice of the Talmud Yerushalmi argues for one of two points of origin. First, powerful and prevailing conventions may have been formed in the earliest stages of the reception and study of the Mishnah, then carried on thereafter without variation or revision. Or, second, the framing of sayings into uniform constructions of discourse may have been accomplished only toward the end of the period marked by the formation of the Talmud Yerushalmi Yerushalmi's units of discourse and their conglomeration into the Talmud Yerushalmi Yerushalmi of the Land of Israel as we know it. This latter possibility is pertinent to the claim of David Weiss Halivni that the Talmud (he speaks of the Bavli, but the Yerushalmi provides a perfectly adequate extension to his position) rests upon prior writings or traditions, and that these writings or traditions are preserved in the document as we have it. Let us examine the two possibilities for explaining the Yerushalmi's authorship's uniformity of discourse.

In the former case, we posit that the mode of reasoned analysis of the Mishnah and the repertoire of issues to be addressed to any passage of the Mishnah were defined early on, then persisted for two hundred years. The consequent, conventional mode of speech yielded that nearly total uniformity of discourse characteristic of numerous units of discourse of the Yerushalmi at which the interpretation of a law of the Mishnah is subject to discussion. In the latter case we surmise that a vast corpus of sayings, some by themselves, some parts of larger

---

deem to be intellectual sloth or mere self-absorption is in fact an established convention in the field of rabbinics, one that Halivni merely replicates.

conglomerates, was inherited at some point toward the end of the two hundred years under discussion. This corpus of miscellanies was then subjected to intense consideration as a whole, shaped and reworded into the single, cogent and rhetorically consistent Talmud Yerushalmi discourse before us. That would seem to me to contradict the position outlined by Halivni in his exegetical work on the Bavli. Indeed, if we see this Talmud (and the other) as a work accomplished essentially in the ultimate phase of its redaction, then there can be no strong case for the authorship's extensively using and preserving prior "traditions" and "sources," in the language of Halivni. In that case, his entire exegetical program rests upon false premises. Seeing the document whole argues strongly in favor of the second of the two possibilities and hence against Halivni's fundamental hermeneutics.

As between these two possibilities, the latter seems by far the more likely. The reason is simple. I cannot find among the Yerushalmi's units of discourse concerning the Mishnah evidence of differentiation among the generations of names or schools. But a null hypothesis, that is, evidence against my position and in favor of Halivni's, would dictate that such differentiation among the putative "sources and traditions" should be much in evidence. To the contrary, there is no interest, for instance, in the chronological sequence in which sayings took shape and in which discussions may be supposed to have been carried on. That is to say, the Talmud Yerushalmi unit of discourse approaches the explanation of a passage of the Mishnah without systematic attention to the layers in which ideas were set forth, the schools among which discussion must have been divided, the sequence in which statements about a Mishnah-law were made. That fact points to formation at the end, like igneous rock, and assuredly not agglutination in successive layers of intellectual sediment, such as Halivni's "sources and traditions" leads us to anticipate.

Once the elemental literary facts make their full impression on our understanding, everything else falls into place as well. Arguments such as the ones we shall now review did not unfold over a long period of time, as one generation made its points, to be followed by the additions and revisions of another generation, in a process of gradual increment and agglutination running on for two hundred years. That theory of the formation of literature cannot account for the unity, stunning force and dynamism, of the Talmud Yerushalmi dialectical arguments. To the contrary, some person (or small group) at the end determined to reconstruct, so as to expose, the naked logic of a problem. For this purpose, oftentimes, it was found useful to cite sayings or positions in hand from earlier times. But these inherited materials underwent a process of reshaping, and, more aptly, refocusing. Whatever the original words – and we need not doubt that at times we have them – the point of everything in hand was defined and determined by the people who made it all up at the end. The whole shows a plan and program. Theirs are the minds behind the whole. In the nature of things, they did their work at the end, not at the outset. To be sure, the numerous examples we shall now inspect may, as I just said, yield one of two conclusions. We may see them as either the gradual and "natural" increment of a sedimentary process or as the creation of single-minded geniuses of applied logic and sustained analytical inquiry. But there is no intermediate possibility.

One qualification is required. I do not mean to say the principles of chronology were wholly ignored. Rather, they were not determinative of the structure of argument. So I do not suggest that the framers of the Talmud Yerushalmi would likely have an early authority argue with a later one about what is assigned only to the later one. That I cannot and do not expect to instantiate. I do not think we shall find such slovenly work in either our Talmud Yerushalmi Yerushalmi or the other one. Our sages were painstaking and sensible. The point is that no attention ever is devoted in particular to the sequence in which various things are said. Everything is worked together into a single, temporally-seamless discourse. Thus if a unit of discourse draws upon ideas of authorities of the first half of the third century, such as Simeon b. Laqish and Yohanan, as well as those of figures of the second half of the fourth century, such as Yose, Jonah, Huna, Zeira, and Yudan, while discourse will be continuous, discussion will always focus upon the logical point at hand.

If Halivni were right, then principles of composition and conglomeration would prove contradictory, so that a discourse or sustained discussion of a problem would appear jerrybuilt and ad hoc. But any analysis of whole units of discourse, as distinct from the sentences that define the arena for Halivni's analysis, shows the opposite. Analysis of any passage beginning to end demonstrates that the whole is the work of the one who decided to make up the discussion on the atemporal logic of the point at issue. Otherwise – again the null hypothesis, that would favor Halivni's position – the discussion would be not the way it is: continuous. Rather, discourse would prove disjointed, full of seams and margins, marks of the existence of prior conglomerations of materials that have now been sewn together. What we have are not patchwork quilts, but woven fabric. Along these same lines, we may find discussions in which opinions of Palestinians, such as Yohanan and Simon b. Laqish, will be joined together side by side with opinions of Babylonians, such as Rab and Samuel. The whole, once again, will unfold in a smooth way, so that the issues at hand define the sole focus of discourse. The logic of those issues will be fully exposed. Considerations of the origin of a saying in one country or the other will play no role whatsoever in the rhetoric or literary forms of argument. There will be no possibility of differentiation among opinions on the basis of where, when, by whom, or how they are formulated, only on the basis of what, in fact, is said.

In my view it follows that the whole – the unit of discourse as we know it – was put together at the end. At that point everything was in hand, so available for arrangement in accordance with a principle other than chronology, and in a rhetoric common to all sayings. That other principle will then have determined the arrangement, drawing in its wake resort to a single monotonous voice: "the Talmud Yerushalmi." The principle is logical exposition, that is to say, the analysis and dissection of a problem into its conceptual components. The dialectic of argument is framed not by considerations of the chronological sequence in which sayings were said but by attention to the requirements of reasonable exposition of the problem. That is what governs.

The upshot is simple. In these two traits the Yerushalmi's character utterly refutes the hermeneutical premises of Halivni's reading of the Talmud. First, the Yerushalmi speaks with a single, fixedly-modulated voice. Second, the Yerushalmi exposes the logic of ideas in a dialectical argument framed without regard to the time and place of the participants. In fact, the Yerushalmi (not to mention the Bavli) is like the Mishnah in its fundamental literary traits, therefore also in its history. Both documents were made up at the end, and whatever materials are used are used to achieve the purposes of ultimate redaction. Any theory of "sources" as against "traditions" will have to explain why some things were changed and some things were not changed. But all Halivni explains is that where he finds "forced interpretations," that imputed trait, which he himself fabricates or posits, identifies the "tradition" as distinct from the "source." And then the exegesis takes on its own momentum.

But, to the contrary, the literary history of the Mishnah, and, by analogy, of the Yerushalmi and the Bavli, begins on the day it concludes. Therefore there can be no distinguishing "sources" from "traditions" on the foundation of the evidence of the document, and that is the only evidence (as distinct from premise or postulate or first principle, to which, these days, intellectual discourse rarely appeals!) that we have. Accordingly, Halivni's basic mode of thought is, in a precise sense, a recrudescence of medieval philosophy, which begins not with data and inductive analysis thereof but from postulates, premises, and first principles. In the case at hand, we know that the Mishnah was formulated in its rigid, patterned language and carefully organized and enumerated groups of formal-substantive cognitive units, in the very processes in which it also was redacted. Otherwise the correspondences between redactional program and formal and patterned mode of articulation of ideas cannot be explained, short of invoking the notion of a literary miracle. Then on what basis shall we know the difference between "sources" and "traditions," unless we know without evidence that the work is composed, indifferently, of sources and traditions? The same argument pertains to the Talmuds. The Yerushalmi evidently underwent a process of redaction, in which fixed and final units of discourse (whether as I have delineated them or in some other division) were organized and put together.

The probably antecedent work of framing and formulating these units of discourse appears to have gone on at a single period. By this I mean, among a relatively small number of sages working within a uniform set of literary conventions, at roughly the same time, and in approximately the same way. These framers of the various units of tradition may or may not have participated in the work of closure and redaction of the whole. We do not know the answer. But among themselves they cannot have differed very much about the way in which the work was to be carried on. For the end product, the Talmud Yerushalmi, like the Mishnah, is uniform and stylistically coherent, generally consistent in modes of thought and speech, wherever we turn. That accounts for the single voice that leads us through the dialectical and argumentative analysis of the Talmud Yerushalmi.

Now let us move on to evidence. We begin with a set of instances which illustrate the fundamental traits of discourse. What we see is that the discussion is coherent and harmonious, moving from beginning to what was, in fact, a predetermined end. The voice, "the Talmud Yerushalmi," speaks to us throughout, not the diverse voices of real people engaged in a concrete and therefore chaotic argument. As in Plato's dialogues, question and answer – the dialectical argument – constitute conventions through which logic is exposed and tested, not the reports of things people said spontaneously or even after the fact. The controlling voice is monotonous, lacking all points of differentiation of viewpoint, tone, mode of inquiry and thought. That is what I mean to illustrate here. To prove this same proposition incontrovertibly, I should have to cite a vast proportion of the Yerushalmi as a whole. A few instances must suffice. I refer to passages translated in my *Talmud of the Land of Israel. A Preliminary Translation and Explanation.*

Y. Horayot 2:1: Once again we have a sustained discussion, this time on the exegetical foundations of a law of the Mishnah. The voice of the Talmud Yerushalmi is undifferentiated; the entire passage concentrates on the substance of matters. A single hand surely stands behind it all, for there is not a single seam or margin. So to give an account of the matter, we must speak in the name of "the Talmud Yerushalmi." That is, "the Talmud Yerushalmi" wants to know the relationship of an anointed priest to a court, the reciprocal authority of autonomous institutions. Scripture has specified several autonomous persons and institutions or groups that atone with a bullock for erroneous actions committed inadvertently. So the Talmud Yerushalmi now raises the interesting question of the rule that applies when one of these autonomous bodies follows instructions given by another. The unit explores this question, first establishing that the anointed priest is equivalent to the community, just as Scripture states, and drawing the consequence of that fact. Then comes the important point that the anointed priest is autonomous of the community. He atones for what he does, but is not subject to atonement by, or in behalf of, others.

A. [If] an anointed [high] priest made a decision for himself [in violation of any of the commandments of the Torah] doing so inadvertently, and carrying out [his decision] inadvertently,

B. he brings a bullock [Lev. 4:3].

C. [If] he [made an erroneous decision] inadvertently, and deliberately carried it out,

D. deliberately [made an erroneous decision] and inadvertently carried it out,

E. he is exempt.

F. For [as to A-B] an [erroneous] decision of an anointed [high priest] for himself is tantamount to an [erroneous] decision of a court for the entire community.

I. A. ["If anyone sins unwittingly in any of the things which the Lord has commanded not to be done and does any one of them, if it is the anointed priest who sins, thus bringing guilt on the people, then let him offer for the sin which he has committed a young bull" (Lev. 4:23-30.)] "Anyone...," "If it is the high priest...," – lo, [the Scripture would seem to imply that] the high priest is tantamount to an individual [and not, vs. M. Hor. 2:1F, to an embodiment of the community and thus not subject to a bullock-offering].

B. [In this case, Scripture's purpose is to say:] Just as an individual, if he ate [something prohibited] at the instruction of a court, is exempt, so this one [subject to court authority], if he ate something at the instruction of the court, is exempt.

C. Just as an individual, if he ate [something prohibited] without the instruction of a court, is liable, so this one, if he ate something not at the instruction of a court, is liable.

D. [To encounter that possible interpretation] Scripture states, "Thus bringing guilt on the people" [meaning] lo, [the high anointed priest's] guilt is tantamount to the guilt of the entire people [just as M. Hor. 2:1F states].

E. Just as the people are not guilty unless they gave instruction [Lev. 4:13], so this one is not guilty unless he gave instruction.

F. There is a Tannaitic tradition that interprets [the matter with reference to] the people [and] the court:

G. Just as [if] the people gave instruction and other people did [what the people] said, [the people] are liable, so this one, [if] he gave [erroneous] instruction and others did [what he said], should be liable.

H. [It is to counter that possible interpretation that] Scripture states, "[If it is the high priest] who sins," [meaning] for the sin that this one himself committed he brings [a bullock], but he does not have to bring a bullock on account of what other people do [inadvertently sinning because of his instruction].

I. There is a Tannaitic tradition that interprets the [matter with reference to] the people [and] the community:

J. Just as, in the case of the people, if others gave erroneous instruction and they [inadvertently] committed a sin, they are liable, so in the case of this one, [if] others gave erroneous instruction and he carried it out [and so sinned], he should be liable.

K. [To counter that possible wrong interpretation,] Scripture states, "[If it is the high priest] who sins," [meaning] for the sin that this one committed, he brings [a bullock], but he does not have to bring a bullock on account of what other people do [inadvertently sinning because of their instruction].

Y. San. 4:9: We find here a further instance in which the argument is so constructed as to speak to an issue, without regard to the source of sayings or the definition of the voices in conversation. A question is asked, then answered, because the rhetoric creates dialectic, movement from point to point. It is not because an individual speaks with, and interrogates, yet another party. The uniform voice of the Talmud Yerushalmi is before us, lacking all distinguishing traits, following a single, rather simple program of rhetorical conventions.

II. A And perhaps you might want to claim, "What business is it of ours to convict this man of a capital crime?"[M. San. 4:9].

B. It is written, "And about sunset a cry went through the army" (I Kings 22:36).

C. What is this cry?

D. Lo, it a song, as it is said, "When the wicked perish, there is a song" (Prov. 11:10).

E. But, on the contrary, it also is said, "[That they should praise] as they went out before the army [and say, 'Give thanks unto the Lord, for his mercy endures for ever']" (II Chr. 20:21).

F. [Omitting the words, "for he is good,"] is to teach you that even the downfall of the wicked is no joy before the Omnipresent.

Y. Makkot 1:5: Here is yet another example in which a sustained conversation on a passage of Scripture, unfolding through questions and answers, conforms to a simple rhetorical program. The voice of the interlocutor is not differentiated from the source of the respondent, for the whole is a single discourse. Not a "real" conversation, but rather an effective presentation of a simple idea is at hand.

I. A. [Scripture refers to the requirement of two or three witnesses to impose the death penalty, Deut. 17:6. Scripture further states, "Only on the evidence of two witnesses or of three witnesses shall a charge be sustained" (Deut. 19.15). The former deals with capital cases, the latter with property cases. Since both refer to two or three witnesses, the duplication is now explained:] Scripture is required to refer to property cases, and also to capital cases.

B. For if it had referred to property cases and not to capital cases, I might have said, In the case of property cases, which are of lesser weight, three witnesses have the power to prove two to be perjurers, but two may not prove three to be perjurers.

C. How do I know that that is so even of a hundred?

D. Scripture states, "Witnesses."

E. Now if reference had been made to capital cases, and not to property cases, I might have said, In capital cases, which are weightier, two witnesses have the power to prove that three are perjurers but three do not have the power to prove that two are perjurers.

F. How do I know that that applies even to a hundred?

G. Scripture says, "Witnesses." [It follows then the Scripture must refer to "two or three" in the context of each matter, since one could not have derived the one from the other.]

All of the units of discourse before us exhibit the same traits. In each instance we see that the conversation is artificial. What is portrayed is not real people but a kind of rhetoric. The presence of questions and answers is a literary convention, not a (pretended) transcription of a conversation. So we may well speak of "the Talmud Yerushalmi" and its voice: that is all we have. The absence of differentiation is not the sole striking trait. We observe, also, a well planned and pointed program of inquiry, however brief, leading to a single purpose for each unit of discourse. While the various units in theme are completely unrelated to one another, in rhetoric and mode of analysis they are essentially uniform: simple questions, simple answers, uncomplex propositions, worked out through reference to authoritative sources of law, essentially an unfolding of information.

Up to this point, we have seen only that the Talmud Yerushalmi takes on a persona, becomes a kind of voice. The voice is timeless. On the face of it, the units we have reviewed can have been made up at any time in the period in which the Talmud Yerushalmi was taking shape, from 200 to 400. The uniformity of style and cogency of mode of discourse can have served as powerful scholastic-literary conventions, established early, followed slavishly thereafter. The bulk of the units of discourse, however, are not anonymous. They constitute compilations of statements assigned to named authorities. These on the surface testify to specific periods in the two centuries at hand, since the authorities mentioned lived at specific times and places. If, now, we observe the same uniformity of tone and dialectic, we shall address a somewhat more refined problem.

This brings us to discourse involving named authorities. The important point in the examples that follow is that, while named authorities and sayings assigned to them do occur, the dialectic of argument is conducted outside the contributions of the specified sages. Sages' statements serve the purposes of the anonymous voice, rather than defining and governing the flow of argument. So the anonymous voice, "the Talmud Yerushalmi," predominates even when individuals' sayings are utilized. Selecting and arranging whatever was in hand is the work of one hand, one voice.

Y. Abodah Zarah 1:5: What is interesting in this account of the language of the Mishnah is that the framer of the entire discussion takes over and uses what is attributed to Hiyya. The passage requires Hiyya's version of the Mishnah-rule. But Hiyya is not responsible for the formation of the passage. It is "the Talmud Yerushalmi" that speaks, drawing upon the information, including the name, of Hiyya. Only the secondary comment in the name of Bun bar Hiyya violates the monotone established by "the Talmud Yerushalmi." And at the end that same voice takes over and draws matters to their conclusion, a phenomenon we shall shortly see again. It is not uncommon for later fourth-century names to occur in such a setting.

1. A. These are things [which it is] forbidden to sell to gentiles:
   B. (1) fir cones, (2) white figs (3) and their stalks, (4) frankincense, and (5) a white cock.

2. A. We repeat in the Mishnah-pericope [the version]: A white cock.
   B. R. Hiyya repeated [for his version of] the Mishnah-pericope: "A cock of any sort."

C. The present version of the Mishnah [specifying a white cock] requires also the version of R. Hiyya, and the version of R. Hiyya requires also the [present] version of the Mishnah.

D. [Why both?] If we repeated [the present version of the Mishnah], and we did not repeat the version of R. Hiyya, we should have reached the conclusion that the sages state the rule only in regard to a white cock, but as to any sort of cock other than that, even if this was all by itself [M. A. Z. 1:5D], it is permitted. Thus there was need for the Mishnah-version of R. Hiyya.

E. Now if one repeated the version of R. Hiyya, and we did not repeat the version before us in the Mishnah, we should have ruled that the rule applies only in the case of an unspecified cock [requested by the purchaser], but [if the purchaser requested] a white cock, then even if this was all by itself, it would be prohibited [to sell such a cock].

F. Thus there was need for the Mishnah-version as it is repeated before us, and there also was need for the Mishnah-version as it is repeated by R. Hiyya.

G. Said R. Bun bar Hiyya, "[In Hiyya's view, if a gentile said, 'Who has] a cock to sell?' one may sell him a white cock, [so Hiyya differs from, and does not merely complement, the version of the Mishnah-pericope]."

H. [Now if the gentile should say, "Who has] a white cock to sell," we then rule that if the white cock is by itself, it is forbidden, but if it is part of a flock of cocks, it is permitted to sell it to him. [This clearly is the position of the Mishnah-pericope, so there is no dispute at all, merely complementary traditions, as argued at D-E.]

Y. Shebuot 3:7: Here is yet another instance, but a more complex and better articulated one, in which topically interesting sayings attributed to two principal authorities, Yohanan and Simeon b. Laqish, provide a pretext for a rather elaborate discussion. The discussion is conducted about what Yohanan and Simeon are supposed to have said. But the rhetoric is such that they are not presented as the active voices. Their views are described. But they, personally and individually, do not express views. Predictably, the language in no way differentiates between Yohanan's and Simeon b. Laqish's manner of speech. Only the substance of what is said tells us how and about what they differ. The reason is obvious. The focus of discourse is the principle at hand, the logic to be analyzed and fully spelled out. The uniform voice of "the Talmud Yerushalmi" speaks throughout.

A. "I swear that I won't eat this loaf of bread," "I swear that I won't eat it," "I swear that I won't eat it" –

B. and he ate it –

C. he is liable on only one count.

D. This is a "rash oath" (Lev. 5:4).

E. On account of deliberately [taking a rash oath] one is liable to flogging, and on account of inadvertently [taking a rash oath] he is liable to an offering of variable value.

I. A. [If someone said], "I swear that I shall eat this loaf of bread today," and the day passed, but then he ate it –

B. R. Yohanan and R. Simeon b. Laqish – both of them say, "He is exempt [from flogging for deliberate failure]."

C. The reason for the position of one authority is not the same as the reason for the ruling of the other.

D. The reason for the ruling of R. Yohanan is on the grounds that the case is one in which there can be no appropriate warning [that what the man is about to do will violate the law, because the warning can come only too late, when the day has already passed].

E. The reason for the ruling, in R. Simeon b. Laqish's view, is that [by not eating] the man is thereby violating a negative rule which does not involve an actual, concrete deed.

F. What is the practical difference between the positions of the two authorities?

G. A case in which he burned the bread and threw it into the sea.

H. If you say that the reason is on the count that the man is not in a position to receive a warning, the man will be exempt [on the same grounds in the present case].

I. But if you say that the reason is that the matter involves a negative commandment in which there is no concrete deed, here we do have a concrete deed [namely, throwing the bread into the sea].

Y. Shebuot 3:9: Here we have a still more striking instance in which the entire focus of discourse is the logic. No rhetorical devices distinguish one party to the argument from the other one. The two speak in rigidly patterned language, so that what is assigned to the one always constitutes a mirror image of what is assigned to the other. That the whole, in fact, merely refers to positions taken by each is clear in the resort to third person and descriptive language, in place of the attributive, "said."

A. "I swear that I shall eat this loaf of bread," "I swear that I shall not eat it" – the first statement is a rash oath, and the second is a vain oath [M. Shebu. 3:9A-B].

B. How do they treat such a case [in which a man has taken these contradictory oaths, one of which he must violate]?

C. They instruct him to eat [the loaf].

D. It is better to transgress a vain oath and not to transgress a rash oath.

E. "I swear that I shall not eat this loaf of bread," "I swear that I shall eat it" – the first is rash oath, the second a vain oath.

F. How do they treat such a case?

G. They instruct him not to eat it.

H. It is better to transgress a vain oath by itself, and not to transgress both a vain oath and a rash oath.

I. "I swear that I shall eat this loaf of bread today," "I swear that I shall not eat it today," and he ate it –

J. R. Yohanan said, "He has carried out the first oath and nullified the second."

K. R. Simeon b. Laqish said, "He has nullified the first and not carried out the second."

L. "I swear that I shall not eat this loaf of bread today," "I swear that I shall eat it today," and he ate it –

M. R. Yohanan said, "He has nullified the first oath and carried out the second."

N. R. Simeon b. Laqish said, "He has nullified the first oath and as to the second, they instruct him to carry it out with another loaf of bread."

O. "I swear that I shall eat this loaf today," "I swear that I shall eat it today," and he ate it –

P. R. Yohanan said, "He has carried out both oaths."

Q. And R. Simeon b. Laqish said, "He has carried out the first, and as to the second, they instruct him to carry it out with another loaf of bread."

R. "I swear that I shall not eat this loaf of bread," "I swear that I shall not eat it today," and he ate it –

S. in the view of R. Yohanan, he is liable on only one count.

T. In the view of R. Simeon b. Laqish, is he liable on two counts?

U. [No.] Even R. Simeon b. Laqish will concede that he [has repeated himself] because he merely [wishes to] keep himself away from prohibited matters [and that is why he repeated the oath, but only one count is at hand].

Y. San. 5:2: The final example does utilize the attributive, with the implication that we have an effort to represent not merely the gist of an authority's opinion, but his exact words. Even if we assume that before us are *ipsissima verba* of Rab and Yohanan, however, we have still to concede the paramount role of "the Talmud Yerushalmi" in the formation and unpacking of the argument. For, as we notice, as soon as Rab and Yohanan have spoken, curiously mirroring one another's phrasing and wording, the monotonous voice takes over. At that point, the argument unfolds in a set of questions and answers, the standard dialectic thus predominating once again. The secondary expansion of the matter, beginning at O, then adduces a piece of evidence, followed by an anonymous discourse in which that evidence is absorbed into, and made to serve, the purposes of the analysis as a whole. Once more the fact that each item is balanced by the next is not the important point, though it is striking. What is important is that movement of the argument is defined by "the Talmud Yerushalmi," and not by the constituents of discourse given in the names of specific authorities. The mind and voice behind the whole are not Rab's and Yohanan's, or, so far as we can see, their immediate disciples'. The voice is "the Talmud's." "The Talmud Yerushalmi" does not tire, as its tertiary explication, testing the views of each and showing the full extent of the position taken by both principal parties, runs on and on. Only at the end, with Mana and Abin, fourth-century figures, do named authorities intervene in such a way as to break the uniform rhetorical pattern established by "the Talmud Yerushalmi."

A. There we learned:

B. He concerning whom two groups of witnesses gave testimony –

C. these testify that he took a vow to be a *Nazir* for two spells,

D. and those testify that he took a vow to be *Nazir* for five spells –

E. The House of Shammai say, "The testimony is at variance, and no Naziriteship applies here at all."

F. And the House of Hillel say, "In the sum of five are two spells, so let him serve out two spells of Naziriteship" [M. Naz. 3:7].

G. Rab said, "As to a general number [the Houses] are in disagreement [that is, as to whether he has taken the Nazirite vow at all]. But as to a specific number, all parties agree that [the testimony is at variance]. [Following the versions of Y. Yeb. 15:5, Naz. 3:7: the sum of five includes two, as at M. 5:2F.]"

H. R. Yohanan said, "As to spelling out the number of vows there is a difference of opinion, but as to a general number, all parties concur that [within the general principle of five spells of Naziriteship there are two upon which all parties concur]. [The testimony is at variance.]"

I. What is meant by the "general number," and what is meant by "counting out the number of specific vows" [the man is supposed to have taken]? [Examples of each are as follows:]

J. The general number – one party has said, "Two," and one party has said, "Five."

K. Counting out the number of vows one by one is when one said "One, two," and the other said, "Three, four."

L. Rab said, "If the essence of the testimony is contradicted, the testimony is not null."

M. And R. Yohanan said, "If the essence of the testimony is contradicted, the testimony is null."

N. All parties concede, however, [that] if testimony has been contradicted in its nonessentials, the testimony [of the first set of witnesses] is not nullified.

O. The full extent of the position taken by R. Yohanan is seen in the following case:

P. For Ba bar Hiyya in the name of R. Yohanan: "The assumption [that a loan has taken place is] confirmed [by testimony] that one has counted out [coins].

Q. "If this witness says, 'From his pocket did he count out the money,' and that one says, 'From his pouch did he count out the money,'

R. "we have a case in which a testimony is contradicted in its essentials [within the same pair of witnesses, who thus do not agree]. [This testimony is null.]"

S. Here even Rab concedes that the testimony is null.

T. Concerning what do they differ?

U. Concerning a case in which there were two groups of witnesses.

V. One states, "From the pocket did he count out the money," and the other says, "From the pouch did he count out the money."

W. Here we have a case in which testimony is contradicted in its essentials. The effect of the testimony [in Yohanan's view] is null.

X. But in the view of Rab, the effect of the testimony is not null.

Y. If one witness says, "Into his vest did he count out the money," and the other says, "Into his wallet,"

Z. in the opinion of all parties, the testimony is contradicted in its nonessentials and therefore the testimony is not nullified. [This testimony is not about the essence of the case.]

AA. If one party says, "With a sword did he kill him," and the other party says, "With a staff did he kill him," we have a case in which testimony has been contradicted in its essentials [just as in a property case, so in a capital one].

BB. Even Rab concedes that the effect of the entire testimony is null.

CC. In what regard did they differ?

DD. In a case in which there were two sets of two witnesses:

EE. One group says, "With a sword...," and the other says, "With a staff..."

FF. Here we have a case in which the testimony has been contradicted in its essentials, and the effect of the testimony is null.

GG. But in the view of Rab, the effect of the testimony is not null.

HH. One witness says, "[The murderer] turned toward the north [to flee]," and the other witness says, "He turned toward the south," in the opinion of all parties, the testimony [of one group] has been contradicted in its nonessentials, and the testimony has not been nullified.

II. The full force of Rab's opinion is indicated in the following, which we have learned there:

JJ. [If one woman says, "He died," and one says, "He was killed," R. Meir says, "Since they contradict one another in details of their testimony, lo, these women may not remarry."] R. Judah and R. Simeon say, "Since this one and that one are in agreement that he is not alive, they may remarry" [M. Yeb. 15:5B-D].

KK. Now did he not hear that which R. Eleazar said, "R. Judah and R. Simeon concur in the matter of witnesses [that where they contradict one another in essentials, their testimony is null]?"

LL. If so, what is the difference between such contradiction when it comes from witnesses and the same when it comes from co-wives?

MM. They did not treat the statement of a co-wife concerning her fellow wife as of any consequence whatsoever.

NN. Said R. Yohanan, "If R. Eleazar made such a statement, he heard it from me and said it."

OO. The Mishnah-pericope is at variance with the position of Rab. All the same are interrogation and examination in the following regard: When the witnesses contradict one another, their testimony is null [M. San. 5:2F]. [Rab does not deem it invariably null, as we have seen.]

PP. Said R. Mana, "Rab interprets the Mishnah-rule to speak of a case in which one witness contradicts another [but not in which a set of witnesses contradicts another such set in some minor detail]."

QQ. Said R. Abin, "Even if you interpret the passage to speak of contradictions between one set of witnesses and another, still Rab will be able to deal with the matter. For a capital case is subject to a different rule, since it is said, 'Justice, [and only] justice, will you pursue'" (Deut. 16:20). [Thus capital trials are subject to a different set of rules of evidence from those applicable in property cases, of which Rab spoke above at L.]

Since this final example is somewhat protracted, we had best review the point of citing it before we proceed. The issue of the interpretation of the passage of the Mishnah, A-F, is phrased at G-H, the conflict between Rab and Yohanan. We note that the former spent most of his mature years in Babylonia, the latter, in the Land of Israel. Accordingly, considerations of geographical or institutional relationship play no role whatsoever. The language of the one is a mirror image of what is given to the other. Then the Talmud Yerushalmi takes over, by providing an exegesis of the cited dispute, I-K. This yields a secondary phrasing of the opinions of the two authorities, L, M, with a conclusion at N. Then the position of Yohanan is provided yet a further amplification, O-R. But what results, S, is a revision of our view of Rab's opinion. Consequently, a further exegesis of the dispute is supplied, T-U, spelled out at W-X, then with further amplification still, now at Y-BB. Once more we attempt a further account of the fundamental point at issue between the two masters, CC-HH, and, in the model of the foregoing exercise with Yohanan, Rab's view is carried to its logical extreme, II-JJ. The final part of the passage, tacked on and essentially secondary, allows for some further discussion of Rab's view, with a late authority, Mana, and his contemporary, Abin, PP-QQ, writing a conclusion to the whole. Up to that point, it seems to me clear, what we have is a rather elegant, cogent, highly stylized mode of exposition through argument, with a single form of logic applied time and again.

When I claim that the Talmud's focus of interest is in the logical exposition of the law, here is a good instance of what I mean. The materials are organized so as to facilitate explanations of the law's inner structure and potentiality, not to present a mere repertoire of ideas and opinions of interest for their own sake. The upshot is a sustained argument, not an anthology of relevant sayings. But Halivni's theory requires the opposite, that is, an anthology of diverse materials, some changed, some not changed, from their "original" formulation. A null hypothesis offered by Halivni should turn up precisely the document as we now have it. A null hypothesis offered by me should turn up the opposite of what the Yerushalmi gives us.

Such a cogent and ongoing argument as we find characteristic of both Talmuds is more likely the work of a single mind than of a committee, let alone of writers who lived over a period of ten or fifteen decades. The role of individuals in the passages we have reviewed is unimportant. The paramount voice is that of "the Talmud Yerushalmi." The rhetoric of the Talmud Yerushalmi may be described very simply: a preference for questions and answers, a willingness then to test the answers and to expand through secondary and tertiary amplification, achieved through further questions and answers. The whole gives the appearance of the script for a conversation to be reconstructed, or an argument of logical possibilities to be reenacted, in one's own mind. In this setting we of course shall be struck by the uniformity of the rhetoric, even though we need not make much of the close patterning of language, e.g., Rab's and Yohanan's, where it occurs. The voice of "the Talmud Yerushalmi," moreover, authoritatively defines the mode of analysis. The inquiry is consistent and predictable; one argument differs from another not in supposition but only in detail. When individuals' positions occur, it is because what they have to say serves the purposes of "the Talmud Yerushalmi" and its uniform inquiry. The inquiry is into the logic and the rational potentialities of a passage. To these dimensions of thought, the details of place, time, and even of an individual's philosophy, are secondary. All details are turned toward a common core of discourse. This, I maintain, is possible only because the document as whole takes shape in accord with an overriding program of inquiry and comes to expression in conformity with a single plan of rhetorical expression. To state the proposition simply: it did not just grow, but rather, someone made it up.

This view is reenforced by the innumerable instances of the predominance of logic over chronology. The Talmudic argument is not indifferent to the chronology of authorities. But the sequence in which things may be supposed to have been said – an early third century figure's saying before a later fourth century figure's saying – in no way explains the construction of protracted dialectical arguments. The argument as a whole, its direction and purpose, always govern the selection, formation, and ordering of the parts of the argument and their relationships to one another. The dialectic is determinative. Chronology, if never violated, is always subordinated. Once that fact is clear, it will become further apparent that "arguments" – analytical units of discourse – took shape at the end, with the whole in mind, as part of a plan and a program. That is to say, the components of the argument, even when associated with the names of specific authorities who lived at different times, were not added piece by piece, in order of historical appearance. They were put together whole and complete, all at one time, when the dialectical discourse was made up. By examining a few units of discourse, we shall clearly see the unimportance of the sequence in which people lived, hence of the order in which sayings (presumably) became available.

The upshot is that chronological sequence, while not likely to be ignored, never determines the layout of a unit of discourse. We can never definitively settle the issue of whether a unit of discourse came into being through a long process of accumulation and agglutination, or was shaped at one point – then, at the end of the time in which named authorities flourished – with everything in hand and a particular purpose in mind. But the more likely of the two possibilities is clearly the latter. Let me first review a passage already set forth. It is at Y. San. 5:2. Here Rab and Yohanan both are assumed to have flourished in the middle of the third century. Placing their opinions in conflict does not violate chronology. There is a Mana who was a contemporary of Yohanan. The first Abin, a Babylonian, is supposed to have flourished about a half-century later. Perhaps Mana's saying at PP stood by itself for a while, and Abin's at RR was added later on. But it is also possible that PP and QQ were shaped in response to one another – that is, at the same time, as yet another layer of argument. The flow of argument from Yohanan and Rab to Mana and Abin is smooth and uninterrupted. The addition at PP-QQ seems to me a colloquy to be read as a single statement. If that is the case, then the whole is a unity, formed no earlier than its final element. This seems confirmed by the fact that the set at PP-QQ is made necessary by the question raised by OO, and that question is integral to the exposition of Rab's position in toto. Accordingly, it would appear that what we have in the names of the latest authorities is an integral part of the secondary expansion of the primary dispute. In that case, part of the plan of the whole, at the very outset, was the inclusion of these final sayings as elements of the amplification of the dispute. If so, the construction will have come into being as whole not much earlier than the early or mid-fourth century. At the same time, we notice that the glosses of the positions of Rab and Yohanan do not reach us in the name of authorities who are assumed to have flourished prior to the times of the principal authorities. The main point must not be missed: The needs of the analysis of the positions of Rab and Yohanan, with attention, in particular, to the logic behind the view of each and the unfolding of the argument to expose that logic, explain the composition of the whole. So a clear conception of the direction and purpose of inquiry existed prior to the assembly of the parts and governed the layout of arguments and the dialectic of discourse. Let us now consider from the present perspective further instances in which the names of diverse authorities figure. What then dictates the composition of a passage? It is logic that forms the governing principle of construction, and that logic is prior to the construction and controls all components thereof.

I take as my example, among innumerable possibilities, Y. Baba Qamma 2:13. In this protracted discussion, we see how one authority cites another, earlier figure, with the result that the question of consistency of the view of the first authority comes under discussion. Simeon b. Laqish's interpretation of the Mishnah-passage is compared with a view of Hoshaiah, yet earlier by a generation and so cited by Simeon b. Laqish. A further discussion has Ami, slightly later than Simeon b. Laqish, interpret Simeon's view. Then an opinion of Hoshaiah – hence prior to both Ami and Simeon b. Laqish – comes under discussion. The reason is not that Hoshaiah is represented as conducting a face-to-face argument with Simeon or Ami. Hoshaiah's position is formulated quite separately from theirs. But it intersects in topic and logic. Therefore the framer of the whole found it quite natural to cite Hoshaiah's views. The context is the main thing. Ilfai-Hilfa was a contemporary of Yohanan. His position in the construction hardly has been dictated by that fact. Rather, what he has to say forms a final topic of discussion, in sequence after the view of Rab, who surely came earlier in the third century than Ilfai.

The main point bears repeating. We do not find that the chronology of authorities bears any important relationship to the arrangement of opinions. We also do not find violation of the order in which authorities flourished. The long argument has been laid out in accord with the principles of logical exposition at hand. For that purpose no attention needs to be paid to the sequence in which people may have expressed their views. But people of different centuries are not made to talk to one another.

A. "How is the tooth deemed an attested danger in regard to eating what is suitable for [eating]" [M. 1:4C]?

B. An ox is an attested danger to eat fruit and vegetables.

C. [If, however] it ate [a piece of] clothing or utensils, [the owner] pays half the value of the damage it has caused.

D. Under what circumstances?

E. [When this takes place] in the domain of the injured party.

F. But [if it takes place] in the public domain, he is exempt.

G. But if it [the ox] derived benefit [from damage done in public domain], the owner pays for the value of what [his ox] has enjoyed.

I. A. [To what does the statement, M. 2:3D-G, "Under what circumstances?" apply?] R. Simeon b. Laqish said, "It applies to the first clause. [If, in the public domain, a beast ate what it usually eats, the owner pays nothing. But if, even in the public domain, it ate clothing or utensils, the owner is liable because people commonly leave things in public domain, and the owner of the beast has the responsibility to watch out for such unusual events.]"

B. R. Yohanan said, "It applies to the entire pericope [including the consumption of unusual items, such as clothing or utensils]. [If someone left clothing or utensils in the public domain, the owner of the beast is exempt, because it is not common to leave such things in public domain.]"

C. The opinions imputed to R. Simeon b. Laqish are in conflict.

D. There R. Simeon b. Laqish has said in the name of R. Hoshaiah, "[If] an ox stood still and ate produce which was stacked in piles, [the owner] is liable." [Hence the owner of the beast is liable if the beast eats what it usually eats in the public domain. M. makes no distinction between the beast's doing so while walking along and while standing still.]

E. And here he has said that [the owner is exempt if the beast eats produce in the public domain, on the grounds that that is common.]

F. They said, "There he spoke in the name of R. Hoshaiah while here he speaks in his own name."

II. A. A statement which R. Simeon b. Laqish said: "[If there were two beasts in the public domain, one walking, one crouched and] the one which was walking along butted the one which was crouching, [the owner] is exempt [because the one which was crouching bore responsibility for changing the normal procedure, and it is not normal for a beast to crouch in public domain]."

B. A statement which R. Yohanan said: "[If] the one which was walking along butted the one which was crouching, [the owner] is liable." [The owner of the crouching beast still may ask, "Who gave your beast the right to butt mine?"]

C. [And, Yohanan further will maintain,] it is not the end of the matter that if the one which was walking along butts the one which was crouching, or the one which was crouching butts the one which was walking along, [the owner of the aggressor is liable].

D. But even if the two of them were walking along, and one of those which was walking along butted the other which was walking along, [the owner] is liable [on the same grounds, namely, while both beasts had every right to be where they were, there is no right for one beast to butt the other].

E. [Dealing with these same matters in behalf of Simeon b. Laqish,] R. Ami said, "R. Simeon b. Laqish's position applies only to a case in which a beast which was walking along butted a beast which was crouching, in which case [the owner] is exempt.

F. "But if a beast which was crouching butted one which was walking along, or one which was walking along butted another which was walking along, [the owner in either case] will be liable."

G. R. Hoshaiah taught, "In all cases, [the owner] is exempt."

H. The basis for R. Hoshaiah's position is that liability for injury done by an ox's horn does not apply in public domain anyhow. [Pené Moshe prefers to read: "This is not a case of damages done by an ox's horn in the public domain."]

I. Rab said, "If the beast stood still [in public domain] and ate up produce which was lying in piles –

J. "now they have made a lenient rule in the case of tooth, in which case an ox walking along consumed produce lying in piles [and so] standing [still],

K. "while they have made a more stringent rule in the case of damages done by the horn,

L. "in which a beast which was walking along has butted a beast which was standing still. [That is, the beast which was walking along does not impose liability on its owner for produce eaten by the way. In this regard a more stringent rule applies to damages done by the beast's horn than those done by the beast's tooth, since if the beast walking along butted one lying down, the owner is liable, while, as we saw, in the case of tooth, the owner is exempt. If, to be sure, the beast had stood still and eaten produce, also in the case of damages done by tooth, the owner is liable.]"

M. Ilfai remarked, "If the beast had stood still and eaten the produce which was lying in piles, [the owner] would be liable.

N. "Now they have made a lenient rule in the case of tooth, in that if the beast which was walking along and ate produce which was lying around, the owner is exempt from paying damages.

O. "But a more stringent rule applies in the case of damages done by the horn when a beast which was walking along butted another beast which was walking along, [and the owner in this case would be liable to damages]."

The upshot is that we may speak about "the Talmud Yerushalmi," its voice, its purposes, its mode of constructing a view of the Israelite world. The reason is that, when we claim "the Talmud Yerushalmi" speaks, we replicate both the main lines of chronology and the literary character of the document. These point toward the formation of the bulk of materials – its units of discourse – in a process lasting (to take a guess) about half a century, prior to the ultimate arrangement of these units of discourse around passages of the Mishnah and the closure and redaction of the whole into the document we now know.

Now, admittedly, the arguments that constitute the exegetical and amplificatory work of the Talmud Yerushalmi often contain names of specific authorities. These figures are assumed to have lived not only at the end of the process of the formation of the document, but at the beginning and middle as well. If we could demonstrate that these authorities really said what was attributed to these authorities really was said by them, we should be able to compose a history of the exegetical process, not merely an account of its end product. And that is what Halivni claims in his *Sources and Traditions* to have accomplished. But as soon as we recognize the simple fact that attributions are just that – not facts but merely allegations as to facts – we realize the remarkably shallow foundations that underlie Halivni's towering construction.

We have very good reason to suppose that the text as we have it speaks within the limited context of the period of the actual framing of the text's principal building blocks. As I have already pointed out, the evidence points to these traits of the writings:

(1) The building blocks – units of discourse – give evidence of having been put together in a moment of sustained deliberation, in accordance with a plan of exposition, and in response to a finite problem of logical analysis.

(2) To state matters negatively, the units of discourse in no way appear to have taken shape slowly, over a long period of time, in a process governed by the order in which sayings were framed, now and here, then and there, later and anywhere else (so to speak). Before us is the result of considered redaction, not protracted accretion, mindful construction, not sedimentary accretion, such as Halivni's theory of matters requires.

As I said at the outset, the traits of the bulk of the Talmud Yerushalmi may be explained in one of only two ways. One way is this: the very heirs of the Mishnah, in the opening generation, ca. A.D. 200-225, agreed upon conventions not merely of speech and rhetorical formulation, but also of thought and modes of analysis. They further imposed these conventions on all subsequent generations, wherever they lived, whenever they did their work. Accordingly, at the outset the decision was made to do the work precisely in the way in which, two hundred years later, the work turns out to have been done. The alternative view is that, some time late in the formation of diverse materials in response to the Mishnah (and to various other considerations), some people got together and made a decision to rework whatever was in hand into a single, stunningly cogent document, the Talmud Yerushalmi as we know it in the bulk of its units of discourse. Whether this work took a day or a half-century, it was the work of sages who knew precisely what they wished to do and who did it over and over again. This second view is the one I take, and on the basis of it the remainder of this book unfolds. The consequence is that the Talmud Yerushalmi exhibits a viewpoint. It is portrayed in what I have called "the Talmud's one voice."

In claiming that we deal not only with uniform rhetoric, but with a single cogent viewpoint, we must take full account of the contrary claim of the Talmud's framers themselves. This claim they lay down through the constant citations of sayings in the names of specific authorities. It must follow that differentiation by chronology – the periods in which the several sages cited actually flourished – is possible. To be sure, the original purpose of citing named authorities was not to set forth chronological lines, but to establish the authority behind a given view of the law. But the history of viewpoints should be possible. As I argued earlier, it would be possible if we could show, on the basis of evidence external to the Talmud Yerushalmi itself, that the Talmud's own claim in attributing statements to specific people is subject to verification or falsification. But all that I can show is a general respect for chronology, not only authority, in the unfolding of discussion. That is, we are not likely to find in Talmud Yerushalmi that an authority of the early third century is made to comment on a statement in the name of a sage of the later fourth century.

But the organizing principle of discourse (even in anthologies) never derives from the order in which authorities lived. And that is the main point. The logical requirements of the analysis at hand determine the limits of applied and practical reason framed by the sustained discourses of which the Talmud Yerushalmi is composed. Now it may well be the case that sayings not reworked into the structure of a larger argument really do derive from the authority to whom they are ascribed. But if the discrete opinions at hand then do not provide us with a logical and analytical proposition, they also do not give us much else that is very interesting. They constitute isolated data, lacking all pattern, making no clear point. The fact that Rabbi X held opinion A, while Rabbi Y maintained position Q, is without sense, unless A and Q together say more than they tell us separately.

To conclude: in a given unit of discourse, the focus, the organizing principle, the generative interest – these are defined solely by the issue at hand. The argument moves from point to point, directed by the inner logic of argument itself. A single plane of discourse is established. All things are leveled out, so that the line of logic runs straight and true. Accordingly, a single conception of the framing and formation of the unit of discourse stands prior to the spelling out of issues. More fundamental still, what people in general wanted was not to create topical anthologies – to put together instances of what this one said about that issue – but to exhibit the logic of that issue, viewed under the aspect of eternity. Under sustained inquiry we always find a theoretical issue, freed of all temporal considerations and the contingencies of politics and circumstance.

None of these traits exhibited by the literature Halivni purports to correct and explain favors Halivni's theory that the document took shape out of prior documents, some changed in the process of later (re)formulation and redaction, some not changed at all ("sources and traditions" once more), which the authorship preserved in such a way that we may identify them. Any claim, such as forms the basis for Halivni's massive exegetical exercise, that we deal with differentiable sources and traditions, contradicts the elementary facts of the Yerushalmi, and, obviously, the Bavli as well. What has gone wrong for Halivni is the simple fact that he never composed a null-hypothesis and told us what sort of evidence would prove the proposition contrary to his own. Having failed to do that, he has built the entire edifice on nothing more than the presupposition that attributions of sayings to named authorities are – must be – valid. Absent that premise, his whole hermeneutics proves hopeless because it contradicts the generative and indicative traits of the text he claims to expound. To dismiss the entire structure Halivni has erected as mere *pilpul* of the old yeshiva type seems to me the only reasonable conclusion, and it is one that, after many years of careful study of his writings, I find myself constrained to adopt.

Let me close with my own view of how we should distinguish, in the Bavli, between sources and traditions, which forms the principal inquiry of Halivni's exegetical *ouevre*. The Talmud of Babylonia, or

Bavli, draws upon prior materials. The document in no way was not made up out of whole cloth by its penultimate and ultimate authorship, the generations that drew the whole together and placed it into the form in which it has come down from the seventh century to the present day. The Bavli's authorship both received out of the past a corpus of *sources*, and also stood in a line of *traditions* of sayings and stories, that is, fixed wordings of thought the formulation and transmission of which took place not in completed documents but in ad hoc and brief sentences or little narratives. These materials, deriving from an indeterminate past through a now inaccessible process of literary history, constitute traditions in the sense defined in the preface: an incremental and linear process that step by step transmits out of the past an essential and unchanging fundament of truth and writing.

Traditions: some of these prior materials never reached redaction in a distinct document and come down as sherds and remnants within the Bavli itself. These are the ones that may be called traditions, in the sense of materials formulated and transmitted from one generation to the next, but not given a place in a document of their own.

Sources: others had themselves reached closure prior to the work on the Bavli and are readily identified as autonomous writings. Scripture, to take an obvious example, the Mishnah, tractate Abot (the Fathers), the Tosefta (so we commonly suppose), Sifra, Sifré to Numbers, Sifré to Deuteronomy, Genesis Rabbah, Leviticus Rabbah, the Fathers according to Rabbi Nathan, Pesiqta deRab Kahana, Pesiqta Rabbati, possibly Lamentations Rabbah, not to mention the Siddur and Mahzor (order of daily and holy day prayer, respectively), and various other writings had assuredly concluded their processes of formation before the Bavli's authorship accomplished their work. These we call *sources* – more or less completed writings. On that basis, what I believe to be a more critical, nuanced, and altogether productive exegetical task finds definition, one that Halivni may well wish to consider as well.

20

The Rabbis of the Babylonian Talmud: A Statistical Analysis[1]

Harold Goldblatt
Independent Scholar, University of Maryland

Abstract

The Babylonian Talmud (BT) has been available in an authoritative English translation since 1948, the Soncino edition, but as yet has not received the attention of many sociologists interested in comparative historical sociology, communications research, or in the sociologies of education, law, knowledge, or religion. Research procedures which are a commonplace in sociology, such as those of survey research and of content analysis, could contribute much to contemporary knowledge and understanding of this ancient monument of literature. To the writer's knowledge, the present research is the first effort at this style of cross-tabulational analysis of statistical data

---

[1]Revised version of paper presented at the annual meeting of the Eastern Sociological Society in Baltimore, March 19, 1989.

I am indebted to David M. Goodblatt, Department of History, University of California at San Diego, for instruction about the talmudic era and for encouragement; to Janet W. Goldblatt, entomologist, St. Croix, U.S. Virgin Islands, for early instruction and assistance in the use of the computer for tabulation of data; to Michael Wagner, Senior Consultant, Behavioral and Social Sciences Computer Laboratory, University of Maryland at College Park, for instruction in SPSS and the UNIVAC and hands-on demonstrations.

Shortcomings of this paper are entirely the responsibility of the writer. The reader is asked to inform me about them at 10900 Bucknell Drive, Silver Spring, MD, 20902, Apt. 622.

about the 1,691 rabbis named in the Mishnah and in the Gemara of the Babylonian Talmud. It is certain not to be the last.

The Babylonian Talmud (hereafter abbreviated as BT) has been available since 1948 in an authoritative English translation prepared under the editorship of rabbi Dr. Israel Epstein for the Soncino Press, London, in seventeen volumes.[2] It could be a fertile source of insights and data for sociologists interested in comparative historical sociology, in educational sociology in the sociologies of religion, of law, and of knowledge and, not least, in socio-cognitive aspects of oral as contrasted with written chains of transmission of knowledge.

Reciprocally, all of these sociological specializations could readily deepen and broaden contemporary understanding of BT among its rabbinic and lay academic students. As yet, however, BT has not received the professional attention of many sociologists. Notable exceptions to this statement include William B. Helmreich, 1982, and Samuel C. Heilman, 1983.

A brief description of BT and terminology associated with it may be useful to readers not as yet acquainted with it.

BT is a compilation of legal discussions, disputations and rulings arrived at by the rabbis in their schools and in Jewish courts of law in Babylonia and in the Land of Israel. To no small extent, BT also includes non-legal narratives about the rabbis and their associates. Some of these narratives are about persons, events, and situations that they themselves participated in; others they learned about through hearsay. Some of the persons, events and situations that they talked about to one another concerned supernatural matters.

Formally, BT consists of the thirty-seven tractates of "The Gemara" which is Aramaic for commentary or interpretation. The Gemara comments upon, interprets "The Mishnah," which is Hebrew for review or repetition. The Mishnah, the earlier text, is a codification of legal rulings based on The Pentateuch, purportedly a repetition of it. The rabbis who are named in the Mishnah are called Tannaim, plural of Tanna, meaning teachers or reciters. Those who contributed to the Gemara are called Amoraim, plural of Amora, meaning interpreters.

According to tradition, the Mishnah was redacted in the Land of Israel by R(abbi) Judah the Patriarch, or Prince, the Great Rabbi, about the year 200 of the era common to Christianity and Judaism

---

[2]There exists also a translation into English of the so-called Jerusalem Talmud, the Talmud of the Land of Israel, undertaken by Jacob Neusner for publication by the University of Chicago Press. The present paper does not relate to this work.

(abbreviated hereafter as C.E.) According to tradition, the Babylonian Gemara was first committed to writing in Babylonia, present day Iraq, in the fifth century C.E. by R. Ashi (d. 429) and R. Ravina II (d. 499),[3] heads of the school at Sura, a town on the Euphrates about 175 miles south of Baghdad on the Tigris. During the intervening centuries, BT existed in the memorizations and unofficial notes of the Babylonian rabbis and their disciples as "the oral law," that is, rabbinic teachings sharply distinguished from "the written law," Biblical traditions of the Pentateuch, the Prophets and the Writings. (Gerhardsson, 1961.)

By modern editorial standards, BT appears to be poorly organized. The work has often been referred to, at once affectionately and despairingly, as "the sea of the talmud." The metaphor appears apt as the Talmud may appear to the student (one does not merely *read* BT) to be almost boundless in scope, bottomless in depth, difficult to navigate to a clear understanding, and may arouse among its discussants turbulent emotions. Thorough mastery of all of its 2,783 folios (Goodblatt, 1979:259) is the preoccupation of a lifetime and such an accomplishment is regarded as a notable feat of heroic scholarship.

Statement of the Problem

The present research has brought to BT empirical research procedures which are a commonplace among sociologists. This research does not relate to the traditions ascribed to the numerous rabbis responsible for the creation of BT. Rather it focuses on the rabbis themselves who are cited in it by name. It has sought to state in quantitative terms findings about the rabbis which have previously existed only as qualitative impressions or intuitions. The research has also sought through cross-tabulational analysis to show interrelationships among findings which while previously suspected could not be confirmed, or which have been assumed to be the case, sometimes mistakenly, or whose existence have never been suspected. Such cross-tabulations can also contribute to our knowledge by raising new questions for further exploration in BT and, not least, more sharply reformulating some very ancient questions. To the writer's knowledge, the present research is the first effort at this style of cross-tabulational analysis of data about the rabbis named in BT. (Of a certainty it will not be the last.)

The statistical questions addressed here are:

---

[3]But see Goodblatt, 1979:314. Goodblatt provides detailed summaries and appraisals of the source-critical, form-critical and redaction-critical researches in BT of historians since 1925. He and other critical historians reject the traditional theory of the redaction of BT.

- How many are the rabbis who are cited by name in the pages of BT? Maimonides guessed at five hundred. Much more recently, Solomon Schechter (1885 and 1945:151) guessed at four to five hundred. J.D. Eisenstein is reported by Hermann Strack (1887, and 1965:105) to have "enumerate(d) 1,812 Amoraim...." Most recently, Jacob Neusner (1972:x) "estimate(d) that about three hundred names of Babylonian Amoraim are mentioned" in BT.
- How many are the cited rabbis who antedate the talmudic era; how many date from the later redactional centuries; how many from the intervening centuries? These data (Table 1) on the chronological distribution of the rabbis are significant for our understanding of the development of BT but have not been available.
- The migrations and itinerancy of scholars from the Land of Israel have been shown by Neusner (1965: I, Chapter IV) to have greatly influenced the making of BT. How many of the rabbis cited in it spent their working lives in each of these countries? How did these proportions vary, if at all, during the centuries of its development?
- As indicated above, the rabbinic roles of Tanna and of Amora differed. The teachings of the Amoraim were often based on the prior teachings of Tannaim as confirmations, rejections or reconciliations. We need to know whether the Tannaim were a small, elite band relative to a large group of followers or whether their numbers were much more substantial. How many were the Tannaim who are cited in BT since they too were its developers?
- Some of the rabbis were Great Sages who are cited repeatedly in a majority of the tractates but very many are known to have been cited in only one tractate but once. How many is "very many"? The frequency of citation is one measure of the relative prestige, influence and fame of the rabbi in the Jewish communities of the Land of Israel and Babylonia. What statistics can be made available on frequency of citation?

The Data

The data in this paper were derived from the Rabbinical Index (abbreviated hereafter as RI) compiled by Judah J. Slotki, published in 1952 in the eighteenth and final volume of the Soncino edition.[4] For

---

[4]An alternative concordance of names, "a monumental work which will be of inestimable value" (Goodblatt, 1979:325) has been completed by B. Kosovsky

each name listed, the RI reported whether the rabbi's major residence was in the Land of Israel, in Babylonia or in both countries; whether his rabbinic role was a Tanna or Amora; the century in which he flourished and the pages of each tractate in this edition on which his name appears.[5]

This research accepted as given the RI's classifications as to rabbinic role, country of residence and century of residence. However, the RI was not intended to be primarily a source for the compilation of statistical data and for the present purpose has the following deficiencies:

Sociologists are, of course, always concerned about large numbers of missing cases, lest generalizations be unrepresentative of the total universe of relevant instances. The number of cases for which information is missing in the RI is large, especially as to century. Cross-tabulations of century by country of residence, as in Table 1 are even more vulnerable to depletion of cases. Slotki explains (1952:621):

> Rabbinic chronology in the Talmud offers numerous and almost insurmountable difficulties. No dates are given and it is therefore, with few exceptions, impossible to give anything more precise than the century in which the sage lived and died. The confusion is intensified by the fact that more than one Rabbi bears the same name, sometimes in the Tannaitic period and sometimes in the Amoraic; sometimes in Palestine and sometimes in Babylonia. When two contemporary Rabbis with the same name live, the one in Babylon and the other in Palestine, the bewilderment is complete.

- Some page-citations which should have been credited to a rabbi have been overlooked. For example, no pages are cited for Eurydemos b. Jose, T 2-3, or for Mesharshia b. Pakod, BA 5. Other such instances may be cited. Hence the citation count underestimates the number of pages on which some rabbis are mentioned.

---

but is available only to readers of Hebrew and Aramaic. Whether the cross-tabulations presented here differ substantially from those derivable from Kosovsky's list of rabbis must await a comparable research using that concordance.

[5]The first entry, for example, is about "Aaron (BA 5) BK 637f, Men 443." He was an Amora, named without patronymic, resident in Babylonia during the 5th century. He is cited in tractate Baba Kama on p. 637 and on the f(ollowing) page and once in tractate Menahoth on p. 443. This citation count was determined from the above entry to be 3 which is the total number of times his name appears. Had he been cited on pp. 637ff, he would have been assigned a page-citation count for 637, 638 and 639, but no more.

- The list of rabbis is also known to be incomplete. For example, Hillel and Shamai, pre-Tannaim of the 1st centuries B.C.E. and C.E., are not listed in RI. (They are listed in the General Index.)
- The country of major residence is not given for each Tanna as it is for each Amora. Not all Tannaim, however, resided in the Land of Israel; some are reported by Neusner (1965: I, 113-48) to have been native Babylonians, others to have emigrated for major periods to Babylonia during troublous times in the Land of Israel.

These are technical difficulties. The remedy applied here is the customary assumption that the cases for which information is missing about century or country of residence would be found to be distributed in the same proportions as the cases for which information is available. That is, the percentages true of the distribution of known cases may be assumed to be true for the unknown as well.

Two historiographical problems must also be mentioned: the accuracy of the text of BT as we have it today, and the attribution of teachings to named rabbis. It is known that the text of BT as we have it today is not identical with that first published in manuscript(s) by its redactors, but rather has been altered by glosses, omissions and additions by later rabbis (Goodblatt:1979) and because of "the persecution of the talmud" (Steinsaltz, 1976:81-85 and Popper, 1969:18) during the Middle Ages. Hence the enumeration of rabbis in the RI need not be identical with enumerations that would have resulted from counts in the earliest manuscript(s). The remedy for this difficulty can be to be wary, as are historians, of drawing anachronistic inferences about BT of the 5th and 6th centuries from research based on the Soncino edition of the 20th century.

More difficult is the problem of attribution raised by William Scott Green (1978). He questions the accuracy of the attributions of teachings allegedly formulated by named rabbis which were "really" formulated by other, now unknown scholars. Since the RI cites both the teacher and the scholar who allegedly transmitted accurately in his name, Green's argument affects both the counts of rabbis and of citations. The present research has no remedy for this problem. There is no way to make case by case corrections in favor of the "real" authors of teachings which have been anachronistically attributed by later, less prestigious authors to Great Sages. (This practice would seem to be an instance in a different historic context of the "Matthew Effect" identified in science by Merton, 1973:439-59.)

Findings

The number of rabbis listed in the RI of the Soncino edition was determined to be 1,691.[6]

This is not necessarily the total number of rabbis who lived during the talmudic era. This number includes, moreover, Tannaim who were cited only in the Mishnah but not in the Gemara.

The number of rabbis resident in the Land of Israel (counting here pre-Tannaim, Tannaim, and Amoraim of the Land of Israel) is 628; those resident in Babylonia 719, or respectively, 47 percent and 53 percent. (Table 1, bottom line.)

These figure suggest the efficacy of the processes of migration and itinerancy by which the scholars of Babylonia acquired familiarity with the teachings of their colleagues and competitors in the distant[7] schools of the Land of Israel.

The "chain of tradition" required for the making of BT extended we are informed in tractate Aboth from Moses to the redactors of Aboth. Table 1 reports the century in which flourished each of the numerous links in the oral and written chains of transmission. The number of rabbis whose century is unknown in 646 or 38 percent of the total of 1,691.

Putting to one side this large source of possible error, the number of sages cited in BT who flourished before or during the first century of the common era is estimated in Table 1 at 95 or 9 percent of the total of 1,044 while the number who lived during the fifth and sixth redactional centuries is estimated at 102 or 10 percent of the total. The modal century of activity clearly appears to have been the third century. There flourished during this one century alone about one-quarter (25.4%) of all the rabbis whose names are reported in the RI.

---

[6]137 names were followed by "*See* (another name)." These were not counted as no page-citations accompanied these listings. 42 names were cross-referenced to other names by "*See also* (another name)". Each of these 42 cross-references was counted, as page-citations accompanied both names. But it is possible that in some instances both names referred to one and same person. E.g., Eliezer, T 1-2 and Eliezer b. Hyrcanus (the Great), T 1-2. In such cases, the citation counts given both names underestimate the number of mentions due the rabbi.

[7]How far from the school at Sura in Babylonia to the school at Tiberias in the Galilee? "...we are told by Strabo (?) that Babylon was considered seventy-two days distance from Antioch...foot passengers would rarely accomplish more than twenty miles in a day, while those on horseback might possibly travel half as far again...we are here trying to estimate the times for ordinary travelers and merchants." (Charlesworth, 1924, and 1961:43,44)

The Soncino edition consists of approximately 16,485 pages.[8]

Had the redactors of BT deemed all of 1,691 named rabbis to be equally noteworthy, each would have been cited on approximately 10 pages. In fact, the frequency with which a rabbi is cited in the text varies from but once on one page of one tractate to more than twenty-eight hundred pages in over thirty tractates. (Table 4) Of the 1,689 rabbis tabulated in Table 2, fully 688 or 41 percent were cited but once, 467 or 28 percent on two to four pages and 188 or 11 percent on five to nine pages. In all, almost 80 percent were cited on fewer than the mean number of pages per "average rabbi." On the other hand, Great Sages (here defined, operationally, as those cited on one hundred or more pages) number 78 or 5 percent of the total. These statistics document the extent to which the distribution of the productivity of the rabbis is skewed and establishes the background of the problem raised by Green as to the authenticity of all of the attributions of traditions to individual rabbis. Is the name of a Great Sage a symbol only of a particular individual or a symbol as well of the school of which he was the master?

Other factors equal, the earlier the rabbi the greater his prestige, fame and influence in the Jewish communities of the Land of Israel and Babylonia. One might suppose from this that the contribution of the Tannaim would have been preponderant. On the other hand, the more proximate the scholar in time and place to the redactors of BT the more accessible their oral transmissions, and one might suppose from this that the contributions of the Amoraim would have been preponderant. The data suggest that both factors, prestige and accessibility, were operative but in opposition to one another. From Table 2: 28 percent (84) of the Tannaim are cited on but one page compared with 32 percent (98) of the Amoraim from the Land of Israel and 37 percent (264) of the Amoraim from Babylonia. For rabbis of relatively low prestige, it appears to have been somewhat easier to gain admittance to the written record if they were Babylonian Amoraim than if they resided in the Land of Israel, and easier for the latter Amoraim then if they were Tannaim.

Table 3 reports on the frequency of citation by century in which the rabbi flourished. Here again, prestige and accessibility appear to have been operative in opposition to one another. The data are suggestive and in support of Table 2, but they are not decisive. Putting aside the pre-Tannaim of B.C.E., the Tannaim of the 1st century and the late Amoraim of centuries 5-6 and 6, whose numbers are relatively small,

[8]Including the extensive footnotes written by the translator-editors to elucidate text.

there is an almost steady increase in the proportions of named rabbis who were cited on only one to nine pages, that is, fewer than the "average rabbi." The proportion of Great Sages cited on 100 pages or more diminishes from 19 percent of those who flourished in the 1-2 century to 3 percent in the 5th century. (Bottom third of Table 3.)

It is largely the teachings and activities of 78 rabbis, Great Sages, which are the subject matter of BT. The names of these rabbis in the rank of their frequency of citation are given in Table 4. The listing does not imply, however, that only they of the 1,691 named rabbis were of consequence among their contemporaries. Rather, as noted above, all of the named rabbis were themselves but a selection from among the total number who lived in the Jewish communities of the Land of Israel and Babylonia during the centuries of the development of BT. The roles of the rabbis in its development and transmission who are cited on but one, two, three or four of its pages are a problem that invites further inquiry.

Summary

The Babylonian Talmud (BT) has been available in an authoritative English translation since 1948, the Soncino edition, but as yet has not received the attention of many sociologists interested in comparative historical sociology, communications research, or in the sociologies of knowledge, of law, of education, or of religion. The present research cross-tabulates four variables utilizing data from the Rabbinical Index (RI) of the Soncino edition. The total number of rabbis named in Mishnah and in BT is estimated at 1,691. The number resident in the Land of Israel is estimated at fully 47 percent, in Babylonia 53 percent. The modal century of activity in the formulation of teachings for oral and written transmission to the redactors of the 5th and later centuries appears clearly to have been the 3d century. Of the total number of named rabbis, fully 80 percent are cited on fewer than 10 pages. It is largely the teachings and activities attributed to 78 Great Sages, 5 percent of the total number of named rabbis, which constitute the subject matter of the Babylonian Talmud.

Table 1 Centuries in Which Flourished, by Rabbinical Role and Country of Residence

Century		Pre-Tanna'im	Tanna'im	Tanna'im-Amora'im	Amora'im Land of I.	Amoraim, Babylonia	Amora'im, Both lands	Amora'im, Country?	Role & Country?	Total
B.C.E.	3	1								1
	2	5								5
	2-1	1								1
	1	4								4
C.E.	1		31		2	2				35
	1-2		47							47
	2		122		12	9	2			145
	2-3		20	1	11	26				58
	3		4	1	120	138	3			266
	3-4				48	124				172
	4				62	144	2			208
	4-5				1	51				52
	5				3	36	1			40
	5-6					1				1
	6					9				9
Total		11	224	2	259	540	8			1,044
Century?			81		51	170	1	279	65	647
Total		11	305	2	310	710	9	279	65	1,691

Table 2 Number of Pages on Which Cited, by Rabbinical Role and Country of Residence

No. of Pages:	Pre-Tanna'im	Tanna'im	Tanna'im-Amora'im	Amora'im Land of I.	Amoraim, Babylonia	Amora'im, Both lands	Amora'im, Country?	Role & Country?	Total
1	1	84		98	264	1	187	53	688
2-4	2	89		88	197	3	76	12	467
5-9	6	39		40	94	1	8		188
10-24		39		33	67		8		147
25-49	2	18		21	36	1			78
50-74		6		6	12				24
75-99		8		4	7				19
100-499		12	2	18	17	1			50
500 or more		9		2	15	2			28
Total	11	304	2	310	709	9	279	65	1,689
No. pp.?		1			1				2
Total	11	305	2	310	710	9	279	65	1,691

Table 3 Number of Pages on Which Cited, By Century in Which Flourished

No. of Pages:	B.C.E.	Century 1	1-2	2	2-3	3	3-4	4	4-5	5	5-6	6	?	Total
1	1	7	6	32	15	71	57	52	19	12	1	5	410	688
2-4	2	12	15	36	16	77	36	62	14	12		4	181	467
5-9	6	8	4	24	4	35	26	33	9	6			33	188
10-24		4	7	23	11	29	19	25	5	4			20	147
25-49	2	2	4	10	3	25	11	15	2	3			1	78
50-74				7		3	4	7		2			1	24
75-99		1	2	4	1	6	2	3						19
100-499		1	6	4	3	14	12	7	2	1				50
500 or more			3	5	4	6	5	4	1					28
No. of rabbis	11	35	47	145	57	266	172	208	52	40	1	9	646	1,689
No. pp. ?					1					1				2
Total Rabbis	11	35	47	145	58	266	172	208	52	41	1	9	646	1,691
No. of pages:														
1-9		77%	53%	64%	61%	69%	69%	71%	81%	74%				
10-99		20%	28%	30%	26%	23%	21%	24%	13%	23%				
100 or more		3%	19%	6%	13%	8%	10%	5%	6%	3%				
Total Rabbis = 100%														

Table 4 Rank Order of Rabbis Cited on 100 or More Pages of the Soncino Talmud

Rank order	Name,* country,* role, century	No. of citation-pages	No. of tractates
1	Raba, BA 3-4	2,889	34
2	Johanan b Nappaha, PA 2-3	2,521	37
3	Rab, BA 2-3	2,149	37
4	Judah b Il'ai, T 2	2,042	61
5	Abaye, BA 3-4	1,936	35
6	Samuel, BA 2-3	1,515	37
7	Meir, T 2	1,386	57
8	Judah b Ezekiel, BA 3	1,353	37
9	Ashi, BA 4-5	1,330	26
10	Simeon b Yohai, T 2	1,299	60
11	Papa, BA 4	1,241	37
12	Joseph, BA 3	1,038	36
13	Nahman b Jacob, BA 4	1,023	36
14	Akiba, T 1-2	987	51
15	Jose, T 2	975	51
16	Hisda, BA 3	952	38
17	Eliezer, T 1-2	947	48
18	Huna I, BA 3	945	36
19	Rabbi Judah the Prince, T 2-3	944	38
20	Simeon b Lakish, PA 3	916	36
21	Rabbah b Bar Huna, BA 3-4	760	39
22	Rabina I, BA 3-4	661	36
23	Zera, BPA 4	618	36
24	Eleazar, PBA 3	573	30
25	Shesheth, BA 3-4	537	37
26	Nahman b Isaac, BA 4	535	35
27	Simeon b Gamaliel, T 2	524	47
28	Joshua b Hananiah, T 1-2	503	57
29	'Ulla, PA 3-4	451	36
30	Eleazar, T	431	32
31	Abbahu, PA 3-4	379	34
32	Joshua b Levi, T and PA 3	369	38
33	Jeremiah, PA 4	369	33
34	Ishmael, T 1-2	355	45
35	Rabbah b Bar Hanah, PA 3	347	33
36	Hiyya, PBA 3	340	35
37	Kahana, BA 3-4	335	34
38	Isaac, PA 3	327	35
39	Gamaliel II, T 1-2	287	45
40	Hiyya b Abba, PA 3-4	277	32
41	Assi I, BA 3-4	248	28
42	Jose b Hanina, PA 3	244	31
43	Assi II, PA 3-4	235	32
44	Eliezer b Jacob, T 1-2	223	44
45	Simeon b Eleazar, T 2-3	220	35
46	Huna b Joshua, BA 4	214	33
47	Jose b Judah, T 2	212	36

48	Dimi, BA 4	208	32
49	Nathan, T 2	200	30
50	Adda b Ahabah, BA 3	200	29
51	Rami b Hama, BA 3-4	197	39
52	Oshaia I, PA 3	197	32
53	Ammi, PA 3-4	190	31
54	Jose the Galilean, T 1-2	183	33
55	Rabbah b Abbuha, BA 3	183	31
56	Abba, BA 3-4	175	31
57	Rabbah b Huna, BA 4	173	31
58	Jannai, T and PA 2-3	169	31
59	Samuel b Nahmani, PA 3	169	28
60	Tarfon, T 1-2	165	42
61	Levi, BA 3	165	32
62	Eleazar b Azariah, T 1-2	154	42
63	Aha b Jacob, BA 3	154	34
64	Mar Zutra, BA 5	154	31
65	Eliezer b Simeon, T 2-3	151	28
66	Hanina, BA 3	151	24
67	Ammi b Nathan, BA 3-4	141	22
68	Nehemiah, T 2	134	32
69	Rabin, PA 4	130	29
70	Kahana I, PA 3	129	27
71	Hamnuna I, BA 3	128	31
72	Zebid, BA 4	128	29
73	Hanina, PA 3-4	126	19
74	Amemar, BA 4-5	124	26
75	Aha b Raba, BA 4-5	112	28
76	Johanan b Zakkai, T 1	110	29
77	Safra, PA 3-4	108	25
78	Hezekiah, PA 4	107	26

*Spelling follows that of the Rabbinical Index. "P" indicates residence in the Land of Israel.

References

Berelson, Bernard, *Content Analysis in Communication Research.* New York: Hefner, 1942, 1971.

Charlesworth, M.P., *Trade Routes and Commerce of the Roman Empire.* Cambridge University Press, 1924. Reprinted by Hildesheim: Georg Olms Verlagsbuchhandlung, 1961.

Gerhardsson, *Birger, Memory and Manuscript, Oral Tradition and Written Transmission in Rabbinic Judaism and Early Christianity.* Translated by Eric J. Sharpe, Copenhagen: CWK Gleerup, Lund, Cjnar, Muskegaard, 1961.

Goodblatt, David M., *Rabbinic Instruction in Sasanian Babylonia.* Leiden: E. J. Brill, 1975.

———, *The Babylonian Talmud in Aufsteig und Niedergang der Romaneschen Welt,* II.19.2, 257-336. Berlin and New York: Walter De Gruyter & Co., 1979.

Heilman, Samuel C., *The People of the Book, Drama, Fellowship, and Religion.* Chicago: University of Chicago, 1983.

Helmreich, William B., *The World of the Yeshiva, An Intimate Portrait of Orthodox Jewry.* New York: The Free Press, 1982

Kaplan, Julius, *Redaction of the Babylonian Talmud.* New York: Bloch Publishing Co., 1933.

Lazarsfeld, Paul F. and Morris Rosenberg, *The Language of Social Research.* New York: The Free Press, 1955

———, *Continuities in the Language of Social Research. With Ann K. Pasanella.* New York: The Free Press, 1972.

Maimonides, Moses, 12th cent.

Merton, Robert K., *On the Oral Transmission of Knowledge in Sociological Traditions From Generation to Generation, Glimpses of the American Experience,* with Matilda White Riley, eds. Norwood, N.J. Ablex Publishing Corporation, 1980, pp. 1-35.

———, *The Matthew Effect in Science in The Sociology of Science, Theoretical and Empirical Investigations,* Norman W. Storer, ed. Chicago and London: University of Chicago Press, 1973.

Neusner, Jacob, *A History of the Jews is Babylonia,* vol. I to V. Leiden: E. J. Brill, 1965.

———, *There We Sat Down: Talmudic Judaism in the Making.* New York: Ktav Publishing House, Inc., 1978.

Popper, Walter, *The Censorship of Hebrew Books. Introduction by Moshe Carmilly-Weinberger.* New York: Ktav Publishing House, Inc., 1899 and 1969.

Schechter, Solomon, *On the Study of the Talmud in Westminster Review*. London CXXII (N.S.L. XVII) republished in Studies in Judaism, Third Series. Phila.: Jewish Publication Society of America, 1885 and 1945.

Slotki, Judah, *Rabbinical Index in Index Volume to the Soncino Talmud*. London: The Soncino Press, 1952, pp. 621-730.

Steinsaltz, Adin, *The Essential Talmud*, translated by Chaya Galai. New York: Bantam Books, 1976.

Strack, Hermann L., *Introduction to the Talmud and Midrash*. New York: Harper & Row, Publishers. Originally published in English in 1931 by The Jewish Publication Society of America. First edition in German, 1887 and 1965.

Zeisel, Hans, *Say it with Figures*. New York: Harper & Row, Publishers. Sixth edition, 1985.

21

Matching Patterns at the Seams: A Literary Study

Herbert Basser
Queens University

According to the first nine chapters of the Book of Genesis God gradually relinquished policing human behavior through Nature. To directly police it would have meant drastic punishments for infractions. Instead, Nature was imbued with ceaseless cycles of behavior. It could not be readily changed to respond to the requirements of punishment. Also, human beings had been endowed with a divine image which allowed them to adjudicate their own affairs as God would have them. Since Nature now followed continuous cycles it could no longer be the rod of punishment as such. As well, God was relieved of being the watchdog of society. The execution of justice was to be a human concern. Yet the responsibility of setting out the processes of justice remained God's. God was still in charge but from a heavenly vantage. He could still interfere in cases where people ignored executing justice such as at Babel or Sodom. It was deemed better for humans to deal with justice than to promote a situation where God would directly become involved.

According to Exodus, God returned at Sinai to take direct control over Israel. For all groups of Jews in antiquity, God's revelation of Torah allowed God once again to manage human affairs through the direct agency of His command. God was king and judge of the community which accurately interpreted the Torah. They were the bearers of covenant through the study of this Torah and obedience to its commandments. The creator God of Genesis brought order, formation, to a heedful society. Through this study one entered the divine life, the realm of holiness, bringing creation to fruition. The transcendent God was brought back as before into society through the teachings of Torah. It therefore became most important to know the best methods of reading Torah.

For the dominant schools of Rabbinic Judaism, these methods were developed through the dialectic of the academies which were communally sanctioned to speak the words of the living God. These words were indeterminate. Torah meant the process of study of these words. What was important was the interpretive process of Torah, not any absolute result. The Torah was not in heaven, not a divine task. It was on earth for humans to work with. The command was God's. The process of dealing with the command was man's way of reaching into the divine realm, the realm of holiness. The study of Torah was holy.[1] God managed human affairs through revealing a process for people to live by. It was the involvement in this process which brought the divinity back into human affairs and allowed Him to bring order into society. The stories and sayings in the literature of the Rabbis of the Rabbinic period (the first six centuries of the Common Era) which highlight this outlook are far too numerous to warrant any analysis here. What we can do here is analyze and categorize some of the methods the Rabbis used in the process of their Torah study.

A Talmudic saying has it that Rabbi Yohanan proclaimed:[2]

> The following verse refers to all who read Scripture without its rhythm and recite Mishnah without its melody: *For yea I have given you statutes which are not good and laws which are not livable.*[3]

The Amora, Abaye, seems to have had difficulty understanding what the verse had to do with those who do not sing their texts. The great medieval commentator, Rashi, explained that the point had to do with those who do not intone their readings with proper punctuation. Someone who does not do this would undoubtedly read the verse as a simple statement. The laws are not good. Indeed, for Rabbinic Jews, this is a fact. One who studies without proper inflection cannot discover the truth of God's laws. On the other hand, one who reads with inflection

---

[1]For the Rabbis, detail was sovereign. According to *b Men.* 29b Moses found God tying crowns to the letters of the Torah. With these Akiba would unravel the sense of mounds of rules. Just as angels could, as if by magic, set crowns upon God in recognition of his authority, so God coronated the letters. See I. Gruenwald, *Apocalyptic and Merkava Mysticism*, Leiden: Brill, 1980, 66 (n. 135). Also see *b Shab.* 88b where it is said that each commandment was made a prince by having two crowns tied to it. As the letter goes, so goes the word, the sentence, the unit, the Torah.

[2]*b Meg.* 32a.

[3]Ez 20:25.

will read the verse to say, *For yea, have I given you statutes which are not good and laws which are unlivable*! For such a one the entire reading of traditional texts will reveal many beautiful laws beneath the simple statements of the texts. Hence, the way in which one chooses to read the verse in Ezekiel indicates one's manner of exegesis and so provides a true indication of what one will find in the Torah: good laws or not good laws.[4]

Rabbi Yohanan further claimed that he who reads the Torah naked is buried naked.[5] One can read the bare lines of Scripture without their delicate fineries, their lavish dressings, and their fitted costumes. Yet to do so is to bury Scripture and oneself in a pile of antiquated documents which have no contemporary meaning. To dwell upon the garb of Scripture, to examine its every shade of fine attire, to probe the forms of its loose or tight apparel, is to see Scripture as a living companion. Whoever marvels at the attire of Scripture is the one who adds rich layers to his ongoing life. His life is not buried with antiquated documents but is enriched anew with each reading of each word in Scripture. Devotees of *midrash, kabbalah, hassidut* have

[4]I am indebted to Prof. Yaakov Shamir, Prof. of Chemistry at the Hebrew University in Jerusalem, for enlightening me about this passage in particular, and for disclosing to me, in general, the secret of analyzing Rabbinic texts through the methods of spectroscopy.

[5]Cf. *b Meg*. 32a and *Shab*. 14a. Once again, it appears that Abaye dismissed the import of Rabbi Yohanan's pithy statement. One might note that Yohanan's words are always laden with meaning although they seem to make little sense on the surface. The best example of this is found in *b Ber*. 14b (bottom). Here we learn, in the name of Rabbi Yohanan that one who reads the *Shma* without *tfillin* **is like one who offers the burnt offering *(olah)* without including the *minha* offering.** The versions vary in the wording here but there can be no doubt that what Rabbi Yohanan meant to say was that reading the *Shma* ***(ol malkhut shamayim)*** was phonetically and conceptually related to the notion of ***olah,*** Temple sacrifice. The ***minha*** of the Temple was now the **hanahat tfillin.** The temple of the head was like the Temple of Jerusalem. The more recent editors of the Talmud mislead us somewhat by dividing this pithy statement from what follows:" And Rabbi Yohanan said that one who wants to accept upon himself ***ol malkhut shamayim*** in its entirety should...***maniah tfillin*** and read the *Shma*." Here the intent of Rabbi Yohanan is made manifest. The commentators were baffled by the juxtaposition of ***olah/minha*** and wondered if there was some specific purpose to this juxtaposition. Rabbi Yohanan's statement contains an entire philosophy of the place of ritual in Judaism and an entire theology of the meaning of Temple/temple in exile. God remains king and the Kingdom of Heaven is no less diminished. We will have reason to further explore the ingenuity of traditions ascribed to Rabbi Yohanan when we discuss *b Meg*. 2a below.

developed systems of making sense of the world. Their particular understandings of the layers of meaning within Scripture have provided the accoutrements of present day Jewish communities.

Marvin Fox has spent his years admiring, analyzing and appreciating the intellects that have helped shape these communities. He has raised students who continue to build upon his insights. He has, in his modest way, contributed to the defining and shaping of these modern day communities. In tribute to him we will look at four of the many techniques the early Rabbis used in their most difficult feats of exegeting invisible threads. We will see how they used particular exegeses (which I term "remez," "fragment," "parallel," and "intertextual") to supply missing information in biblical verses, thus assigning the text to specific referents.

Remez-exegesis (provides information not found in Scripture):

In the Talmuds, Scripture plays a key role. The Rabbis were not primarily concerned with the elucidation of rules or events which are clearly discernible in Scripture. Their main interest lay with the elucidation of that which is not clearly discernible.[6] The Rabbis also associated laws and lore that had long been part of their culture with specific verses even though they were aware of the artificiality of such activity. By associating accepted laws and lores with scriptural verses, the Rabbis infused these traditions with the divine authority of Scripture, an authority taken as axiomatic by all Jewish groups of their era. Moreover, such association connected particular verses with ancient and Rabbinic traditions so integrally that the very details of the verses could be used to limit or expand those laws associated with them. An example of this is the limiting of the rule "The Torah shows concern over the expenses of Israelites." This rule will be discussed below.

The dynamic development of *halachic* and *aggadic* traditions depended to some extent upon their verse associations (henceforth *filing*). Where verses were used to *justify* extra-biblical traditions, they could also be used to *discover* important parameters governing the application of these traditions.[7] This method of "filing" also allowed the Rabbinic curriculum to be taught in conjunction with the teaching of Torah portions.[8] The study of Scripture could therefore encompass the

---

[6]Cf. *j Rosh Hash.* 3:5 (The words of the Torah are poor in their place and rich in another place) and *Tanhuma Hukat* 23 (The words of the Torah are interdependent).

[7]See below n.23.

[8]Hence the format of the halachic midrashim and the *She'iltot* is that of commentary on biblical verses in sequence.

study of Rabbinic law and lore. The Rabbis used great ingenuity in associating their own enactments with Scriptures. Students of the Talmud are sometimes at a loss to determine which associations were understood by the ancient masters to be intended by Scripture and which were simply pegs upon which to hang extra-biblical law and lore.

Our task here is to consider some of the more difficult interpretive procedures of the Rabbis in dealing with what they saw as insufficient data in scriptural verses. One such procedure, ***remez-exegesis***, could be a very serious method to elucidate scriptural verses. The medieval scholars, in their commentaries and novellae, divided *remez-exegesis* into several categories. Below we present a table which indicates all the possibilities of understanding *remez-exegesis*. It is not to be taken for granted that all medieval students of Talmud worked with all four categories. Some may have posited all four while others may have posited only two, such as A,C or B,D. It is not possible to completely reconstruct their systems.

Status	**Not In Scripture**	**In Scripture**
Divine	A	B
Human	C	D

One category (B,D) expressed the actual intention of the verse's "author" concerning some rule of God's or some widely practiced custom. Another category served as a "filing" device for the Rabbis to recall divinely given oral laws or to legitimate Rabbinic enactments. This latter type was not understood to exegete the intended meaning of the verse. Sometimes this type of exegesis was referred to as "mere." The medieval commentators apparently categorized only the exegesis as "mere," not the status of the law. We should not confuse literary categories with legal ones. It may be that such distinctions are indeed very ancient.[9]

[9]In *b Moed Katan* 5a distinctions are made between laws handed down orally from Moses but hinted at through close readings of Scripture and specific laws which will be legislated but also are only hinted at. In both cases the term "remez" is deemed appropriate because in neither case is the wording of the original legislation present. Rashi, to *b Sotah* 16a remarks that occasionally laws, which were handed down from Moses at Sinai and were unknown from Scripture, were nonetheless associated with verses as "mere allusion" (A). This is consonant with *b Nidah* 32a which provides examples of such allusions to orally received laws.

This style of exegesis is introduced by the phrase, "Where is the hint," *(heikha remiza).*[10] Let us now look at a specimen of this usage. A rule stated in Proverbs is said to be hinted at in the Pentateuch, "Is there anything written in the Hagiographa which is not hinted at in the Pentateuch!"[11] This enthusiastic claim is illustrated by associating Pr 19:3, *"The foolishness of man perverts his way: and his heart frets against the Lord,"* with its hint in Gen 42:28, *"And their heart failed them, and they were afraid, saying one to another,'What is this that God has done to us.'"* The verse in Genesis is taken as a specific instance of a rule stated in Proverbs. Genesis illustrates the rule which is unknown as a universal principle until stated in Proverbs. Once the rule is known we see the specific case alludes to the rule's general validity.[12] The case is said "to hint" at the general rule.

We now consider another example. "Where is the hint from the Torah requiring the erection of grave markers?"[13] The answer was given: "When anyone sees a man's bone, then he will set up a sign by it." (Ezekiel 39:15). The Amoraim were divided in their approach to the possibility of discovering relevant, divine commandments in Ezekiel 39:15. Some saw *only* a scriptural reference to a law which was for the period after Ezekiel's proclamation, if not actually for the Messianic Era (thus, any similar laws in force today are not of Mosaic origin). Others saw a law which was known from Mosaic, oral sources (applying to the Current Era as well as to the Future) and alluded to by Ezekiel (B). According to Rashi, as read in the *eyn ya'akov* version, Ezekiel 39:15,[14] at first seemed to the Talmud to state what will be done by common practice in the Future Era. It did not appear to allude to

---

[10]The more usual and general phrase is "From where do we know," *(menalan).*

[11]*b Ta'an.* 9a. The question, by its very nature, defines *remez-exegesis* here to refer to finding information nowhere explicitly stated in the Pentateuch. Generally, the term refers to finding information nowhere explicitly stated in Scripture.

[12]Usually *remez-exegesis* points towards rules operative in society but unstated directly in Scripture. If the context of the verse is consonant with the context of the law then the hint is said to be seriously intended by Scripture. If it is not consonant then we say the rule is known from extra-biblical sources (Moses at Sinai or from Rabbinic legislation) and the exegesis is "mere," unintended by Scripture.

[13]*b Moed Katan* 5a.

[14]It is not clear in this passage of Talmud if "Where is the hint of *law x* from the Torah?" means "From the Torah (=Scripture) where is the hint of *law x*?" or if it means "Where is the hint of *law x,* which is a law from the Torah?" One suspects the former generally but Rashi's excellent analysis suggests the latter in this instance.

any law legislated in and for biblical times. Rashi, considering the argument of the Talmud, proceeds to demonstrate that the law of markers had been passed down orally from the time of Moses. While Ezekiel neither legislated nor forecast the legislation of "the law of markers" he does refer to it. That is to say, Ezekiel alluded to the orally known law by referring to an instance of its application in the Future. "People will set up markers in accordance with known oral law." In a similar way to Rashi some Tosafists explained the flow of *b Ta'an.* 5a:

> Although this verse is specifically written to refer to the Future and not to Ezekiel's period; nevertheless, the Talmud argues that the Mosaic basis of the law can be associated with the words of Ezekiel....Now you may wonder how the law can be of Mosaic origin if the Holy One, blessed be He, did not notify us in the Torah about the duty to erect markers. The Talmud responds by indicating that there are many things which are forbidden us from Torah (i.e. Mosaic, hence divine) legislation which were nowhere mentioned in Scripture until Ezekiel alluded to them. However they were known through the halachic oral tradition.[15]

Other sources relate further ideas of the Tosafists. These other opinions may not be in conflict with the above which merely describes a passage without judging its final legal status. According to these other sources the Talmud's entire repartee is meant to indicate that the erection of grave markers is an enactment of the Rabbis and not of Scripture.[16] These Tosafists reconciled data from elsewhere in the Talmud. *b Nidah* 57a states that the duty to erect such markers was solely Rabbinic. These Tosafists took the fact that *b Ta'an.* 5a produced a further scriptural source for the law of markers as a sign of rejection. The claimed *remez* source for the law in Ezekiel must have been too difficult to maintain. The Talmud also abandoned this further source and found no others. The Tosafists reasoned that the Talmud itself had no choice but to accept that the law of markers was not of Mosaic origin and *b Nidah* 57a verifies this explicitly. Nevertheless, for our purposes, *b Ta'an* is instructive in showing us that the term **remez min hatorah** (hint from the Torah) was apparently taken to allude to laws promulgated in Mosaic times.

Another example: "Where is the hint of visiting the sick from the Torah?"[17] The answer is Nu 16:29, "If these men die the common death of all men or if they be visited after the visitation of all men...."

---

[15]Tosafot to *b Moed Katan* 5a.

[16]See Tosafot to *b Baba Batra* 147a.

[17]*b Ned.* 39b.

Although "visitation" seems to mean "manner of death," the Rabbis tried to avoid seeing exact repetitions in verses. They therefore saw that the second half of the verse defined the first half. Common death is when one is first sick and lies in bed while others visit. Rosh described this type of exegesis as "a specific hint."[18] Both Rabbenu Yonah and Ritva understood this obligation of visiting the sick to be a rule of Torah, that is of divine origin (B). Their point appears to be that Nu 16:29 refers to "all men" and therefore refers to a universal rule, which, if not legislated explicitly, is assumed as normative by Scripture. Maimonides, in his *Mishneh Torah,* ruled the ordinance was completely Rabbinic (C).[19] Meiri's comment to *b Nedarim* 39b is interesting: "It is a positive commandment from the words of the scribes to visit the sick **and not withstanding** it is hinted at in the Torah" (D). Meiri means that the legislation is certainly of Rabbinic origin. The verse in Scriptures shows us that the practice is very ancient and hinted to the Rabbis that such legislation, beyond voluntary norm, would be in order. Meiri thus brings the positions of the others closer together.

In discussing the law of one who steals a Temple utensil, the Mishnah claims that the law of zealots applies.[20] "And where is the hint."[21] Nu 4:20, "But people came not expecting to be seen when the things were stolen and they could die," provides an answer. According to Rashi the verse really refers to the priests covering or packing Temple utensils, an act not to be witnessed by the Levites. We cannot reconcile the hint meaning with its context in Scripture. Rashi called this "mere hint." We do not know if Rashi meant that although the literary sense of the verse precludes any such reference, nevertheless the law is divine. That is, it was part of oral tradition (A). It may well be that Rashi meant that the law was devised by the Rabbis and filed under this verse (C). In a passage previous to this passage Rashi spoke of "remez-mikzat," partial allusion. That case concerned permission for a court to induce death, through neglect of proper diet, in a habitual

---

[18]See *perush haRosh* to *b Ned.* 39b. His point is that elsewhere (*b Baba Kam.* 100a and *b Baba Mez.* 30b) the obligation to visit the sick is said to be derived from Ex 18:20, "And you shall inform them of the way they shall go." The context of this verse is too general to see the specific exegesis. Rosh points out that Nu 16:29 can be read as a specific reference to visiting the sick.

[19]See the discussion of these sources in J.D. Eisenstein, *Jewish Laws and Customs,* New York, 1938, *s.v. bikur holim,* 49.

[20]The law of zealots refers to extraordinary provision excusing the behavior of zealous righteousness. One, in hot blood, may kill another who is desecrating the sanctity of God and Israel.

[21]*b Sanhed.* 81b.

offender of a serious crime where technicalities prevented a capital judgment. Rashi understood the law here was known from oral tradition passed down from Moses at Sinai. The Talmud had found a hint in one of the Psalms to allude to such a case. The law was not enacted by the Psalmist but Rashi apparently saw reason to suppose that Psalms could be so construed, in some partial way, as if it were alluding to it. It were as if the Psalmist, aware of the rule, subconsciously phrased his words in such a way that we can find some weak allusion to "the rule of extra-procedural execution." If so, the allusion was to an oral rule, not a scriptural one. For Rashi, in the present case, Numbers was certainly not even "subconsciously" referring to "the rule of zealots"(execution through righteous indignation). Nevertheless, Rashi may well have maintained that the rule of zealots, though nowhere referred to in Scripture, including Numbers, is in fact of divine authority. It was handed down orally from Moses at Sinai (A). Ramban argued a similar position (A or B) against Maimonides who saw the law of zealots as of Rabbinic origin (C). For Maimonides, the Rabbis had simply and artificially filed their own legislation in Numbers.[22]

We have noted the most constant use of *remez-exegesis* is to refer to data in verses which supply illustrations of unstated rules. The rules are extrapolated from considering circumstances not addressed in the verses. Where the verse is better set in a context which in fact, does not illustrate a rule, the hint is said to be "mere." In instances of this type the medieval commentators took this to mean one of two things. Either that the rule was known from oral tradition beginning with Moses, the Rabbis using the verse for filing purposes (A); or the rule was noted to be of Rabbinic legislation (C). In both cases the use of the *remez-exegesis* was for filing purposes. We can also note cases where the medievals understood that *remez-exegesis* was the mechanism intended by the "author" to understand the verse in question (A,D). The precise usages of the Talmud are somewhat difficult to determine and all that can be said is that our chart above contains all possibilities.

---

[22]The entire issue of the status of *remez-exegesis* is discussed by Moses Nachmanides in his glosses on the *Sefer Hamitzvot* (s.3) of Moses Maimonides. Nachmanides, or Ramban as he is commonly called, adopts the position so manifest in his *Commentary to the Torah.* No one, not even a prophet, can create new commandments of divine status; yet, God enabled the Sages to discover the real nature of the commandments of the Torah. He therefore argues that many laws developed through *remez-exegesis* were understood to be divinely ordained and argues the present case is certainly among them. His arguments are thoroughly analyzed by other commentators to the *Sefer Hamitzvot.*

Two *remez* derivations of type "B" are worthy of attention. "So you shall give the congregation and ***their*** beasts drink." (Nu 6 20:8) This verse is supposed by the Talmud to refer to a law, unknown through any tradition except by use of *remez-exegesis,* whereby religious authorities are to show concern for the property of all Israelites. That is, in cases where the property of all Israelites is concerned, as in the case of large public expenditures, authorities are to find means to reduce the financial burdens. Since the biblical verse was concerned with the property of all Israelites this verse is taken as a specific instance to establish the use of cheap wheat in public offerings which call for wheat.[23] The commentators note this to be an instance of type "B" *remez-exegesis.* The parameters of the exegesis limit the concern to large public and frequent expenditures. The principle could otherwise be subject to abuse.

A more intricate instance is the passage in *b Makkot* 2b and *b Sanhedrin* 10a. The passage defines "hint" as a reference to a rule that is not explicitly stated in the biblical text. Deut 25:1,2 asks judges to condemn the guilty and clear the innocent. It also introduces the laws of administering lashes. The Rabbis of the Talmud were perplexed that such a trivial statement could serve to introduce the laws of lashes. They therefore claimed that the verses were referring to the treatment of false witnesses. The innocent victim had to be cleared and the guilty witnesses had to be punished in the way they would have had their victim punished. When such punishments, for technical reasons, could not apply then lashes were to be administered. That is to say, the verses make passing reference to a rule known in no other way (B). There is no particular allusion in the verse to witnesses. However, the context can be surmised in the light of all the information given in the verse. Ramban notes that Scripture reveals the law by means of a hint. Meiri, like all commentators, notes that the verse is meant to be explicated in terms of "lying witnesses" (B).

A most interesting case of *remez-exegesis* is to be found at the beginning of *b Megillah.* The editor of the passage justifies his position (here placed in bold letters) that an unspecified exegesis which was current in the academies was in fact *remez-exegesis.*

---

[23]See *b Men.* 76b. Since Nu 20:8 is in the context of all Israel and involves great loss, the principle of *hasa torah al mamonan shel yisrael* is limited to this context.

Mishnah:

The Scroll of the Book of Esther is read on one of the 11th, 12th, 13th, 14th, 15th days of Adar; no less and no further.[24]

Gemara:

"The Scroll of the Book of Esther is read on one of the 11th...." From where do we know this? **From where do we know this! [We need no verse,we know this] Because of what is stated later: The Sages[25] eased the rule [limiting Purim celebrations to only the 14th and 15th]....in order for the villagers to provide water and food for their brethren in walled cities![26] [No, we rejected this as an original source for] our very question implied: "Since it**

---

[24]According to Esther 9:21 only the 14th and 15th days of Adar were to be used for celebrating. LXX Esther 9:17,18 and Josephus, *Antiquities,* (ed. Whiston) 11, 6, 13, imply that all were to observe the 14th while some were *also* to observe the 15th. *j Meg.* 1:1 preserves a statement wherein Rabbi Yonah argues that the word "times" in Esther 9:31 refers to discreet times. Those who observe the 15th were not to observe the 14th as well. LXX intimates that the 14th was generally observed as a rest day; while those who observed the 15th were joyful. It does not appear that they rested on that day as well. Josephus omits all mention of resting and seems, like the Rabbis, to maintain that neither day was observed as a rest day. While the reading of the Scroll is nowhere attested until the time of the Mishnah, it is possible that many communities were accustomed to doing that. The extra days of Purim mentioned in the Mishnah are unknown from sources prior to the Mishnah.

[25]We have above what appears to be the citation of the Mishnah tradition with an appended explanation. This forms an early layer, quite possibly of Palestinian origin, which a Babylonian editor comments upon. It is unusual for *b* to recite a Mishnah at the opening of a Talmud tractate although it does happen more often in *j*, see n. 31 below. The editor sees in the question certain proof to show that courts do not change the rulings of earlier authorities. The search for a scriptural source implies that the Rabbis of the Mishnah did not originate these extra times to celebrate Purim. The editor therefore prods us to consider that no verse would be necessary if the legislation were entirely the work of the Rabbis of the Mishnah. Therefore *b Meg.* 5b cannot mean that the Rabbis of the Mishnah did legislate these extra times.

[26]See *b Meg.* 5b. The point is that if farmers had to spend two days a week at market (Mondays and Thursdays) and celebrate Purim on the 14th and then tend to those who celebrated on the 15th they would have only two days to spend in the fields. By stipulating that they could celebrate Purim, even not on the 14th, on the closest previous market day, the Rabbis made it possible for the farmers to provide for those who celebrated on the 15th. The farmers would still have three days in the fields. This *baraita* refers to the Sages of the Mishnah, a reference which, at first blush, seems to render the search for a verse as a source for the rule as inappropriate.

has to be claimed that the Men of the Great Assembly ordained all the times....

> **For if you entertain the notion that the Men of the Great Assembly ordained just the 14th and the 15th,[27] could the Rabbis of the Mishnah come and uproot an ordinance of the Men of the Great Assembly? Have we not learned, "A court cannot annul the enactments of another court unless it supersedes it in wisdom and in number"! Surely it is obvious that all the times [in the Mishnah] were ordained by the Men of the Great Assembly....**

where is their hint [of these times]?"[28] –

"Rabbi Shimon the son of Abba related that Rabbi Yohanan explained: Scripture states, "To ordain these days of Purim in their times." (Esther 9:31) Many times they (the Sages)[29] ordained for them."

---

[27]It was thought that the Men of the Great Assembly both wrote the Book of Esther and legislated the rules for Purim observances. *b Baba Batra* 15a refers to Ezra (one of the members of the Assembly) as the author of Esther. Thus Esther 9:21 seems to indicate that the Assembly sanctioned only the two days for Purim observances. What is placed between the dots here is simply a parenthetical elaboration showing that The Sages of the Mishnah could not have changed the original legislation concerning the days on which Purim is celebrated. It is therefore indented.

[28]Here ends the interpolation. The editor has established that a verse is necessary to show that the original Purim rules incorporated the possibility of celebrating on days other than the 14th and 15th. He has also established that the Men of the Great Assembly ordained (TKN) all the times possible to celebrate. This claim will push Rabbi Yohanan's statement to mean that "the Sages" who ordained (TKN) the extra times of Purim were in fact the Sages of the Great Assembly. Finally, he has refined the general search for a verse to a particular, specific genre of exegesis. Since it is obvious that only the 14th and 15th were operative days for Purim in the Book of Esther, we are looking for some hint that will allow us to discover that permission was given to increase the times. We note that at the end of the Talmudic period there was an enterprise to define types of exegesis in terms of existing categories.

[29]When "times" in Esther 9:31 is compared with "time" in Esther 9:21, we assume that extra days are intimated. There seems to be two ways of understanding this passage. The Spanish commentators read "Sages" here and this appears to be the reading. It is attested as early as Alfasi and all versions of *b Yeb. 13b* show it to be the original reading. Rashi, likely sensing the real import of the passage understood that the reference here was not to the Sages of the Mishnah but to the Assembly. It is therefore possible that, in the light of Rashi's excellent understanding, the troublesome word fell out in many texts (if it had not already fallen out). The Spanish commentators understood the word to refer to the Sages of the Mishnah who received permission from the Great Assembly to add the extra days. Rashi's understanding seems better suited to

The above italicized sections represent what I take to be the original citations of Mishnah and Gemara while the bold represents probable later additions.[30] What originally stood before the redactor was a passage very much like the opening of *j Megillah* 1:1:

> *The Scroll of the Book of Esther is read on one of the 11th....Rabbi Ilah said in the name of Shimon*[31] *bar Abba who cited Rabbi Yohanan: "To ordain these days of Purim in their times."...Rabbi Yosah said it refers to the times that the Sages ordained and these are they....*[32]

This statement claims the use of "times" and not "time" expands the set time of the 14th and 15th days of Adar to celebrate Purim. The term *leqayem* used in Esther is rendered as *tiqnu* in *b* and as *qav'u* in *j*, perfectly acceptable renditions.[33] Times were to be set for the celebrations. The redactor of *b Megillah* 2a has interpolated a section to sharpen the precise mode of exegesis used in this tradition.[34] After justifying the need to adduce a verse,[35] the redactor set out to make clear the precise nature of the exegesis used by Rabbi Yohanan, *remez-exegesis*. That is, he needed to clarify "From where do we know this" *(menalan)*, and to define it precisely: "Where is the hint?"

The positions of the medieval commentators are interesting. Rashi, Meiri, Ritva see the hint as very serious exegesis (B). The word "times"

---

the editor's view; the Spanish commentators seem to provide us with a truer view of the original intent of the Yohanan tradition.

[30]I.e. a statement of the tradition found in the Mishnah with a proof text supplied by Rabbi Yohanan. It is not common to find such restatements of Mishnah in *babli* although we do find them in *yerushalmi* as a glance through *j Peah* (beginning with 1:1) will indicate.

[31]SM'WN in *j* is the same person as SMN in *b*. In *j* the students of Yohanan argue about his intent. *b* agrees with the position of Yosah but attributes it directly to Rabbi Shimon in the name of Rabbi Yohanan.

[32]"Sages" here appears to refer to the Sages of the Mishnah. The editor of *b Meg.* 2a has "fudged" this sense in his version of the tradition so that it could refer to the Men of the Great Assembly.

[33]*QB'* means establish as law; e.g. see Tosefta *Hag.* 2:2(end): *niqba'ah halakhah kedivre bet hilel.* In general it parallels *TKN;* e.g. see Rabbenu Hannanel to *b Suk.* 49a: *bizman shelo nitqav'u hashanim ketikunan.*

[34]He informs us that the exegesis is serious even if it not obvious. By showing us that we have *remez-exegesis* before us he removes our doubts that the exegesis is forced and allows us to see the exegesis as a serious derivation. The genre of *remez-exegesis* allows that obscure references can be intentional allusions in the verse.

[35]No court would presume to change the original ordinance of the Men of the Great Assembly and so they must have promulgated the allowance for extra Purim days on which the Scroll of Esther could be recited.

shows that the authors of the laws of Purim considered the need for extra days and allowed for them in their legislation. "Times" in *Esther* 9:31 refers directly to this legislation and must be seen as a purposeful allusion. True, the text of the verse says nothing about extra days but we can reconstruct the rule from the use of the plural "times." Rashi is clearest on this point,"They certainly hinted." Rabbenu Hannanel sees the hint here as the type which does inform us of a rule. The rule was known orally, passed down by the Assembly (a form of A), and the hint is simply an allusion to the rule, not a way of deriving it. Rosh refers to it as *remez be'alma,* a term which may mean that the verse is simply referring to something known already from oral sources (a form of A).

It is difficult to know exactly what Rabbi Yohanan and his students intended to tell us. That is why the editor introduced his gloss. He believed that the Men of the Great Assembly did ordain the extra days. It would seem that he either thought the rule was inherent in the verse (B), although somewhat covertly; or, less likely, that the rule was known orally and that the verse alluded to it (A). His gloss instructs us as to the activity at the close of the Talmudic period. The nature of early exegesis was under scrutiny with the aim of classifying types of exegesis more precisely. Most likely the editor indicates to us that he took "remez" to be a form of exegesis which discloses ancient law, and not simply an interpretive ruse. He could not have used the term in the context he did had he thought otherwise. That context requires a serious form of exegesis. He puts much weight on this passage for the tractate concludes with the statement:

> Moses ordained (TKN) for Israel that they should inquire and formally elucidate the pertinent rules of conduct for festive days.

Here we have the parallel to our opening tradition:

> Many times they (the Sages) ordained for them.

The redactor of tractate *b Megillah* wants us to know that just as Moses ordained the study of God's festivals on their respective days so did the Men of the Great Assembly ordain the reading of *Esther* on the **days** of Purim. While *Megillah* may be the only tractate dealing with a festival that deals with one not prescribed in the Torah of Moses, it dreams the same dreams as found in every festival tractate: the eternal glory of Israel under the sovereignty of God.[36]

---

[36]The Talmud seems to have found meaning in the placement of these days at the head of the tractate. The Talmud makes the point that because Israel is not sovereign, any prolongation of a festival celebrating Jewish victories over their enemies would be dangerous. The readings of *b Meg.* 2a-b as given by Alfasi

Thus far we have examined passages of the Amoraic period which have legal import. We discovered that the term "hint" could be used in a manner to indicate serious exegetical implications. This term has a long history of usages in Rabbinic tradition. The Aggadic use of "remez" is noteworthy. In the tannaitic midrashim we find the term "remez" used to indicate true information obtained through close readings of texts.[37] It is also possible that Josephus considered such techniques legitimate since he indicated some biblical passages were thickly veiled.[38] In the Middle Ages "remez" was also used to refer to exegesis based on numerologies *(gematria)* and mneumonics *(notorikon)* and more

---

and Meiri refer to danger, SKN. Also, *j Meg.* 1:4 and *Tosefta Meg.* 1:3 support this contention. So too the allusions to these days as dependent upon certain conditions which existed in the time of Joshua stress one point: Even though Israel's glory is lost, Purim remains the symbol of God's readiness to save his people wherever they may be. The Talmudic Rabbis saw in the Mishnah's opening statement here a message of renewing the mood of covenant. The Mishnah's law was designed for times of sovereignty. It still remains viable because Israel is eternal and will ultimately be vindicated.

[37]E.g. see *Sifre Deuteronomy* (ed. Finkelstein, Berlin 1939), 379, *piska* 329.

[38]See *Antiquities* 1:24. Likewise *Genesis Rabba* begins by indicating that some explanations of Torah are based on passages whose sense is very hidden. This indication is based upon a fine reading of Pr 8:30. Based on insights of Y. Elman of Bar Ilan University I suggest that Wisdom is portrayed in that passage as God's personal artistic designer *(etslo amon)*. The hypostasis of Wisdom is then spelled out in detail:

And I was the artist with Him;
And I was Entertaining daily
Playing in His presence;
Playing in His world
Entertaining with people.

The chiastic form stresses how Wisdom is at once the entertainment of the divine realm and whose play there is mirrored in the human world. To play with the Torah is then *imatatio dei*. From the human perspective Torah operates on several levels, some of which are clear and some of which are remote. Josephus progresses in his description of the art of Torah (*Ant.* 1:24) from that which is veiled to that which is plain while the midrash progresses from that which is plain to that which is hidden. One wonders if Josephus was aware of Pr 8:30 as a description of the nature of Torah's style. Prof. C. Hospital of Queen's University has informed me that Hindu sources also see the acts of Creation as the play of the gods. Play is divine activity. For Jews it is shared with humans through their play with the Torah.

generally to refer to a philosophic typology (as opposed to homiletic or mystical discourses).[39]

The Amoraim used the phrase "Where is the hint?" in aggadic passages as well. Thus Gen 48:19, "And his seed shall be a multitude of nations." perplexed the Rabbis as this blessing to Ephraim might seem to indicate that Ephraim would come to be removed from the nation of Israel. The Rabbis read it as an elliptical passage: The offspring of Ephraim shall be *known* to a multitude of nations. The context of an offspring of Ephraim is now supplied.[40] It is Joshua who became known to all the nations when he caused the sun to stand still. Gen 48:19 hints about the feat of Joshua. Here again a context is supplied that is not known from the verse and the verse is now read as if in reference to that context.

We have seen one type of exegesis by which insufficient data in a biblical text is supplied in such a way as to give meaning to the fine details of the text. *Remez-exegesis* deserves serious study as its usage is limited to a handful of passages in the Talmud. From the examination of limited details one sheds light on the much larger picture of hermeneutics in Rabbinic literature. What has emerged from our study is the idea that the Rabbis understood that biblical verses could allude to information known from outside the text. At least sometimes, these allusions were understood to be the intended meaning of the text. The literatures of Qumran, Philo, Apocrypha, Apocalyptic, Josephus; in short the general literature of Jews in antiquity and afterwards illustrates such understanding to be at the center of the Jewish approach to Scripture. That, in time, the various types of exegesis became formalized with specific terminology and phraseology need not surprise us. As this happened the formulas became applied more and more to those cases which suited the definitions.

We shall now consider other types of exegeses which also supply information not observable in the biblical text as such. Although we will look at only one example of each type the reader should note that these types are not rare in midrashic literature.

Fragment-exegesis (provides information from isolated phrases):

Tannaitic midrash is capable of using dual readings of verses to inform the reader of the actual intent of a particular passage. Part of a

---

[39]See *b Zeb.* 115b for an Amoraic usage of "Where is the hint?" to refer to the formula "Don't read...but rather read..." That passage is somewhat corrupt but even here the commentators find reference to a context which was unstated in the verse at hand.

[40]See *b Avodah Zarah* 25a. Nu 13:8 identifies Joshua as an Ephramite.

verse will be read without regard for the entire verse. This section, read on its own terms without regard to the syntax of the rest of the verse, will be exegeted in terms of information not supplied by the verse. Then this understanding will be transferred back to the verse as a whole. There are halachic usages of this technique[41] but here we will dwell on the aggadic usages.[42]

> *And Moses stretched out his hand against the Sea [and he caused, the Lord, to come back....]:*[43] The Sea defied him. Moses spoke to him in the name of the Holy One, blessed be He, to split but he did not accept that authority. He showed him the staff[44] but he did not accept that authority...[45] until the Holy One, blessed be He, arrived in his *doxa*. When the Holy One, blessed be He, arrived in his *doxa* and *dynamis*[46] the Sea speedily fled as Scripture says: *The Sea saw and fled.*[47] Moses said to him, "All day I might have spoken to you in the name of the Holy One, blessed be He, without you accepting that authority. Why now do you flee? *What happened to you, O Sea, that you flee?"*[48] He (the Sea) replied,"Not before you, son of Amram, do I flee but rather *before the face of the Lord – who made the Earth tremble; before the face of the Lord – who turned the rock into a standing water, the flint into a fountain of waters."*[49]

In view of the fact that God in Ex 14:16 asks Moses to "lift his rod and stretch his hand over the sea and divide it " one would naturally assume that in 14:21 that is precisely what God expects Moses to do. On

---

[41]E.g. *b Pes.* 21b, ascribed to the Tanna, Rabbi Meir.

[42]Specifically, we will dwell upon *Mekhilta Beshallah, Vayehi parashah 4. Ed. Horowitz-Rabin 102.*

[43]Ex 14:21. The bracketed section is omitted in the Mekhilta texts but is essential to the understanding of the midrash. The full verse requires the syntax that the one who caused the coming back was God. He caused the Sea to come back in order to expose the dry parts beneath it. However, if we read the verse so that we understand Moses caused the Lord (and not the Sea) to come back, then we will derive a fresh insight. Such a reading corrects the apparent impression left by the text.

[44]According to tradition, the staff was inscribed with the letters of the divine name. The use of divine names and seals to accomplish theurgic acts is well known from the Heikhalot literature. Our midrash denies such techniques can be efficacious.

[45]Omitted here is a story in which a buyer of the king's property is denied entry until the purchaser *summons* the king and he comes. Then the watchman immediately gives way.

[46]The "Glory" and "Power" are used in Heikhalot literature to signify the Royal Location of God in some type of visible manifestation.

[47]Ps 114:3.

[48]Ps 114:5, the reference is to the Sea that split for the Israelites.

[49]Ps 144:7,8.

the other hand one might be concerned that Ps 114 relates that the Sea gave way before the presence of the Lord, literally before "the face of the Lord." The midrashist is happier with this version where power is ascribed directly to God and not to Moses' magic use of his staff. The solution of the midrashist to this state of affairs is to read Ex 14:21 in a partial manner: *And Moses stretched out his hand against the Sea and he caused the Lord to come back.* Whatever can be read now in the text about Moses is simply to instruct Moses that he might try all sorts of things to part the Sea but ultimately only the presence of God will suffice to do it. Indeed, vs. 21 does not mention the staff. The midrashist stands on firm ground in his exposition. The partial reading explains that Moses' rod was of no avail and so he raised his hand (the stance of prayer) to *summon* God directly. The partial reading is not seen to be at odds with a close reading of the entire passage. It explains details not otherwise comprehensible to the mind of the midrashist. Only God is the source of all awe and power over nature.

Here the Rabbis introduced the context of the exegetical reading into the context of the primary reading. In doing so they unified the various accounts in Scripture concerning the splitting of the Red Sea and promoted their views of the inefficacy of theurgic or magic acts.[50] God taught Moses not to rely upon ritual acts but upon the Godhead itself. The reading of the Rabbis is offered in all seriousness as the way to understand Scripture. *Fragment-exegesis* is not meant to be read out of context but rather to reshape the context of the surrounding verses in Scripture. It expands and refines the primary meaning of Scripture by discovering hidden messages within the syntax of the verse. What we find then is that the Rabbis used small detail and peculiarities in syntax of minor units to explain the larger framework of verses. Yet, in other instances the Rabbis would use the broader framework of Scripture to understand the detail and syntax of smaller units in the biblical text. Such mechanisms might well be called *parallel-exegesis.*

Parallel-exegesis (provides information from parallel passages):

From ancient times Jews had studied the linguistic and grammatical structures of units of Scripture to determine the referents in verses which lacked specific information. Whole units were organized under specific themes. By looking at Rabbinic traditions and comparing them with whatever ancient traditions have survived, we can

---

[50]See E.E. Urbach, *Hazal*, Jerusalem, 1977, 105 n.13. Urbach sees our midrash in opposition to other midrashim which claim that the tetragrammaton was inscribed on Moses' staff and the Sea split upon witnessing it. See also D. Boyarin, "An Exchange on the Mashal," *Prooftexts* 5, 1985, 269-280.

reconstruct the early methods of exegesis which the Rabbis inherited. Let us examine a section of writing from those early writings known as Pseudepigrapha.

> And you, do not rush to make your deeds evil through lust after gain and to convince yourselves through words of vanity. For should you silence these through pure- heartedness you will know how to become strong in the will of God and to despise the will of Belial.
>
> **Sun and moon and stars do not change their order. Thus, you also, do not change the law of God through the disorder of your doings. Gentiles, erring and leaving the Lord, changed their order and followed after wood and stones and spirits of error.**
>
> **Not so you, my children, who know through the heavens and the earth and the sea and all creation that God has made them in order that you should not be like the Sodomites who perverted their order.**
>
> **So also did the giants pervert their order such that God cursed them at the time of the Flood and laid waste the earth, on their account, its inhabitants and all that grew upon it.**[51]

Reflection upon the motifs here will allow us to conclude that this passage is based upon a *parallel-exegesis* in the 32nd chapter of Deuteronomy.[52] To understand exactly what has been done let us begin by noting the presentation in *The King James Version* of Deut 32:1-7:

> (1) Give ear, O ye heavens, and I will speak; and hear, O, earth, the words of my mouth. 2) My doctrine shall drop as the rain, and my speech shall distill as the dew, as the small rain upon the tender herb, and as the showers upon the grass: 3) Because I will publish the name of the Lord: ascribe ye greatness unto our God. 4) He is the Rock, his work is perfect: for all his ways are judgment: a God of truth and without iniquity, just and right is he. 5) They have corrupted themselves, their spot is not the spot of his children: they are a perverse and crooked generation. 6) Do ye thus requite the Lord, O foolish people and unwise? is he not thy father that hath bought thee? hath he not made thee, and established thee?

---

[51]*Testament of Naphtali,* 3:1-5. Cf. 1 *Enoch,* 1:1-3. See also H.W. Hollander and M. de Jonge, *The Testaments of the Twelve Patriarchs: A Commentary,* Leiden: Brill, 1985, 305-309.

[52]Deut 32 refers to "leaving the Lord" (vs 15), "obeying spirits" (vs 17), "disobeying God through lack of wisdom" (vs 28). Lars Hartman, *Asking for a Meaning: A Study of 1 Enoch 1-5* (Coniectanea Biblica, New Testament Series 12: Lund: Gleerup, 1979) connects the midrash on Deut 32, *Sifre Deut* 306, with 1 *Enoch* 2:1-5:3 (see pp 29, 86-7). He also connects this midrash to *T Naph* chs. 3 and 4 (pp 54-5).

> (7) Remember the days of old, consider the years of many generations: ask thy father and he will hew thee; thy elders, and they will tell thee.

A quick glance will show us we have two imperatives: "Give ear" and "Remember." The parallel grammatical forms suggest the same audience; namely, Israel. Thus (1) can be rendered, "Give ear about the heavens and I will declaim; and hear the words of my mouth about the earth." Now the passage is more intelligible. Moses invokes a lesson from nature and a lesson from history to instruct Israel not to change her order which has been divinely set. The Rabbinic midrash paraphrases here:

> The Holy One, blessed be He, instructed Moses: Tell Israel, "Consider the heavens which I created to serve you. Perhaps it has changed its order...how much more so you must not change your order."[53]

The "order" is meant to refer to God's instruction. If we could discover why the midrashist insisted that the lessons have to do with "changing order" we could well appreciate that this is not altogether an unreasonable rendering of the passage. God's instruction is compared to nature's order, rain and dew.

We know Israel is to be instructed through paying attention to the heavens and the earth (vs. 1). What we do not know is what lesson they are to learn from "the days of old" (vs. 7). The Rabbinic midrash is perplexing:

> Remember what I did...you do not find a generation in which there is not the likes of the people of the generation of the Flood nor the likes of the Sodomites....[54]

It is not clear why these generations are singled out or indeed where there is any allusion to them in the verse. Inspection of the verse shows us that what was translated above as "many generations" in fact is "generation and generation." Thus the midrashist knew the reference was to two generations. But we also know something else. The reference to "years" is problematic in the biblical text. The word is "shenot." While "years" is a possible translation, "perversions" suits the context much better.[55] The Rabbinic midrash makes no mention of this point in

---

[53]*Sifre Deut* 306, ed. Finkelstein, 332.

[54]*Sifre Deut* 310, ed. Finkelstein, 350. The introductory part of this tradition adds "the generation of the Dispersion." It appears that, in concert with the predilection of folklore for triads, an extra villain has crept into the earlier format.

[55]See the discussion of *shinah* and *shina* in H. Yalon, *Studies in the Hebrew Language*, Jerusalem, 1971, pp 150-1. *Shina* is the word used in *1 Enoch* 2:4

its comment to Deut 32:7. Yet, only if we read Deut 32:7 as "Consider the perversions of the generation and the generation." can we explain the stress the Rabbis put upon "changing order" in their comment to Deut 32:1. At some time the two verses must have been read together as a parallel structure. There is no other way to account for the midrashic comment to Deut 32:1. Moses asked Israel to reflect upon both nature and history to learn the consequences of "changing one's order." Nature taught obedience while history showed what happened in the case of disobedience. This supposition is confirmed through comparing the text of *T. Naph.* to the midrash. Here we also see the instruction of the heavens and the earth which teach one not to change one's order and we also see what happened to the generations of the Flood and Sodom which did change their order. Both the midrash and the pseudepigraphic text refer to "changing one's order."[56] There is no likely way to explain this unless we posit that both sources drew from a

---

(SNYTN) which passage is equated with *T Naph* 3 by its author (see *T Naph* 4:1). This is also the sense used in the midrash: *shinah midah* (the reading in ms Vatican, Assemani 32), *shinah seder* (the variant reading in ms Berlin, Acc. Or. 1928, 328 and *Midrash Hakhamim*). While "change order" is quite literal the import of the term is "perversion." The term for "order" is *midah* which is the normal word for "conduct." Thus *j Hag.* 2:2 reads "memidah lemidah yatsa," departed from one order to another, while b Hag 15a reads "yatsa letarbut ra'ah," departed to evil conduct. In the variant reading in Sifre Deut, that we noted above, we find *seder* can have this sense of "rules of conduct" as demonstrated in *b Ket.* 103b *(sidrei hokhma, sidrei nesi'ut)* and b Shab. 53b (sidrei bereshit). *Gen. Rabba* 33:11 refers to the Flood generation: "hem qilqelu silonot shelahem af hamaqom shinah lahem siduro shel olam": They ***perverted*** their sexual channels so God ***changed the order*** of the world. Hartman *(Asking)*, 57, notes *midah* in the Sifre midrash is paralleled by *taxis* in T Naph 3. *Taxis* generally refers to a set order or duty to be performed in good will. This set order is what the evil generations perverted.

[56]The sense of this phrase is understood by H.C. Kee ("The Ethical Dimensions of the Testaments of the XII as a clue to Provenance," *NTS* 24, 1978, 262), to refer to the universal natural law of the Stoics. D. Slingerland ("The Nature of Nomos (Law) within the Testaments of the Twelve Patriarchs," *JBL* 105, 1986, 39-48), disputes Kee's assertion. He claims "the order" referred to is Israel's entire legal corpus (the wider sense of *Torah*). In the view of the midrash, this is certainly the case.

common tradition[57] which used *parallel-exegesis* to explicate Deut 32. Hence this technique is very ancient.[58]

Rabbinic midrash draws upon early sources and develops themes in its own style. These sources point to an enterprise in which disparate information is sifted and reconstituted into a unified structure. Elsewhere it has been shown that Josephus engaged in this very activity.[59] It is not always an easy task to reconstruct the trigger mechanism of midrash. A case in point will provide an example of what may well be termed "intertextual-exegesis."

Intertextual-exegesis (provides information from other contexts):

Let us look at an early midrash:

> Rabbi Eleazar the Moda'ite says: **And Amalek came** (Ex 17:8) - Amalek entered underneath the Wings of the Cloud and kidnapped Israelites and killed them. This is as it says, **who met you on the way** (Deut 25:18).[60]

One is hard put to explain how Eleazar equated Amalek's **coming** (in Ex) with his **meeting Israel on the way** (in Deut) so as to prove that Amalek came to *kidnap and kill.* We might consider the problem in all its aspects. In Exodus we are nowhere told why Amalek came and what he did. We are only told that he waged war against Israel and that his war will be carried on throughout the generations until he is utterly destroyed.[61] In Deuteronomy we are not given much more information to warrant this obligation of utterly destroying Amalek and his seed. What did Amalek do that was so reprehensible? The midrash tells us that his crime was kidnapping and murder. It provides proof. In Deut we see that Amalek **met Israel on the way.** Now this "meeting on the way" can be treated as a technical phrase. A phrase connoting a situation where one is tempted to kidnap offspring from under the mothers presence.

> When you **meet on the way** a bird's nest...you shall not take **the young when the mother is over the young.**[62]

---

[57]For further examples of commonality between midrash and Pseudepigrapha see J. Klausner, *The Messianic Idea in Israel,* New York, Macmillan, 1955, 342-44 and E. Urbach, *Hazal,* Jerusalem, 1978, 395 n.95, 202 n.44, 147ff.

[58]*The Testament of the Twelve Patriarchs* originates in the pre-christian period. See A. Kahana, *HaSefarim Hahitsonim,* Jerusalem, Maqor, 5730, 144-146.

[59]H. Basser, "Josephus as Exegete," *JAOS* 107 (Jan. 1987), 26.

[60]*Mekhilta Beshallah, Amalek parashah 1.* Ed. Horowitz-Rabin 176.

[61]See Ex 17:16.

[62]Deut 22:6.

This verse occurs in a chapter preceding the notice that Amalek **met Israel on the way**. When we look at the midrash carefully we find traces of the "law of the dam." Amalek took Israel from under the Wings of the Cloud according to the midrash. The two verses have been read together as a structured unit. God's presence is described as a cloud in Scripture. Eleazar mentions wings on the cloud as if it were a mother bird. Amalek transgressed the grounds of decency by grabbing Israel from under the presence of God and killing them. We now know what Amalek did to warrant such biblical response: "You shall blot out the remembrance of Amalek from under Heaven."[63] Tit for tat.

We can now summarize our investigation as follows. 1) *Remez-exegesis:* Interpretation of an obscure passage in the light of information nowhere explicitly available in Hebrew Scriptures. 2) *Fragment-exegesis:* Interpretation of a passage whose apparent sense is unacceptable and is accomplished in the light of information available from reading a segment of a verse and then reading larger sections in terms of this segment. 3) *Parallel-exegesis:* Interpretation of an ambiguous passage in the light of information available in a close-by passsage which shares formal structures with the ambiguous passage. 4) *Intertextual-exegesis:* Interpretation of a passage which lacks sufficient information for cogency; it is accomplished in the light of relating words or phrases in the problematic passage with other passages which contain these words or phrases in specific contexts. The specific context is then read into the problematic passage which then becomes clarified.

The configuring of legal and narrative texts to yield a more complete understanding of Scripture is justifiable since Scripture intermingles the two regularly. We are ignorant for the most part as to how this mixture came about. The methods of the Rabbis show not only attention to detail but awareness of the larger biblical style. Where sufficient information was lacking to make sense of the details of a passage, the Rabbis were confident that such information could be found or fathomed.

Indeed, the enterprise was even more complex. Every expressed commentary we know of in late antiquity that emanated from Jewish circles followed a predictable format. It is observable in the pesher commentaries of Qumran and the allegories of Philo. It can be seen in New Testament and it is commonplace in our corpora of midrash. The

---

[63]Deut 25:19. See the pertinent remarks of Prof. Harry Fox concerning the terms "Wings of the Shekina" and "Wings of Heaven" in the midrash, "Simhat Bet Hashoeva," *Tarbits*, 5746, 213-216.

format is simply this: A verse is given; Something to be proved from this is intimated; An exegetical technique is employed to supply the proof (if only another verse). The Euclidean midrashic enterprise has a specific goal. The exegetes know that Scripture, Torah, *points* to a wider truth which lies implicit in the letters of Scripture. This wider truth can be shown using the mathematics of midrash. Midrash *seeks* to establish the larger truth which is reflected in Scripture. The question arises, as it does for Euclid, "How did they know what they were supposed to prove so that they could begin to seek proof?" Perhaps the answer is that they knew a great deal from practical experience and naive intuition concerning the discipline in which they were engaged. They knew what to expect and then they demonstrated it formally to remove any doubts as to the truth of the matter. This did not mean that proofs could not be challenged from the standpoint of the formal requirements of proof and from the standpoint that the nature of what was being sought was contrary to the system as a whole. The enterprise was guarded by the boundaries of an inherited culture (axioms) and a consensus as to what constituted acceptable teaching (propositions). The teaching was an intellectual feat, a very serious play as all intellectual feats are, through which the group understood the world.

By categorizing the techniques of the Rabbis we are lead to a profound appreciation of their astuteness as we become aware of the vast energy expended in pursuit of joining God's play.[64] The material in Scripture is indeed many-colored. Rainbow Bibles, or "Jezebel Bibles" as Solomon Schechter referred to them, put disparate passages (assigned to different sources) into varying colors. But long before this, Jewish exegetes had matched the seams so that all the shades of meaning in Scripture blended into a harmonious pattern. They never held an unclad Scripture or failed to intone it with enchanting harmony.

---

[64]For a complex attempt to illustrate the exegetical techniques of the Rabbis one may refer to the detailed work of E.Z. Melamed, *Bible Commentators,* Jerusalem, 1978, 1-128. More systematic in attempts to categorize the techniques is the work of M.L. Malbim, *Ayelet HaShachar, HaTorah VeHamitzvah,* Jerusalem, 1956. For much earlier attempts one may consider the *13 Attributes of Rabbi Ishmael* appended to the beginning of Sifra and the *Baraita of 32 Principles of Rabbi Eliezer the son of Rabbi Yosi the Galilean* (see Melamed, *op. cit.* 1061-1083).

22

Recent and Prospective Discussion of *Memra*

Bruce Chilton
Bard College

In his recent book, *Divine Revelation and Divine Titles in the Pentateuchal Targumim,*[1] Andrew Chester sides with George Foot Moore, in seeing מימרא as a phenomenon of translation, rather than of theology.[2] Where Moore was resisting the tendency to see in מימרא a precursor of λόγος in Christian theology, Chester sets himself against the more sophisticated schemes of Domingo Muñoz Leon and Robert Hayward. Chester's resistance to a theological understanding of מימרא is especially striking, in that it appears in a work in which exegetical and theological aspects are elsewhere, in respect of other terms, held to be complementary. Observing, for example, that the verb אתגלי is used as a verbal replacement in theophanic contexts, Chester speaks of the usage quite categorically:

> It is not, then, merely a negative device, but is used with positive exegetical and theological purpose, to indicate one way in which God can be spoken of as active and present in the world.[3]

---

[1]Number 14 in the series, Texte und Studien zum Antiken Judentum (Tübingen: Mohr, 1986).
[2]Chester, *Divine Revelation*, 308-9.
[3]P. 243, cf. 152, 245, 261, 262. It may be noted that I had earlier made a similar argument for the usage of the same verb in Targum Zechariah 14.9, in "Regnum Dei Deus Est," *Scottish Journal of Theology* 31 (1978) 261-270, 265 (now reprinted in *Targumic Approaches to the Gospels. Essays in the Mutual Definition of Judaism and Christianity:* Studies in Judaism [Lanham: University Press of America, 1986] 99-107, 101). As a note there observes, Dalman and Moore had already traced the cognate usage within Rabbinica.

Given that Chester is fully capable of a nuanced co-ordination of the exegetical and theological strands of a usage, we may ask, Why does he bifurcate them in the case of מימרא, and then unequivocally give preference to the exegetical strand?

Chester proceeds in his work by means of a careful evaluation of the history of discussion in regard to the various sorts of revelational language in which he is interested. Indeed, the care of his historical description is such that sometimes the value of his book transcends the merits of the particular case which he argues. In the instance of מימרא, Chester's lucid resumé is capped by the observation that recent discussion has polarized:

> Thus from the recent work of Muñoz Leon and Hayward on the one hand (even allowing for the important differences between them) and Aufrecht on the other, we appear to be presented with two diametrically opposed interpretations of Memra and its significance. The one holds that Memra is an important creative theological concept, above all in N[eophyti], the other that it is simply a limited type of translation, basically a metonym, with no theological significance whatever.[4]

Faced with a choice between the poles of a dichotomy, Chester prefers the exegetical alternative to the theological one.[5]

Chester is brought to his choice by means of an analysis of the arguments of Muñoz Leon and Hayward, both of which he finds seriously wanting. Muñoz Leon, in Chester's estimation, imposes a scheme upon Neophyti I which is, at the end of the day, apologetic:

> That is, he imposes a theological system on N and its usage of Memra, and reads theological significance into this usage both in detail and in general, without taking proper account of the inconsistencies that do not fit this theory. Further, the theological categories he uses appear preconceived; thus, his characterization of Memra as "the creative, revealing and saving Word" fits his understanding of the Johannine Logos but not at all obviously the evidence of the Targumim themselves.[6]

---

[4]P. 305. The references are to: Domingo Muñoz Leon, *Dios-Palabra. Memra en los Targumim del Pentateuco:* Institución San Jerónimo 4 (Granada: Santa Rita-Monachil, 1974); C.T.R. Hayward, *The Use and Religious Significance of the Term Memra in Targum Neofiti I in the Light of the Other Targumim* (Oxford: D.Phil., 1975), a revised form of which was published as *Divine Name and Presence: The Memra:* Oxford Centre for Postgraduate Hebrew Studies (Totowa: Allanheld, Osmun and Co., 1981); W. E. Aufrecht, *Surrogates for the Divine Name in the Palestinian Targums to Exodus* (Toronto: Ph.D., 1979).

[5]Cf. pp. 308-9, 313.

[6]P. 306.

It should be noted, before Chester's evaluation is accepted at face value, that the suspicion of an incipiently Christological understanding of מימרא in the work of Muñoz Leon is not consistently supportable, in that he adamantly corrects against the tendency of earlier discussion to conceive of מימרא as independent of God.[7] Nonetheless, there is a persistent recourse in his work to the language of substitution, and even of hypostasis,[8] which must seem odd in the wake of Moore's definitive assertion that "nowhere in the Targums is *memra* a 'being' of any kind or in any sense, much less a personal being."[9] Chester rightly discerns the weakness in the analysis of Muñoz Leon, which finally fails to engage Moore's classic assertion that "*memra* is purely a phenomenon of translation, not a figment of speculation."[10] The unavoidable result of Moore's study is that מימרא should not, without argument, be taken as the object of systematic reflection among meturgemanin.

Just the last criterion of recent discussion is ignored, even more comprehensively than by Muñoz Leon, by Robert Hayward. His study is the most daring attempt ever to fasten a univocal meaning upon מימרא. He was inspired by the work of Pamela Vermes on Martin Buber, in which a link between מימרא and the divine name as disclosed in Exodus 3 is explored. Indeed, Chester's basic problem with Hayward's argument is its aetiology; he complains that Hayward "takes over uncritically the argument of P. Vermes connecting Memra with the divine name, and builds his whole thesis on hers."[11] In justice, it must be observed that Hayward does attempt to honor Moore's position:

---

[7]We might give the example of the category, "Sustitución Memrá en lugares que expressan reacciones divinas," pp. 57f. Essentially, the emphasis upon God's unity is manifest here, cf. B. D. Chilton, *The Glory of Israel. The Theology and Provenience of the Isaiah Targum:* Journal for the Study of the Old Testament Supplements Series 23 (Sheffield: JSOT, 1982), 56-69 and 140-146, and Hayward, *Divine Name*, 6.

[8]Cf. Hayward, *Divine Name*, 6, 7.

[9]G. F. Moore, *Judaism in the First Centuries of the Christian Era. The Age of the Tannaim* I (Cambridge: Harvard University Press, 1927) 419 and "Intermediaries in Jewish Theology," *Harvard Theological Review* 15 (1922) 41-85, 53, 54.

[10]*Judaism*, 419; "Intermediaries," 54.

[11]*Divine Revelation*, 307. Hayward has taken issue with Chester in a review, claiming that he worked independently of Mrs Vermes (*Journal of Jewish Studies* 38 [1987] 261-266, 265). That clarification would appear to contradict the "Preface" of *Divine Name* (p. ix).

> ...the *Memra* is neither an hypostasis, nor a pious periphrasis for the Name of YHWH, but...an exegetical term which stands for the Name revealed by God to Moses at the burning bush, the Name 'HYH I AM/I WILL BE THERE."[12]

What Hayward appears not to have recognized, however, is that such a specific locus of meaning, generated within a profoundly resonant passage and distributed generally through the Targumim, makes מימרא no longer an "exegetical term," but the engine of a systematic idea. What is at issue at this point in Hayward's thesis might more accurately be called an exegetical theology, and the more generally it is imputed to the Targumim as a whole, the less plausible it appears. Hayward's own characterization of the meaning of מימרא in Neophyti makes it evident that his understanding is far from Moore's:

> N's point is therefore clear: the covenant with Jacob at Bethel is God's assurance that He, in His *Memra*, will be with Jacob and the Jerusalem Temple is the outward and visible proof of the fulfilment of that oath, since it is the point of contact between earth and heaven, the place where God's presence in His *Memra* is most keenly apprehended.[13]

Hayward so restricts the meaning of מימרא, that in order to explain its actual appearances elsewhere in the Targumim, he must rely on the expedient of supposing that its original meaning had been forgotten.[14] Essentially, Hayward appears unaware of the conceptual difficulties of his own thesis.[15]

Confronted, then, with two unsuccessful attempts at a systematic understanding of מימרא in the Targumim, Chester's preference for a genuinely exegetical approach is understandable:

> It is in fact more plausible to see Memra (in form a substantival infinitive) as basically a translational and exegetical term, drawing on the various senses of the underlying verb אמר and its related noun forms, with connotations such as "utterance, speech, word, promise, command."[16]

---

[12]Hayward,, "The Holy Name of the God of Moses and the Prologue of St John's Gospel," *New Testament Studies* 25 (1978-9) 16-32, 17.

[13]*The Use,* 113.

[14]For these and other criticisms, cf. *The Glory of Israel,* 67, 68 and 143-4 n. 31; 144-5 n. 38; 145-6 nn. 39-46.

[15]There is, it must be said, a certain naïveté in his bland assertion of his own, unproven case, cf. "Memra and Shekhina: A Short Note," *Journal of Jewish Studies* 31 (1980) 210-13.

[16]*Divine Revelation,* 308-9, citing V. Hamp, *Der Begriff "Wort" in den aramäischen Bibelübersetzungen. Ein exegetischer Beitrag zur Hypostasen-*

Chester is at pains to stress that מימרא is not a "theologically sophisticated" usage; and he argues that "it simply portrays one main mode of God's activity, intelligible at a popular level and intended primarily as an interpretation of the biblical text."[17]

Chester's last statement is offered by way of conclusion; conceptually, it serves only to highlight the paradox of his position. On the one hand, מימרא is held not to be a usage of a theological nature, while on the other it is described as portraying a "main mode of God's activity." If the term in fact conveys a reference to divine action, then it is not simply exegetical or – in Moore's language – translational. Of course, Chester's pre-emptive defence against such an objection is to insist that, even if technically theological, the usage is not sophisticated: the activity of God simply falls within an ordinary range of the associations of אמר.

Just at this point, however, a fundamental objection to the procedure used by Chester, along with Hayward and Muñoz Leon, may be registered. We have long since passed the point when all Targums may be supposed to adhere to a single sense of מימרא, be it unsophisticated or otherwise. Some such basic meaning as "speech" or "utterance" is – of course – assumed, and has been recognized by scholars otherwise as much at variance as Moore and Hayward.[18] But the effort has persistently been made to typify that meaning further, and so to arrive at the underlying sense of מימרא. Hayward represents the most extreme case of attempts to typify the whole from a particular part: Neophyti Exodus 3:14; 4:12 are for him paradigmatic. Because מימרא is associated with אהיה there, it is everywhere. Moore represents a far more adequate procedure of typing, from general usage to overall sense. He observes the usage in Onqelos and Jonathan especially, in the interests of "brevity and simplicity."[19] He concludes that the types of use include command,[20] the obedience of command,[21] the acceptance of a command,[22] divine speaking,[23] divine meeting with others,[24]

Frage und zur Geschichte der Logos Spekulation (München: Filser, 1938) 79-102. Cf. also *The Glory of Israel,* 144 (the continuation of n. 31).

[17]*Divine Revelation*, 313

[18]Cf. Moore, "Intermediaries," 47; Hayward, *Divine Name*, 1.

[19]"Intermediaries," p. 60 n. 7. In fact, the usages cited below, from Moore's study, are all taken from Onqelos, with occasional reference to Pseudo-Jonathan.

[20]P. 47.

[21]Pp. 47-8.

[22]P. 48.

[23]Pp. 48-9.

oracles,[25] swearing by God,[26] his fighting for Israel,[27] his protection,[28] his establishing covenant.[29] Whatever may be said of Moore's contribution conceptually, he represents a procedural advance in permitting the Targums to typify their own sense of מימרא. That is precisely what Chester, Hayward, and Muñoz Leon do not do.

Chester offers the possibility of an important distinction of usage between Onqelos and the so-called Palestinian Targumim, but he does not himself explore that possibility. In a work published in 1982, the present writer offered a typology of מימרא in the Isaiah Targum, based upon Moore's approach, but applying it to new material (cf. n. 19).[30] In that study, however, the refinement was introduced, that the order of categories was determined by the order of appearance of the first instance of each category. The types present מימרא as an occasion for rebellion,[31] an agent of punishment,[32] a demand for obedience,[33] an edict,[34] a voice,[35] divine protection,[36] an eternal witness,[37] an intermediary of prayer.[38] The overlap with Moore's categories is evident, but not complete. His typology, on the basis of Onqelos, included categories and a precedence of categories not found in Jonathan's Isaiah, and vice versa. The possibility emerges that Targum Isaiah is distinctive in its usage of מימרא, precisely by virtue of its focus upon Israel's disobedience, and God's demand for a reversal on the basis of his election of his people. In other words, literary variation might appropriately be built into our characterization of מימרא, rather than explained away or ignored.

The testing of any such hypothesis is obviously impossible, if it must rely solely upon the comparison of, say, Moore's analysis of the

---

[24]P. 49.
[25]Pp. 49, 50.
[26]P. 50.
[27]Pp. 50-1.
[28]P. 51.
[29]P. 51. In all of these classifications, I have categorized on the basis of Moore's own, characteristically discursive, descriptions.
[30]*The Glory of Israel*, 56-69.
[31]Pp. 57-8.
[32]Pp. 58-60.
[33]P. 60.
[34]P. 61.
[35]Pp. 61-2.
[36]Pp. 62-3.
[37]P. 63.
[38]Pp. 63-4. It should be clearly understood that I immediately cited Hamp's observation, that an intermediary need not imply a hypostasis, cf. p. 143 n. 31.

Pentateuch in Onqelos, and my analysis of Isaiah in Jonathan. What is required is a comparison of cognate documents, preferably from demonstrably related streams of tradition. The so-called Palestinian Targumim, of course, make just that comparison practicable.[39] By comparing Neophyti I and Pseudo-Jonathan from Targum to Targum, and also from document to document within each Targum, we will be in a position to say whether there is in fact a significant variation in the types of usage of מימרא.

The more technical requirements of the comparison include access to critical editions of the two Targums which are cognate in their policies of textual criticism, and which are indexed even-handedly. For that reason, the five volumes of Roger LeDéaut have been been used as the basis of the collation.[40]

Because, in the nature of the case, we must move from book to book within Torah, it is impracticable to employ my earlier method, of ordering the categories according to the precedence of appearance within the text. At the same time, it is necessary within the logic of a typological analysis that the text (rather than the interpreter) in some way establish precedence. For that reason, the lead will be taken from the *frequency* of types within each book of each Targum.[41] As a rule of

---

[39]Moore, needless to say, did not have access to Neophyti I, and he simply evinced no strong interest in Pseudo-Jonathan.

[40]*Targum du Pentateuque. Traduction des deux recensions palestiniennes complètes avec introduction, parallèles, notes et index* 1-5: Sources Chrétiennes 245, 256, 261, 271, 282 (Paris: Les editions du Cerf, 1978, 1979, 1979, 1980, 1981). By their very nature, the Fragments Targum and the materials from the Cairo Genizah are not sufficiently comprehensive for such a comparison as is proposed here.

[41]In this connection, it might be noted that, had the same procedure been followed in the instance of the Isaiah Targum, the result would actually have been to heighten thematically central usages, and to reduce the attention given to less prominent concerns:

demand for obedience	22
divine protection	22
edict	19
rebellion against	12
witness	12
agent of punishment	10
voice	7
intermediary	2

The usages have been tabulated on the basis of my previous survey, as presented in *The Glory of Israel*, pp. 56-69. The last two usages are in fact of little conceptual importance within the Isaiah Targum. The arrangement by frequency, rather than precedence, gives greater emphasis to the imperative

thumb, only types consisting of 10% of the total usages of מימרא within the document will be considered to characterize the usage of the document in question.[42] That additional constraint will considerably help us to resolve a portrait of מימרא document by document, because there are not eight, but fifteen types in play throughout Neophyti and Pseudo-Jonathan.[43]

In Neophyti's Genesis, מימרא is characteristically portrayed as:

speaking	13 of 62 occurrences
involved in worship	10 of 62 occurrences
influencing	9 of 62 occurrences
involved in covenant	8 of 62 occurrences
creating	8 of 62 occurrences.

Lest it be thought Genesis simply demands such usages by virtue of its subject matter, it must be borne in mind that Pseudo-Jonathan's Genesis delivers a different impression of מימרא:

aiding	13 of 50 occurrences

("demand for obedience") and positive ("divine protection," "edict") aspects of מימרא, rather than the negative aspects of rebellion and punishment. Such an emphasis probably does greater justice to the theology of the document (cf. *The Glory of Israel*, 97-111).

[42]Were that rule applied to the Isaiah Targum, with its 106 usages, the types of voice and intermediary would be omitted, which are precisely the types of least conceptual import (cf. the previous note). During the development of the present exercise, usages representing only slightly less than 10% of the total were also considered.

[43]The types present מימרא as speaking, blessing, creating, a voice, giving law, involved in worship, deliberating, acting, influencing, aiding, being with others, involved in covenant, swearing, demanding obedience, occasioning revolt. The arrangement and designation of the categories is heuristic. Their meaning is largely self-explanatory, although reference might be made to the distinction operative between "acting" and "influencing." The former includes transitive acts of direct impact, such as striking, throwing, taking, closing, protecting, etc., while the latter is concerned when the action involved indirectly makes itself felt, as when the מימרא manifests itself, appears, converses, realizes, causes descent, gratifies, gives sons, tempts, etc. Obviously, no hard and fast division between these two categores has been possible to draw. Indeed, all of the categories need to be applied elastically, once usage establishes them, if a typological approach is to be developed at all. Moreover, a single use may sometimes be said to invoke more than one category, although in the present paper double counting is avoided, provided one category is used with emphasis. A tabular list of all the usages surveyed is included as an appendix. It must be stressed that the typologies here explored are provisional, and were evolved by assessing the sense of each passage in its context, not by means of a dictional or semantic analysis.

deliberating	7 of 50 occurrences
involved in covenant	7 of 50 occurrences
influencing	7 of 50 occurrences.

Only the types involving covenant and influence present points of obvious overlap, and only the first of the two may be regarded as generated by the content of Genesis, in that the second proves to be distributed generally within the Pentateuch. Neophyti's Genesis, alone of all the Targums we shall consider, gives priority to the מימרא as speaking,[44] but then also imagines it as acted upon in worship,[45] as involved in covenant,[46] as well as influencing (the typically Targumic portrayal) and creating.[47] The conception in Pseudo-Jonathan is more unequivocally active,[48] although a certain reflexivity, manifest in deliberation,[49] is also apparent.

Both Targums alter their usage in Exodus. Neophyti I gives us a largely new list:

being with others	13 out of 43 occurrences
influencing	9 out of 43 occurrences
deliberating	5 out of 43 occurrences
involved in worship	5 out of 43 occurrences
demanding obedience	4 out of 43 occurrences.

The first, fourth and last of these may be regarded as required by the content of Exodus,[50] since they also show up among the prominent types of usage in Pseudo-Jonathan, and are not featured in Genesis:[51]

acting	10 out of 51 occurrences
demanding obedience	7 out of 51 occurrences
being with others	7 out of 51 occurrences

[44] 1:3, 5, 6, 8, 9, 10, 11, 20, 24, 28; 17:3; 18:17; 20:6. Such usages would be vastly augmented, were marginal variants taken into account. It is striking that the מימרא's speaking is made more prominent in Neophyti by virtue of its importance in chapter one (cf. the type, "creating").

[45] 4:26; 8:20; 12:7, 8; 13:4; 15:6; 16:13; 21:33; 22:14; 26:25.

[46] 9:12, 13, 15, 16, 17; 17:7, 8, 11. Other covenantal moments might obviously have occasioned the usage: the covenants involving Noah and Abraham are of especially concern to the meturgemanin. The distribution in Pseudo-Jonathan is virtually the same.

[47] 1:9, 11, 16, 25, 27; 2:2; 14:19, 22.

[48] Cf. the portrayal of the מימרא as "aiding," 21:20, 22; 26:28; 28:15, 20; 31:3, 5; 35:3, 5; 39:2, 3, 23; 48:21; 49:25.

[49] 6:6, 7; 8:1, 21; 29:31; 41:1; 50:20.

[50] As a matter of fact, the correspondence between Neophyti and Pseudo-Jonathan within these categories is fairly high (cf. the appendix).

[51] Only the type of involvement in worship shows up there, and even then in Neophyti alone.

involved in worship	7 out of 51 occurrences
influencing	6 out of 51 occurrences.

"Influencing" is so far common to all four lists, and may be held to be endemic within the ethos of Neophyti I and Pseudo-Jonathan. That leaves very little that is distinctive within Exodus. Deliberating appears to be the emphasis of Neophyti I at this point,[52] while acting is stressed most emphatically in Pseudo-Jonathan.[53] It is not obvious why deliberating should be stressed in Neophyti, especially when it appeared only once in Genesis (against seven usages in Pseudo-Jonathan): evidently, the emphasis is not mere convention, but reflects how the meturgemanin understood divine activity in Exodus in particular. Pseudo-Jonathan, however, seems consistent, so far, in a portrayal of מימרא as comparatively active.

Leviticus occasions the fewest number of references to מימרא in both of the Palestinian Targums.[54] In both cases, the by now conventional portrait of the מימרא as influencing is obvious. On the other hand, Neophyti I manifests its greater concern for the involvement of מימרא in worship,[55] while Pseudo-Jonathan breaks new ground in its focus on the מימרא as giving law[56] and as demanding obedience:[57]

Neophyti	
influencing	8 out of 14 occurrences
involved in worship	2 out of 14 occurrences
Pseudo-Jonathan	
influencing	4 out of 13 occurrences
giving law	3 out of 13 occurrences
demanding obedience	3 out of 13 occurrences.

It appears clear that the meturgemanin of Pseudo-Jonathan are here concerned for a reading of מימרא within Leviticus in particular which is more prescriptive, as compared both to other books in Pseudo-Jonathan and to Neophyti at this point.

---

[52]3:17; 15:2; 17:1, 16; 18:11. Of these usages, 17:1 hardly represents deliberation in any substantial sense, but formal emphasis is perhaps for that reason all the more apparent.

[53]2:5; 7:25; 12:23, 29; 13:8, 17; 14:25; 15:1, 8; 33:22.

[54]That Hayward does not explain this distributional factor, in making his case of a cultic association of מימרא , is unfortunate.

[55]16:8. 9. The numbers are far too small to bear much weight in isolation, but the coherence with the usage in Neophyti's Genesis (and, to a lesser extent, Exodus) supports the generalization.

[56]9:23; 24:12; 26;46. The ground broken, however, is not broad (cf. the last note).

[57]8:35; 18:30; 22:9; cf. the previous note.

The deliberation involved in מימרא,[58] and its demand for obedience,[59] which surfaced in Neophyti in Exodus, also characterizes Neophyti in Numbers:

deliberating	12 out of 55 occurrences
demanding obedience	12 out of 55 occurrences
influencing	10 out of 55 occurrences
being with others	6 out of 55 occurrences
occasioning revolt	5 out of 55 occurrences.

The aspect of influencing is, again, consistently a feature of Neophyti's portrayal of the מימרא, but the appearance of the type of מימרא as occasioning revolt may be determined by the content of Numbers, as it also appears in Pseudo-Jonathan:[60]

demanding obedience	17 out of 50 occurrences
influencing	10 out of 50 occurrences
occasioning revolt	6 out of 50 occurrences
deliberating	5 out of 50 occurrences.

Of course, the types of deliberating and demanding obedience also appear in Pseudo-Jonathan, but those types are established as typical of Neophyti before Numbers. What is striking in Pseudo-Jonathan is the more deliberative, deuteronomistic aspect of the מימרא in Numbers,[61] as compared to the more dynamic portrayal earlier.

Both Targums evince a fresh, distinctive and vigorous view of מימרא in Deuteronomy. Although Neophyti's usual emphasis upon the מימרא as influencing is present, for the first time its function as a voice is significantly present, and in fact predominates:[62]

voice	26 out of 117 occurrences
influencing	21 out of 117 occurrences
acting	11 out of 117 occurrences
demanding obedience	10 out of 117 occurrences.

The dynamic quality of מימרא is here also suggested by the presence of acting as a type of usage, for the first time in Neophyti.[63] On the other hand, by this stage the type of demanding obedience appears simply to be characteristic of both Targums after Genesis. Pseudo-Jonathan also

---

[58]9:18, 20; 10:13; 11:20; 14:41; 20:24; 22:18; 24:13; 27:14; 33:2, 38; 36:5.

[59]3:16, 39, 51; 4:37, 41, 45, 49; 14:24; 20:12, 21; 32:12, 15.

[60]As the appendix indicates, the overlap between the two Targums is impressive, although not complete.

[61]Just this aspect is reminiscent of the Isaiah Targum (cf. n. 41).

[62]4:12, 30, 33, 36; 5:23, 24, 25, 26; 8:20; 9:23; 13:5, 19; 15:5; 18:16; 26:14; 27:10; 28:1, 2, 15, 45, 62; 30:2, 8, 10, 20; 34:10.

[63]3:21; 4:3; 5:24; 9:4, 19, 20; 11:23; 29:22, 23; 32:39; 33:27.

averts to the vocal sense of מימרא in Deuteronomy,[64] and presents it as even more active than Neophyti does:[65]

acting	21 out of 75 occurrences
demanding obedience	17 out of 75 occurrences
occasioning revolt	9 out of 75 occurrences
voice	8 out of 75 occurrences.

Clearly, the vocal associations may be triggered by the content of Deuteronomy, although the reference of Pseudo-Jonathan to revolt[66] may be considered a characteristic convention.

As the types of usage are viewed within Neophyti and Pseudo-Jonathan, and compared to one another, so that distinctive elements are identified, a profile of each Targum emerges:

Neophyti:

Genesis	**Exodus**	**Leviticus**	**Numbers**	**Deuteronomy**
speaking involved in worship creating	deliberating	involved in worship	deliberating	voice

Pseudo-Jonathan:

Genesis	**Exodus**	**Leviticus**	**Numbers**	**Deuteronomy**
aiding deliberating	acting	giving law demanding obedience	demanding obedience	occasioning revolt

Neophyti, at the beginning and end of the Pentateuch, presents מימרא in its vocal association, but also portrays it as creating (Genesis), involved in worship (Genesis, Leviticus), and deliberating (Exodus, Numbers). Pseudo-Jonathan proceeds in a more sequential manner, from the activity of מימרא in aiding, deliberating, and acting (Genesis, Exodus) to its demanding obedience to the law (Leviticus, Numbers), and thence to the inevitable revolt (Deuteronomy). That מימרא is to be related to the verb אמר, and assumes a divine subject, is indeed a necessary occasion of such usages, but the patterns of types manifest within Neophyti and Pseudo-Jonathan suggest that the association is not the sufficient condition of the usages. Rather, the immediate inference from the

---

[64]4:33, 36; 5:5, 24, 25, 26; 26:14; 34:10. (All usages but 5:5 are included within Neophyti.)

[65]1:30; 2:21; 3:22; 4:3, 24; 5:24; 11:23; 18:19; 19:15; 24:18; 26:5; 28:20, 22, 27, 28, 35; 29:22; 32:39, 43; 33:27; 34:6.

[66]1:26, 32, 43; 8:20; 9:23; 21:20; 25:18; 32:18, 51.

patterns of distribution observed is that God is portrayed as speaking in different ways and at different points within Neophyti and Pseudo-Jonathan. In other words, מימרא is not simply a metonym for God, or even for God understood as speaking, but is the term which conveys the sense of God's distinctively vocal, deliberative, creative, and worshipped aspects in Neophyti, and his distinctively active, demanding, and resisted aspects in Pseudo-Jonathan.

In the most general of terms, one may therefore infer that מימרא is the Targumic category of God's activity of commanding. Within that activity, a meturgeman might think of commanding as what is ordered, as the response to the order, or as what is behind the order. There are a range of emphases, both interior to the act of commanding, informing the decision of command, and exterior to the act, devolving from it, which מימרא might theoretically convey.[67] At just this point, however, it is crucial not to mistake the categories with which we are dealing. Although מימרא is used variously, there is no warrant for saying that there is such a thing as a *concept* of God's מימרא which can take distinctive forms. Following the lead of Moore, we may say that מימרא is not a personal being, a being, a figment of speculation (so far Moore), or even (we now conclude) a systematic idea, consistent from Targum to Targum. What links the Targumim, in their usage of מימרא, is not a theological thought, but a theological *manner* of speaking of God.

But having spoken in largely negative terms, we must also guard against the recent tendency, so to discount the coherent reference of מימרא, as to deny the sensibility of its usage. It has now become evident that מימרא in Neophyti and Pseudo-Jonathan (as in the Isaiah Targum) evinces patterns of usage. Obviously, those patterms do not amount to a systematic theology. But it is equally obvious that מימרא within a given Targum is not invoked haphazardly when some verb of speaking happens to be used of God in the Hebrew text which is rendered. The

---

[67]Precisely because the usage of מימרא is flexible, and has to do with effective command, it seems unwise to discount the possibility of a relationship with Philo's use of λόγος, which refers to the more interior, or intentional, aspects of command, cf. Chilton, *Glory*, 145, 146 (n. 46), and "Commenting on the Old Testament (with particular reference to the pesharim, Philo, and the Mekilta)," *It is Written: Scripture Citing Scripture. Essays in Honour of Barnabas Lindars, SSF* (eds D. A. Carson and H. G. M. Williamson; Cambridge: Cambridge University Press, 1988) 122-140, 129, 130, 131-3. Indeed, the procedure defended here, of reading מימרא inductively, and inferring a sense therefrom, is analogous to H. A. Wolfson's in respect of the Philonic λόγος , cf. *Philo: The Foundations of Religious Philosophy in Judaism, Christianity, and Islam* I, II (Cambridge: Harvard University Press, 1947, 1948) I.229f., 235f., 240, 244f., 253f., 291, 331; II.32 and Muñoz Leon, 34, 49.

Targums to hand suggest an alternative hypothesis for the understanding of מימרא: *the usage of the term reflects the manner in which given meturgemanin conceive of God's activity of commanding, whether from the point of view of God's intention in the command, or the human response to what is effected (or affected) by the command.* Within the history of each Targum's development, the typologies of usage vary, and the principal variables at issue are (1) the notion of how God commands (and what response his command elicits), and (2) the complex of ideas triggered by a given book. מימרא might therefore be understood as covering the conceptual field[68] of divine speaking, inclusive of the deliberation behind, and the results of, that speaking. The term performs taxonomically, invoking the possibility that a range of terms within the appropriate lexical field might be employed. In the Masoretic Text, the same *sorts* of action or event may be described, but the taxonomic system is not as well regulated.[69]

---

[68]Cf. Georges Mounin, *Les problèmes théoretiques de la traduction* (Paris: Gallimard, 1963) 71-112. A personal conversation with Koenraad Kuiper suggested the description of the use of מימרא in terms of taxonomy.

[69]By contrast, דבור in Neophyti and Pseudo-Jonathan is a later development, restricted to particular disclosures of God, usually involving Moses (cf. Exodus 29:3; Leviticus 1:1; Numbers 7:89 in Neophyti, and Exodus 33:11; Leviticus 1:1; Numbers 7:89; Deuteronomy 4:12; 5:22, 23; 18:16 in Pseudo-Jonathan). Both Targums associate the usage with Jacob at Genesis 28:10.

Appendix

Typologies of Usage, by Book and Targum

Genesis: Neophyti 62; Pseudo-Jonathan 50
speaking – Neophyti 14 (1:3, 5, 6, 8, 9, 10, 11, 20, 24, 28; 17:3; 18:17; 20:6)
Pseudo-Jonathan 1 (20:6)
blessing – Neophyti 3 (1:22; 24:1; 26:3)
Pseudo-Jonathan 2 (24:1; 26:3)
creating – Neophyti 8 (1:9, 11, 16, 25, 27; 2:2; 14:19, 22)
Pseudo-Jonathan 0
voice – Neophyti 2 (3:8, 10)
Pseudo-Jonathan 2 (3:8, 10)
giving law – Neophyti 0
Pseudo-Jonathan 1 (3:24)
involved in worship – Neophyti 10 (4:26; 8:20; 12:7, 8; 13:4; 15:6; 16:13; 21:33; 22:14; 26:25)
Pseudo-Jonathan 4 (4:26; 15:6; 18:5; 21:33)
deliberating – Neophyti 1 (29:31)
Pseudo-Jonathan 7 (6:6, 7; 8:1, 21; 29:31; 41:1; 50:20)
acting – Neophyti 1 (20:13)
Pseudo-Jonathan 4 (7:16; 12:17; 16:1; 20:18)
influencing – Neophyti 9 (12:7; 15:1; 16:3; 17:1; 18:1, 19; 19:24; 20:3; 46:4)
Pseudo-Jonathan 7 (11:8; 15:1; 16:13; 19:24; 22:1; 27:28; 48:9)
aiding – Neophyti 2 (31:5; 49:25)
Pseudo-Jonathan 13 (21:20, 22; 26:28; 28:15, 20; 31:3, 5; 35:3; 39:2, 3, 23; 48:21; 49:25)
being with others – Neophyti 2 (28:15; 31:3)
Pseudo-Jonathan 1 (46:4)
involved in covenant – Neophyti 8 (9:12, 13, 15, 16, 17; 17:7, 8, 11)
Pseudo-Jonathan 7 (9:12, 13, 15, 16, 17; 17:2, 7)
swearing – Neophyti 0
Pseudo-Jonathan 2 (21:23; 31:50)
demanding obedience – Neophyti 3 (22:18; 24:3; 26:5)
Pseudo-Jonathan 3 (22:18; 24:3; 26:5)
occasioning revolt – Neophyti 0
Pseudo-Jonathan 0

Exodus: Neophyti 43; Pseudo-Jonathan 51
speaking – Neophyti 0
Pseudo-Jonathan 2 (10:29; 33:12)

blessing – Neophyti 0
Pseudo-Jonathan 0
creating – Neophyti 1 (12:42)
Pseudo-Jonathan 0
voice – Neophyti 2 (19:5; 23:22)
Pseudo-Jonathan 0
giving law – Neophyti 1 (15:25)
Pseudo-Jonathan 2 (13:17; 15:25)
involved in worship – Neophyti 5 (4:31; 5:23; 14:31; 17:15; 34:5)
Pseudo-Jonathan 7 (14:31; 17:15; 20:7; 26:28; 33:19; 34:5; 36:33)
deliberating – Neophyti 5 (3:17; 15:2; 17:1, 16; 18:11)
Pseudo-Jonathan 3 (2:23; 3:17; 15:2)
acting – Neophyti 3 (12:23; 15:1, 8)
Pseudo-Jonathan 10 (2:5; 7:25; 12:23, 29; 13:8, 17; 14:25; 15:1, 8; 33:22)
influencing – Neophyti 9 (3:8, 12, 14; 6:3; 11:4; 19:9, 20; 20:4; 31:17)
Pseudo-Jonathan 6 (1:21; 3:8; 12:27; 13:15; 31:17; 33:9)
aiding – Neophyti 1 (18:4)
Pseudo-Jonathan 3 (3:12; 10:10; 18:19)
being with others – Neophyti 13 (3:12; 4:12, 15; 8:18; 10:10; 12:12; 13:21; 25:22; 29:43, 45; 30:6, 36; 31:17)
Pseudo-Jonathan – 7 (4:12, 15; 25:22; 29:43; 30:6, 39; 31:17)
involved in covenant – Neophyti 0
Pseudo-Jonathan 0
swearing – Neophyti 0
Pseudo-Jonathan 3 (6:8; 13:5; 17:16)
demanding obedience – Neophyti 4 (15:26; 17:1; 19:5; 23:22)
Pseudo-Jonathan 7 (5:2; 14:7; 15:26; 17:1, 13; 19:5; 23:22)
occasioning revolt – Neophyti 0
Pseudo-Jonathan 1 (16:8)

Leviticus: Neophyti 14; Pseudo-Jonathan 13
speaking – Neophyti 0
Pseudo-Jonathan 1 (1:1)
blessing – Neophyti 0
Pseudo-Jonathan 0
creating – Neophyti 0
Pseudo-Jonathan 0
voice – Neophyti 0
Pseudo-Jonathan 0
giving law – Neophyti 1 (26:46)
Pseudo-Jonathan 3 (9:23; 24:12; 26:46)
involved in worship – Neophyti 2 (16:8, 9)
Pseudo-Jonathan 0

deliberating – Neophyti 1 (26:42)
Pseudo-Jonathan 0
acting – Neophyti 0
Pseudo-Jonathan 1 (9:23)
influencing – Neophyti 8 (9:4; 16:2; 19:2; 20:23; 25:38; 26:9, 12, 45)
Pseudo-Jonathan 4 (20:23; 26:11, 12, 30)
aiding – Neophyti 0
Pseudo-Jonathan 0
being with others – Neophyti 0
Pseudo-Jonathan 0
involved in covenant – Neophyti 1 (26:46)
Pseudo-Jonathan 1 (26:46)
swearing – Neophyti 0
Pseudo-Jonathan 0
demanding obedience – Neophyti 0
Pseudo-Jonathan 3 (8:35; 18:30; 22:9)
occasioning revolt – Neophyti 1 (26:23)
Pseudo-Jonathan 0

Numbers: Neophyti 55; Pseudo-Jonathan 50
speaking – Neophyti 2 (1:1; 22:12)
Pseudo-Jonathan 0
blessing – Neophyti 4 (6:27; 10:29; 23:8; 24:5)
Pseudo-Jonathan 3 (6:27; 23:8, 20)
creating – Neophyti 0
Pseudo-Jonathan 0
voice – Neophyti 0
Pseudo-Jonathan 0
giving law – Neophyti 1 (13:3)
Pseudo-Jonathan 1 (14:35)
involved in worship – Neophyti 1 (18:9)
Pseudo-Jonathan 0
deliberating – Neophyti 12 (9:18, 20; 10:13; 11:20; 14:41; 20:24; 22:18; 24:13; 27:14; 33:2, 38; 36:5)
Pseudo-Jonathan 5 (9:18, 23; 14:41; 22:18; 24:13)
acting – Neophyti 1 (23:5)
Pseudo-Jonathan 2 (21:6; 22:28)
influencing – Neophyti 10 (11:17; 14:14; 17:19; 18:20; 22:9, 20; 23:3, 4, 12, 16)
Pseudo-Jonathan 10 (12:6; 17:19; 21:35; 22:9, 20; 23:3, 4, 16; 24:23; 27:16)
aiding – Neophyti 0
Pseudo-Jonathan 4 (14:9, 43; 23:21; 31:8)

being with others – Neophyti 6 (6:27; 14:9, 21, 28; 23:19, 21)
Pseudo-Jonathan 2 (25:4; 23:19)
involved in covenant – Neophyti 0
Pseudo-Jonathan 0
swearing – Neophyti 1 (11:21)
Pseudo-Jonathan 0
demanding obedience – Neophyti 12 (3:16, 39, 51; 4:37, 41, 45, 49; 14:24; 20:12, 21; 32:12, 15)
Pseudo-Jonathan 17 (3:16, 39, 51; 4:37, 41, 45, 49; 9:20, 23; 10:13; 13:3; 20:12; 21:8, 9; 33:2, 38; 36:5)
occasioning revolt – Neophyti 5 (11:20; 14:11, 43; 21:5, 7)
Pseudo-Jonathan 6 (11:20; 14:11; 16:11; 20:24; 21:5; 27:14)

Deuteronomy: Neophyti 117; Pseudo-Jonathan 75
speaking – Neophyti 9 (5:5, 28; 9:10; 10:4; 17:16; 31:2; 32:12; 33:2; 34:4)
Pseudo-Jonathan 2 (31:2; 32:49)
blessing – Neophyti 5 (5:28; 8:10; 15:4; 21:5; 33:7)
Pseudo-Jonathan 1 (24:19)
creating – Neophyti 1 (32:15)
Pseudo-Jonathan (8:3)
voice – Neophyti 26 (4:12, 30, 33, 36; 5:23, 24, 25, 26; 8:20; 9:23; 13:5, 19; 15:5; 18:16; 26:14; 27:10; 28:1, 2, 15, 45, 62; 30:2, 8, 10, 20; 34:10)
Pseudo-Jonathan 8 (4:33, 36; 5:5, 24, 25, 26; 26:14; 34:10)
giving law – Neophyti 4 (1:1; 4:23; 8:3; 34:9)
Pseudo-Jonathan 0
involved in worship – Neophyti 6 (4:7; 18:5, 7, 19, 20, 22)
Pseudo-Jonathan 2 (4:7; 18:7)
deliberating – Neophyti 7 (1:1; 12:14; 17:10; 32:23, 26; 33:27; 34:5)
Pseudo-Jonathan 6 (12:5, 11; 26:18; 32:23, 26; 33:27)
acting – Neophyti 11 (3:21; 4:3; 5:24; 9:4, 19, 20; 11:23; 29:22, 23; 32:39; 33:27)
Pseudo-Jonathan 21 (1:30; 2:21; 3:22; 4:3, 24; 5:24; 11:23; 18:19; 19:15; 24:18; 26:5; 28:20, 22, 27, 28, 35; 29:22; 32:39, 43; 33:27; 34:6)
influencing – Neophyti 21 (1:27; 4:20, 27; 5:24; 8:18, 19, 20; 9:4, 23; 10:5, 15; 11:17, 21; 13:18; 26:17, 18; 30:3; 31:4; 32:30; 34:1, 11)
Pseudo-Jonathan 34 (1:10; 4:20; 5:24; 11:12; 28:7, 9, 11, 13, 21, 25, 48, 49, 61, 63, 65, 68; 29:1, 3; 30:3, 4, 5, 7, 9; 31:5, 15; 32:12, 36, 39, 50; 33:29; 34:1, 5, 6, 11)
aiding – Neophyti 3 (31:8, 23; 32:9)
Pseudo-Jonathan 4 (2:7; 20:1; 31:8, 23)
being with others – Neophyti 2 (32:39, 40)
Pseudo-Jonathan 0
involved in covenant – Neophyti 1 (4:23)

Pseudo-Jonathan 0
swearing – Neophyti 0
Pseudo-Jonathan 2 (5:11; 31:7)
demanding obedience – Neophyti 10 (1:36; 2:1; 6:2; 7:4; 10:8; 13:5, 11; 25:18; 29:17; 31:27)
Pseudo-Jonathan 17 (4:30; 11:1; 13:5, 19; 15:5; 26:17; 27:10; 28:1, 2, 15, 45, 62; 30:3, 8, 10, 20; 31:12)
occasioning revolt – Neophyti 7 (1:26, 32, 43; 9:7, 23; 32:18, 51)
Pseudo-Jonathan 9 (1:26, 32, 43; 8:20; 9:23; 21:20; 25:18; 32:18, 51)

23

The *Am Ha'Arets* as Literary Character

Peter Haas
Vanderbilt University

When reconstructing the ethics of early Rabbinic Judaism we are forced to rely on written documents. Yet in the face of impressive advances in hermeneutic theory and literary analysis the texts of early rabbinic Judaism are still treated all too often as accurate historical descriptions, not as literature. In the following I wish to explore the results for descriptive ethics that emerge if we apply literary theory to our examination of early rabbinic documents. For this purpose I wish to look at the "am ha'arets," an outstanding example of a literary character that has been taken as an historically accurate description. Since the am ha'arets appears in contexts having to do with proper (or improper) Judaic behavior, it will serve as a useful term for examining what effect a literary approach has on our study of early Rabbinic ethics.

Although I propose to treat the phrase "am ha'arets" as a literary creation, I do not mean thereby to deny that such folks existed. What I am claiming is that the ethical meaning of the term is not to be found in a supposed historical referent, but in the function the phrase has in the overall literary program of its text. As we shall see, this difference of approach yields significantly different results as to the meaning of the term. In particular, our survey will reveal that the am ha'arets mentioned in these texts symbolize the type of person who is unethical, that is, who does not conform to the behavior or character-patterns which the rabbinic authorship of each text wants to advocate. Thus the character of the am ha'arets will vary from text to text as the operative theory of the good life varies. In fact it appear that the am ha'arets are ascribed traits that define the systemic opposite of what the author wishes to promote. Thus far from being a description of an actual social group, the rabbinic am ha'arets, though fashioned out of historical material, is the creation of an author's mind and reflects in a clear, albeit inverse way the image that author has of the good life.

The above discussion establishes one methodological parameter that we must note before proceeding. That is that any such analysis must respect textual boundaries. This means that we must examine the function and so meaning of the phrase independently for each document in which it appears. If the portrayal of the am ha'arets appears to vary from text to text, we must not suppress that datum but must take it to mean that the underlying conceptions of the good life in the documents in question are not the same. By preserving the unique literary character of the phrase in each text, we discover, as we shall see, a much richer side to the rabbinic tradition and so of the diverse ways in which the creators of early rabbinic Judaism conceived of the model Jew.[1]

To indicate how different the results of a literary analysis of these texts are for our understanding of rabbinic ethics, we shall look first at what traditional positivistic readings have produced. Scientific attempts to deal with the am ha'arets go back to the seminal work of Abraham Geiger.[2] In his reconstruction of ancient Judean society, Geiger posited the existence of two clearcut social classes, a depiction heavily reminiscent of popular conceptions of medieval European society. On the one hand were the political and social elite, the natural aristocracy, who were concerned with the political and cultural life of their community. These, in Geiger's scheme were the Pharisees and Saducees. On the other hand were the peasant masses which remained largely indifferent to political struggles, following whomever promised them the most.[3] These people, the am ha'arets, did not share

---

[1]My claim here parallels J. Neusner's claim as regards the legal traditions found in diverse Rabbinic texts. Neusner argues that each legal text establishes its own contours of the law. These various legal systems are not to be blended into each other to achieve a unitary view of "the" law. I make this same claim now as regards literary data. An exposition of this view and its development in Neusner's work can be found, for example, in "New Problems, New Solutions: Current Events in Rabbinic Studies," in *Method and Meaning in Ancient Judaism* (3rd Series) (Chico: Scholar's Press, 1981), pp. 61-82.

[2]*Urschrift und Uebersetzungen der Bibel* (Breslau, 1857), pp. 150f.

[3]The exact opposite conclusion is reached by M. Friedlaender. He argues that the Am Ha'arets represents in fact the patriotic and nationalistic common folk of Judea. The animosity which developed between them and the Pharisees was due largely to the establishment of the academy at Yavneh, according to

the elite's concern with religious or national identity. From the point of view of the preservation of Judaic culture, these am ha'arets were not really different from foreigners, that is resident in Judea but not committed to the particular religious character of the nation.

In a curious way, Geiger's reading reflects the social position of Jews in Germany at his own time. A small band of rabbis and intellectuals were dedicated to maintaining the true character of Jewish civilization while the masses were becoming indistinguishable from the surrounding Gentiles. It is quite possible that Geiger's reconstruction of ancient Judaism was simply a recasting of what he was witnessing in his own time.

Adolf Buechler at the turn of the century attempted a fresh look at the am ha'arets and in so doing moved the discussion to a more rigorous methodological level.[4] While he still assumed the term was to be taken as referring to a definite social grouping, he at least recognized that we know of them only through the writings of the partisan rabbinic class. According to Buechler, the label am ha'arets was used by the rabbis to denote those in the community who refused to conform to rabbinic teachings. Although Buechler could concede on these grounds that some of the connotations of the term may be a function of the rabbinic depiction, he takes for granted the basic historical fact that such people as a group actually existed. He still regards them as basically members of the landed peasantry. Thus while Buechler recognized that the term had religious and ideological connotations and so was a literary device, he had at the same time no doubt that behind the term was a definite socio-economic group.[5]

By the early twentieth century, Judaic scholarship began to flourish in America. American scholars who dealt with the issue of the am ha'arets tended to draw more heavily on the early positivistic *Wissenschaft*, represented by Geiger, than on the later, more literary understanding of Buechler. Both Solomon Zeitlin and Louis Finkelstein followed Geiger's lead in casting the am ha'arets as a distinct peasant class opposed to the ruling aristocratic elite represented by Saducees

---

Friedlaender. The Am ha'arets, who supported the war against Rome, saw Yohanan ben Zakkai's deal with Vespasian as traitorous. After the war, the people could not reconcile themselves to Pharasaic rule. See his *Zur Entstehungsgeschichte des Christenthums* (Vienna, 1894), pp. 37-58.

[4]Adolf Buechler, *Der Galilaische 'Am-Ha'ares des Zweiten Jahrhunderts* (Georg Olms V.: 1906, repr. 1969) and *The Political and Social Leaders of the Jewish Community of Sepphoris in the Second and Third Centuries* (Jew's College Pub #1, 1909).

[5]*Ibid.*, pp. 236-237.

and the Pharisees.[6] For both scholars, Geiger's treatment needed to be updated only in the details of the role the am ha'arets played in the class struggle in Roman Palestine.

Finkelstein had the less radical interpretation. He argues that the am ha'arets were simple peasant farmers who did not accept the Pharisaic legal codes. They, like peasants everywhere, did not share a particular ideology or compose a philosophical school. They simply preferred to be left alone to work their fields and orchards. Thus while agreeing that the am ha'arets were a distinct economic and social class, he did not link them with any religious movements or ascribe any particular content to their opposition. In this he is reminiscent of Geiger.

Zeitlin on the other hand constructed a much more complex picture of ideological struggles in Roman Palestine and the role of the am ha'arets in these.[7] Like Geiger, Zeitlin seems to have projected medieval European Jewish experiences back on to the second century, and with it an array of attitudes and ideological disputes. His depiction of the tension between am ha'arets and the Sadducean/Pharisaic elite is strikingly reminiscent of the struggle a century before between the medieval Jewish masses and the Polish Rabbinate, and in fact produced remarkably similar results.[8] In the seventeenth and eighteenth centuries, masses of East European Jews rebelled against what they conceived to be the aristocratic and elitist demands of the orthodox rabbinate. They turned instead to popular healers, preachers such as the "baale shem" (masters of the good [or divine] name), messianic pretenders such as Shabbtai Tsevi, or simply to the emerging secular cultures around them. In all cases, they seemed eager to throw off "the yoke of the law." In parallel fashion, Zeitlin argues, the am ha'arets in Late Antiquity turned away from the aristocratic and intellectualizing priests and scholars to follow the charismatic leaders of the Jewish-Christians, the Zealots or the early apocalyptic movements. As in the early modern period, the rebels were lead to various forms of antinomianism.[9]

Zeitlin's attempt to link the am ha'arets to early Christianity shaped much subsequent research. Such an identification did, after all, enjoy a certain surface plausibility: the am ha'arets seem to have been

---

[6]See Solomon Zeitlin, "The Am Haarez," *JQR* 23:1932-33, pp. 45-61. Louis Finkelstein's views are expressed in his massive study *The Pharisees* (Philadelphia: JPS, 1962). See especially Volume II, pp. 754-761.

[7]Zeitlin, *op. cit.*, pp. 47-48.

[8]*Ibid.*, pp. 53-54.

[9]*Ibid.*, pp. 53-58.

on the fringes of society, to be questioning rabbinic authority and to have rejected the law. These characteristics sounded to the nineteenth century ear as virtually congruent with early Christianity.[10] Further, such an identification met the needs of many Christian who were attempting to find the Jewish roots of Christianity. The am ha'arets might just fit the bill. Since the essence of early, and certainly Pauline, Christianity was escape from the law and since the am ha'arets are a Jewish group of rabbinic times characterized by their lack of regard for the law, it would seem to follow that it is to the am ha'arets that we must look for the social origins of early Jewish-Christianity. Even the recent massive study of the am ha'arets conducted by Aaron Oppenheimer was very much influenced by this line of reasoning.[11]

Oppenheimer's study both builds on Buechler's insight into the term as a literary creation while at the same time attempting to correct Buechler's narrow definition and late dating of the am ha'arets. Oppenheimer claimed rightly that Buechler, and others such as Zeitlin, conceived of the term "am ha'arets" in too monolithic a way. The term is used much more loosely than these scholars have acknowledged. The needed corrective, says Oppenheimer, is to reexamine how the phrase is used throughout the rabbinic literature and on the basis of such a survey to construct a picture of the am ha'arets that takes account of the diverse meanings the term had. Yet, his goal in reevaluating this term is, finally, "to shed light on its social manifestation." Thus despite his apparent flexibility, Oppenheimer is just as committed to the assumption that the term finally can be understood as a real social group as were his predecessors. His one real advance is that he is much more sensitive to the changes that apparently occurred in this group over time and less tied to ascribing to it a particular view or program.[12]

The shortcomings of trying to tie the term am ha'arets to a real social class is nicely illustrated by Shmuel Safrai. Let me cite part of his argument here because it is a good example of the limitations of this strategy. In the following passage Safrai tries to account for the fact that in the Mishnah the am ha'arets is usually one who does not keep the laws of tithing or purity while in the Talmud, the am

---

[10]See for example W. Bousset, *Die Religion des Judenthums in NT Zeitalter* (Berlin, 1903), pp. 166ff. The same connection is drawn on the Jewish side by Heinrich Graetz, *Geschichte der Juden* (Leipzig, 1888) III:1, p. 289.

[11]A. Oppenheimer, *The Am Ha'aretz* (Leiden: Brill, 1977), pp. 4 f.

[12]*Ibid.*, p. ix. Oppenheimer admits in his article in the *EJ*, however, that "Am Ha-aretz is not to be regarded as a distinctive social classification..." *EJ* (Jerusalem: Keter, 1971), III, p. 834.

ha'arets is often one who simply is not a scholar. Safrai, of course, wants to find continuity across these documents, assuming, in good positivistic style, that a single social group lies behind the term:

> With regard to the am ha'arets, it is possible to suggest various explanations for the diminution of this phenomenon and its final elimination. To a large extent, the gradual ceasing of the practice of purity and impurity in the later Amoraic period brings this about. The observance of the purification rites involved the possibility of cleansing oneself from severe impurity, such as follows from touching a dead body, by sprinkling waters of purification, that is, pure waters from the spring, together with scattering a small amount of the ashes of the red heifer on the water. Following the destruction of the Temple, a small quantity of these ashes was preserved for a few generations, but since the Temple was not standing, they were unable to prepare new ashes and so the supply dwindled and with it the purification practices disappeared as well. Strictness in the law of purity was one of the causes of the tension between the Haverim and the amme ha'arets, and thus the discontinuance of these laws in practice naturally led to the end of the conflict.[13]

Safrai makes a good point here. The am ha'arets as one who disregards tithing and purity is the characteristic am ha'arets of the Mishnah. This type of am ha'arets loses salience in the Gemara, where the am ha'arets is just as likely to be one who is identified solely on the basis of ignorance of Torah. Safrai goes awry, however, in trying to account for this not in literary terms, but in historical terms. The result is a reconstruction that is entirely conjectural. It posits practices and changes in Jewish religious practice in the post-Temple period for which there is no evidence whatsoever. It is true that purity does not occupy the center of attention in the Talmud as it does in Mishnah. But this need not be due merely to the loss of ashes of the red heifer. A much more fruitful explanation is that the very nature of Judaism was different for the Babylonian rabbis, and so different emphases surface in their religious texts.

The above shows that taking the term semiotically, that is as pointing to and descriptive of a single social referent, leads into a dead end. In the first place, the various documents in which the term is used were written in different places and at times centuries apart. The Mishnah, for example, took shape in Palestine about the year 200 C.E. The Babylonian Talmud received its present form in approximately seventh century Persia. It seems highly unlikely that a social group of

---

[13]S. Safrai, "Elementary Education, Its Religious and Social Significance," in *Cahiers d'Histoire Mondiale* XI:1-2, 1968, pp. 167-168.

some sort in Roman Palestine could "evolve" into a social group in Persia.

Further, in neither corpus do we find the term actually presupposes a specific economic or social group. What defines an am ha'arets for Mishnah is the disregard of tithing and purity laws. But this is a judgment placed on others by Mishnah's insiders, not a marker of any specific socio-economic class. An am ha'arets in Mishnah's sense could logically be a peasant, a landowner, or even an urban businessman with a garden plot. His socio-economic status is not indicated by the term itself. The traditional conviction that the am ha'arets were peasants drew on earlier models of social theory, as we saw earlier. Similar things can be said for the Talmudic am ha'arets. Again, no social or economic status is indicated, the terms simply reflecting a judgment by the talmudic authorship.

The point is that the character of the "am ha'arets" has become so conjectural that it can serve no real function in helping us understand the ethical thought of the early rabbis. To the contrary, as I have tried to show, the am ha'arets that emerge from scholarly studies often reflect most clearly the worldview of the later writer, not the author of the early text.

My aim in what follows is to review again the data about the am ha'arets reported by the Tannaitic and Amoraic literature, but to treat it now as a literary term, not as a description of an actual social class. There is no need to collate the references, since Oppenheimer's own work in gathering together and discussing these data cannot be materially improved upon. What I want to show is that a literary approach to understanding the am ha'arets not only avoids the methodological dead end described above, but allows to emerge a characterization of the term that is useful for the study of Jewish ethics.

Before proceeding, I wish briefly to alert the reader to my methodology for laying out the data. The chart below identifies each location in Mishnah of the use of the word am ha'arets.[14] Following the reference to the passage is a brief summary of the content or theme of the unit. This allows the reader to see the context in which the author has placed the am ha'arets. In some cases the term appears several times in a single discussion. In those cases, I catalog the discussion itself, not each use of the term. The reader should also be aware that many Mishnaic and Talmudic passages appear to be talking

---

[14]For purposes of this survey I consider Pirqe Avot to be a distinct literary creation and not an integral part of the Mishnah. I therefore do not include references in it to the am ha'arets.

about an am ha'arets without actually using the term. In the interest of methodological rigor I have not included such instances in the following catalog. I analyze here only passages in which the term actually occurs.

I find reference to the am ha'arets in some twenty-six passages in Mishnah. These are as follows ["AH" denotes Am Ha'arets; Haber is a strict follower of Mishnah's laws]:

Location		*Theme*
Demai	1:2	May be given demai[15]
	1:3	Need not tithe dough offering of an AH
	2:2	May an AH lodge with a follower of Mishnah?
	2:3	Restrictions on commerce with an AH
	3:4	We entrust tithed food to an AH
	6:9	AH and haber may share an inheritance
	6:12	AH buys produce for a haber
M.S.	3:3	Do not consecrate produce of an AH
	4:6	Do not give consecrated money to an AH
Sheb	5:9	Wife of a Haber may borrow from wife of AH
Hag	2:7	Clothes of an AH convey uncleanness (=Gittin 5:9)
Eduyot	1:14	AH renders vessels unclean
Hor	3:8	Scholarly mamzer precedes an AH High Priest
Kin	3:7	Old AH compared to elder of Torah
Toh	4:5	Clothes of an AH convey uncleanness
	7:1	Clean goods left in care of AH
	7:2	" " " "
	7:4	Haber's wife grinds grain with AH's wife
	7:5	Goods left with unsupervised AH are unclean
	8:1	" " " "

[15]"Demai" refers to produce which may have had tithes and other priestly gifts already removed. It is contrasted to produce which is known to have been tithed, on the one hand, and to produce which we know has not been tithed, on the other. The former, fully tithed food, is the only food that Mishnah allows its followers to eat. Untithed food may not be eaten, nor may it be given to someone, such as the amme ha'arets, who we suspect will not separate tithes before eating it. Demai is produce which falls into neither category and which is therefore anomalous. See R. Sarason, *A History of the Mishnaic Laws of Agriculture*, pp.1 f.

	8:2	" " " "
	8:3	" " " "
	8:5	AH's wife does not render house unclean
	10:1	AH conveys uncleanness
Makh	6:3	AH usually trusted to preserve cleanness
TY	4:5	Do not assume goods of an AH are consecrated

Of these twenty-six entries, twenty-four clearly place the discussion of the am ha'arets in the context of purity or tithing laws. That is, the am ha'arets in these passages is implicitly, if not explicitly, assigned the role of one who does not conform to the Mishnaic laws of purity or tithing. In only two cases, Hor. 3:8 and Kinnim 3:7, does the literary context create a different sense for the term. In both these later cases, the governing contrast is between the am ha'arets and a scholar. That is, in both cases the opposing character is one marked by the author as a sholar of Torah. But over 90% of the Mishnaic pericopae invoking the am ha'arets do so in the context of tithing and purity. Less than 10% see the am ha'arets in others terms. The Mishnah as a document, then, has assigned a remarkably consistent meaning to the term.

When we turn to the Gemara, we find a significant shift. Now there are numerous references to an am ha'arets which assume that the identity of this group is established by its lack of knowledge of Torah, not explicitly with any failure to abide by laws of tithing or purity. In fact, this characterization of the am ha'arets has roughly equal representation with the Mishnaic portrayal. On purely literary grounds, we must conclude that the terms means something different now than it did for the framers of Mishnah.

The data are summarized below. In the interest of space, I have not summarized the theme of the passage in each case, but have simply indicated whether the places the am ha'aretz in the context of Mishnaic rules of tithing and purity (= M) or in the context of learning and knowledge of Torah (= T). In ambiguous cases, I follow the semantics of the passage. That is, when the am ha'arets in the overall discussion is set overagainst "sages" or "scholars," I list the reference as "T," even if the details deal with matters of table fellowship. If the governing contrast is to "haber," I mark the discussion with "M."[16]

[16]In the following data sample I have been governed by certain principles which I should now spell out. As I have said, I am interested here in the proportion of legal discussions in which the am ha'arets of one kind or the other enters the text. For this reason I have chosen to list thematic units in which the am ha'arets appear, not individual occurrences of the term. This

Passage	*Type*	*Passage*	*Type*
Ber 43b	T[17]	Sot 21b-22a	T
Ber 47b	M (=Git 61a)	Sot 48a	M
Ber 47b	T (=Sot 22a)	Git 61b-62a	M
Ber 52b	?[18]	Git 62a	M
Ber 57a	T	Qid 70b	T
Ber 61a	T (=Erub 18b)	BQ 95b	T
Shab 13a	M	BM 33b	T
Shab 32a	T	BM 85a	T
Shab 32b	M	BM 85b	T
Shab 63a	T	BB 8a	T
Shab 114a	T	BB 57b-58a	T
Shab 152a	T	BB 168a	T
Erub 32a-b	M	Sanh 20b	T
Erub 37b	M	Sanh 52a-b	T
Erub 39a	T	Sanh 90b	M
Pes 42b	M	Sanh 94b	T

leads to two difficulties, however. First, in many cases what appears at first to be a single discussion turns out in fact to be a chain of smaller discussions. In such cases, I have tried to be guided by the thematic development of the material in deciding whether to list the material as a single discussion, or as two or more discussions that happen to be juxtaposed. If the entire block of material addresses and develops a single theme, beginning to end, I count this as a single discussion. If, on the other hand, the component discussions are not in conversation with each other and seem to take up recognizably different themes, I list them separately. The second problem has to deal with material that is repeated in substantially the same form in other parts of the Talmud. In such cases, I have chosen to list the discussion only once. In these ways I hope to keep attention focussed on the number of legal themes in which the am ha'arets are invoked, not the proportion of overall talmudic material devoted to the term. I realize that some of my decisions may be subject to disagreement, but I feel it yields a reasonably close approximation of presence of each concept of the am ha'arets in the Talmudic corpus.

[17]The text deals with matters of table fellowship. I list this as "T" because the passage claims to be listing things that are unbecoming to a "scholar." It is to "scholars," then, that the am ha'arets is compared.

[18]This passage is not clear cut. The subject has to do with table-fellowship, and in particular with cleaning up crumbs after the main meal. Since the concern is with one who will know which size crumbs are significant, I am inclined to see this as a matter of contrasting scholars to those who are ignorant, but other conclusions are possible.

Pes 49a-b	T	Sanh 96a	T
Pes 49b	T (=Ned 14a)	Makkot 17a	M
Suk 39a	M	AZ 39a (=Bekh 30b)	M
Suk 43b	M	AZ 70b	M
Betsah 11b	M	AZ 75b	M
Betsah 35b	M	Sheb 16a	M
Meg 18a	T	Sheb 18a	T
Meg 28a	T	Sheb 30b	T
Taanit 14b	T	Men 99b	T
Hag 20a	M	Hul 15a	M
Hag 20b	M	Hul 92a	T
Hag 22a-b	M	Hul 130b	?[19]
Hag 23a	M	Bekh 22a	M
Hag 26a	M	Bekh 23b	M
Yeb 114a	M	Bekh 30b	M
Ket 66b	T	Bekh 36a	M
Ket 111b	T	Arakh 15b	T
Ned 14a	T	Nid 30b	M
Ned 20a	T	Nid 33b	M
Ned 84b	M	Nid 33b-34a	M

The above table shows that the use of the term am ha'arets in the Babylonian Talmud is radically different from its use in Mishnah. In the Mishnah, as we saw, the term refers with only two exceptions to a person who ignores Mishnah's laws of purity or tithing. In the Talmud it is used this way in only one out of every two instances. Of approximately seventy-two discussions involving the am ha'arets in the Gemara, roughly thirty-four (47 percent) depict the am ha'arets to be so on account of his laxness in the laws of table-fellowship (= M) but a slightly greater thirty-six (50 percent) define the am ha'arets in terms of lack of knowledge of Torah (= T). In the remaining two cases (3 percent), the context is too ambiguous to allow for a firm determination as to the nature of the am ha'arets.

The distinction noted here is not new. We have already mentioned Safrai's attempt to account for it. Scholars use two terms to distinguish

[19]This passage can be classified either way. We are told here that the am ha'arets is not to be given the priestly gifts – suggesting M – because he is not sufficiently versed in the rules of Torah – suggesting T.

between these two characterizations of the am ha'arets. The first, *am ha'arets lemitzvah,* describes people who are suspected of being lax about the laws of tithes, purity and the like. The second, *am ha'arets letorah,* refers to those people who are not (sufficiently) versed in the Rabbinic tradition and Torah. At issue then is not the fact that the Mishnah and the Gemara see the am ha'arets in different ways, but how to account for that fact.

As we have seen, earlier scholars were forced by their methodological assumptions to deal with this phenomenon either by homogenizing the data, or by explaining the shift in social and historical terms. At the one extreme on the spectrum stands Buechler who took textual contexts seriously and so who correctly recognized that the terms had different significations in different documents. His positivistic assumptions, however, finally forced him to conclude there must have been two historically distinct groups of am ha'arets to whom the rabbis were pointing. He actually went so far as to claim that the "am ha'arets lemitzvot" were located in Galilee while the "am ha'arets letorah" dwelt in Judea.[20]

On the other extreme stand the bulk of Talmudic scholars, who treat the two terms as referring in all cases to a single group of peoples, albeit highlighting different aspects. For them, there is a single social reality behind any use of the phrase "am ha'arets," a peasant group that was both ignorant of Torah and recalcitrant in the laws of tithing and purity. Of this group, only Oppenheimer is more cautious, trying to acknowledge that the term does take on different implications at different times, while yet holding on to the affirmation that the term points to a single relatively coherent referent. He is willing to agree that each term has a distinct signification (along with Buechler), but he is not willing to go so far as to claim that therefore we must assume the existence of two different social groups. Rather, Oppenheimer asserts, we have to do with two different conceptualizations of the single phenomenon of the am ha'arets. The preference for one view or the other is "dependent either on the identity of the sage who defined and dealt with it or on the historical changes and circumstances of the periods in which the concept occurred."[21]

This compromise situation, partially historical, partially literary, allows Oppenheimer to have it both ways, and so neither way. Once he has admitted that the two usages appear at the same

---

[20]This view has been generally rejected. A good critique is by Gedaliah Alon, *Toldot HaYehudim beErets Yisrael bitqufat ha-Mishnah ve-ha-Talmud* (Tel Aviv: 1952-55) I, pp. 318-323.

[21]Oppenheimer, *op. cit.,* p. 114.

time, he can not invoke "historical changes" to explain why one kind of am ha'arets is described in one place and why another kind in another. Conversely, by arguing that historical change is a factor, he undercuts his ability to explain why one sage will have one kind of am ha'arets in mind while a contemporary will have the other kind in mind.[22] There is, then, no way Oppenheimer can satisfactorily account for the emergence and use of these two distinct concepts given the methodological limits he has set for himself.

We avoid all of these myriad problems, and still achieve useful data, by treating our texts as literature and interpreting references to the am ha'artes accordingly. On these grounds we can simply say that the phrase "am ha'arets" has different meanings in Mishnah and Talmud because it is used by different authors in different contexts to make different points. Our focus then shifts from speculations about the socio-economic make-up of Roman Palestine to understandings of how the authors of the early rabbinic documents conceived of and described their world. As I shall now show, the different connotations of the am ha'arets in Mishnah and Gemara reflect differing theories of the nature of the good life within Judaism.

For the early authorities of Mishnah, the center of proper Jewish life in the absence of the Temple was managing one's table in a way reminiscent of the Temple altar. Foods eaten by Jews had to be properly tithed and maintained in a requisite state of holiness. Thus each household would become a sort of Temple. This is the lifestyle to which Mishnah's heroes, the Haverim, devoted themselves. The dangerous person was the one who refused to do this, that is, who lead a life that ignored the ritual demands of Torah. These are the people the Mishnah labels as am ha'arets.

The religious conception of the Babylonian Talmud reflect a different situation and so new urgencies, naturally giving rise to a different negative role model. Its authors did not live in the holy land where tithing laws were applicable nor where the land on which a house stood was part of the holy land occupied by the Temple. For its authors, the study of Torah and its application to other aspects of life –

---

[22]The Houses contrast the am ha'arets to scholars in Berachot 52b, but clearly have amme ha'arets lemitzvot in mind in Hag. 22a-b, for example. Similarly, R. Judah talks about amme ha'arets lemitzvot in Pes. 42b, but about amme ha'arets letorah in Ned 20a. As a third example see Rabbi's remarks as regards amme ha'arets lemitzvot in Ber 47a and his remarks concerning amme ha'arets letorah in Ned. 14a.

civil law, commerce, etc. – become the vehicle for preserving Judaism.[23] This shift in concern is manifest in a number of ways. First is the lack in Gemara of a sustained effort to develop the laws of tithing and purity in the same way civil law, family law and festival law is developed. We do not in Talmud have an order of seeds or of purity. Second, is the nature of the books themselves. Mishnah primarily develops a system of practice. It has as its agenda more or less practical questions for which it proposes answers. Talmud on the other hand primarily develops a system of discourse, of argument. It teaches us how to think about law, how to ask questions of Scripture, how to adjudicate cases. This shift is carried over to the Talmud's conception of the quintessential outsider – the am ha'arets. For Gemara, this one now becomes the type person who does not care to know or to study properly the Torah and its oral tradition. It is a person, in short, who rejects that virtue which the Talmudic authors hold to be definitive of the model Jewish life. Thus as in the Mishnah the am ha'arets stands for the type of person who does not do what the rabbis regard as essential. The differences between the am ha'arets in these two texts points to the difference in what the rabbis in each case regarded as essential. The gemara's particular use of the "am ha'arets" image points not to an evolution within a social class but to a different understanding, on the part of the authors, of what constitutes true Judaism.

Judaism from Mishnah to Gemara has gone from being a particular sect (with a peculiar style of maintaining Temple purity) among other Jewish groups to an ethnic group living in a foreign and alien culture. In these two documents, the use of the signifier "am ha'arets" has undergone concomitant change, namely, from meaning one who refuses to keep Temple purity (or at least refuses to do so in what the authors regard as the proper way) to one who refuses (or is unable to) understand rabbinic law in all its applications. Through this change we can see at work an internal development that generated within Judaism two very different theories of, among other things, the ethical life.

The search for the historical am ha'arets, I believe, has diverted scholarly interest into an area that is ultimately arid. Even if we could identify such a social group and adduce a valid social definition of them, it would not help us understand emerging rabbinic Judaism. At best, describing such a social stratum can only give us some predictable answers about why certain classes of people might reject rabbinism. What I have tried to do here is indicate that a literary approach to the am ha'arets leads us into the core of rabbinic thinking about right

[23]See J. Neusner, "In Praise of the Talmud," in Alan Corre, *Understanding the Talmud* (N.Y.: KTAV, 1975), pp. 403ff.

and wrong, and so about the character of the good life to which Jews are called. If we see the am ha'arets as a literary devise used in the religious discourse established by rabbinic thinking, we gain insight into how the rabbinic estate at different times and different places conceptualized the nature of Judaism in the world, and the kind of life values they called on Jews to adopt. This in turn gives us a much more useful insight into the patterns of thought that give structure to the various forms of rabbinic ethics.

Part Eight

JUDAISM IN THE MIDDLE AGES: THE ENCOUNTER WITH CHRISTIANITY

24

The Christian Position in Jacob Ben Reuben's *Milḥamot Ha-Shem*

Robert Chazan
New York University

Narrated dialogue between representatives of two or more religious faiths or world views is one of the most popular literary forms for medieval polemical literature. This literary technique affords a number of obvious advantages for illuminating the superiority of one religious system over its competitors. In the first place, the narrated dialogue provides dramatic tension and interest. The excitement of intellectual jousting and the flow of argumentation hold the interest of the reader more readily than a straightforward and direct presentation of doctrine. The second advantage of this literary format is the interplay of thrust and parry. By setting the stage for claim, refutation, and counter-claim, this literary vehicle enables the author to present in greater depth, yet without unduly taxing the patience of the reader, the inevitable intricacies of religious argumentation.

In medieval western Christendom, major polemical works written in this style are known from both Christian and Jewish authors. Gilbert Crispin's *Disputatio Iudei et Christiani,* Peter Abelard's *Dialogus inter Philosophum, Iudaeum et Christianum,* or Raymond Lull's *Libre del gentil e dels tres savis* afford outstanding examples of exploitation of this literary technique by Christians. Medieval Jews were similarly aware of the advantages of the dialogue format. Probably the best known of medieval Jewish polemical works is Judah ha-Levi's *Kitāb al-Ḥujja waal-Dalīl fi Naṣr al-Dīn al-Dhalīl* (more popularly known as *Sefer ha-Kuzari*), written in extended dialogue form. Less well-known, but significant are Jacob ben Reuben's *Milḥamot ha-Shem,* the *Sefer ha-Berit,* attributed to Rabbi Joseph Kimḥi, and the dialogues in Rabbi Meir ben Simon's *Milḥemet Mizvah*.

In polemical dialogues, depiction of competing religious systems varies widely. In some instances there is serious grappling with these competing worldviews, with the author treating the spokesmen for these faiths with sympathy and dignity; in other cases the competition is simplistically lampooned. We might also note a distinction in fundamental arrangement of these literary encounters. On occasion debate is conducted among a number of spokesmen, each addressing a neutral outsider. This pattern of organization by and large tends to produce a fairly high-level and sympathetic presentation of the alternative faith systems. More frequently the clash takes place directly between representatives of two views, resulting often in fairly crude treatment by the author of the competing religion. An interesting and important exception to this general tendency is provided by Jacob ben Reuben's treatise, the *Milḥamot ha-Shem.*[1]

The importance of the *Milḥamot ha-Shem* has been noted by many observers, although it has not yet received the full treatment that it deserves.[2] It may well be the earliest Hebrew polemical work from medieval western Christendom, seemingly stemming from the middle decades of the twelfth century.[3] The backdrop to the emergence of Jewish polemical works at this juncture is of course the marked vitalization of Christian society that began during the latter decades of the tenth century and progressed with accelerating force through the eleventh and into the twelfth century. The *Milḥamot ha-Shem* is also important for containing the first significant translations and critique of materials from the New Testament. Chapter eleven of the book is devoted to a series of questions raised by the Jew, based on extensive citations in Hebrew from the Gospel of Matthew. David Berger, in his

---

[1]While I clearly lack the philosophic training and expertise to do full justice to Jacob ben Reuben's *Milḥamot ha-Shem,* the invitation to submit an essay to this volume in honor of Professor Marvin Fox emboldened me to make some preliminary observations on a text that has for many years fascinated me. I hope that my long-time colleague and friend will see in this preliminary study an expression of my esteem and warmth for him.

[2]Jacob ben Reuben's *Milḥamot ha-Shem* has been carefully edited by Judah Rosenthal (Jerusalem, 1963). Rosenthal's introduction to his edition of the text affords the fullest study of the work to date. Important also is David Berger, "Gilbert Crispin, Alan of Lille, and Jacob ben Reuben: A Study in the Transmission of Medieval Polemics," *Speculum* XLIX (1974): 34-47.

[3]On the dating, see Rosenthal's remarks in his introduction to the text, p. viii. *Sefer ha-Berit,* attributed to Rabbi Joseph Kimḥi, may be roughly contemporaneous to the *Milḥamot ha-Shem.*

valuable study of the *Milḥamot ha-Shem,* argued that it likewise provides the first Hebrew translations of medieval Christian polemical materials, selections from the aforementioned disputation penned by Gilbert Crispin.[4] I would suggest further that the *Milḥamot ha-Shem* merits serious examination of some of its salient characteristics. It adopts from the outset a tone of high intellectuality; it accords respectful consideration to the Christian point of view; its understanding of contemporary Christianity is clearly well grounded in the realities of twelfth-century Christian thought. I shall attempt to argue these characteristics in this brief examination of the dialogue.

Jacob begins his opus with a sharply focused and valuable introduction. In addition to spelling out his goals and the circumstances that gave rise to the composition, the author, *en passant,* alerts us to some of the qualities that will distinguish his work. He begins by delineating the concerns that led him to compose his polemical treatise. Convinced of the truth of Judaism but concerned with the danger of Christian inroads among his Jewish contemporaries, Jacob ben Reuben set out to compose a manual of Christian claims and Jewish rebuttals. After beginning his introductory remarks with emphasis on the unity of God, proven by both rational and scriptural testimony, Jacob ben Reuben attacks the Christian doctrines of Trinity and Incarnation, both of which contravene, for him, the unity of God. While, for the Jewish author, the error of Christian belief is patent, danger exists nonetheless.

> It is known to every rational being that it [Christian doctrine] is futile and pursuit of wind, so much so that the ear cannot hear it nor the eye see it. However, the mouth must report their arguments and claims to many of our people, for whom intelligence does not penetrate to the depths of their heart. We must be concerned lest their hearts be led astray when they hear the words of those in error [expounded] strongly and lies [expounded] vigorously. For they [the Christians] buttress their error subtly and they reinforce their deceitful ways with deception and untruth. They bring proofs from all the writings of our Torah, which never taught thus and never intended [such things]. For all these reasons we are obligated to fashion responses, to distinguish the language of truth from the expression of falsehood and to distinguish the essential from the peripheral, to destroy wicked constructs and to obliterate futile creations, through clear proofs and refutations.[5]

Thus, for Jacob ben Reuben, many of his fellow Jews, while possessed of the truth, stood in danger of being subverted by powerful – albeit

---

[4]Berger, "Gilbert Crispin, Alan of Lille, and Jacob ben Reuben."

[5]Jacob ben Reuben, *Milḥamot ha-Shem,* p. 4.

erroneous – Christian teaching. It was for the deflection of this pressure that Jacob composed his manual.

Jacob claims that, in fact, his own personal experience had contributed both to his desire and his capacity to write such an opus. This personal experience had included extended contact and conversation with a learned Christian cleric.

> There, in the place of my habitation, a certain Christian – one of the nobles of the city and one of the scholars of the generation – became enamored of me. Indeed he was a priest, accomplished in logic and learned in theology, except for the fact that our Creator had glazed his eyes that they not see and his heart that it not understand, so that his soul cleaved to its idolatry and his will and reason worshipped his sticks and stones. Since I was regularly with him, to learn from him wisdom and knowledge, he asked me, saying: "How long will you hesitate on the threshold and not concentrate your hearts to understand and your eyes to see and your ears to hear – you and all your brethren who are designated by the name of Jacob, who clearly are increasingly impoverished and humiliated and weakened, who decline in numbers daily, while we continue to grow, to the point where our horn stands high and our enemies are trampled under our feet and our allies are like the emergent sun in its strength. Now, if there is evil in your hand, remove it; but if there is truth on your lips, respond with it. Speak freely and fear not. I shall ask you and you shall inform me...." I inclined my ear to all his questions, I understood his claims, I directed my heart to hear and understand, to seek out and discover responses to his errors.[6]

There is, of course, no guarantee that the personal backdrop sketched by Jacob ben Reuben is in fact true. This could conceivably be merely a literary device. We have no way of checking the veracity of this statement, although there is surely nothing implausible in it. In any case, the personal portrait – whether real or fictitious – that emerges is an interesting one. It reinforces the general sense of Christian aggressiveness and Jewish defensiveness. It was his Christian associate who took the initiative and challenged the Jew to abandon his faith; it was the Christian who mounted arguments and the Jew who was put in the defensive posture, very much along the more general lines noted earlier.[7]

---

[6]*Ibid.*, pp. 4-5.

[7]In his fine study, "Mission to the Jews and Jewish-Christian Contacts in the Polemical Literature of the High Middle Ages," *American Historical Review* XCI (1986), 576-591, David Berger notes the recurrent claim on the part of Christian polemicists of Jewish aggressiveness in argumentation with Christians. It may well be that aggressiveness was manifested from both sides. It is also possible that justification of polemical literature impelled such portraits. That is to say, authors anxious to dispel any impression that writing

A number of important further elements emerge from the personal portrait as well. The relationship between the Christian and the Jew (again whether real or fictional) involves human warmth and intellectual respect. The Jew depicts himself as beloved of his Christian adversary and intellectually dependent upon him. It is the Christian who is the teacher of wisdom and the Jew who is his student. I suggest that this backdrop is useful in understanding some of the major characteristics of the dialogue. While the Jewish author is thoroughly convinced of the truth of his own religious faith and the error of Christian doctrine, he maintains the exchange on a fairly high level and relates respectfully throughout to his Christian adversary. The sense conveyed of an intellectually vital ambiance, with Christian and Jew studying seriously and at a high level together, is reflected in the broad sophistication of the work. This dialogue was penned by a man of erudition and the level at which the discussion is conducted is a high one. The human warmth and the intellectual sophistication suggested in the author's personal statement are in fact manifested throughout the opus. While in works of this kind there is an inevitable pull toward presenting the opposition as weak and laughable, the Christian spokesman in the *Milḥamot ha-Shem* – as we shall see – is made to speak at length and persuasively. In a number of instances he is portrayed as mounting strong counter-arguments to the Jew's case. In a general way, he is portrayed sympathetically and is never reduced to a stock figure. Finally the personal reflections in the introduction suggest that the Jewish author had first-hand experience of the twelfth-century European intellectual ambiance and that the Christianity depicted in his *oeuvre* is likely to correspond to the realities of Christian thinking at that particular juncture.

The work is organized into twelve chapters. The first deals with "proofs that he [the Christian] brought from reason, not from Scripture, rather from the depth of the heart."[8] The subsequent nine chapters involve proofs based on verses in a series of biblical books, with the Christian again mounting his claims and the Jew rebutting. Only in the closing two chapters does the Jew speak independently. In order to illustrate the tone, the fullness of depiction of Christianity, and the accuracy of that depiction, we shall emphasize the first chapter, drawing only occasional data from the rest of the book.

The intellectual tone that we have surmised from the introductory observations of Jacob ben Reuben is in fact borne out by the rest of the

---

polemics bespeaks lack of certainty on their own part shift the focus by invoking the aggressive other in explaining the genesis of their works.

[8]Jacob ben Reuben, *Milḥamot ha-Shem*, p. 7.

composition. We might note immediately that the first of the twelve chapters deals with claims for the truth of Christianity drawn from rational considerations and with the Jewish rebuttals of these claims. Throughout this initial chapter there is heavy emphasis on the importance of rationality and recurrent utilization of technical philosophic terminology and argumentation. When we turn to the second chapter, which initiates the arguments drawn from close examination of Scriptures, we are again struck by the insistence on a high intellectual tone. Rather than plunging into immediate discussion of biblical verses, the Christian is made to open with a methodological statement as to how the biblical text must be read. Thus, in general, the promise of serious intellectual exchange held out in the introductory remarks is in fact realized throughout Jacob's opus.

More interesting yet is the Jewish author's commitment to a full presentation of both the Christian and Jewish points of view. Let us illustrate with a close look at the central issues that play through the first chapter. This chapter opens with a lengthy and compelling speech placed in the mouth of the Christian adversary by the Jewish author. The Jewish author allows his Christian antagonist to emerge as a man of religious sensitivity and intelligence, with whose views to be sure the Jewish author disagrees.

> At the beginning I shall begin to speak and to elucidate concerning the [being who is the] beginning of all beginnings and the first whom nothing precedes. I shall offer a prayer to the end of all ends. I believe and acknowledge concerning him that he created everything from nothing and was created for the redemption of his creatures at the time of his choosing. He created all that has been created and was created in the form of flesh at the proper time as one of us, in order to save his creatures from descending to Hell, but not for his own sake, for he is in need of nothing. I – who have been set apart from the vanities of the world on his behalf and who fasts and dresses in black so that he might set me aside for the knowledge of truth – know that he brings into being and was brought into being, that he is the father and the son, that he is the one who is designated as two and became three, that trinity does not disrupt unity, and that unity does not contradict trinity....Knowledge of these matters is beyond most of mankind who do not understand the issue in a fundamental way. However, to all men of discernment and understanding the matters of the godhead are sweeter than oil and purer than milk. I shall show you these things through the understanding of the intellect, for every man of understanding must believe truly in the worship of the Trinity. I shall bring you proofs from created things, so that you understand through them the greatness of the Creator. Through his wonders you shall comprehend and know some of his majesty.[9]

---

[9]*Ibid.*, pp. 7-8.

The Christian protagonist concludes his opening speech with the first of a series of metaphors intended to illuminate Christian doctrine. In this instance the image is one of a burning coal, which is a unity and, at the same time, separable into matter, fire, and flame.

The Jewish response to this opening statement is to agree with part of the Christian statement and to highlight the area of disagreement. The Jew is quite comfortable with the notion of God as without beginning and end, utterly beyond the influence of time, and the creator of all things. These are fundamental beliefs which the Jew is pleased to share with his Christian friend and adversary. What is not acceptable to the Jew, of course, is the notion of God as a created being, whatever the purposes of such createdness might be. To the Jew the notion of fashioning of the divinity into human form entailed a series of implications that are unacceptable to reason.

> All the philosophers and men of reason ridicule you and ask concerning this [the notion of fashioning of God into human form]. If the Creator, may he be blessed, was created, tell me if he was created prior to his existence or subsequent to his existence? If prior to his existence, then you have contradicted yourself, for you said that he was the beginning of all beginnings and the first without precedent. If you say that subsequent to his existence he was fashioned in fleshly form at the time that he willed, then during that time [the interval between his existence and his emergence in fleshly form] he lacked flesh and bones and sinews which he received at the time that you suggest and that is not correct.[10]

This same tack is taken in slightly altered form, with an emphasis on the semantic.

> Now tell me both from your reason and your belief: Was he called "the son" prior to his birth or subsequent to his birth? If you say prior to this birth,, this is not possible, for there is nothing in the world for whom the term "son" can be used prior to its birth. Rather subsequent to his birth he was called "the son." If this is so, then your words are found to be untrue. For you said that unity does not diverge from trinity. But, on this occasion, surely that time that he existed prior to being born from the womb of a virgin, his unity was not equivalent to trinity, rather it was a duality, for the designation "son" had not yet been applied to him.[11]

The Jewish thrusts are not original. They do, however, indicate an author – and an anticipated audience – that is sophisticated and erudite. The terminology reflects, as we have suggested, substantial immersion in philosophic discussion and issues.

---

[10]*Ibid.*, pp. 8-9.
[11]*Ibid.*, p. 9.

What is yet more striking is the full response which the Jewish author provides for his Christian antagonist. While the issue might well have been dropped at this juncture, with the Jewish protagonist clearly and simply victorious, the Christian is made to present a well formulated counter-statement. In this speech, the Christian argues that in fact the deity stands altogether outside the normal categories of time, thereby depriving the Jew's case of all its force.

> You said that, all that time that he [the divinity] existed prior to the time that he willed to take on fleshly form and human appearance, unity was not equivalent to trinity, for the designation "son" had not been initiated for him. What you have said is pointless. For one of the created beings over which time passes, it is possible to give the response that you have given, namely that the mouth cannot use the designation "son" except for what the eye sees as having been born and exiting into the atmosphere. For time passes over us, sometimes in ways that are obvious and sometimes in ways that are not obvious until the time comes for the thing to appear. But with respect to the Creator, may he be blessed, you and all who comprehend the findings of reason must understand that all this world – before it was created and subsequent to being created – and all created things – those that were created and that will be created – and all that has passed and all that is fated to pass stand before the view of the Creator as he looks upon us. Indeed you testified concerning him that time does not pass over him.[12]

Thus the Christian is made to argue that the categories of time simply do not apply to the divinity, thereby stripping the Jewish claim of its impact. What is so striking is the willingness of the Jewish author to accord such a follow-up statement to an antagonist whose views he is attempting to rebut. Clearly the Jewish author chose not to take the low road of ready dismissal of Christian claims. Instead he was willing to extend the argument and accord the Christian position significant consideration. There is of course no hint that this reflects serious doubts on the part of the Jewish author. It seems to reflect, rather, the ambiance within which he moved, an ambiance of real give-and-take, and a sense that Jewish readers should be equipped to meet sophisticated Christian argumentation.

The Jew is of course provided with the last word. In his speech he claims that, by virtue of accepting earthly form, the divinity thereby subsumed itself under the categories of material existence, including the category of temporality.

> You said that, with respect to created things, over which time passes, it is possible to respond as I did to you. However, with respect to the Creator it is not possible. For time does not pass over him and

---

[12]*Ibid.*, p. 11.

> accident and contingency do not adhere. However, at time that he willed, when you say that he descended to earth and was fashioned in our form, it is proper to respond that time changes for him from one category to another. Indeed when he reached the gates of death, surely he was affected by accident and contingency.[13]

What the reader is left with is something of a standoff, with the Christian claiming that the categories of time and contingency do not apply to the divinity at all, either in its other-worldly or in its this-worldly form. The Jew, on the other hand, argues that, upon taking human form, the divinity would be subjected to normal categories of time and contingency and that, as a result, Christian doctrine proves to be logically absurd. While the Jewish author has surely raised an important issue and projected a powerful Jewish stand, he has refrained from creating a Christian straw-man opponent. Instead he has fashioned for the Christian spokesman a reasonable set of arguments, in particular a strong rebuttal to the initial Jewish thrust.

The issue of the inherent logic of the doctrines of Incarnation and Trinity is, at this juncture, abandoned, and Jacob ben Reuben turns his attention in another, albeit related, direction. This tack involves the basis asserted by the Christian spokesman for the need for Incarnation. The Jewish protagonist alters the direction of the discussion with the following observations:

> I shall further respond to what you have said, namely that the world lacked the capacity to be saved from Satan until he [the divinity] passed into the womb of the virgin. Indeed you are correct, that the world lacked the capacity, however the Creator has the capacity to save his world, for he had already created it ex nihilo....Subsequent to creation, when all was created according to his will, how could one of his creatures bring him to the point of control, so that he could not save the rest of his creatures from his [Satan's] hands, until he was born like one of us and turned himself over to him [Satan] on our behalf, so that he was crucified and they were saved? Indeed we have not even seen this salvation. For in the very same way that Satan killed the created beings, similarly he still kills them.[14]

The Jewish claim that God's omnipotence is compromised by the notion of Incarnation as the only means for saving mankind from the grasp of Satan constitutes the second and last major issue confronted in the first chapter of *Milḥamot ha-Shem.* The Christian attempts to build his case for the need for such action by emphasizing the inscrutability of divine behavior. Let us gain a sense of this set of exchanges by looking at the earliest in the series. The Christian begins

---

[13]*Ibid.*, p. 12.
[14]*Ibid.*, pp. 12-13

his response by once more identifying points of agreement. Like the Jews he believes fully in creation *ex nihilo,* in a world that God fashioned entirely according to this will. Like the Jew, he affirms that God

> created everything in six days and on the seventh day he rested. Regarding the basis for that resting I have a question for you. Indeed it has been readied by me until the appropriate time for its asking. Tell me, while the Creator, may he blessed, created his world in six days, who forced him so that he not create it in one day?...Indeed this world of ours has existed for only a short time from the point of its creation till now, [a time] which has not yet reached five thousand years according to your reckoning. Who forced the Creator that he not create it [the world] a long time previously, prior to our being? You ask, how did one of his creatures bring to the point of control; then tell me, who brought him to all these points of control? Rather you must acknowledge that everything developed in his will so that it be done in such fashion. No force was exerted upon him. It is not our place to ask the reason for his deeds, for everything was according to his will. Thus, just as all these things [creation of the world in six days, resting on the seventh, creation of the world at a precise time] were done according to his will, so too it was his will and intention to save his world in this manner. It is not our place to ask why.[15]

Jacob ben Reuben's Jewish spokesman acknowledges the principle of God's freedom of action. He draws, however, an important distinction. While God's freedom of action is not circumscribed, there are styles of action that can be reasonably attributed to the divine and others that are so remote from his nature that to attribute them to God is erroneous. To elucidate the Jew resorts to a parable.

> An earthly king goes out at the time when kings go out, dressed in royal finery, with a golden crown on his head and his officers and troops running before him. He deals with them in all the matters of the kingdom. There is in such behavior nothing surprising. We need not ask why....
>
> On another occasion the king rises from his throne, removes his royal apparel, puts on sackcloth and ash, and walks about barefooted. He sits in a place closed off from light. All his officers who sit before him and his servants stand about and look and tremble mightily and are astounded. They place their hands on their mouths. They stride to and fro. All of them whisper and gossip and ask, "What is this and why is our lord the king no longer like yesterday and the day before?" Why all this astonishment? Because it is not the way of kings to behave mournfully and to seat themselves in the recesses of darkness. Now tell me, why did they tremble and react with astonishment over the mournful behavior while they did not tremble and react with

---

[15]*Ibid.,* pp. 14-15.

> astonishment over the imperious and royal behavior? Rather, whether you wish or not, one is appropriate behavior and the other is not.[16]

We might note that the argument has evolved away from issues of pure logic into the realm of appropriate metaphors. The Jew has contended that the Christian set of metaphors is ultimately inappropriate to the majesty of the divine.

Once more Jacob ben Reuben does not create a passive Christian partner to the dialogue. He allows the Christian disputant again to make a strong counter-claim, advancing his own metaphor for appropriate divine behavior.

> Now in the same fashion of an allegory shall I respond, [an allegory] of a king of flesh and blood who has a son born in his old age, intended to reign after him and to occupy the throne of his kingdom. He [the son] is handsome and pleasant, respected by all creatures. He went out to play with his fellows. When his chariot began to run the course of the race, it happened to fall into the bog of dirt and clay. There it sank to its extremities. Following him all the lads who were with him fell into the bog. Those wishing to help were powerless and failed to assist. None had the requisite strength to aid his fellow. The scout on the city tower saw all these things and cried out loudly, sounding the horn that indicated: "Assist the prince who is sinking in the bog." The king trembled at the report. He went forth by foot, thoroughly discomforted. He went to the bog, he quickly removed his shoes, and he entered the dirt, to save his son. He did not wait for the assistance of his servants, because the lad was beloved to him. [He strove] until he extricated him [the prince]. You should attend carefully to this matter. There is in it no cause for astonishment. There is no cause to ask for a reason. For the hour and the circumstance brought about that it be done this way, even though it is not normally the manner of kings to do such a thing, to go our into dirt and clay.[17]

The Christian's point is clear: The metaphor of a concerned God is as reasonable as the metaphor of a majestic God. Once again Jacob ben Reuben accords the last word to his Jewish protagonist. However, also once more he has accorded his Christian disputant a dignified role and has set up a clash that does not resolve itself decisively into right and wrong. On both of the major issues that play through the first chapter of *Milḥamot ha-Shem* the Jewish author has argued vigorously for the Jewish point of view, while at the same time refraining from lampooning the Christian point of view. To the contrary, on both issues he accords the Christian argumentation an extended and full hearing. Again the introductory report of extensive and sympathetic contact

---

[16]*Ibid.*, p. 16.
[17]*Ibid.*, p. 18.

between the Christian cleric-teacher and the Jewish polemicist-student is amply demonstrated within Jacob's narrative.[18]

Finally I suggested that the same introductory remarks imply a Jewish author who was well aware of contemporary currents of thought in Christian society. This implication is realized in the body of the text as well. As noted early on, Jacob in the first place provides us with the first substantial translation and critique of New Testament materials in medieval western Christendom, indication of a man who was aware of much more than internal Jewish folklore concerning Christian belief. David Berger's insightful analysis of materials that appear in parallel form in Gilbert Crispin, Jacob ben Reuben, and Alan of Lille shows clearly that Jacob ben Reuben was aware of more than Christian Scriptures – he was conversant as well with medieval Christian polemical literature. This is surely not the norm for medieval Jewish polemicists, particularly at this early juncture in time.

Both the substance and the style of the *Milḥamot ha-Shem* confirm the Jewish author's immersion in the intellectual environment of the twelfth century. We have already noted that the first chapter of this polemical dialogue is devoted to proofs adduced from rationality. Given the more normal predilection for religious discussion based on scriptural grounds, the very organization of the work, with its opening devoted to rational argumentation, alerts us to the general ambiance of late-eleventh- and twelfth-century western Christendom. This was, after all, the very period in which new forms of argumentation and speculation were transforming broad areas of traditional teaching and doctrine. That Jacob ben Reuben chose to begin his work as he did suggest strongly his awareness of and immersion in the new cultural environment of his period.

In this first chapter, the first issue addressed is the Trinity, with the Christian claiming the rationality of this doctrine and the Jew mounting arguments against its reasonability. The reasonability of the doctrine of the Trinity is indeed a major concern of late-eleventh- and twelfth-century Christian thought. Anselm, with whom the aforecited Gilbert Crispin enjoyed important intellectual links, set out as a major objective of his late writing to address in rational terms the doctrine of the Trinity. It was the dialectical implications of this doctrine that formed the essence of the challenge mounted by the secular master Roscelin, necessitating on the part of Anselm the composition of his *De*

---

[18]By way of contrast we might note the simplistic presentation of the Christian position in such works as *Sefer ha-Berit* or in the dialogues in the *Milḥemet Mizṿah*.

Incarnatione Verbi.[19] The issues involved in this important internal Christian dispute were much the same as those aired by the Christian and Jewish protagonists in *Milḥamot ha-Shem* – the reasonability of the teaching of three persons and one substance. Jacob ben Reuben has not created an internal Jewish caricature of Christian doctrine with which to interact; he is aware of the issues on the Christian agenda, introduces them, and mounts against standard eleventh- and twelfth-century Christian claims his own Jewish counter-arguments.

The same is true for the second major issue confronted in the first chapter of Jacob's opus, the doctrine of Incarnation. R. W. Southern in particular has noted the importance of the Jewish opposition to this doctrine in the energetic effort of key Christian theologians like Anselm to construct meaningful rationales for the necessity for incarnation of the divine in human form.[20] Here we might note an interesting curiosity. While in the second chapter of the *Milḥamot ha-Shem* Jacob borrows from Gilbert Crispin, in the first chapter he underplays the somewhat older stance of Crispin on Incarnation in favor of emphasis on a position closer to the important innovation of Anselm. I refer to the differing views between these two friends and colleagues on the manner in which incarnation of the deity functions in overcoming Satan's control of mankind. According to the traditional view repeated by Crispin, it was only by tricking the Devil into taking into his control the sinless deity that the hold of the Devil over humanity could be eliminated. Anselm broke with this traditional view of Incarnation, emphasizing instead the impact of the willingness of the God-Man for sacrifice. According to Anselm, it was that willingness – not legal niceties – that broke Satan's power over mankind. During the late eleventh and twelfth century, the new Anselmian position displaced the older view represented by Crispin, among others.[21] Indeed, Jacob's Christian protagonist is made to explicate a position roughly akin to that of Anselm on this issue. As in the Anselmian position, stress is placed on the deity's essential desire to save mankind from its predicament. As we have seen, the image is that of a king who is willing to compromise his honor and sully himself physically by descending into the mud in order to save his beloved son from disaster.[22] While this image does not by any means capture the complexities of Anselm's position as laid out in *Cur Deus Homo*, it is

---

[19]There is a voluminous literature on Anselm. See in particular the magisterial analysis of R. W. Southern, *Saint Anselm and His Biographer* (Cambridge, 1963). On the dispute between Roscelin and Anselm, see pp. 77-82.
[20]*Ibid.*, pp. 88-91.
[21]*Ibid.*, pp. 93-121.
[22]See above.

certainly closer to the Anselmian formulation than to the earlier view which Anselm contested. More important, this exchange again suggests that the Jewish author was in fact quite *au courant* with the major streams in Christian thinking at this juncture.

Finally even the use of metaphors and parables, while in many ways quite traditional in Jewish thinking, shows remarkable similarity to the argumentational style of the late eleventh and twelfth century. The writing of Anselm, for example, abounds in the use of images drawn from feudal realities, images that are much like the parables which pervade both the Christian and Jewish presentations in the first chapter of the *Milḥamot ha-Shem*. Here too the sense is that Jacob was fully immersed in the intellectual environment of the twelfth century and that the issues with which he chose to deal and the style in which he addressed these issues stem from that vibrant period in the history of European Christendom and its Jewish minority.

This is far from a complete study of Jacob ben Reuben's *Milḥamot ha-Shem*. I have attempted only to alert others to the enormous interest of a work insufficiently analyzed heretofore. Jacob ben Reuben's dialogue represents an unusual achievement in its broad sophistication, its full treatment of the opposing viewpoint, and its clear reflections of contemporary intellectual issues and trends. Whether these characteristics flow from an actual relationship of the kind depicted in Jacob's introductory remarks or not, they suggest a Jew open to his general environment in unusual measure. A thorough study of this important treatise, done out of full appreciation of the major intellectual currents of the late eleventh and twelfth centuries would, I contend, bear rich rewards. I hope that this exploratory investigation might stimulate a colleague or advanced student to accord the *Milḥamot ha-Shem* the full attention that it so richly merits.

Part Nine

JUDAISM IN THE MIDDLE AGES: THE ENCOUNTER WITH SCRIPTURE

25

Tradition or Context: Two Exegetes Struggle with Peshat[1]

Martin I. Lockshin
York University

The twelfth century was an exciting one in the field of Jewish Bible interpretations. Many literary works of a lasting nature were produced. Many different authors, some bolder and some more conservative, were attempting to apply the idea of peshat – the attempt to uncover the plain, contextual meaning of the biblical text – to the exegetical enterprise.

Curiously, peshat exegesis was flourishing in the Jewish world at the same time in two very different arenas – in Moslem Spain and in Northern France. The cultural and intellectual gulf that separated these two Jewish communities was formidable. The intellectual Jews of Moslem Spain thrived on philosophy; the leaders of the Jewish community in Northern France weren't quite sure what a philosopher was.[2] Sephardic interests in such areas as secular poetry, the study of natural sciences or the field of comparative semitics find no direct parallels in twelfth-century Ashkenaz.

And yet in the twelfth century, Jews – both in Moslem Spain and in Northern France – began to take seriously the idea of peshat biblical exegesis, the idea that it is possible and worthwhile to try to determine the simple meaning of a biblical text without making use of

[1]This article is dedicated to my teacher, Professor Marvin Fox, who guided me in my studies of medieval biblical exegesis, who supervised my doctoral dissertation on Rashbam and who taught me the true value of peshat.
[2]See Tos. Shabbat 116a, s.v. *philosopha'*.

traditional midrashic exegesis.[3] There is no reason to assume that one of these Jewish communities borrowed or imported the concept of peshat from the other. There is a history in each community of fledgling interest in peshat, developing independently, well before the twelfth century.[4]

The two twelfth-century *pashṭanim* who left the most popular and lasting literary legacies were Abraham ibn Ezra, originally from Moslem Spain, and Samuel ben Meir (Rashbam) from Northern France. They wrote their commentaries at the same time, they read and reacted to many of the same earlier Jewish works[5] and they reached conclusions that were often, but not always, quite similar to each other's. Still Margaliot[6] has argued well that it is most reasonable to see their works as independent – i.e. that Rashbam probably wrote all his works without ever seeing ibn Ezra's works and that ibn Ezra wrote the grand majority of his exegetical works without seeing Rashbam's. When two *pashṭanim* reach the same interpretive conclusion, argues Margaliot, there is no cause for surprise and no reason to posit any influence.

While Rashbam and ibn Ezra both blazed new trails in exegesis they knew that in many ways their works would be seen as derivative of the works of Rashbam's maternal grandfather, Rashi, who, justifiably or not, owned then (and owns still now in many circles) the reputation of being the founder and greatest practitioner of the art of peshat exegesis. Both Rashbam and ibn Ezra pointed out to their

---

[3]Defining what peshat exegesis really meant for various Jewish authors is a very difficult task. See the excellent summary and critique of the scholarly positions in Sarah Kamin's *Rashi: Peshuṭo shel miqra' umidrasho shel miqra'* (Jerusalem, 1986).

For the purposes of this paper it is sufficient to say what peshat exegesis is not. In this study of Rashbam and ibn Ezra, the term peshat will be used to describe exegetical conclusions reached without recourse to traditional midrashic exegesis.

[4]See the historical overviews of N. Sarna, "Hebrew and Bible Studies in Medieval Spain," in *The Sephardi Heritage*, ed. by R. Barnett (London, 1971), pp. 323-366 and by S. Poznanski *"Mavo' `al ḥakhme ṣorfat mefarshe ha-miqra',"* in his *Perush `al yeḥezkel utere `asar lerabbi Eliezer mi-Beaugency* (Warsaw, 1913).

[5]For lists of sources used by these two exegetes, see D. Rosin's introduction to his edition of Rashbam's commentary (Breslau, 1881/2), pp. xxiii-xxxii and Rosin's *R. Samuel ben Meir als Schrifterklärer* (Breslau, 1880; henceforth RSBM), pp. 57-77; and Y. Krinski's introduction to his *Meḥoqeqe Yehudah* (Reprint edition: Jerusalem, 1961/2), pp. 33-45 and A. Weiser's introduction to his *Ibn Ezra `al ha-Torah*, vol. 1 (Jerusalem, 1976), pp. 59-71.

[6]E. Margaliot, *"Ha-yaḥas she-ben perush ha-Rashbam leferush ha-Ra'va` `al ha-Torah,"* in *Sefer 'Asaf*, ed. by U. Cassuto (Jerusalem, 1953), pp. 357-369.

readers that Rashi's works were not the be all and end all of peshat exegesis and that something was left for them to accomplish. Rashbam delicately claimed that his grandfather had himself admitted that his commentary was incomplete and required revision.[7] Ibn Ezra more audaciously wrote:

> The later generations have made midrash into the primary and most important concern. For example, the late Rabbi Solomon [i.e. Rashi] wrote a commentary on the Bible following [standard] midrashic methods. He thought that his commentary was following peshat methods but only one comment out of a thousand in his works represents peshat. Contemporary scholars take great delight in such works.[8]

So both Rashbam and ibn Ezra shared the realization that, as *pashṭanim,* they were living in the shadow of Rashi and that they had to argue for the need for their own works to be written.

While there are many possible areas of comparison between the works of Rashbam and of ibn Ezra, this paper will concentrate on the way these two scholars offered explanations of legal passages in the Bible in a way that is at odds both with traditional exegesis and with halakhah. Traditional Jews, both medieval and modern, have often felt that more latitude can be given to a commentator to be innovative when dealing with narrative passages that have no legal ramifications.[9] Rashbam and ibn Ezra agreed, on some level, with that premise and exercised some restraint when dealing with legal passages, as I shall argue below. But they went farther than any other rabbanite Jews of their time in offering novel non-halakhic interpretations of biblical passages.

They did not, to be sure, create the field of non-halakhic peshat. Even Rashi occasionally interpreted a legal passage not according to its standard halakhic interpretation.[10] Nevertheless, the sheer volume of non-halakhic peshat in Rashbam and ibn Ezra's works is unprecedented.

---

[7]Rashbam's commentary to Gen. 37:2.

[8]*Safah berurah,* ed. by G. Lippmann (Furth, 1839), p. 5a.

[9]See e.g. Joseph Bonfils' defense of Abraham ibn Ezra's heterodox views about the authorship of Gen. 12:6, *"...ve'af ki bedavar she-'enennu miṣvah raq sippur devarim she-`averu,"* cited in N. Leibowitz's *Limmud parshane ha-miqra' uderakhim lehora'atam* (Jerusalem, 1975), pp. 221-222 and M. Mendelssohn's introduction to his Torah commentary where his admiration for Rashbam's loyalty to peshat clearly does not extend to Rashbam's approach to legal passages.

[10]See e.g. Rashi's comm. to Ex. 23:2 or his preference for Shamai's view over Hillel's (see Besah 16a) in his comm. to Ex. 20:8.

There are times when ibn Ezra and Rashbam both offer the same interpretation and both acknowledge that they are diverging from rabbinic opinion. Exodus 22:13-14 says that when a borrowed animal becomes injured or dies, the borrower is responsible, unless "its owner was with it." The talmudic discussion of this passage considers and rejects the plain meaning of the text.[11] According to the Talmud, responsibility for the damages is in no way dependent on the place where the owner was when the damages took place. Rashi's Torah commentary simply reiterates that talmudic position. Rashbam and ibn Ezra, though, both write that "according to the peshat" the borrower is absolved of responsibility when the owner of the animal is actually physically "with" the animal.[12] Rashbam unabashedly uses the phrase, *bimelekhet 'otah behemah,* echoing the language used by the Talmud to summarize the position that it ultimately rejects.

In a similar manner, following the plain meaning of Deut. 25:6, *yaqum `al shem 'aḥiv,* the son who is born from a levirate marriage should bear the name of his deceased uncle. The Talmud[13] acknowledges that this interpretation is the plain, contextual interpretation[14] but frontally rejects this conclusion because of a non-contextual application of the hermeneutic principle of *gezerah shavah*[15] (thereby not requiring the son to bear the same name). Rashi again toes the talmudic line while Rashbam and ibn Ezra[16] again offer the peshat explanation, without apologies.

At times only one of these *pashṭanim* offers a non-traditional interpretation, while the other remains silent. For example, the rabbis use the beginning of Exodus 13:7, "no leavened bread should be found with you *(lekha),*" to prove that a non-Jew living among Jews may own

---

[11]BM 95b. See the position of Rabbi Himnuna there, which is rejected on that same page.

[12]In his shorter commentary to Exodus (Y. Fleischer's edition [Vienna, 1925/6], p. 183), ibn Ezra suggests that what the rabbis said is "also true" *(gam hu' nakhon).* In his longer commentary he mentions only the peshat interpretation.

[13]Yevamot 24a.

[14]Or, at least, pashṭeh *[diqera'].* See Kamin's discussion of the meaning of this term in classical rabbinic literature, in her *Rashi,* pp. 32-48.

[15]*`Al shem* in Gen. 48:6 refers to inheritance laws and not to the naming of children, so too *`al shem* in this verse must refer only to inheritance laws.

[16]Rashbam's use of the phrase, *lefi ha-peshaṭ,* makes it clear that he knows that the Talmud came to a different conclusion. There is no similar qualifier in ibn Ezra's commentary. The possibility that ibn Ezra does not realize the heterodoxy of his own interpretation cannot be ignored. See the discussion below about the extent of ibn Ezra's knowledge of halakhah.

ḥameṣ on Passover (*"'aval 'attah ro'eh shel 'aḥerim")*.[17] In his longer commentary to that verse, ibn Ezra cites the end of the verse, "no leaven shall be found in all your territory *(bekhol gevulekha),"* to prove the opposite conclusion, that a non-Jew living among Jews must not eat *ḥameṣ* around Jews. In the same comment, ibn Ezra writes that a *ger toshav* living among Jews must observe the Sabbath, again contradicting the talmudic law.[18] Neither of these halakhically anomalous interpretations is found in Rashbam.

Rashbam, but not ibn Ezra, reacts to the troubling inclusion of *baqar* in Deuteronomy 16:2 in an apparent reference to the paschal sacrifice (which, following Exodus 12:5, had to be a sheep or goat) by trading one religious problem for another. He suggests that the word actually refers to those free-will offerings that can be offered on Passover and other festivals, "for, according to the peshat, they used to bring their *nedarim* and *nedavot* on pilgrimage festivals." Rashbam knows that the Talmud says the precise opposite – that "everyone" concedes that nedarim and nedavot cannot be offered on a festival[19] but that does not stop him. (Perhaps he finds a conflict between two passages in the Written Law – one in Deuteronomy and one in Exodus – more troubling than a conflict between a passage in the Written Law and one in the Talmud.)

Similarly a man who lets his livestock graze on someone else's property must make restitution that accords with *meṭav sadehu* (Exodus 22:4). Rabbi Ishmael, in the Talmud,[20] suggests that *sadehu* refers to the field that was damaged, yielding the sense "he shall pay according to the quality of the damaged field." Rabbi Aqiva, whose opinions are considered authoritative,[21] explains that *sadehu* refers to the field of the person whose animal caused the damage – i.e. "he shall pay from the best of his own fields." Rashi naturally follows Rabbi Aqiva. Ibn Ezra's position is unclear.[22] Rashbam outlines the accepted rabbinic opinion and then tells his readers what the peshat is – the position suggested in the Talmud by Rabbi Ishmael.[23]

---

[17]Pesahim 5b.

[18]Of Sanhedrin 58b, which forbids a non-Jew from observing the Sabbath.
See also ibn Ezra's shorter commentary to Ex. 20:10 (Fleischer's edition, p. 144).

[19]"Divre ha-kol." Besah 19a.

[20]BQ 6b.

[21]*Halakhah ke-rabbi `Aqiva' me-ḥavero* (Eruvin 46b and passim).

[22]In his longer commentary he says nothing. In his shorter commentary, in a pericope difficult to understand, he seems to try to have it both ways.

[23]Actually, Rashbam's position is even more cavalier here. The opinion that he follows is not only that of an unauthoritative *tanna'*, Rabbi Ishmael, it is also, according to the Talmud, the wrong way of understanding what Rabbi Ishmael

Neither Rashbam nor ibn Ezra was a Karaite and there are definite limits to their willingness to offer non-halakhic interpretations. Neither is willing to suggest that the Torah's words (Exodus 21:29) that "the owner [of an ox, with a reputation for goring, who kills a man], too, shall be put to death" are to be taken literally. They must mean only that *God* will put him to death.[24] Similarly, "an eye for an eye" (Exodus 21:24), according to our *pashṭanim,* could not possibly be understood literally.[25] Each insists on saying, following the Mekhilta,[26] that some of the laws referring to slaves in Exodus 21 refer to Jewish slaves while others refer to non-Jewish slaves – although the text uses the same word, *`eved,* for both.[27] Both claim, again following the Mekhilta,[28] that the word *uvishalta,* relating to the paschal sacrifice, means roasting.[29] (The rabbinic abandonment of the peshat of Deuteronomy 16:7 is based on a desire to adhere to the peshat of Exodus 12:8-9, where roasting is described as the only legitimate way to prepare the sacrificial meat.) There are other examples. They say that the paschal sacrifice was to be slaughtered any time shortly after noon, despite the text's use of the term *ben ha-`arbayim.*[30] Neither is willing to consider the possibility of a woman slave becoming a "slave in perpetuity" despite the straightforward meaning of the words, "Do the same with your female slave."[31] In short, on many occasions both our *pashṭanim* prefer to follow standard rabbinic exegesis of legal passages and *not* the peshat.

Ibn Ezra at times allows his readers to see his processes of exegesis – of weighing the peshat against the traditional interpretation. The Torah writes that a criminal deserves to be flogged *kede rish`ato bemispar* (Deut. 25:2). It would be reasonable, says ibn Ezra, to interpret that phrase as meaning that the severity of the crime should determine the number of lashes given. However, continues ibn Ezra, we have learned from tradition, the only reliable source of truth, that

---

really meant. See the question of Rava' and the "more correct" understanding of Rabbi Ishmael's position proposed by R. Aha b. Jacob in BQ *ibid.*

[24]Following Mekhilta *Neziqin* 10 (J. Lauterbach's edition [Philadelphia, 1935], vol. 3, pp. 85-86) and Sanh. 15b.

[25]Following Mekhilta *Neziqin* 8 (Lauterbach's edition, vol. 3, pp. 67-68) and BQ 83b-84a. See further discussion of ibn Ezra's attitude to these verses below.

[26]*Neziqin* 6 (Lauterbach's edition, vol. 3, pp. 56-58).

[27]See both commentaries ad Exodus 21:20, for example.

[28]*Pisḥa'* 6 (Lauterbach edition, vol. 1, p. 49).

[29]See Deut 16:7 and Rashbam and ibn Ezra, there.

[30]See Ex. 12:6, Mekhilta *Pisḥa'* 5 (Lauterbach's edition, vol. 1, p. 43), both of ibn Ezra's commentaries to Ex. 12:6, and Rashbam ad Ex. 23:18.

[31]Deut. 15:17 and see Qiddushin 17b.

See also similarly Rashbam and ibn Ezra ad Ex. 21:11.

that is not the case.[32] Similarly, according to ibn Ezra, many thought to interpret the phrase *ha-davar ha-zeh* in Exodus 12:24 as referring, as context seems to require, to the ceremony of applying blood to the doorposts and lintel. Using only logical criteria, continues ibn Ezra, that interpretation would be correct, but the true tradition[33] tells us otherwise.

While ibn Ezra writes such statements about tradition outweighing peshat only on a few verses in his commentary, it is reasonable to assume that both he and Rashbam went through such a process – of determining peshat and then setting it aside for the sake of tradition – on numerous occasions. As shown above, there are many passages where Rashbam and ibn Ezra both follow the halakhic line. On the other hand it is clear that neither does so consistently. As shown above, there are many passages where Rashbam, ibn Ezra or both of them suggest non-halakhic readings of legal texts.

Neither *pashṭan* advances an explanation of when he will be willing and when he will be unwilling to offer non-halakhic readings of legal texts. To my mind, no objective criteria for such distinctions can be unearthed in either exegete's works. Why would Rashbam be willing to offer a non-halakhic explanation of the laws of borrowing animals (ad Exodus 22:13-14) but not of the laws of "slaves in perpetuity" (Deuteronomy 15:17)? How could ibn Ezra explain his willingness to offer a non-halakhic – even an anti-halakhic[34] – interpretation (that a *ger toshav* is required to refrain from working on the Sabbath) when he often claims that halakhah must overrule peshat?

On a subjective level, each exegete must have weighed his sensitivities as a *pashṭan* and his sensitivities as a halakhic Jew and decided which sensitivities to sacrifice on an ad hoc, verse-by-verse basis. Although it is difficult – perhaps impossible – to determine their subjective criteria, it is worth considering the question of which of the two exegetes was more willing to offer non-halakhic peshat and why.

---

[32]Ibn Ezra there, following Makkot 3:10.

[33]Mekhilta *Pisḥa'* 11 (Lauterbach edition, vol. 1, p. 89). See also Pesahim 9:5.

[34]For a discussion of the distinction between *non*-halakhic peshat and *anti*-halakhic peshat, see M. Berger's doctoral dissertation, *The Torah Commentary of Rabbi Samuel ben Meir* (Harvard, 1982), pp. 271ff.

While all traditional exegetes presumably find *non*-halakhic peshat less heterodox than *anti*-halakhic peshat, the distinction ultimately cannot be considered to be the criterion used by either Rashbam or ibn Ezra. I purposely cited in this paragraph examples of the willingness of both ibn Ezra and Rashbam to offer *anti*-halakhic peshat.

There are many reasons to think that ibn Ezra would be likely to be more daring and innovative in offering non-halakhic readings. First of all, ibn Ezra had broad secular knowledge and was an accomplished philosopher. Rashbam had some contact with Christian contemporaries but for the most part lived the life of a relatively insulated Northern French Jew. As Rosin put it:

> How different were Rashbam and ibn Ezra! The one a Frenchman and the other a Spaniard. The one was brought up by his fathers to a life of Torah and Talmud; the other from his youth stood in the middle ground between Torah and the wisdom of the Arabs in Spain.[35]

Both Rashbam and ibn Ezra were interested in grammar. Still ibn Ezra had easier access to the great classics of Hebrew grammar, which were written in Judeo-Arabic, than Rashbam had. Furthermore, ibn Ezra had an additional linguistic tool, the knowledge of another semitic language (Arabic), at his disposal.

Rashbam was an accomplished halakhist, author of many Talmudic commentaries and an important Tosaphist. What was the extent of ibn Ezra's Talmudic acumen? There are good reasons to suspect that there were significant lacunae in his halakhic training. It is not even clear that he himself claims to be a great halakhist. He writes that he does not know[36] whether the instruction to take the paschal lamb specifically on the tenth day of the first month applies only to the first Passover celebrated in Egypt or to all Passovers. The issue is discussed in the halakhic literature and the conclusion – that the law applies only to that first Passover – is never disputed and is spelled out openly in the Mishnah.[37] Ibn Ezra proudly announces having combed the Torah to find twenty-three different crimes that are punished by *karet*, or cutting off.[38] What purpose could he have in knowingly ignoring the Mishnah that enumerates thirty-six such crimes?[39]

Other comments of his are similarly problematic. Ibn Ezra seems to think, erroneously, that there is an explicit halakhah that in the case of an attempt to tempt someone to worship idols, the victim *(nissat)*

---

[35]Introduction to his edition of Rashbam's Torah comm., p. xxx.

Full biographies of either exegete have not been written but see e.g. the appropriate sections of M. Segal's *Parshanut ha- miqra'* (Jerusalem, 1971) and E. Urbach's *Ba`ale ha-tosafot* (Jerusalem, 1980) and see also the bibliography cited in my *Samuel ben Meir's Commentary on Genesis* (in press).

[36]Or, perhaps, "we do not know," i.e. nobody knows. *("Lo' yada`nu.")* Longer comm. to Ex. 12:3.

[37]See Pesahim 9:5 and Mekhilta *Pisḥa'* 3 (Lauterbach edition, vol. 1, p. 25).

[38]Longer comm. ad Ex. 12:47.

[39]Keritot 1:1.

may not testify against his tempter *(massit)*.[40] He also quotes an interpretation of Deuteronomy 15:22 according to which a damaged first-born animal may be eaten by both priests and lay people and he labels that interpretation farfetched.[41] If ibn Ezra had known that that is the halakhically authoritative understanding[42] it is hard to imagine that he would have expressed himself so strongly.[43]

If ibn Ezra falls short of the level of Rashbam's halakhic erudition, he does outshine his French contemporary in the sophistication of his theology. Compare their respective understandings of Deuteronomy 13:2-4:

> If there appears among you a prophet or a dream-diviner and he gives you a sign or a portent, saying "Let us follow and worship another god"...even if the sign or the portent that he named to you comes true, do not heed the words of that prophet or dream-diviner. For the LORD your God is testing you to see whether you really love the LORD your God....

According to Rashbam, the way in which God tests us is by creating such a world in which magic really does work and it is possible to ascertain true knowledge of the future through various impure means;[44] nevertheless we are asked to refrain from availing ourselves of such shortcuts. According to ibn Ezra's interpretation, on the other hand, the false prophet has not performed and indeed cannot perform miracles.[45] God tests us by allowing false prophets to walk the face of this earth, but not by giving any powers to those false prophets.

In another question of theology, ibn Ezra takes pains to prove that God is beyond all corporeality and that all biblical language referring to God's "hand," "anger" etc. must not be understood literally.[46] Rashbam describes God as being difficult to see – the type of image that a partially blind man might see – but still visible and presumably corporeal.[47] Good people do not strive to see Him,[48] just as good people

---

[40]See his comm. ad Deut. 13:10. For a discussion of the halakhic issue, see R. Margaliot's *Margaliot ha-yam*, vol. 2 (reprint edition: Jerusalem, 1977), p. 57, s.v. *umakhminim lo.*

[41]*Vezeh raḥoq be`enay.*

[42]Following the opinion of Bet Hillel in Bekhorot 5:2.

[43]On the subject of the extent of ibn Ezra's halakhic knowledge, see further J. Reifmann, *`Iyyunim bemishnat ha-Ra'va`* (Jerusalem, 1961/2), pp. 89-93.

[44]*She-yode`im `atidot `al yede ruaḥ ṭum'ah uterafim ve'ov veyidde`oni.*

[45]Hence ibn Ezra's tortuous explanation of *'ot* and *mofet* as meaning only symbolic, and not supernatural, actions.

[46]See e.g. his longer comm. ad Exodus 19:20 or ad Exodus 33:21.

[47]See his comm. to Gen. 48:8.

[48]Comm. to Ex. 33:18.

do not avail themselves of the forces of magic, but that does not mean that they cannot see Him.

So Rashbam was less sophisticated and less knowledgeable than ibn Ezra in secular, rational and speculative pursuits. He also lacked many of the tools that a *pashṭan* requires. On the other hand, Rashbam was more sophisticated and knowledgeable than ibn Ezra in halakhic texts, and was famous for his deep piety.[49] One would naturally expect Rashbam to side more often with the halakhic reading and ibn Ezra to promote the textual reading that is more based on logic and independent inquiry. That is, however, not the case.

Time and time again Rashbam is the one who offers the bolder, more innovative reading of a legal text while ibn Ezra supports the traditional halakhic reading. Rashbam has no qualms about saying that, despite the halakhah that a "slave in perpetuity" actually is freed during the jubilee year,[50] the literal implication of *le`olam* in Exodus 21:6 is that a such a slave remains a slave for all his life. Ibn Ezra, however, does not admit that there is tension between peshat and halakhah here but argues that the word *le`olam* can legitimately be understood to mean "until the jubilee year."[51]

Rashbam sees the literal meaning of *ve`onatah* in Exodus 21:10 as referring to the obligation of a slave owner to provide housing for his slave. Ibn Ezra, at least in his longer commentary, (the one probably written later and after ibn Ezra had read Rashbam's commentary[52]) sets aside that reading for the sake of the rabbinic understanding[53] that *`onah* is a term for conjugal rights. Rashbam feels at ease saying that the "deep peshat" of "a sign on your hand and a reminder on your forehead" (Exodus 13:9) has no connection to *tefillin*. Ibn Ezra, again only in his longer Exodus commentary, indignantly explains the methodological shortcomings of such an approach (which he, himself, in his shorter commentary, had labelled one of two possible readings of the text) and supports the halakhic reading.[54]

Ibn Ezra writes that he realizes that a reasonable reading of Leviticus 21:1-4 might yield the conclusion that a priest is not allowed to defile himself when his wife dies. Nevertheless, since he finds that

---

For a different view of Rashbam's attitude to God's corporeality, see Rosin's RSBM, pp. 114-115.

49 See Urbach, *ibid.*, p. 42.

50 Mekhilta *Neziqin* 2 (Lauterbach's edition, vol. 3, p. 17) and Qiddushin 15a.

51 The argument is made more clearly in his longer comm. to Exodus.

52 See E. Margaliot, *op. cit.*

53 Mekhilta *Neziqin* 3 (Lauterbach's edition, vol. 3, p. 27) and Ketubbot 47b.

54 Mekhilta *Pisḥa'* 17 (Lauterbach's edition, vol. 1, pp. 150-157).

the rabbis have said the precise opposite,[55] he claims that his first interpretation is now cancelled or retracted.[56] Rashbam has no such second thoughts. He merely juxtaposes the two mutually exclusive readings in his commentary and gives top billing to the heterodox understanding.

Perhaps the most famous example of Rashbam and ibn Ezra disagreeing about the appropriateness of a non-halakhic reading of a biblical text relates to the verse, "And there was evening and there was morning, a first day" (Genesis 1:5). Rashbam sees here a reference to a day that ends at sunrise, not at sunset as halakhah would have it.[57] While most scholars agree that the brunt of ibn Ezra's objections[58] to such a reading is not directed at Rashbam,[59] it is still obvious that ibn Ezra objects to a reading which, for Rashbam, is acceptable.

Part of the solution is that, for ibn Ezra, one of the primary purposes of his commentary is to refute the views of the Karaites.[60] (Rashbam's commentary has no such goal.) One who engages in polemics against Karaites must be careful about how much non-halakhic peshat he offers. Yet ibn Ezra is, as I have shown, willing to offer non-halakhic readings of some biblical texts. Furthermore, there is no one-to-one correspondence between those verses where ibn Ezra shows exegetical timidity and those verses where he is engaged in anti-Karaite polemics. Some further explanation for his relative conservatism must be found.

Both ibn Ezra and Rashbam make some general comments about the relationship between peshat and traditional halakhic exegesis. Ibn Ezra insists that the rabbis must have always known the peshat of biblical texts even if they indulged in midrashic exegesis.[61] Rashbam does not think so. He tells us of Rabbi Kehana in the Talmud who (following Rashbam's understanding of that text) admitted to having learned the entire Talmud without knowing that there was any value to the peshat level of exegesis.[62] Ibn Ezra mocks those rabbis who have

---

[55]Yevamot 22b.
[56]*Baṭel ha-perush ha-rishon.*
[57]See e.g. Hullin 5:5 and Berakhot 2a.
[58]In his longer comm. to Ex. 16:25 and in his *'Iggeret ha-shabbat.*
[59]See e.g. Poznanski, *Mavo'*, p. 43, footnote 2 and P. R. Weiss, *"'Ibn `ezra' ha-qara'im veha-halakhah,"* in *Melilah* I-IV (1944-1950). However, cf. the reasoned arguments of E. Margaliot, in his *"Ha-yaḥas,"* pp. 366-367 and footnote 30, that ibn Ezra *is* referring to Rashbam.
[60]See Weiss's article, cited above.
[61]*Safah berurah*, p. 4b: *"ve'en safeq she-hem yade`u ha-derekh ha-yesharah ka'asher hi'."*
[62]Comm. ad Gen. 37:2, citing Shabbat 63a.

no appreciation of peshat,[63] while Rashbam comes to their defense. He says that it is "due to their piety" that great rabbis of the past never became attuned to the peshat level of meaning.[64]

From reading both introductions that Ibn Ezra writes to his Bible commentary, it is clear that he thinks (like most exegetes over the years) that his Bible commentary was the most important one yet to have been written. Curiously Rashbam does not make such claims for his own commentary. On numerous occasions he says that midrashic halakhic exegesis is much more important than the study of peshat, which is after all the goal of his own commentary.[65]

While one might be tempted to see Rashbam's minimizing of the importance of peshat as either false modesty or as an attempt to deflect attention from his heterodoxy, I take his statement quite literally. I do not think that Rashbam feels that peshat is that important. He is a gifted practitioner of peshat exegesis but he is also an accomplished halakhist. He considers the halakhists' approach to the biblical text the more important one. The question of why a person would dedicate so much effort to an enterprise he considers of but secondary importance requires some good explanation.[66] Nevertheless the claim of a halakhist that peshat is secondary is not, in itself, surprising.

Ibn Ezra, who believes in the value and usefulness of intellectual inquiry and in the ability of human beings to figure things out on their own,[67] sees peshat as crucial, as something that worthy rabbis, ancient or modern, must be acquainted with and must take into account in their own exegesis. As a loyal rabbanite Jew he then finds conflicts between peshat and halakhah disturbing. For Rashbam, though, if one can be a good halakhist without knowing peshat, and if peshat really is of secondary value when compared to midrash halakhah, then conflicts between peshat and halakhah are less disturbing.

---

[63] *Safah berurah*, p. 5a.

[64] Rashbam, *ibid.*

[65] See e.g. his comm. ad Gen. 1:1 and 37:2 and his introduction to his commentary on Ex. 21.

[66] For attempted solutions, see e.g. E. Touitou, *Shiṭato ha-parshanit shel ha-Rashbam `al reqa` ha-meṣi'ut ha-hisṭorit shel zemano*, in *Studies in Rabbinic Literature, Bible and Jewish History*, ed. by Y. Gilat, Ch. Levine and Z. Rabinowitz (Ramat-Gan, 1982), pp. 48-74; D. Halivni, *Midrash Mishnah and Gemara* (London, 1986), pp. 105-107; and my "Truth or Peshat" to appear in *Law in its Social Setting in the Ancient Mediterranean World* (provisional title) ed. by B. Halpern and D. Hobson.

[67] See e.g. in his lengthy excursus on Exodus 20:1, in his longer Exodus comm., the section beginning *she'alani rabbi Yehudah ha-levi* (Krinski edition, p. 301; Weiser edition, pp. 131-132).

So Rashbam can allow himself to offer an anti-halakhic peshat interpretation more often than ibn Ezra does. Rashbam can juxtapose two mutually exclusive readings of a biblical text in his commentary – one peshat and one halakhah – when ibn Ezra cannot.[68] And Rashbam does not need to harmonize peshat and midrash halakhah or to explain what value the peshat level of interpretation might have when it does not represent halakhah. Not surprisingly ibn Ezra does.

Rashi had already realized the conflict between the peshat view of Exodus 23:2 ("do not blindly follow the majority") and the traditional rabbinic understanding (*'aḥare rabbim lehaṭot* – "the majority rules"). Ibn Ezra, not Rashbam, was the one to follow in Rashi's footsteps, struggling to suggest some way of getting the peshat reading to lead naturally into the desired halakhic conclusion.[69]

While "an eye for an eye" and "the owner shall also be put to death," as discussed above cannot, even according to ibn Ezra, be taken literally, he still has some respect for the literal sense of those troubling words. He appears to suggest on a few occasions that such words have value of a didactic nature – pointing out the gravity of the offence and the punishment that is "really" deserved – although the Torah has no intention of allowing such punishment to be implemented.[70]

Ibn Ezra becomes so caught up in this approach that he even tries to find some value in the literal sense of the verse, "You shall cut off her hand; show no pity" (Deuteronomy 25:12). He makes the disturbing suggestion that chopping off a woman's hand (interpreted by the rabbis as a euphemism for monetary payment)[71] is meant to be taken literally and would be applied by the courts if the offending woman didn't have any money.

In any case ibn Ezra does not abandon the rabbinic interpretations of these verses for the sake of peshat. He, along with the rabbis, introduces the idea of monetary compensation into his understanding of Exodus 21:24, Leviticus 24:19 and Deuteronomy 25:12 – verses where, on the peshat level, there appears to be no mention of money. But he feels a need to justify the peshat of the words. Rashbam does not.

Rashbam also does not make use of ibn Ezra's other major tool for resolving the peshat-halakhah problem – the concept of *'asmakhta'*.

---

[68]E.g. ad Ex. 21:6 or ad Lev. 21:1-4, both discussed above.

[69]See both his longer and shorter commentaries to Exodus and see also *Safah berurah*, p. 6a, *"vehinneh ḥakhamenu berov sikhlam hevinu davar mittokh davar...."*

[70]See his comm. to Ex. 21:24 (shorter and longer commentaries), Ex. 21:29 (shorter and longer commentaries) and Lev. 24:19.

[71]BQ 28a.

On numerous occasions when the tension between the simple meaning of the words and the rabbis' understanding of them becomes too great, ibn Ezra comments that the rabbinic midrash halakhah was not meant as exegesis. For ibn Ezra, it is too remote to claim that Numbers 27:11 really *means* that a husband inherits his wife's estate. When the rabbis said that, they were using an *'asmakhta'*, artificially attaching a binding legal principle to some biblical verse. The rabbis, argues ibn Ezra, never meant to claim that that is what the verse meant.[72] So when midrash conflicts with peshat, sometimes it is because midrash is not a form of exegesis at all. For Rashbam, though, midrash *is* a form of exegesis and the most important type of exegesis. The *'asmakhta'* answer is not an option for him because he does not want to apologize for the midrash, which he sees as the organic, true explanation of the text.[73]

Rashbam may be the "better" peshat exegete – the less apologetic one, the more daring one and the least troubled by conflicts between peshat and midrash. Paradoxically it is because he finds peshat to be relatively less important that he reaches such unrestrained heights of interpretation. In the twelfth century, at least, the scholar who truly values peshat, who feels that it is a crucial tool of the human intellect, applies peshat to the biblical text in a more cautious and circumspect manner.

---

[72]See ibn Ezra's lengthy excursus on this verse in his shorter commentary to Ex. 21:8 (Fleischer's edition, pp. 162-3) and see also his discussion of *'asmakhta'* in *Safah berurah*, pp. 4b-6a. Other verses that ibn Ezra explains according to the *'asmakhta'* principle include Ex. 21:8, Ex. 23:2 and Lev. 21:4.

[73]For further discussion of this issue, see my "Truth or Peshat."

26

"Introduction to the Commentary on Song of Songs Composed by the Sage Levi ben Gershom"[1] – An Annotated Translation

Menachem Kellner
University of Haifa

Said Levi ben Gershom: we have seen fit to comment on this scroll, the Scroll of Song of Songs, as we understand it, for we have not found any [other] commentary on it which could be construed as a [correct]

[1]In what follows I present an annotated translation of Gersonides' (1288-1344) introduction to his commentary on Song of Songs. It was my original intention to preface this translation with an introductory essay but the limitations of space available in this tribute made that impossible. Readers are therefore referred to my forthcoming essay on Gersonides' commentary on Song of Songs to appear in *Gersonide en son Temps* to be published jointly by the National Center for Scientific Research (Paris) and the Center for Jewish Studies at the Sorbonne. I edited the text on which this translation is based while on a sabbatical leave supported by the University of Haifa and the Memorial Foundation for Jewish Culture. To them both, I express my deep gratitude. The Hebrew text of Gersonides' introduction to his commentary on Song of Songs is due to be published, God willing, in a forthcoming issue of *Da'at*. Readers are referred to that publication for information concerning the mss. on which my text is based and for an updated bibliography of writings about Gersonides. Due to technical limitations, I transliterate Hebrew terms here without diacritical marks. I would like to thank Tyra Lieberman, Zev Harvey, and Avraham Melamed for their help.

explanation of the words of this scroll.[2] Rather, we have seen that all the commentaries which our predecessors have made [upon it] and which have reached us adopt the midrashic approach, including interpretations which are the opposite of what was intended [by the author of Song of Songs]. These midrashic explanations,[3] even though they are good in and of themselves, ought not to be applied as explanations of the things upon which they are said midrashically. For this reason one who wishes to explain these and similar things ought not to apply to them the derashim said about them; rather, he should endeavor to explain them himself according to their intention. He also ought not to combine those derashim with his explanations, for this will either confuse the reader and cause him to misunderstand what he intended, most especially with deep things such as these, or because this will bring [the reader] to despise the words of the author. This [latter] is so for two reasons: [a] the [excessive] length of the matter, or [b] the confusion in them of essential and accidental matters, for all this causes things to be despised.[4]

---

[2]Gersonides' claim here that he is the first correctly (which, as will become clear, means philosophically) to explain the meaning of Song of Songs indicates that he was unaware of earlier attempts to explain Song of Songs along similar lines. Abraham ibn Ezra, in his introduction to his commentary on Song of Songs, refers to certain philosophic interpretations of the text. In a number of places Maimonides interprets verses from Song of Songs in ways which anticipate Gersonides' approach. See, for example, Maimonides' citations from Song of Songs in *Guide of the Perplexed* III. 51 and III. 54 and his comments in "Laws of Repentance," X. 3. Two full commentaries on Song of Songs which read the text much as Gersonides does have reached us. The first is by a North African contemporary of Maimonides, Joseph ben Judah ibn Aknin, whose commentary was published for the first time, with a Hebrew translation from the original Arabic, by A. S. Halkin in 1964 (Jerusalem, Mekize Nirdamim). Halkin called his translation *Hitgalut ha-Sodot vi-Hofa'at ha-Me'orot.* Moses ibn Tibbon is the author of a second fully worked out philosophic commentary on Song of Songs. This commentary was published in Lyck in 1874. I have found no signs that Gersonides actually read these two commentaries and there is no reason to doubt his assertion here that he was not familiar with any "correct" commentary on Song of Songs other than his own (Maimonides' scattered comments, of course, excepted).

[3]Literally, "things."

[4]Compare Gersonides *Wars of the Lord* I. 6 (Leipzig, 1866, pp. 46-7; Seymour Feldman [trans.], Levi ben Gershom, *The Wars of the Lord,* Vol. I [Philadelphia: Jewish Publication Society, 1984] p. 161; these texts will be referred to as "Leipzig" and "Feldman" respectively). Gersonides there analyzes our propensity to confuse accidental for essential matters.

For this reason we have set as our intention to write what we understand of this scroll without mixing with it other things which vary from the [author's] intention. We have made no attempt in our commentary to mention what the Sages have said about some of the words of this book. This is so because it has already been made clear that what they said midrashically ought not to be cited in this commentary, despite their being very good things in and of themselves. [Further,] that which was reported from [the Sages] which does not accord with the intention of the scroll is so deep that it needs more of a commentary than all that upon which they commented. The weight and burden of commenting on the words of this book – because of their depth themselves and even more the fact that they were expressed in symbolic representations[5] and deep allegories[6] – is enough for us without adding a burden to our burden, [especially] when we add to this what it would involve in the matter of length! Furthermore, the meaning of those statements will not remain hidden after the intention of the book is made clear.[7]

We will devote a separate treatise to the explanation of the statements by the Sages in connection with this scroll and others whether by way of midrash or by way of commentary if God wills and

---

[5]Hebrew: *hikkuyim.* This term, deriving from the Hebrew root meaning "to portray" (see Ezekiel 8:10) and in medieval and modern Hebrew used in the sense of "imitation" is not easy to translate. Gersonides uses it as a synonym for *mashal* (translated here as "allegory"): in *Wars of the Lord* II. 6 (Leipzig, p. 109 and Feldman, Vol. II, p. 56) Gersonides defines *hikkuy* as *hiddah* ("riddle" or "enigma") or *mashal.* Feldman translates it as "representation," offering "symbol" as an alternative. I think that translation is a bit too vague (although it nicely catches the senses of portrayal and imitation from the Hebrew) and does not emphasize sufficiently that we are dealing with a figure of speech. I therefore use "symbolic representation."

[6]Hebrew (sing.): *mashal.*

[7]Note must be taken of the implication of Gersonides' words here. He is claiming that rabbinic interpretations of Song of Songs will be rendered clearer by his own commentary on the scroll. The implication is that the Rabbis meant through their midrashic exegesis to hint at the philosophic import of Song of Songs. In this, of course, Gersonides is following in the footsteps of Maimonides, who maintained that the Rabbis were actually philosophers as well as halakhists. On this, see my *Dogma in Medieval Jewish Thought* (Oxford: Oxford University Press, 1986), p. 234, n. 169, and the analysis of Maimonides' "Parable of the Palace" (*Guide,* III. 54) in my *Maimonides on Human Perfection* (Decatur, Georgia: Scholars Press, forthcoming).

decrees that I live.[8] This appears to us as the most appropriate way: to explain those statements all together in their [proper] places.

We now begin one presentation which encompasses everything included in this book. It is evident from the perspective of the Torah and the Prophets and from the perspective of [philosophic] speculation that man's *summum bonum*[9] resides in cognizing and knowing God to the extent that is possible for him. This will be perfected through the observation of the state of existent beings, their order,[10] their equilibrium,[11] and the manner of God's wisdom in organizing them as they are. This is so because these intelligibles direct one to knowledge of God to some extent, for an activity gives some indication concerning its agent; i.e., absolutely perfect activity indicates that its agent is absolutely perfect, insofar as it is an agent.

From this perspective we can cognize and know God, i.e., from the perspective of His actions, these being the things which are consequent upon Him for He has no antecedent causes at all; rather, He is the first cause of all existent beings. It is thus evident that He has no antecedent causes better known than Him.[12]

This is [even] more evident according to what Aristotle thought concerning His apprehension, that He is the nomos of existent beings, their order, and their equilibrium. This is so because it is necessary according to this position that he who knows the nomos of some of the

---

[8]Gersonides, like Maimonides before him, both promises to devote a separate treatise to the philosophic exposition of rabbinic midrashim and, so far as we know, fails to keep that promise. For Maimonides, see his Introduction to the tenth chapter of Mishnah Sanhedrin *(Perek Helek)* (in the edition of Rabbi J. Kafih [Jerusalem: Mossad Ha-Rav Kook, 1965], Vol. IV, p. 140) and his Introduction to the *Guide of the Perplexed,* translated by Shlomo Pines (Chicago: University of Chicago Press, 1963), p. 9.

[9]Hebrew: *ha-hazlahah ha takhliti'it*. Compare Wars I. 13 (Leipzig, p. 90 and Feldman, Vol. I, p.225).

[10]Hebrew: *sidduram.*

[11]Hebrew: *yoshram. Yosher* has been translated in a variety of ways. Various scholars have chosen "organization," "arrangement," "regularity" and "rightness." My own choice reflects that of Harry A. Wolfson, *Crescas' Critique of Aristotle* (Cambridge: Harvard University Press, 1929), p. 349. On this term see the important comments of Gad Freudenthal, "Cosmogonie et physique chez Gersonide," *REJ* 145 (1986), p. 305.

[12]We know God, that is, not as the effect of better-known causes, but as the cause of empirically-known phenomena. It was a staple of medieval philosophy that the examination of nature (=the natural sciences) yields a measure of knowledge concerning God. See, for example, Steven Harvey, *Falaquera's "Epistle of the Debate"* (Cambridge: Harvard University Press, 1987), p. 88.

existent beings apprehends God's essence to some extent. We have already made the truth concerning this clear in *Wars of the Lord;* its investigation does not concern us here.[13] However it may be, God's existence and perfection is clearly, evidently, and strongly shown by what can be seen of the magnitude of wisdom in the existence of all existent beings as they are, since it cannot be said of these things – in that they are found in the state of utmost possible perfection for them and in constant order – that their existence could have come about by accident, without an efficient cause as Epicurus and his followers maintained. Aristotle explained this in the *Physics.*[14]

It has been shown in *On the Soul* that our passive intellect is without concepts at all at the beginning of its creation and it is thus possible for it[15] to cognize them all, as glass can become all colors since it lacks them all.[16] The matter being so, all the concepts which we cognize are acquired.

---

[13]In introducing his discussion of God's knowledge of particulars (*Wars* III. 1 [Leipzig, p. 121, Feldman, Vol. II] p. 90) Gersonides writes:

> There are two mains views on this topic among the ancients that are worthy of discussion: (1) the views of Aristotle and his followers, and (2) views of the great sages of the Torah. Aristotle maintained that God (may He be blessed) does not know particular things in the sublunar world. Those who followed him are divided into two camps on this question, the first group maintaining that Aristotle believed that God (may He be blessed) has no knowledge of these things in the sublunar world, either universals or particulars....The second camp holds that Aristotle's view is that God (may He be blessed) knows the things in the sublunar world with respect to their general natures, i.e., their essences, but not insofar as they are particulars, i.e., contingents. Nor is there any multiplicity in His essence on this view, since He knows only Himself and in this knowledge He knows all things with respect to their general natures. For He is the principle of law, order, and regularity in the universe...." (Feldman translation, Vol. II, p. 90)

See further Feldman's notes *ad. loc.; Wars* V, iii, 3 (Leipzig, p. 241), where Gersonides argues that this second interpretation of Aristotle is correct; Charles Touati, *Les Guerres du Seigneur, III-IV* (Paris: Mouton, 1968), p. 42; and Norbert Samuelson, *Gersonides on God's Knowledge* (Toronto: Pontifical Institute of Medieval Studies, 1972), p. 90.

[14]Aristotle, *Physics* ii, 4-6.

[15]Literally, "the passive intellect."

[16]Aristotle, *On the Soul* iii, 5. Compare Jesse Stephen Mashbaum, "Chapters 9-12 of Gersonides' Supercommentary on Averroes' Epitome of the De Anima: The Internal Senses," Ph.D. Diss., Brandeis University, 1981 (Xerox University Microfilms Order No. 8126886), p. 126 (henceforth, "Mashbaum").

It has been shown in the *Posterior Analytics* that in order to acquire any concept a person needs prior knowledge.[17] This [prior knowledge] is of two types: primary concepts and secondary concepts, these [latter] being acquired syllogistically from the primary concepts. We acquire the primary concepts through our sense by way of repetition.[18] This is carried out by our faculties of memory and imagination, for the imagination acquires for us the sensed notion upon its being revealed by the senses, and the faculty of memory perfects the repetition by virtue of which the universal judgment is completed. Thus these two faculties are to some extent a cause of our acquiring all the concepts [which we acquire]. There is another, worthier agent which plays a role in the process of our acquiring concepts: this is the Active Intellect, as was shown in *On the Soul*.[19] No concept can be acquired without it for through it we become aware of the matter of repetition which is presented by the senses, whether [or not] it is essential to those things. We [then] make an infinite judgment because of this defined multiplicity, apprehension of which comes from the senses; i.e., on this basis we judge the continuation of the judgment concerning each individual member of that species and in every particular time, without end.[20]

It has already been shown in *On the Soul* and in *Parva Naturalia* that there are [different] levels of spirituality among the impressions which reach the soul from the senses, these latter being outside of the soul.[21] The first [of these] is the impression which is presented by the sensation of any of the individual senses. The second level is the impression presented by the form in the sensation of any of the individual senses to the common sense. The third level is the

[17]See Aristotle, *Posterior Analytics* i, 1-3 generally and the opening of the book (p. 71a1) in particular. Compare *Wars* I. 9 (Leipzig, p. 55 and Feldman, Vol. I, p. 174).

[18]Hebrew: *hishanut*. Compare *Wars* I. 6 (Leipzig, p. 46 and Feldman, Vol. 1, p. 161), Wars I. 10 (Leipzig, p. 68 and Feldman, Vol. I, p. 195), and Mashbaum, p. 37.

[19]*On the Soul*, iii, 5.

[20]Compare *Wars* I. 6 (Leipzig, p. 46-7 and Feldman, Vol. I, p. 162).

[21]Gersonides' sources here are not in Aristotle's writings themselves but in Averroes' commentaries upon them. With respect to the first, see Mashbaum, pp. 30-31. With respect to the second, see *Averroes' Epitome of Parva Naturalia*, translated by Harry Blumberg (Cambridge: Medieval Academy of America, 1961), p. 26. Compare Wars I. 3 (Leipzig, p. 21 and Feldman, Vol. I, p. 122). See further Mashbaum, p. liv. In his discussion here Gersonides explains how our sense perceptions are rendered more and more abstract (="spiritual") as they are transmitted from one internal sense of the soul to the next.

impression which is presented by the sensations in the common sense to the faculty of imagination. The fourth level is the impression which is presented by the impression in the imagination to the faculty of discrimination. The fifth level is the impression which is presented by the [faculty of] discrimination to the [faculty which] preserves and remembers. These [impressions] are more spiritual than all the others because the other faculties have already abtracted from them many of the hylic attributes of the sensed object by virtue of which it was distinctively particular.[22] Thus the impressions in the faculty of memory are potentially the sensible form. So also with the impressions in the imagination, i.e., that they are potentially in the sensible form, since these impressions reach [the soul] through these faculties from the sensed objects, [after] many of the hylic attributes of the sensed object outside of the soul were abstracted from them. So also it ought to be considered of these faculties of the soul in connection with the faculty of the soul which precedes it, as if you were to say that the imaginative forms are potentially in the impressions which are [in turn] potentially, not actually, in the common sense since they are more abstract and more spiritual.

You ought to know that the intelligible form is also potentially in those forms which are in these faculties, even if the potentiality is more distant. For example, after the intellect abstracts the hylic attributes – by virtue of which this apprehended thing was distinctively particular – from the imaginative form, that form appears to it[23] in a universal way;[24] i.e., it is the universal nature common to the individuals of that species infinitely. In this manner one may solve the problem which prompted the ancients to posit forms and numbers or to deny the possibility of knowledge, as was made clear in the *Metaphysics*.[25]

One ought not to ignore [the fact] that there is great difficulty in acquiring this stupendous felicity towards which we are disposed; so much so that its acquisition is very unlikely for any particular human being; [indeed], only very few individuals can acquire a large measure

---

[22]Hebrew: *perati vi-ramuz elav.*

[23]i.e., the soul.

[24]Hebrew: *she-bah ha-zurah bi-einah kolelet.*

[25]Aristotle, *Metaphysics*, i, 6; i, 9; xiii, 4-5 (especially p. 1078b). Compare *Wars* I. 6 (Leipzig, p. 46-7 and Feldman, Vol. I, p. 162). It is Gersonides' point here that Aristotle's account of knowledge (summarized in the preceding paragraphs) solves those problems which led the skeptics to claim that knowledge as such was impossible and which led Plato, rejecting the claim of the skeptics, to the theory of forms.

of it. This is for two reasons: first, the difficulty in perfectly apprehending the states of existent beings; second, the multiplicity of impediments which impede our attempts properly to achieve this apprehension.

The first of these impediments is the effervescence of our natures while we are young which attracts us to physical desires.[26] The second is the misleading [nature] of imagination and opinion[27] which brings us to confuse substantial and accidental matters and to think that what exists does not, and vice versa.

The difficulty in perfectly apprehending the states of existent beings has many causes. First, the difficulty in finding the method which will [correctly] bring us to the apprehension of each subject which we investigate; as if you were to say, moving to it on the basis of the essential matters specific to[28] that subject-matter.

Second, our ignorance at the beginning of our study of the method which will cause us perfectly to apprehend the states of existent beings because only through this defined ordering can this apprehension be perfected; as if you were to say that one should study first what ought to be studied first. There is a difficulty about this which does not disappear, especially when we take into account the great desire which humans have to achieve the end, for this brings them to destruction by studying first what is last in order. In this manner, not only do they not acquire perfection, but, rather, add deficiency to their deficiency.

Third, our ignorance of many of the things which ought to be investigated, which makes it such that we cannot [even] strive to reach the truth concerning it for one who does not know the subject under the discussion certainly does not know the method which will bring him to the acquisition of the truth concerning it.

Fourth, the difficulty in acquiring from the senses what is needed for the apprehension of many of the existent things.[29]

Fifth, the subtlety of the matters themselves, and their depth.

Sixth, the many objections which may be raised concerning each of the alternatives in a contradiction.[30]

---

[26]Compare Maimonides, *Guide of the Perplexed* I. 34 (Pines translation, pp. 76-7).

[27]Hebrew: *mahshavah*.

[28]Hebrew: *ha-meyuhasim li-*.

[29]i.e., the difficulties involved in empirical observation.

[30]Hebrew: *helkei ha-soter*.

Seventh, the confusion of conventional truths[31] concerning it[32] with the truth itself, for much of what we believe is what we have grown accustomed to hearing from our youth.

Eighth, the great differences of opinion concerning the subject which are found among those who have studied it, each of them bringing many arguments in support of his position.

Generally, acquiring felicity is inordinately difficult because of the reasons just mentioned and others like them. Therefore, the Prophets and Sages never ceased guiding individuals to the way in which they could acquire felicity, each according to his ability. With respect to this guidance the Torah is absolutely the most perfect among all the guides; because it contains absolutely perfect guidance for both the masses and for individuals. If we wanted to make this clear on the basis of the words of the Torah we would need a long book; but we will be brief and adduce from this [only] enough according to our intention in this place.

We say that since what we ought to be guided towards first is moral perfection, the Torah guides us towards this perfection in many of the commandments. However, that which it contains concerning the improvement of the soul was kept hidden because of its distance from the masses. Most of what the Torah guides us [toward] concerning speculation deals either with the speculative principles the apprehension of which for the scholar is very difficult, or with the great principles, mistakes concerning which greatly distance a man from human perfection. Since it is fitting that every activity directed towards some end should be so directed from its beginning, so that the activity altogether may be directed by its end, and since this is impossible for the masses with respect to what the Torah commanded concerning moral perfection, for they do not know what the human end is, the Torah cunningly collected both things together.

It hinted at this end and commanded it – it being cleaving to God – and referred to many of the wonderful speculative matters in some of the narratives and commandments and in describing the sanctuary and its implements as if guiding the elite to [the realization that] the rest of the Torah commandments are for this end.[33] It said for the multitudes, concerning many of the commandments, that they who observe them will thereby achieve length of days and many [other] fanciful felicities, and the opposite concerning those who do not observe

---

[31]Hebrew: *mefursam*.

[32]i.e., the subject under study.

[33]See Gersonides' commentary on the weekly reading *Terumah*, third lesson *(to'elet)*; in the Venice, 1547 edition of his Bible commentary, pp. 104a-105b.

them, even though the Torah commandments are not for this purpose. This is so since the multitudes cannot picture the purpose of the Torah commandments and since a man will not desire to perform some action if he cannot picture its advantage for him; thus the Torah guided [the multitudes] to fulfill these commandments first for this purpose and through performing this worship first not for its own sake they will be guided to doing it afterwards for its own sake. The Torah did not strive to teach us these things perfectly according to their methods, because this is not the [objective] of a prophet in his capacity as a prophet, but, rather, in his capacity as a savant.[34] And thus the Prophets and those who speak by virtue of the holy spirit never ceased from guiding men to perfection, either to the first perfection, or to the final perfection, or to both. This [will be accomplished] when what is understood by the multitudes from the words of the Prophets guides one to moral perfection and what is understood by the elite[35] guides [one] to conceptual perfection. The book of Proverbs is of this latter type.

But this book, Song of Songs, guides the elite only to the way of achieving felicity and thus its external meaning was not made useful to the masses. In it, according to our understanding of his words, he first referred to the overcoming of impediments consequent upon moral deficiency, for this is what ought to come first, as [was noted] above. After this, he referred to the overcoming of impediments consequent upon the failure to distinguish between truth and falsehood. After this, he referred to the preparation[36] for speculation according to the proper order of three kinds, as Aristotle mentioned in many places: one kind deals with body and what is abstracted from body in speech [only], not in reality, as you will find concerning mathematical things; one kind deals with body and what is not abstracted from body in speech, as in

---

[34]This is a difficult passage since the Hebrew seems to imply that a prophet need not be a savant (Hebrew: *hakham*), contradicting Gersonides' expressly stated position in *Wars*, Introduction (Leipzig, p. 4 and Feldman, Vol. I, p. 94) and VI, ii, 11 (Leipzig, pp. 453-4). See further Haim Kreisel, "Hakham vi-Navi bi-Mishnat ha-Rambam uvnei Hugo," *Eshel Beersheva* 3 (1986), pp. 149-69. A more literal translation of the passage here would be: "because this is not the [objective] of a prophet qua prophet but [of a prophet] qua savant, to the extent that he is one."

[35]Hebrew: *yehidim*.

[36]Hebrew: *derikhah*. This term, which Gersonides may have coined (he uses it frequently, other writers almost not at all, as may be seen from the references in the dictionaries of Klatzkin and Ben Yehudah), derives from the Hebrew root, *d-r-kh* (to step or stamp down, as in squeezing grapes; to bend or draw a bow). It connotes readiness, preparation, process, transition, tendency, passage, passing through, transition, moving in the direction of.

the case of physics, for the study there of form deals with it insofar as it is a perfection of matter, and matter is studied in physics insofar as it is a substratum for form; one kind does not deal with body at all, neither in speech nor in reality, as is the case with metaphysics.[37]

Now the nature of things in themselves necessitated that the stages in the study of existent beings follow this order. This is so because what the mathematical sciences investigate is body qua absolute body, not as some body or other; as if you were to say, heavy or

---

[37]While this classification of the sciences is indeed Aristotelian, its presentation is not. Gersonides presents the sciences in the following order: mathematics, physics, and metaphysics. Aristotle usually presents them in the order: physics, mathematics, metaphysics. On this see the studies of H. A. Wolfson, "The Classification of Sciences in Medieval Jewish Philosophy," "Additional Notes to the Article on the Classification of Sciences in Medieval Jewish Philosophy," and "Note on Maimonides' Classification of the Sciences," in Wolfson, *Studies in the History and Philosophy of Religion* Vol. I (Cambridge: Harvard University Press, 1973), pp. 493-545, 546-550, and 551-560. On p. 516 of the first article Wolfson takes note of different orderings of the sciences and explains it "by the distinction between the arrangement of these sciences according to the order of importance and their arrangement according to the order of study." This solution does not hold good for Gersonides' arrangment here which, as he will argue immediately below, not only reflects the proper order of study, but also the order of existence. Furthermore, Gersonides presents the sciences in the same order in the Introduction to the *Wars of the Lord* (Leipzig, p. 3; Feldman, p. 92). Joseph ben Judah ibn Aknin presents a similar classification of the sciences in chapter 27 of his (Arabic) "Hygiene of the Soul." An English translation of the passage in question may be found in Jacob R. Marcus, *The Jew in the Medieval World* (Cincinnati: UAHC, 1938), p. 375: "These studies are divided into three groups. The first group is normally dependent upon matter, but can, however, be separated from matter through concept and imagination. This class comprises the mathematical sciences. In the second group speculation cannot be conceived of apart from the material, either through imagination or conception. To this section belong the natural sciences. The third group has nothing to do with matter and has no material attributes; this group includes in itself metaphysics as such." This passage is reprinted in Norman Stillman, *The Jews of Arab Lands* (Philadelphia: Jewish Publication Society, 1979), p. 227. The text was originally published in German translation by Moritz Guedemann, *Das Juedische Unterrichtwissen waehrend der spanisch-arabischen Periode* (Vienna, 1873 and Amsterdam, 1968), p. 68 and in Hebrew translation by S. Eppenstein in the Nahum Sokolow festschrift (Warsaw, 1903), pp. 371-88. On ibn Aknin's book see A. S. Halkin, "Classical and Arabic Material in ibn Aknin's 'Hygiene of the Soul,'" PAAJR 14 (1944): 25-147. It is a safe assumption that Gersonides and ibn Aknin ultimately drew their formulations from the same source; the identity of that source is unknown to me.

light, or, not heavy and not light. Physics investigates a particular body insofar as it is body; as if you were to say, changing body, or heavy or light, or not heavy and not light. Now the investigation of the attributes of absolute body [must] precede the investigation of the attributes of some body [or other] for the general matters ought to be studied before the specific matters, especially since the general matters are better known to us, as was made clear in the first book of the *Physics*.[38]

In general, that which many things share is better known to us than what is particular, and thus the study of this science precedes [the study of] physics; [this is all the more the case when we] add to it the strength of our knowledge of this science since it is not involved in matter. Further, it trains our intellect, actualizes it and causes it to acquire the [proper mode of] speculation, [thus] guarding it from error in other sciences due to the strength of the proof[s] based on this science, since most of the proofs [in it] are absolute proofs.[39] Further, the mathematical sciences guide [one] to some extent to physics and metaphysics, as was made clear in the first part of the *Almagest*.[40]

Physics necessarily precedes the divine science which is metaphysics since metaphysics goes further than it on the path of perfection and purpose.[41] It also assumes the existence of the separate

---

[38]*Physics* i, 1 and i, 5 (especially p. 189a). Gersonides' comments on mathematics and physics here seem to mean that while the mathematical sciences deal with concepts such as "weight" in the abstract, physics deals with the actual weight of specific bodies. Compare Metaphysics iv, 2, 1004b: "For, just as numbers have peculiar attributes, such as oddness and evenness, commensurability and equality, too much and too little, and as these belong to numbers in themselves or in relation to one another, so what is solid, what is unmoved, what is moved, what is heavy, and what is not heavy, each has its properties, which differ from those of the others" (I quote from the translation of Richard Hope [Ann Arbor: University of Michigan Press, 1960], p. 65).

[39]Hebrew: *mofetim muhlati'im*. Absolute demonstrations proceed from causes to effects, from prior to posterior, where what is prior to us in knowledge is also prior in existence. See Steven Harvey, "The Hebrew Translation of Averroes' Prooemium to His *Long Commentary on Aristotle's Physics*," *PAAJR* 52 (1985), p. 81.

[40]Ptolemy, *Almagest* I, 1; in Robert M. Hutchins (ed.), *Great Books of the Western World* Vol. 16, pp. 5-6.

[41]Hebrew: *takhlit;* also translated here as "goal" or "end" depending upon the needs of English style. This final clause of this sentence reads as follows: *lifi she-hokhmat mah she-ahar ha-teva holekhet mimenah mahalakh ha-shelemut vi-ha-takhlit*. It may be that we are dealing here with an Arabism, *yelekh mimenu mimadregah,* in which case the sentence should be translated

causes, which are neither physical things nor physical forces, something which is established in physics. The [level] of verification which can be reached in physics is below the [level] of verification which can be reached in the mathematical sciences, since most of its proofs are *a posteriori* and it is not the way of causes discovered through *a posteriori* proofs to affirm existence if it was unknown. For this reason, this science requires a more settled mind than do the mathematical sciences.[42] Thus, of those who wish to plunge deeply into this science and will not believe something unless it is impossible to disagree with it, many fall by the way [and do not achieve perfection] in this science.

The verification we achieve with metaphysics, despite its [higher] degree, is weaker, in that it is taken from remote commonly accepted premises.[43] In particular [this is so] in what it investigates concerning those things which are neither a body nor a physical force, this being the fruit of that science and its end.

The verification we achieve in physics is based upon particular appropriate premises.[44] It is the way of commonly accepted premises

---

as follows: "Physics necessarily precedes the divine science which is metaphysics since metaphysics stands to it in the relation of [its] perfection and purpose." On the phrase in question, see Isaac Husik, "Studies in Gersonides," in Strauss and Nahm (eds.), *Philosophical Essays of Isaac Husik* (Oxford: Oxford University Press, 1952), pp. 186-254, p. 202. This important study, with is many valuable discussions of Gersonides' usages, first appeared in *JQR* 7 (1916-17): 553-94 and *JQR* 8 (1917-18): 113-56, and 231-68. On the notion of priority raised here see Feldman's note in Vol. I, pp. 99-100 and the lengthy discussion in Jacob Staub, *The Creation of the World According to Gersonides* (Chico, California: Scholars Press, 1982), pp. 173-8.

[42]Since having a "settled mind" *(yishuv ha-da'at)* comes only after one overcomes the "effervescence of youth," Gersonides is implying here that the sciences are best studied at different ages. See above, note 26.

[43]*Hakdamot mefursemot rehokot.* The point is that the premises of metaphysics are based on commonly accepted opinions which are "those which commend themselves to all or the majority of the wise – that is, to all of the wise or to the majority or to the most famous and distinguished of them" (Aristotle, *Topics* i, 1, 100b; I quote from the translation of E. S. Forster [Cambridge: Harvard University Press, 1960], p. 275). Compare *Wars of the Lord,* Introduction: "our knowledge of the essence of the First Cause is very slight" (Leipzig, p. 2, Feldman, p. 92); i.e., because of the limitations of our knowledge, metaphysics cannot be based on apodictic proofs. See further, *Wars* VI, i, 5 (Leipzig, p. 307).

[44]*Hakdamot meyuhadot u-meyuhasot.* On the question of the different levels of certainty achieved in the different sciences, compare Maimonides, *Guide* I. 31 (p. 66) and see Steven Harvey (above, note 12), p. 43.

that they lead to two contraries or contradictories. Thus this science is impossible for one who is not strongly settled on the true views from the perspective of Torah and speculation, and for one the effervescence of whose nature has not quieted, lest his yearning to follow after his desires brings him to make his views in this science accord with what he sees fit, as is well known concerning Elisha Aher when he entered *Pardes*,[45] adding to this [the fact that] the smallest mistake which occurs in this science is great from the perspective of the degree of the subject matter and [also] since the object of this science is the utmost human felicity.

As the object of this book is to make known the way to achieve felicity, and since there are great doubts concerning whether it is possible to achieve it, it was necessary that these doubts be resolved at the beginning. This is what concerned the author, as we see it, from the beginning of the book to the beginning of the third paragraph,[46] where it says, *To a steed* (1:9). Included here also is the name of the book, the name of the author and his rank, his method of approaching [the subject], the subject under investigation, and its purpose.[47]

From the beginning of the third paragraph to the beginning of the fifth paragraph, where it says, *Hark! My beloved!* (2:8) he indicates the effort necessary to overcome the impediments [to perfection] from the perspective of moral deficiency.

From the beginning of the fifth paragraph to the beginning of the eighth paragraph, where it says, *on my bed* (3:1), he indicates the effort necessary to overcome the impediments [to perfection] from the perspective of imagination and thought, until he knows how to escape from error and distinguish between truth and falsehood.

From the beginning of the eighth paragraph to the beginning of the thirteenth paragraph, where it says, *Come with me from Lebanon, my bride* (4:8), he indicates the attainment of the mathematical sciences.

---

[45]For the story of Elisha ben Abuyah, the notorious apostate Tanna, see Hagigah 15a. The phrase translated here as "with what he sees fit" is *lifi mah she-ya'ut lo*. A possible alternative is, "in accordance with what pleases him." The point is that Elisha, led astray by his lusts, allowed his desires to determine his metaphysical conclusions instead of basing them on objective reality. Compare Maimonides, *Guide of the Perplexed* I. 32.

[46]The Hebrew text of the Bible is divided into *parashot* or paragraphs; it is to these that Gersonides refers here.

[47]Compare Averroes' approach to the writing of introductions; see the article by Steven Harvey cited above in note 39.

From the beginning of the thirteenth paragraph until *Who is this who cometh up from the wilderness, leaning upon her beloved?* (8:5), he indicates the attainment of physics in the order appropriate to it.

From the statement, *Who is this who cometh up from the wilderness*...to the end of the book, he indicates the attainment of metaphysics.

This is what we wish to present. We have seen fit to preface it to our commentary on this book. It is a great gateway for what we wanted since the difficulty in explaining this book arises from one of two perspectives: the depth of the matters themselves, and the depth of the symbolic representations found in this book. Having first guided [the reader] to an understanding of these matters, what remains is the understanding of the depth of the symbolic representations. This is not something which is exceptionally difficult for us. But if we had burdened ourselves with both matters at the same time it would have been exceptionally difficult for us. The activity here is of the degree of one who found his burden too heavy to carry all at once and [therefore] divided it into two parts, making it easy for him to carry those parts, one after the other. Furthermore, in this way it will be easier for the reader of our words to understand them and determine their truth; they will not confuse him because of their length or because of their combining the understanding of the two matters together.

From this point we will begin to explain generally many of the symbolic representations and allegories found in this book so that we will not have to explain them separately in each place where they occur. This is [also] a valuable guide towards the understanding of the words of this book.

We say that it is self-evidently clear that this Sage used *Jerusalem* (6:4) as an allegory in this book for 'man' for man alone among all compound entities is distinguished by worship of God as Jerusalem was distinguished by this from other cities and places. There is another reason for this: [the word] "Jerusalem" is derived from *shelemut* [perfection] and thus it is called *Shalem*, as it says, *king of Shalem* (Genesis 14:18) and *In Shalem also is set His tabernacle* (Psalms 76:3). Since man is the most perfect of all the existents in the sublunar world, so much so that he is likened to a microcosm, he is called *Jerusalem* allegorically.

For this reason the faculties of the soul were allegorically called *daughters of Jerusalem* (1:5, etc.). The intellect was allegorically called *Solomon* (1:5, etc.) since he was the king of Jerusalem and so the intellect is ruler of the man. So much [is the intellect ruler of the man] that he used Solomon to indicate the perfection of this part since it is derived from *shelemut*.

Since Zion was the worthiest part of Jerusalem, the Temple and the king's palace being there, he allegorically called the faculties of the soul most closely related to the activity of the intellect, *daughters of Zion* (3:11).

It is known that the Temple was in *the forest of Lebanon* (I Kings 7:2, etc.); and thus the Temple is called *Lebanon,* as it says, *Lebanon is ashamed, it withereth* (Isaiah 33:9). You will thus find that in this book, in an allegory connected to this one, he calls that which originates in an activity of the intellect, *from the woods of Lebanon* (3:9), and *flowing streams from Lebanon* (4:15), [and] *Come with me from Lebanon, my bride* (4:8). The repetition of this allegory was [intended] to arouse the reader of his words to understand his intention in this wonderful allegory according to his ability, understanding with this [the need for it] to be hidden from the masses by virtue of the symbolic representations and allegories in which he couched his words.

We also say that he allegorically compares the beginning of the time when a person prepares himself to move in the direction of one of the speculative perfections to the [time] when plants begin to bear fruit or to the [time] when the shadows of the night begin to pass. The allegory in this is clear, for then the darkness of ignorance passes and the light of wisdom begins to be seen. Then the soul strives to bear its fruit when it acquires this perfection to which it has been directed by those premises on the basis of which one can grasp the matters of that science. Allegories of this sort are found repeatedly in this book.

Since he allegorically compares scientific perfection[48] to "fruit" he allegorically compares that which potentially is the fruit to flowers and lilies since the flowers and lilies are potentially the fruit or the seed, which is the primary end. They are also that which the plant puts forth first in its attempt to bear its fruit or its seed. Thus he says of the intellect concerning that which reaches it from the imagination, *that [it] feedeth among the lilies* (2:16, 6:3), for the intelligible form is found in potential in the imaginative forms. The imagination is also called *that feedeth among the lilies* with respect to that which it reaches it from the senses for this very reason itself, as we mentioned above.

Connected to this allegory, he allegorically compared beneficial speculative, physical, and metaphysical matters to spices and distilled oils because of their merit and because they arouse one to grasp their truth from what one smells of them at first. These are matters which are posterior to them in that they wonderfully show the perfection of their agent, just as a person is aroused to pay attention to

---

[48]Hebrew: *ha-shelemut bi-hokhmah.*

the spice when he senses the goodness of its fragrance. This is so because his sensing the goodness of its fragrance causes him to pay attention to the place where the spice is found, and arouses in him a desire to search for it until he reaches it. This is also repeated often in this book.

Since perfection of the intellect comes from the Active Intellect by way of those imaginative forms which the imagination emanates upon it, and this is perfected – i.e., the presentation to the intellect by the imagination of what it needs from the senses in each subject of study – when it so wonderfully desires to be subservient to the hylic intellect that it places all of its activities in the service of the intellect so far as it can, he allegorically compared this desire to the desire of the male and female who desire each other in order to indicate the great extent of this desire. He allegorically compared the intellect to the male since it is on the level of form relative to the imaginative faculty.[49] This is something which continues throughout this book.

He likened the influence of the hylic intellect to suckling from breasts [8:1] because this is a very appropriate allegory concerning female influence and also because milk is similar to a substance which is potentially consumed and is on the level of hyle relative to it. So it is also with respect to the imaginative forms [relative to] the intelligible forms.

You must not fail to note that some of the attributes with which the lovers described each other relate to the allegory and some to its intended meaning; of these there are many. Some of them relate only to the intended meaning, as when he said, *thy hair is as a flock of goats* (4:1; 6:5), for this is not a fitting indication of beautiful hair if it were according to the allegory. So also, *thy belly is like a heap of wheat* (7:3), and *we have a little sister [and she hath no breasts]* (8:8). After that he said, *and if she be a door, we will enclose her with boards of cedar* (8:9), *if she be a wall [we will build upon her a turret of silver]* (8:9),[50] for this does not fit the allegory at all. This is also found often in this book. He did this in order to indicate the hidden meaning, so that one would not mistakenly think that the statements in this book should be taken according to their external sense.

In a small number of places, as we see it, those attributes relate to the allegory only. This was done for the perfection of the text and its improvement, as if to combine the hidden and the open, for this adds obscurity to his words, perfecting them as they ought to be in such cases,

---

[49]For the Aristotelian source of the doctrine that the male contributes the form, the female the matter, see *On the Generation of Animals,* Part I, Book 2, chapter iii, p. 732a.

[50]Gersonides reverses the word order in the verse.

namely, keeping them hidden from those who are not fit for them and open to those who are fit.

We must not fail to note that this beloved man is first called *Solomon* (3:7) and after that *King Solomon* (3:9) – he said, *behold, it is the litter of Solomon* (3:7), *King Solomon made himself a palanquin* (3:9), *upon King Solomon* (3:11) – for this is the sort of thing which ought to have significance, certainly in so wonderfully structured[51] an allegory.

We ought to be aware of the different names by which this beloved woman is called and their various degrees. Thus, in the beginning, he called her *my beloved* (1:9); after that he called her *my beloved, my fair one* (2:10, 13); after that he called her bride (4:8, etc.);[52] after that he called her *my dove* (2:14); after that, *my dove, my undefiled* (5:2); after that he called her *Shulammite* (7:1) and *prince's daughter* (7:2). For this also ought to have significance.

We ought to be aware that in her adjuration of *the daughters of Jerusalem* the first and second time (2:7 and 3:5) she said, *by the gazelles and by the hinds of the field that ye awaken not* and the third time (8:4) she did not say *by the gazelles and by the hinds of the fields* and she did not say *that ye awaken not;* rather, she said, *why should ye awaken.*

We ought to be aware of the different orderings in which the praise of this beloved woman and her beauty are described in this book. Thus, the first time he began his praises from her head and descended with them gradually to her breasts. The second time he began his praises from her head and the praises never left her head, i.e., they never descended below her head. The third time he began his praises with her legs and did not cease ascending with them until he reached her head. For this could not possibly be without significance in so perfectly structured an allegory.

We ought to be aware of the wisdom expressed in his allegorical expression of the perfection which one passes through at the beginning of one's approach as the ascent *upon the mountains of spices: Until the day breathe, and the shadows flee away, turn, my beloved, and be thou like a gazelle or a young hart upon the mountains of spices* (2:17); and in his allegorical expression of the perfection which one passes through afterwards, as his arriving at the ascent upon *the mountain of myrrh* and *the hill of frankincense:* he said, *Until the day breathe, and the*

---

[51]Hebrew: *bi-tikkuno;* the root *t-k-n* in Mishnaic Hebrew can mean edit, sytematize, arrange, or bring to order. See Saul Lieberman, *Hellenism in Jewish Palestine* (New York: Jewish Theological Seminary, 1950), p. 90.
[52]This verse is cited out of order (appearing here between 2:10 and 2:14).

shadows flee away, I will get me to the mountain of myrrh and to the hill of frankincense (4:6); and in his allegorical expression of the perfection which one passes through at the end as the ascent *upon the mountains of spices* (8:14). What is intended here relates to the differences concerning the mountains, why the first and last were expressed in the plural – he said, *upon the mountains of spices*[53] (2:17) and *upon the mountains of spices*[54] (8:14) – while the second was in the singular – he said, *mountain of myrrh* and *hill of frankincense* (4:6). Further, why did he specify specific spices in the second description, while in the third taking *spices* generally? For this is also something which ought to have significance.

We ought to be aware of that which we have found to be unique in the passage *come with me from Lebanon, my bride* (4:8) with respect to this beloved's garden and what the beloved plucked from his garden, concerning the word *with* – which indicates combination and generality – which is repeated here often. He said, *a park of pomegranates with precious fruits; henna with spikenard plants; spikenard with saffron, calamus and cinnamon, with all trees of frankincense; myrrh and aloes, with all the chief spices* (4:13-14); *my myrrh with my spice; I have eaten my honeycomb with my honey; I have drunk my wine with my milk* (5:1). See how the word *with* is repeated here; you will not find it [repeated] so in this book except in this passage. [It is] as if to awaken the somnolent with this wonderful repetition so that they will be aware of what he intended by this. This reflects his perfection and his desire that his words be [both] understood according to the ability of those fit to understand them and kept hidden from the masses, as he must do.

This is what we have seen fit to present as an introduction concerning the symbolic representations and allegories found in this book. Through this, coupled with the previous introduction, the content of this book has almost been made perfectly clear. Having completed this we commence the explanation of this scroll as we intended.

---

[53]Hebrew: *betar.*

[54]Hebrew: *besamim.*

27

Late-Fourteenth Century Perception of Classical Jewish Lore:
Shem Ṭob ben Isaac Shapruṭ's Aggadic Exegesis

Lester A. Segal
University of Massachusetts – Boston

By the time Shem Ṭob ben Isaac Shapruṭ of Tudela had come to write a full-length commentary on talmudic aggadah, his *Pardes Rimonim,* he had already given evidence of his concern with the proper exposition of this rabbinic material in two previous works which have remained unpublished. In both of them, *Eben Boḥan,* a comprehensive Jewish apologetic treatise written in 1380-1385 which had grown out of his debate in Pamplona with Cardinal Pedro de Luna – latter antipope Benedict XIII – and in *Ṣofenat Pa'aneiaḥ,* an explanatory work on Abraham ibn Ezra's Pentateuchal commentary, Shem Ṭob's attention to aggadah occupies a notable place. In *Eben Boḥan* Shem Ṭob expressed his concern with the sizeable number of former co-religionists who, having defected from the Jewish ranks attempted to ingratiate themselves with the Christians by debating the meaning of various biblical verses and aggadot. Shem Ṭob reports that some engaged in debate and questioning to find support for their newly adopted religion while others utilized this as a forum for exhortations intended to slander Jews. All this apart from the "many among the Christian scholars who wish to debate with us."[1]

---

[1]*Eben Boḥan* (Bodleian Library, Ms. Opp. Add. 4to, 72). Folio 1v. Hereafter cited as *E.B.* There are several manuscripts of this work. I wish to thank the

In preparing the *Eben Boḥan* Shem Ṭob drew on the earlier apologetic work by Jacob ben Reuven, *Milḥamot Ha-Shem*, but he found it necessary to comment at the outset that the author "had not introduced anything concerning aggadot although he had very great need to do so."[2] Indeed in the *Eben Boḥan* Shem Ṭob devoted an entire book to some two dozen problematic aggadic texts[3] which were used by Christians to support their faith or to demonstrate presumed Jewish animosity towards its followers. Access to such rabbinic material had long since been made available through various Christian polemical compendia, notably the *Pugio Fidei* (Dagger of the Faith) by the thirteenth-century Dominican Raymond Martini.[4] That on the Jewish side polemicists were not derelict in their acquaintance with Christian sources and particularly with the New Testament, is obvious from Shem Ṭob himself who even included a translation of *Mathew* in the *Eben Boḥan*.[5]

In his response to the Christian challenge, articulated in the *Eben Boḥan* by the anonymous "trinitarian" ("ha-meshalesh") who personifies the Christian spokesman, Shem Ṭob counters with an aggadic exposition by the "unitarian" ("ha-meyaḥed") intended to uphold Jewish doctrine. The dialogue format for such polemics is not original with Shem Ṭob. His "'amar ha-me-shalesh" and "'anah ha-meyaḥed" resemble for example, "the heretic" and the believer" in the twelfth-century treatise *Sefer Ha-berit* by Joseph Kimhi ("'amar ha-min" and "'amar ha-ma'amin") and especially "the denier" and "the unitarian" in Jacob b. Reuven's *Milḥamot Ha-Shem* ("'amar ha-

---

Curators of the Bodleian Library, Oxford for permission to cite *E.B.* and the other manuscripts that I have utilized in this study.

[2]*Ibid.* Shem Ṭob erroneously attributes *Milḥamot Ha-Shem* to Joseph Kimhi.

[3]*Ibid.*, Folios 148v-159r. In the brief introduction to this section he refers to his own present lack of "a book composed on this [subject]" (Folio 148v).

[4]Martini's influential polemical role and the character of *Pugio Fidei* have in recent years been re-examined in Jeremy Cohen's *The Friars and the Jews – The Evolution of Medieval Anti-Judaism* (Ithaca and London: Cornell University Press, 1982), 129-156.

[5]See Alexander Marx's discussion of the versions of *Eben Boḥan* and also his comparison of a section from Shem Ṭob's translation with other Hebrew versions of Mathew, in "The Polemical Manuscripts, etc." in *Biographical Studies and Notes on Rare Books and Manuscripts in the Library of the Jewish Theological Seminary of America* ed. M.H. Schmelzer (New York: Ktav Publishing House, 1977), 462-470. See too Shem Ṭob's obvious adaptation of certain New Testament passages in his *Pardes Rimonim* (Sabbioneta: 1554, Repr. Israel, 1968), 34a. Hereafter cited as *P.R.*

mekhaḥed" and "heishiv ha-meyaḥed").[6] Both these earlier works however were primarily in response to Christological interpretation of Hebrew scripture. Shem Ṭob on the other hand was in his book XI of *Eben Boḥan* specifically concerned with Christian appropriation or misrepresentation of rabbinic lore.

Shem Ṭob begins with an aggadah from the tractate *Sanhedrin* which reports that the sons of R. Ḥiyyah, Judah and Hezekiah, sitting once in the presence of R. Judah the Patriarch, observed that the son of David (i.e. Messiah) would not appear until the two ruling houses in Israel – the Babylonian Exilarchate and the Palestinian Patriarchate – had ceased to exist. Citing this narrative, the Christian disputant in Shem Ṭob's *Eben Boḥan* concluded that at present there was neither Patriarch nor Exilarch and "if so the messiah has already come."[7] The claim concerning Jesus' messiahship could, in other words, be validated on the assumption that the two branches of Davidically descended Jewish leadership had long since ended; indeed the implication of the Christian spokesman's argument was that the two offices had ostensibly ceased to function even long before the time of R. Judah the Patriarch.

The text of this passage as cited by "the trinitarian" omits the reaction of R. Judah. Distressed by the suggestion drawn from the book of Isaiah, that the coming of the son of David would be "for a stone of stumbling and for a rock of offense to *both* the houses of Israel," (i.e. Patriarchate and Exilarchate) he said to R. Ḥiyyah's sons: "You have placed thorns in my eyes."[8] The Christian polemicist's version appears to have ignored the obvious fact implicit in R. Judah's response that the patriarchate was still a vigorous and assertive force at the time that the exchange recorded in the talmudic narrative took place. Shem Ṭob's "unitarian" reminded his opponent of some elementary historical facts. R. Judah the Patriarch had lived long after the destruction of the Temple, and following him the Patriarchal line had continued down through the time of even his great-grandsons. In which case, the messiah had not yet come in their days, and Jesus, having come prior to a long succession of Patriarchs, cannot have been the messiah. Shem Ṭob pressed the historical side of his argument even further, noting that "even at present there are Patriarchs and Exilarchs."[9] He was no doubt

---

[6]See Kimhi, *Sefer Ha-berit,* ed. F. Talmage (Jerusalem: Mosad Bialik, 1974), and Jacob b. Reuven *Milḥamot Ha-Shem,* ed. J. Rosenthal (Jerusalem: Mosad Ha-Rav Kook, 1963).

[7]*E.B.,* Folio 149v, and see *B. Sanhedrin,* 38a.

[8]*B. Sanhedrin,* 38a.

[9]*E.B.,* Folio 149v.

aware that even in the late thirteenth century Jewish spokesmen and polemicists in Christian lands had continued to extol the greatness and dignity of the contemporary Exilarch,[10] and that the title of Nasi persisted down to his own age. Apart from the hereditary Nasi of Narbonne, whatever the origins of that position may have been, Shem Ṭob may even have been aware of the contemporary Sar Shalom Nasi ben Pinhas in Egypt, and then Baghdad, who had apparently succeeded in demonstrating his Davidic origin.[11] That the patriarchate like the exilarchate was by his time but a shadow of its former self did not deter Shem Ṭob, in his capacity as a polemicist, from attempting to establish as decisively as possible from the actual continuity of the two offices over the centuries, the Jewish doctrinal implications of the aggadic passage in dispute.

From an argument which he viewed as based on historical considerations, Shem Ṭob nonetheless felt compelled to take the matter several steps further. He noted that the language of the narrative itself, "until the two ruling houses in Israel ceased to be," suggested that there might in fact be an interval between the cessation and the actual arrival of the messiah. He then added that Ḥiyyah's son had been neither a sage nor a prophet but a mere lad and one could derive absolutely no proof from his assertion.[12] In effect, the potential challenge of the aggadic passage as appropriated by the Christian disputant was so serious that Shem Ṭob felt compelled to provide the most comprehensive range of explication: all the way from presenting the most precise historical frame of reference within which the narrative in question had to – or could – be understood, to demonstrating on the basis of the unreliable authority cited in it that this aggadah was purely speculative and could not sustain the Christian's argument.

But even before responding to the Christian disputant's appropriation of this aggadah – and the almost two dozen others that follow in book XI of the *Eben Boḥan* – Shem Ṭob first introduced a statement of principle as to the status of aggadah in general. Echoing the position already suggested by talmudic sages, elaborated by geonic spokesmen, and refined further by later medieval authorities such as Maimonides, the "me-yaḥed" declared: No argument should be made

---

[10]See e.g. Salo W. Baron, *A Social and Religious History of the Jews* (Philadelphia: Jewish Publication Society, 1957), V, 8, and 294, n.4.

[11]See Jacob Mann, *The Jews In Egypt and in Palestine Under the Fātimid Caliphs*, (Oxford University Press, 1920), I, 174. Regarding Narbonne, see S.W. Baron, *The Jewish Community* (Philadelphia: Jewish Publication Society, 1948), III, 68, n. 12a.

[12]*E.B.*, Folio 149v.

on the basis of aggadah because all aggadic dicta are metaphorical in nature, hinting at hidden matters; they are not to be taken literally in as much as they merely present an exterior[13] – which, Shem Ṭob no doubt meant, is intended to convey something other or more profound than what is apparent at the surface level.

To what extent Shem Ṭob intended this characterization to refer in fact to "all aggadic dicta" is somewhat problematic; certainly not all of his Jewish predecessors and contemporaries who were concerned with the subject of aggadah were prepared to be quite so inclusive. In the thirteenth century Naḥmanides for example, had allowed for a nonliteral understanding of an apparently very broad range of aggadic material; at times he even sought in his halakhic work to sort out rabbinic pronouncements which he deemed to be purely hyperbolic in intent.[14] Yet in the discussion of divine retribution in his *Torat Ha-adam* he was insistent that a particularly vivid aggadic description of Gehinnom attributed to the amora Joshua b. Levi must not be assigned to the category of "metaphor and riddle" because it was so explicit in its detail and because it had a bearing on Jewish religious law.[15] Naḥmanides younger contemporary and student Solomon ibn Adret, who composed a special work to explain some aggadot, clearly viewed certain extremely anthropomorphic talmudic passages concerning God as metaphorical in intent, declaring that "they are all parables" intended to facilitate a person's perception.[16] But in this same, partially preserved commentary where he refers in various instances to the use of parable he attempted to establish the credibility of some rather extraordinarily imaginative aggadot. Shem Ṭob, as we shall see, found much to criticize in ibn Adret's commentary but made some use of it himself.

Both ibn Adret and Shem Ṭob seem in fact to have broadly subscribed to a position essentially similar to that set forth earlier by Maimonides. In the well-known passage in his *Commentary to the Mishnah, Pereq Ḥeleq,* Maimonides had indicated his intention to compose a treatise which would explain "all of the *derashot* in the Talmud and other sources." He proposed to interpret them in a manner "corresponding to the truth," disclosing those to be understood according

---

[13]*Ibid.*

[14]See Chaim Tchernowitz, *Toledoth Ha-Poskim* (New York: Jubilee Committee, 1947) II, 109, and n. 2.

[15]*Kitvei Rabbenu Mosheh ben Naḥman*, ed. H.D. Chavel (Jerusalem: Mosad Ha-Rav Kook, 1963), II, 285.

[16]See *'Ein Ya'akov, Berakhot*, 59a, where Jacob ibn Ḥabib quotes ibn Adret, in his commentary *Ha-kotev*. See too the opening line to ibn Adret's commentary in *'Ein Ya'akov, Berachot*, 6a.

to the plain meaning, those to be taken as parables, and still others as events experienced in a dream but which the sages reported as if they had occurred in a wakeful state.[17] Later on when he had decided against this plan, he noted in the *Guide* that he had previously promised to write a work that would "explain all the difficult passages in the *Midrashim* where the external sense manifestly contradicts the truth and departs from the intelligible," and he asserted that "They are all parables."[18] Ibn Adret appears to have applied this formulation to that which was blatantly anthropomorphic in the aggadot, while elsewhere attributing concrete reality to supernatural or miraculous phenomena in the aggadah where he viewed it as theologically defensible or spiritually justified to do so.

In a polemical work for example, where he recorded his responses to a Christian interlocutor's exploitation of aggadic material – apparently the Dominican polemicist and author of the *Pugio Fidei,* Raymond Martini – ibn Adret addressed the following issue: The Christian, having raised a question regarding the rabbinic idea of the pre-existence of the Torah prior to the creation of the world, asked how it was possible that the Torah should have been written, as an aggadah had it, "with black fire on white fire," for fire would presuppose physical matter. And since space did not yet exist, how was such matter possible for matter cannot exist in the absence of space. To this ibn Adret replied that white and black fire as used here were to be understood as "parables and figures of speech...the black and the white hinted at punishment and reward," while "the writing" hinted at the idea of preserving awareness and memory of the message being conveyed. If however, one wished to insist on the literal intent of this aggadah, as ibn Adret apparently sensed the Christian was doing, then the question he had raised of "matter" and "space" presented no obstacle in the rabbi's opinion. For God, Ibn Adret argued, who was after all the very "existence of the world" and had created "a space" in advance for the celestial spheres and the earth, had similarly brought the "standing place" into being to sustain the substance of the "writing" referred to in the aggadah.[19] Contemporary Christian polemics directed against Judaism certainly played a role in ibn Adret's

---

[17] *Mishna 'Im Perush Ha-Rambam,* trans. J. Kafaḥ (Jerusalem: Mosad Ha-Rav Kook, 1963), *Nezikin, M. Sanhedrin,* commentary, 140.

[18] *Guide of the Perplexed,* trans. Sh. Pines (Chicago: Chicago University Press, 1963), I, 9f.

[19] "Perushei Aggadot la-Rashba," in *R. Salomo ben Abraham ben Adreth,* ed. J. Perles (Breslau, 1863), 48f. Regarding this aggadah, see e.g. *Y. Sheqalim,* 6:1.

formulation of a response which included affirmation of this aggadah in its literal sense. Still, he apparently felt assured that in so doing he did not compromise his own intellectual integrity nor that of the classical Jewish tradition.

He no doubt felt equally assured in his exposition, in the commentary on talmudic aggadot, of the account regarding Leviathan and the feast prepared for the righteous in the world to come – the distinctly corporeal aspects of which he sought to uphold while simultaneously describing how that corporeal reality was intended to help realize spiritual purpose. "Do not be disposed to dismiss [the idea of] the righteous having a feast in the world to come according to the literal meaning of the words presented by the sages, of blessed memory, in some of the haggadot in the Talmud and the midrashot." Ibn Adret then followed up his reference to "seudah kefeshatei ha-devarim" with a long analysis intended to establish the credibility of the future feast as a prior physical stage which would facilitate the spiritual fulfillment of the soul. The stirring of the bodily powers through the means of food and drink and the resulting joy of heart, would help to effect the strengthening of the intellectual power of the soul. And the ingredients of the future feast, having been prepared from the very period of creation were, by virtue of their pure nature, especially suited to achieve this spiritual objective.[20] It is of interest to note that this exposition also occurs, in virtually identical language, in a manuscript of Todros Abulafia's late thirteenth-century qabbalistic commentary to talmudic aggadah, *Ọsar Ha-kavod*.[21] If the transposition of the one author's work into that of the other was not entirely inadvertent, one wonders whether it was perhaps the spiritual meaning given by ibn Adret to the Leviathan aggadah which led it to be associated with a leading qabbalistic commentary of the period.

Ibn Adret in any event, in asserting that "we take these [aggadic] matters in their literal sense ("bifeshatan") – a point he reinforced in various ways along the line in his analysis – set forth an interpretation which clearly presupposed Naḥmanides' position on the matter of "the world to come." "Olam ha-bah" according to ibn Adret, was to be experienced by the righteous while they were still in their corporeal condition; in this condition, and following the promised feast, they

[20]Leon A. Feldman, "Perush Ha-aggadot la-Rashba le-massekhet Bava Batra," *Bar Ilan Sefer Ha-shanah* (1970), VII-VIII, 140ff. and see *B. Bava Batra*, 74b.

[21]*Ọsar Ha-kavod*, (Ms Bodleian Arch. Seld A50), Folio 204v. See too Feldman's comments in the *Bar Ilan* study (above, n. 20), 139, but also his "Ọsar Ha-kavod Ha-shalem le-massekhet Ketubot Le-Rabbenu Todros Abulafia MiTulitula," *Sefer Ha-Yovel Le-Khevod Shalom Baron* (Jerusalem: American Academy for Jewish Research, 1974), III, 298.

would finally achieve a level of spirituality something like that of Moses during the Sinaitic revelation, or like that of Elijah and Enoch at the time of their ascension.[22] On the purely metaphorical side however, insofar as corporeal things were constituted so as to correspond to spiritual ideas and facilitated rational perception thereof, ibn Adret understood the Leviathan story as hinting at issues of "matter and form" ("ha-ḥomer ve-haṣurah") and more specifically at the joining of the intellect with the soul in the body – and he proceeded at some length to deal with the relationship of the two. The term "Leviathan" according to ibn Adret, meant "joining," and was ostensibly related to the verb *"yilaveh"* in *Genesis* 29:34, and, as a metaphor for the adornment of intellect, to the phrase "*livyat* ḥen" in *Proverbs* 1:9 ("a graceful *wreath* upon your head").[23]

The merits of these etymological associations apart, the metaphorical side of ibn Adret's explanation of the Leviathan and of God's disposition of the male and female pair of this species according to the Talmud, is suggestive of the speculative aspect of his aggadic exegesis. Shem Ṭob Shapruṭ had in fact already acknowledged this dimension of his predecessor's commentary, when, in the introduction to his *Pardes Rimonim* he called attention to ibn Adret's praiseworthy intention to interpret aggadot by resorting to a conjunction of philosophy with the plain meaning of the Torah. The plan however, had gone awry according to Shem Ṭob as a result of the undue influence of qabbalah on ibn Adret – an influence Shem Ṭob viewed as detrimental to clarity. Previous authors' efforts to deal with aggadah along purely qabbalistic lines, "ten sefirot [suspended over] emptiness" he caustically added, had resulted in a body of commentary which was even vaguer and more impenetrable than the aggadic material itself.[24] Shem Ṭob probably had in mind Abulafia's *Ọsar Ha-kavod* or even the earlier thirteenth-century qabbalistic commentaries of Azriel of Gerona and Ezra of Gerona. But as for the mingling of mysticism with philosophical rationalism, Shem Ṭob obviously believed this could only further aggravate matters. For "philosophy and qabbalah" he observed, "are in truth two opposites between which there is no mediator and this has been the cause of confusion fo serious students [of the subject]."[25] Whether it was this introductory critique that Shem Ṭob had in mind when he later referred to ibn Adret's "outlandish explanations" of the Leviathan aggadah is not quite clear. But he was

[22]Feldman, "Perush Ha-aggadot la-Rashba," 143f. and 144, n. 78.
[23]*Ibid.*, 144, 146.
[24]*P.R.*, Author's Introd. 2a.
[25]*Ibid.*

very firm in asserting that "aliens had come through the portals" in this piece of aggadic exegesis and that in most of what ibn Adret had here proposed the element of truth was mixed up with the nonsensical. When it came down to detail Shem Ṭob directed his criticism at what he perceived to be a confusion on ibn Adret's part regarding the nature of "the rational soul," which distinguishes man from all other sublunar beings, and "the vegetative soul," which man has in common with the vegetable realm of being. Ibn Adret had presumably merged the two into one in his analysis, and since it was unthinkable that anyone should have said such a thing, the rabbi, Shem Ṭob declared, must not have been fully alert when he made this assertion or someone else was responsible for it.[26]

The Leviathan aggadah was in fact one which Shem Ṭob himself addressed not only in the *Pardes Rimonim,* but before that in his super-commentary to Abraham ibn Ezra's work, *Ṣofenat Pa'aneiaḥ* – although there without any reference to ibn Adret's handling of it. Following the main text of the latter work, in which he also had occasion to address various aggadic passages, there is a kind of appendix which Shem Ṭob intended as "an explication of some aggadot" referred to but not clarified by ibn Ezra in his Pentateuch commentary.[27] In the two dozen or so folios which make up this section of the *Ṣofenat Pa'aneiaḥ* manuscript, there are any number of aggadic interpretations which, in very similar although not necessarily identical language, later recur in the *Pardes Rimonim.* Shem Ṭob would in such instances indicate that he had already explained the particular passage in the "sha'ar ha-aggadot" of his work on ibn Ezra.

Proceeding from a purely metaphorical point of view, Shem Ṭob noted that the sages had hinted at "the secret of the relationship between body and soul" and had used the term "Leviathan" to designate the rational soul which endows man with his unique being as distinguished from other living creatures. He resorted here to at least one of the biblically-based etymologies previously utilized by ibn Adret: the rational soul being the "crown" with which the human was adorned, the sages had referred to it as "Leviathan" by association with the phrase in *Proverbs* 1:9, "*livyat* ḥen le-roshekha." He described the relationship between the human being's corporeal and rational faculties in the light of the talmudic imagery about the creation and disposition of the male and female pair of Leviathan,[28]

---

[26]*Ibid.*, 9a-b.
[27]*Ṣofenat Pa'aneiaḥ* (Bodleian Library Ms. Opp. Add. 4to107), Folio 270r. Hereafter cited as *Ṣ.P.*
[28]*Ibid.*, Folios 276 v-r and *P.R.*, 9b.

presumably rectifying the confusion that ibn Adret had introduced into this relationship in his attempt to deal metaphorically with the same aggadah. Whatever similarities there may be however, between the two interpreters in this metaphorical understanding of the aggadah, Shem Ṭob's exegesis in this matter is entirely devoid of any suggestion of literalism.

Indeed it would appear from his sharp criticism of what he characterized as the *strange* and *absurd* features of ibn Adret's interpretation, that Shem Ṭob was not only dismissing its confused account of the rational and vegetative soul relationship, but also ibn Adret's effort to uphold both literal and metaphorical meaning. Shem Ṭob commented on the fact that of all the problematic aggadot in the talmudic tractate *Bava Batra,* especially those reported by Rabba bar Bar Ḥanna, the literal sense of which was in his opinion even more difficult to deal with than the Leviathan story, ibn Adret had chosen only to explicate the latter. Of the fantastic stories reported by Rabba b. Bar Ḥanna Shem Ṭob had written that "No person is able to assert that he experienced [any of] this in reality."[29] And in a manuscript passage on the same subject – a passage – missing in the sixteenth-century printed version of *Pardes Rimonim* – Shem Ṭob reminded the reader that "[With respect to] all these aggadot *your rational faculty* will instruct you as to how to interpret them."[30] These sentiments undoubtedly applied to the Leviathan story as well.

What no doubt also precipitated Shem Ṭob's criticism in this particular matter is that, given ibn Adret's view of the Leviathan aggadah and of the future feast, he obviously subscribed to Naḥmanides' opinion that there would be both corporeal and spiritual reward in the world to come.[31] This condition would come about following the resurrection when body and soul would exist in conjunction forever after in that future world, with the corporeal part of man having been purified by God beyond the need for food and drink. Shem Ṭob however, in this area of Jewish doctrine, clearly held the opposite position, which had been enunciated by Maimonides. In the well-known passage in his *Mishneh Torah* Maimonides observed that the sages had metaphorically referred to the future bountiful condition

---

[29]*P.R.*, 9a.

[30]*Pardes Rimonim* (Bodleian Library Ms. Mich. 212) Folio 14r. Hereafter cited as *P.R.* (Ms.). This is a much shorter version of the work than the printed (1554) edition. Maharsha's much later insistence on the literal meaning of the Leviathan aggadah may be noted: "Ve-dah ki yesh lanu le-ha'amin be-khol ha-devarim ha-eileh bi-feshatan...'ein ha-devarim yoṣe'im mimashma'an."

[31]See *Sha'ar Ha-gemul* in *Torat Ha-adam, Kitvei Rabbenu Mosheh ben Naḥman*, II, 300f., 302f., 304, for some of Naḥmanides' discussion of this point.

prepared for the righteous as a "feast" and it is this state, he added, which they everywhere designated as "the world to come."[32] This future reward was understood by Maimonides to be purely spiritual, and conferred upon the soul only in the everlasting life of the world to come – a condition which would follow the corporeal state of the time of the resurrection.

Commenting on the aggadot in *Pereq Ḥeleq* in his *Pardes Rimonim,* Shem Ṭob observed that Maimonides had so validly interpreted the matter of the world to come that there was nothing further to be said about it; he noted moreover that he had previously explained all this in his *Eben Boḥan* to which he referred the reader.[33] Indeed in that work, in his discussion of the Messiah for example, Shem Ṭob had occasion to discuss the aggadah from *Pereq Ḥeleq* which said that those righteous whom God would resurrect in the future were destined never to return to the dust. This meant, said Shem Ṭob, that their corporeal being would ascend and would be transformed into spiritual form as in the case of Enoch and Elijah.[34] It is instructive that Shem Ṭob made do with these two biblical examples alone and was careful not to include the instance of Moses at the Sinaitic revelation to illustrate the spiritual transformation of the righteous – which ibn Adret had indeed done in interpreting the Leviathan aggadah. While there might be some ambiguity about the conditions surrounding Enoch's and Elijah's ascension, Moses experience, despite the temporary detachment from the mundane at Sinai, was still too clearly associated with corporeality to serve the purpose of Shem Ṭob's analysis. Equally instructive is Shem Ṭob's choice of words to characterize the phenomenon in question. Ibn Adret had said: "*sheha-olam ha-bah yikansu bo ha-ṣadikim bequfoteihem ve-yiheyu bo ke-inyan Mosheh beSinai,* ve'im tirṣeh 'emor ke-inyan Eliyahu veḤanokh, she'amru za"l shena'aseh besaram lapid eish."[35] Shem Ṭob on the other hand wrote in the *Eben Boḥan: "sheyit'aleh gufam veyithapeikh leruḥani* keguf Ḥanokh veEliyahu;" and in his *Pardes Rimonim:* "shelo yishlot bahem rimah vetole'ah rak *yithapeikh hagufim leruḥaniyut kevesar Eliyahu*...shehaKadosh barukh Hu 'oseh lahem kenafayim, kelomar

---

[32]*Mishneh Torah, Hilkhot Teshuvah,* 8:4.

[33]*P.R.,* 14b.

[34]*Eben Boḥan* (Bodleian Library Ms. Mich. 137 [ol.4]), Folio 178v. This is a second copy of *Eben Boḥan* and will be here designated as *E.B. (2).* And for the aggadah see *B. Sanhedrin,* 92 a-b.

[35]Feldman, "Perush," *op. cit.,* 143f. Emphasis added.

'eini 'omeir shehagufim ya'amdu rak sheyithapkhu leruḥaniyut vehu ha-nirṣeh bemilat kenafayim.[36]

Apart from the fanciful language of the aggadah in *Pereq Ḥeleq* – which also spoke of God as endowing the righteous with wings that they might then "move to and fro above the waters" – it was "clear" for Shem Ṭob for a number of doctrinal reasons, that it could not have been meant literally. Among other things, as he also explained in the *Pardes Rimonim* along Maimonidean lines, unless one were to ascribe greater delight to corporeal than to spiritual existence – which would give the lie to the very foundations of the Torah – the aggadah could only be understood as referring to "the world of the souls." Resurrection itself after all was *only* intended to allow for that perfection of the souls and that spiritual perception which had not been possible during the earthly life.[37] In all this it is of some interest to note that Shem Ṭob's explication of aggadic terms or vocabulary in the *Pardes Rimonim* is not always precisely identical with what one finds in the *Eben Boḥan* or in the *Ṣofenat Pa'aneiaḥ* – although the overall analysis of the particular passage is similar. Thus with respect to the "wings" to be given to the righteous he informed the reader in the *Eben Boḥan* that "You are already aware that 'wing' is analogous with perception and 'water' with the Torah" – meaning that their perception of the Torah would thus enable the righteous to cleave unto God and be spared the upheavals of the day of judgement under individual providence.[38] In the *Pardes Rimonim* there is a more general statement about the transformation of corporeal into spiritual existence "which is what is intended by the word 'wings'."[39]

Shem Ṭob had undertaken to prepare his *Pardes Rimonim* motivated by what he perceived as the current dearth of clarity in the exposition of aggadic material. His plan was to interpret those aggadot which appeared to require clarification, "in accordance with Toraitic opinions known to us from the words of our great teacher Maimonides...and Abraham ibn Ezra." Such opinions being reasoned conclusions, akin to philosophy, one would then be able to carry on informed public discussion on the subject of aggadah.[40] That such exposition and discussion continued to be for Shem Ṭob no mere academic exercise may readily be gathered from what he says in the *Pardes Rimonim* of his zealousness on behalf of the talmudic sages. The *Pardes*

[36]*E.B.(2)*, Folio 178v; *P.R.* 15a. Emphasis added.
[37]*P.R.*, 15a.
[38]*E.B.(2)*, Folio 178v.
[39]*P.R.*, 15a.
[40]*Ibid.*, Introd. 2a.

Rimonim appears to have been in direct response to those whom he describes in his introduction as scorners of the sages' words. Shem Ṭob like various Jewish authors – Maimonides, Isaiah di Trani the Younger, and others – who complained of such scorners no doubt had certain Jews in mind. But his mention of those who compiled works in which aggadot had been selected with the purpose of utilizing them to slander Jewish religious tradition appears to refer especially to Christian and apostate polemicists.[41]

Having already taken on the task of responding to the Christian appropriation of aggadah for polemical use, Shem Ṭob then proposed to address the subject from the much broader perspective of a full-length commentary on the Babylonian Talmud which would selectively consider some of the most enigmatic aggadot, and those most likely to be misunderstood in the light of what they narrated or the imaginative language they employed. Although others had preceded Shem Ṭob with commentaries organized according to the order of the talmudic tractates – notably Azriel of Gerona, Todros Abulafia, ibn Adret, and also the thirteenth-century Provençal author Isaac b. Yedaiah[42] – his was at the very least unique in that it was the first to appear in print as a volume unto itself long before the modern age.

Rationalism informs much of Shem Ṭob's aggadic exegesis. Predictably not denying the reality of miracles *per se,* he deemed it far preferable to explain aggadic matters rationally rather than resort to the miraculous.[43] And as with miracles, so too with the esoteric: Shem Ṭob does not appear to have rejected the possibility of esoteric meaning as such, but, viewing himself as one whose task it was to "interpret the Torah according to its plain meaning...leaving secret things behind,"

---

[41]*Ibid.,* The extensive Christian interest in and utilization of such works is well illustrated from Shem Ṭob's own disputant the cardinal – legate Pedro de Luna, who made a specialty of çollecting them; of Martini's *Pugio Fidei* alone he possessed three different copies. See Baron, *Social and Religious History,* IX, 99, and 287, n.2.

[42]See: *Perush Ha-aggadot Le-Rabbi Azriel,* ed. I. Tishby (Jerusalem: Mekize Nirdamim, 1945); Feldman's work on ibn Adret, previously cited (n.20) and references there and in his Abulafia paper (above N. 21) to other published parts of Adret's commentary; *Oṣar Ha-kavod* was, in part, first published in Nowy Dwor, 1808; on Isaiah b. Yedaiah, see Mark Saperstein, *Decoding The Rabbis – A Thirteenth-Century Commentary on the Aggadah* (Cambridge: Harvard University Press, 1980). Extensive extracts from Adret's work were published by ibn Ḥabib in his *Ha-kotev* to his *'Ein Ya'akov* (1516) and other parts by his son Levi b. Ḥabib.

[43]e.g. *P.R.,* 21b commenting on the first chapter of tractate *Yoma* about the "miracles" which transpired when throngs of pilgrims had assembled in the Temple precincts.

the esoteric, as he asserted, was not his kind of concern.[44] "Plain meaning" *('al derekh ha'peshat)* as an exegetical procedure or principle, must be understood here with reference to a body of doctrinal, moralistic, or philosophical truths assumed by an exegete such as Shem Ṭob to have been aggadically cast by the ancient sages in the manner of "riddle and metaphor" *(be-derekh ḥidot u'meshalim).*[45] Although the recognition of such aggadic device or manner of expression long predates Shem Ṭob, he was perhaps especially emphatic in insisting that this literary format had been utilized by the sages as a way of communicating ideas to the enlightened, too subtle and profound for the masses to grasp adequately. If not concealed from the latter these ideas and truths might lead them to imagine certain fallacious opinions, damaging to their faith.

One needed to recognize therefore that "the more bizarre the riddle the more impossible its literal meaning" and that the objective of such usage by the sages was that the enlightened would strive to get at the lesson inherent in the riddle while the fool's lack of understanding would drive him to abandon the effort.[46] The intellectual disparity between the two groups is stated even more strongly in the manuscript version of the *Pardes Rimonim,* where one finds perhaps an earlier draft of Shem Ṭob's introduction: The sages had intended to conceal certain secrets and wondrous matters "in husks, in order that the fool flee from them, since they are unfit for one such as he; whereas the intellectually cognizing individual will remove the husk and the veil and consume the choice fruit."[47]

Shem Ṭob's extensive attention to aggadic exegesis suggests that learning just how to "remove the husk and the veil" was a very demanding task – especially given, what he sometimes refers to as, the proclivity of *many people* to "pursue the literal meaning of the aggadot." Commenting on the tractate *Sanhedrin* for example on the subject of demons *(sheidim),* he goes on to indict these "many people" because, being literalists, they have concluded without any reservations that demons are beings endowed with bodies who come to men when certain invocations have been pronounced. Almost apologetically Shem Ṭob declared that he had gone on at great length on this subject because in his experience almost everyone subscribed to

---

[44]*Ibid.,* Introd. 2b.

[45]*Ibid.,* 2a.

[46]*Ibid.;* "Sheha-maskil noten 'el libo le-havin ha-nimshal bo ka'asher yir'eh she-peshuto nimnah ve-hasheinit shelo yavin ha-sakhal bahem davar veya'azveim."

[47]*P.R.* (Ms.), Folio 1v.

these views, including even a certain class of talmudists, and he considered this extremely detrimental to religious belief. What Shem Ṭob meant when he added briefly that he himself indeed believed in "the existence of demons" while vigorously denying that they came to man or performed either beneficent or malevolent acts[48] – "all the invocations in the world" notwithstanding – can best be gathered from his *Ṣofenat Pa'aneiaḥ*. There he explained "sheidim" as an imagination and fear – presumably self-induced – which enters the heart of the rationally deficient causing their confused mind to conceive of frightening forms which ostensibly communicate with them. Shem Ṭob further confirmed this condition, as it were, by reference to Maimonides' explanation in his *Guide* of the "sheidim" mentioned in *Deuteronomy* 32:17, those *"imaginary beings"* by which people in Moses' time had been led astray.[49]

In his denunciation of demonology, which he equated with pagan worship, there is also a polemical aspect. Explaining certain passages in *Sanhedrin* which he believed exemplified the sages' rejection of demonology as nonsense and utter vanity, he referred to its wide dissemination "among the nations as a result of the spread of *many beliefs* whose fundamental principle and pivotal point was that their (i.e. the believers) *guardian angel* had come to save men from their (i.e. the demons) power." The words italicized here read in the manuscript of *Pardes Rimonim* as: "Christian belief," and "deity"[50] – a version which either no longer existed in the manuscript which the sixteenth-century printer in Italy had before him, or which was changed at the time due to censorship.

Rationalism did not necessarily dispose Shem Ṭob to uphold whatever the ancient philosophers and naturalists had claimed, nor did he appear to see any contradiction between explaining the manifestations of nature according to what he – and presumably the talmudic sages – understood the empirical circumstances of their occurrence to be *and* simultaneously linking such natural phenomena in a cause and effect relationship with moral accountability to God. In discussing certain rabbinic dicta in the last chapter of tractate *Berakhot* Shem Ṭob observed that the sages *had attributed* various natural phenomena to God and even couched them in anthropomorphic language in order to instill acceptance of His authority and providence.[51] He considered it beyond doubt for any "intellectually

---

[48]*P.R.*, 13b-14a. Emphasis added.

[49]*Ṣ.P.*, Folio 264v, and see Maimonides' *Guide*, ed. Pines, II, 587.

[50]*P.R.*, 13b and *P.R.* (Ms.) Folio 15v.

[51]*P.R.*, 43b.

cognizing individual who is learned in the Torah" that God bestows His goodness on His people because of the observance of the Torah commandments. However metaphorically he might view aggadah, Shem Ṭob clearly understood Pentateuchal statements regarding promise of divine rewards literally – and therefore while rain for example, was "a natural thing," when Israel fulfills God's will rain falls at the most opportune time. Beyond this divine role in the manifestations of nature however, Shem Ṭob went on to describe some of these phenomena in the light of natural causes and he urged his readers not to be troubled by the fact that the sages might have held opinions with respect to nature which did not conform to what Aristotle and his followers had claimed. For Aristotle himself had disagreed with certain views preceeding his own and in these matters most of what he himself had asserted was by no means definitively proven.[52] Shem Ṭob did not however provide specifics here as to which aspects of ancient Greek natural science and philosophy he may have found problematic. What is however most striking, or at least most exegetically informative, in this entire discussion is its conclusion: On the purely aggadic side Shem Ṭob drew the reader's awareness to the fact that the sages' *attribution* of certain actions to God which, ostensibly accounted for the physical phenomena – the figurative language, in other words which they had employed to describe such actions – represented a key to the comprehension of rabbinic dicta: "And understand this very well, and give it your attention for it is a major principle in interpreting aggadot."[53]

Regarding the aggadot in *Berakhot* too, there is an element of contrast with the commentary of ibn Adret, although perhaps less pronounced than with those previously considered. Ibn Adret had taken careful note of the metaphor and imagery in these aggadic passages and he asserted further that the phenomena of nature are perennial, having been part of the original order of creation. Beyond this however, he did not find it necessary, or appropriate, as did Shem Ṭob, to transfuse the plain words of the aggadic statements into the realities of celestial physics, as then understood (e.g. "God kicks at the firmament" presumably meant that thunder resulted from the entry of gaseous vapor, generated by the dry condition of the earth, into the body of the cloud and its subsequent eruption with great force). Ibn

---

[52]*Ibid.* 43a-b. Regarding God's beneficence as reward for observing the Torah, Shem Ṭob elsewhere clarifies that this is entirely beyond the natural scheme of things; such reward, or punishment, is not compelled by the natural order, indeed it is contrary to it (*P.R.* 25a).
[53]*Ibid.*, 43b.

Adret places much greater emphasis on the correlation between the extreme or destructive form of natural phenomena *and* human sin and shortcoming. For ibn Adret the sages' dicta were intended to represent usual manifestations of nature as in a state of periodic dysfunction resulting from divine displeasure with man's falling away from the Torah – especially since the destruction of the Temple and its absence as an instrumentality of atonement.[54]

Still, with respect to Shem Ṭob's relationship to the aggadic exegesis of ibn Adret it needs to be pointed out that he was not disinclined to draw on his predecessor's work – in several instances in the form of long, verbatim extracts.[55] He would sometimes highly commend ibn Adret's interpretations when presenting them,[56] but several are included in the *Pardes Rimonim* without attribution. Thus, although Shem Ṭob insisted on naturalistic explanation of miracles wherever possible, he in one instance concurred with ibn Adret's confirmation of the miraculous. According to the tractate *Ḥullin* the saintly R. Phineas b. Yair commanded a certain river to divide itself for him, and some fellow-travellers, because the sage was en route to perform a very worthy religious deed. The river acquiesced, and ibn Adret understood this to be one of the many instances reported by the sages where, in time of special need on behalf of the people at large, and by virtue of their elevated spiritual condition, the very pious were able to effect something miraculous which involved a departure from the normal course of nature. Ibn Adret did however underscore that short of such great need (in this instance, redeeming of captives) such action was inappropriate. Shem Ṭob included ibn Adret's analysis word for word without comment in the *Pardes Rimonim*.[57] Only in a following, second round of commentary to this tractate did Shem Ṭob himself address the same aggadah, this time much more briefly and directly, although retaining the main point of ibn Adret's presentation. Here Shem Ṭob noted that no one, not even "the philosophers," would deny that the spiritually whole individual was capable of initiating "signs and wonders" when great necessity required it. Shem Ṭob did however reduce at least the one aspect of this aggadah involving R. Phineas encounter with the patriarch R. Judah to purely metaphorical

[54]See ibn Adret as quoted in ibn Ḥabib's *Ha-Kotev, 'Ein Ya'akov, Berakhot,* 59a, and cf. *P.R.* 43a.

[55]*P.R.*, 38b-39a; 43b-44a, 44b-45a.

[56]*Ibid.*, 33a; 47b.

[57]*Ibid.*, 43b-44a, and cf. ibn Adret as quoted in *Ha-kotev, 'Ein Ya'akov, Ḥullin,* 7a.

expression, even attempting to interpret it in the historical context of the patriarch's duties in relation to Roman officialdom.[58]

No one, Shem Ṭob had asserted early on in the *Pardes Rimonim,* would deny the reality of miracles except for one who denied the law of Moses.[59] However, the conditions specified with respect to the Phineas b. Yair story represent the essential limits within which he was prepared to acknowledge literal truth in aggadic accounts of the miraculous. Otherwise, he almost invariably discounted miracles, divination, hyperbole, supernatural communications and visitations of all sorts that he encountered in the aggadah. To accord them acceptance in literal form would in his opinion be offensive to the rational sense and an impediment to correct religious faith and understanding. They were instead made to issue various philosophical, moral, or doctrinal truths; if at all conceivable within the realm of reasonable human experience they were accommodated to the mundane; where the advice or guidance they proffered were minimally useful or defensible, or even potentially delusive, he had no hesitation to classify them as vanities which were best avoided.[60]

One further observation needs to be made in the matter of earlier exegetical works on aggadah which Shem Ṭob appears in some instances to have drawn on. There is some irony in the fact that for all of his criticism of how qabbalistic authors had hopelessly obfuscated the meaning of aggadah – and his approach certainly does contrast sharply with theirs – comparison of texts suggests that he utilized material from Todros Abulafia's *Ọsar Ha-kavod* in several places. Thus, some of Shem Ṭob's analysis of the four sages who entered the "Pardes", as reported in the tractate *Ḥagigah,* has distinct affinities with Abulafia's, even though the arrangement and wording of the material differs. Regarding Ben Azzai for example, the following partial comparison is instructive:

Pardes Rimon reads:
"...hinei ha-Pardes romeiz
le-fardeis ha-hokhmah veha-
'iyun vehi hokhmat ha-'elohut.
U'ven Azzai heiṣiṣ vera'ah
sheha-hokhmah hi ha-'ikar
u'she'ar kinyenei ha-'olam
sheheim hevel venatan

Ọsar Ha-Kavod reads:
"...r"l le-fardeis ha-hokhma
hi hokhmat ha-'elohut.
Ben Azzai heiṣiṣ u'meit
mitokh shedavqah nafsho
be-'ahavah u'deveiqut
'amiti ba-devarim ha-
'elyonim sheheim yesodah...

[58] *P.R.*, 47a.

[59] *Ibid.*, 14b.

[60] On the very last point here, see *P.R.*, 15b-16a.

'aṣmo lilmod u'pireish
mei'inyenei ha-'olam...
shehiniaḥ kol ta'avotav
hagashmiyo'.. 'o r"l
meit shelegodel ha-devequt
davqah nafsho bemeqorah
vera'atah menuḥah ki tov
venifredah meiha-guf velo
yasfah shuv 'eilav 'od."[62]

be-'otah sha'ah ra'atah
menuḥah ki tov velo shavah
'od lemeqomah..."[61]

In addition Shem Ṭob's commentary on the aggadah in tractate *Ḥullin* regarding the one-horned ox which Adam brought as a sacrifice consists of a long discussion taken verbatim from ibn Adret, although in this instance not identified as such. This analysis too, the opening line of which in *Pardes Rimonim* – and in ibn Adret – reads "There is in this [aggadah] a hidden secret and we shall disclose it,"[63] parallels the material in *Ọsar Ha-kavod* in many ways, again with differences in arrangement and formulation. In both for example, the single horn is identified with the notion of God's unity. In *Ọsar Ha-kavod,* the commentary occurs in the section on tractate *Shabbat* where the same aggadah is recorded.[64] Whether this material is original with ibn Adret and inadvertently was inserted into the *Ọsar Ha-kavod,* as with the commentary on the Leviathan story cited previously, is not clear.

By way of conclusion something may be said regarding the printing of the *Pardes Rimonim* in sixteenth century Italy and some spirited contemporary response to its appearance in print. From the point of view of an unmitigated champion of literalism such as the talmudist Joseph Ashkenazi, writing in the 1560's, metaphorical meaning of aggadic texts when their religious integrity presupposed and demanded, according to him, no more nor less than the plain sense of the words, was to contribute to the subversion of the tradition. Although reserving his most bitter denunciation for Shem Ṭob, he was simultaneously disturbed by ibn Adret's approach which he viewed as encouraging doubt about anything in the tradition which could not be immediately grasped. Ironically, like Shem Ṭob, Ashkenazi singled out ibn Adret's effort to employ a kind of syncretic exegetical method in the exposition of aggadah as inherently flawed. But with respect to a

---

[61]*Ọsar Ha-kovod,* Folio 112v.
[62]*P.R.,* 31a, and see *B. Ḥagigah,* 14b.
[63]*P.R.,* 44b, and cf. ibn Adret as quoted in ibn Ḥabib's *Ha-kotev, 'Ein Ya'akov, Ḥullin,* 60a.
[64]*Ọsar Ha-kavod,* Folio 52v.

main element in this approach, philosophy, the two represented diametrically – opposed positions. For Shem Ṭob, a philosophically-oriented understanding of the profundities which "our earliest sacred Fathers" had related through the means of aggadic parables and riddles[65] was vital and essentially self-sufficient. For Ashkenazi philosophy was not only entirely dispensable, but it needed to be vigorously rejected for it obscured the fact that the unadorned sacred dicta of the sages were self-sufficient. Ashkenazi could not comprehend what had possessed the great rabbinic authority ibn Adret who after all "believes in the plain meaning of the majority of the sages' words..., to ride on two steeds simultaneously, following in the path of the accursed philosophers...And behold all those who came after him...added to his words, for he believed in the literal meaning of the [aggadic] matter even though he presented it as 'form', while they found a pretext, on the basis of his words, not to believe in the entire Torah with respect to whatever is not [immediately] within their grasp from the very outset of their speculation."[66] And ibn Adret himself after all, as Ashkenazi too noted in passing, had been a central figure in the well-known early fourteenth-century controversy in Provence over the study of philosophy and what appeared to some at the time as the threat of religious rationalism. He had finally agreed to issue the ban in 1305 which proscribed the study, before the age of twenty-five, of the works of the Greeks on natural science or metaphysics and public instruction in this subject matter. What may especially have rankled Ashkenazi, the bitter opponent of Maimonidean philosophy and of secular studies, was the fact that ibn Adret had however defended the works of Maimonides and had actually exempted them from the ban.[67]

As for Shem Ṭob, Ashkenazi viewed his *Pardes Rimonim* as directly inspired by ibn Adret's work on aggadah, and anyone who took the trouble to examine it would find that it was but a pack of errors and vanities. He essentially accused Shem Ṭob of having unscrupulously attempted to demonstrate that miracles *per se* were untenable by using extraneous arguments to invalidate the literal sense of every aggadic

---

[65]*P.R., Introd.* 2a.

[66]See Gershom Scholem, "Yediot Ḥadashot 'Al R. Yosef Ashkenazi Ha'tana' MiṢefat," *Tarbiz* 28 (1958), I-II, 233. The citation is from the manuscript treatise published here by Scholem, apparently composed by Ashkenazi in the 1560's during a stay in Italy and prior to his departure for Safed.

[67]See the discussion in Abraham A. Neuman, *The Jews In Spain* (Philadelphia: Jewish Publication Society, 1948) II, chap. XVI, espec.130ff., and Yitzhak Baer, *A History of the Jews in Christian Spain*, trans. L. Schoffman (Philadelphia: Jewish Publication Society, 1966) I, 288, 301f.

miracle he had undertaken to interpret. The end result of all this according to Ashkenazi, was that the Torah had been made out to be nothing more than an account of innumerable, staggering problems, presumably unworthy of credibility – a villainous characterization for which he held "this wicked heretic, author of *Pardes Ha-minim(!)*" responsible.[68] Ashkenazi was not alone in these sentiments. Writing just some years earlier the well-known Italian rabbi and qabbalist Moses Basola bemoaned the recent appearance of Shem Ṭob's commentary on aggadah, and other rationalistic type works. He considered it a pity that they had survived, being in his view, "vanities which deserve to be burned and which it is forbidden to read."[69]

The contrast between all this and the effusive praise heaped upon both author and treatise in the preface and in the concluding remarks to the sixteenth-century printing of the *Pardes Rimonim* is very striking. The remarks are those of one, Solomon Isaac ben Menahem Yerushalmi – or Zekel Ashkenazi, as he informs the reader he was generally called – who described the manuscript in his possession as a singular copy of the work. This he had held on to zealously in the course of the tribulations of his wanderings, finally seeing it printed in 1554 in the Sabbioneta press of Ṭobias Foa.[70] Referring to the fact that Jewry was then trembling in agony and in the aftermath of the "blazing conflagration which had overtaken the house of Jacob," – and he of course had in mind the recent (1553) papal condemnation and consequent burning of enormous numbers of Hebrew books in Italy – Zekel Ashkenazi noted the substantial measure of spiritual relief which Shem Ṭob's *Pardes Rimonim* could afford his co-religionists. Virtually associating the contemporary disaster in a type of cause and effect relationship with a lack of knowledge in the Jewish ranks and a preoccupation with "alien wisdom," not an uncommon complaint at the time, he goes on to extol Shem Ṭob's commentary and its prospective role in the reaffirmation of Jewish religious life and learning.[71] He treats it with a kind of pietistic rhetoric that one might almost expect, in that age, to be conferred on a widely acknowledged moralistic treatise. That Zekel Ashkenazi viewed the *Pardes Rimonim*, which "had straightened out the thorny [subject matter] of the aggadot," as a

---

[68]Scholem, 77f. quoting Ashkenazi's treatise.

[69]See Meir Benayahu, *Haskamah U'reshut Bedefusei Veneșiya* (Jerusalem: Mosad Ben Șvi-Mosad Ha-Rav Kook, 1971), 86, and see 88.

[70]*P.R.*, concluding two pages – not numbered – following 51a of Shem Ṭob's text.

[71]*P.R.*, opening page, before 2a of Shem Ṭob's Introd.

work so worthy that he who devoted himself to it "will always be exalted...and in whose light we will see light,"[72] may be described, with not too much exaggeration, as light years apart from the assessment of his namesake, only a decade or so later.

---

[72]*P.R.*, concluding page following 51a.

Part Ten

JUDAISM IN THE MIDDLE AGES: PHILOSOPHY AND THEOLOGY

28

Creation in Medieval Philosophical, Rabbinic Commentaries

Norbert M. Samuelson
Temple University

Introduction

This essay analyses the concept of creation in Genesis 1:1 through 2:3 of the Hebrew Scriptures as that concept was interpreted in the biblical commentaries of medieval Jewish philosophers. It would not be possible in a single essay to deal with every commentary. However, I believe that the selection made for study here is representative of the diversity of interpretations in medieval rabbinic tradition and, with one qualification, sets the parameters for determining the classical Jewish doctrine of creation. The qualification is that this essay will not give an equal voice to all genres of rabbinic interpretation.

Every rabbinic commentator on the Hebrew Scriptures sought to explain the biblical text in any or all of the following ways: He explained its simple and/or its hidden meaning.[1] The former dealt primarily with linguistic questions, viz., semantics and grammar. The latter was homiletic, philosophical and/or mystical.[2] All four kinds of

[1] I.e., he dealt with the פשט of the text and/or he gave a פרוש נסתר. The different categories of rabbinic biblical commentaries given below are taken from the different terms that Nachmanides uses in his commentary.

[2] I.e., the commentator (המפרש) in this case presented a homily(אגדה) and/or he gave a reason (יתן טעם) for what the text says, and/or he revealed a secret (סוד יגלה) of the text. The tradition of rabbinic Judaism that concentrated on these "secrets" was the Kabbalah.

interpretation are important to understanding how the rabbis understood Scripture. Often these different approaches produce contrary explanations, and most commentators recognized the contradictions. However, for most[3] rabbis this diversity of meaning was not problematic. God expresses His truth in multiple ways in His written word. While one kind of hidden meaning may not seem to agree with another kind, the conflict is not real. The difference lies only in the mode of expression. Just as the statements "1+11=12" in base 10 and "1+11=100" in base 2 look as if a different answer is being given to the same question, in fact the problems are different and the statements, when set in their appropriate context, are mutually coherent, so a homiletic and a philosophical statement, for example, may seem from their language to be dealing with the same question and reaching different conclusions, when in fact each kind of statement is dealing with a different question, and for that very reason there need not be any conflict between them. This is not to say that the rabbis advocated any kind of multiple truth theory any more than modern mathematicians believe that clear mathematical problems have multiple, incoherent answers. Without exception these rabbis believed that the one God of the universe is the source of only one truth. However, this epistemological unity has diverse expressions. Consequently, within each kind of commentary there is a need to determine, in keeping with the logical rules of that language, coherence and consistency. Hence, two philosophical interpretations that violate the law of the excluded middle cannot both be true. However, to give a reason is not the same thing as to give a homily, and what the language of a text explicitly says[4] or what that explicit statement logically entails[5] need not be consistent with what the text alludes to or how the text is used in a homily. Allusions or hints[6] are subject to their own distinct kind of grammar.

This essay is primarily interested in what the classical rabbinic commentators determined to be the linguistic and philosophical meaning of Genesis' account of creation, so that ultimately[7] constructive Jewish theologians will be in a more informed position to compare what

---

[3]"Most" but not all. Marc Saperstein presents an excellent discussion of the attitudes of thirteenth century commentators to earlier homiletic biblical interpretations in *Decoding the Rabbis: A Thirteenth-Century Commentary on the Aggadah*, Cambridge, Harvard University Press, 1980.

[4]I.e., פשט.

[5]Which is another way of stating what a philosophical interpretation is.

[6]What the rabbis sometimes call the text's "inner meaning" (פנימיה); what I am here calling the "mystical interpretation."

[7]Beyond the scope of this single essay.

Judaism teaches about creation with the teachings of contemporary Western science. What the commentators say as linguists and as philosophers is comparable, but what they say as preachers and mystics is not. In the latter cases the languages simply are too different. In this instance a comparison would be the proverbial error of comparing apples and oranges. Hence, midrash and Kabbalah will largely be ignored in this essay. However, there is no intent to diminish the importance of this kind of rabbinic literature, and they will not be ignored entirely. All of the commentators to be discussed were familiar with and used midrash, and at least one of them[8] emphasized Kabbalah. To the extent that these materials relate to the commentators' consideration of the linguistic and philosophical meaning of creation in Genesis, they will be dealt with in this essay.

The body of this essay will explore the interpretations philosophically-oriented commentators recorded in the מקראות גדולות.[9] The מקראות גדולות are the standard printed rabbinic bibles that present the Hebrew text of Scriptures together with the Onkelos Aramaic translation and selected commentaries. While the commentators presented in this set of volumes have changed over the centuries, and "making it" into an edition is in no formal sense a process anything like canonization, still, these commentators have a special status in consequence of their inclusion that testifies to their legitimacy as major voices in determining what is the Jewish understanding of Scripture. Whether they have this authority because they were included in these editions or they were included because they have the authority is an issue of scholarship that once again need not concern us in this essay. Whatever the historical causes are, it is legitimate to look to these commentaries on Genesis as expressions of the rabbinic understanding of creation. The three presented are Abraham ben Meir ibn Ezra,[10] Moses Ben Nachman Gerondi,[11] and Obadiah Ben Jacob Sforno.[12]

---

[8]Viz., Nachmanides.

[9]How Jewish philosophers interpret creation outside of their biblical commentaries within their general philosophical works will be discussed in a separate essay where particular attention will be given to the writings of Saadia, Maimonides and Gersonides.

[10]Henceforth referred to as "Ibn Ezra." b. 1092 C.E. in Toledo. d. in 1167 C.E. in Rome. Lived in Cordova until 1140 C.E. The last twenty-seven years of his life were spent as a travelling scholar, mostly in Christian Provence, Northern France and Italy.

[11]Known to the Jews as "Ramban." b. 1194 C.E. in Gerona. Believed to have died in the Holy Land around 1270 C.E. Henceforth referred to as "Nachmanides."

[12]b. around 1475 C.E. in Cesena. d. 1550 C.E. in Bologna. Henceforth referred to as "Sforno."

Each commentator presents a distinct kind of biblical interpretation that reflects the best of Jewish thought about creation at the time that he lived. Ibn Ezra was a twelfth-century Andalusian poet and philosopher, a contemporary of such philosophic giants as Judah Halevi, Joseph ibn Zaddik and Abraham ibn Daud. Although his commentary was written near the end of his life when he travelled in the southwestern regions of Christian Europe, it represents the best of Jewish philosophical thought in the Muslim world. Nachmanides was a twelfth-century European rabbi, steeped in Kabbalah, who played an important spiritual and political role in the so-called "Maimonidean controversy"[13] and represented the Jewish community in the disputation with Pablo Christiani in Aragon in 1263. Nachmanides reflects a sophisticated European rabbinic reading of Scripture informed by the commentaries of Rashi, ibn Ezra and Jewish mysticism. Finally, we encounter in the early sixteenth century physician-rabbi Sforno an excellent representative of how a committed and informed rabbinic Jew of the Italian renaissance interpreted creation in the light of the entire tradition of classical rabbinic commentaries.

This essay will not examine every aspect of these commentaries. Rather, they will be discussed in detail only to the extent that they deal with creation, i.e., with a picture of how the universe came into being and what the initial universe looked like. The commentaries will be presented in relationship to each other verse by verse in their respective genealogical order.

The Explanation of Ibn Ezra, Nachmanides and Sforno

Day One (1:1-5)

According to Ibn Ezra, verses one and two constitute a single sentence that says, when[14] the revered primary judge[15] together with the next level of judges,[16] all of whom are immaterial entities, decreed His desire[17] that limits be imposed on the pre-existing materials[18] in order to transform them into something new,[19] these materials became this

[13]See Daniel J. Silver, *Maimonidean Criticism and the Maimonidean Controversy, 1180-1240*. Leiden, E.J. Brill, 1965.
[14]Which is what "בראשית" means.
[15]Which is what "אלהים" means.
[16]Viz., the angels.
[17]חפץ, which is what God's "רוח" means.
[18]Viz., the תוהו.
[19]Which is what "ברא" means.

physical universe. God's "desire" is the element, air.[20] תוהו and בוהו are pure capacities of the element, earth. The World To Come is an immaterial, eternal region in which reside incorporeal, unchanging angels. Like the angels and the World To Come, these capacities are not created, but neither are they real or of any value. Solely through His desire, God actualizes them into the yet undifferentiated material universe,[21] whose subsequent physical inhabitants will be subject to birth and death. This domain consists of three primary territories. There is a region composed from the element earth, that is covered by a region of water, that itself is covered by air. Subsequently these three spaces – earth, sea and sky – will be further divided into distinct areas. Light will be made explicit on the first day, sky on the second, vegetation on the third, stars on the fourth, and the souls of the living things on days five and six.

Basing himself almost exclusively on the grammar of the terms within the Hebrew Scriptures, Ibn Ezra rejects the claim that "ברא" must mean bringing something into existence out of nothing. His analysis of the term "אלהים" reconciles the grammatical data that the form of the subject is plural and the form of the verb is singular. The verb is singular because the referent of the subject is God. The noun is plural because its sense makes reference to the angels. It is not a proper name. Rather it is a disguised description for the master of the masters who more directly govern the physical universe. On his view there are only two worlds – the World To Come,[22] which is an immaterial, unchanging region in which the angels reside, and This World[23] of material change.

In contrast, according to Nachmanides, at the very first moment of[24] the universe,[25] the power that is the source of the power of everything[26] brings forth matter from absolutely nothing at all by an act of will without the imposition of any intermediary.[27] At this stage the universe was nothing at all except space predisposed to be made

[20]Note that the Stoics made the element air the active causal agent of all biological activity. While Ibn Ezra may be influenced in this case by Hellenistic thought, it is not an unreasonable interpretation of Scripture itself.

[21]I.e., "This World" (העולם הזה).

[22]העולם הבה.

[23]העולם הזה.

[24]Which is what "בראשית" means.

[25]Which is what "את השמים ואת הארץ" means.

[26]Which is what "אלהים" means.

[27]Which is what "ברא" means.

into something. As such it was a first body composed from prime matter[28] and form[29] into the elements fire,[30] air,[31] water[32] and earth.

According to Ibn Ezra, the physical universe becomes a unified, revolving sphere of earth, surrounded by water, surrounded by air. The sphere in turn becomes encompassed by an area of light that blends into an area of dark. As the sphere of the universe revolves through these regions, it passes from a period in light without dark to a period where both are indistinguishably present, to a period in dark without light, to a period where both are again present but now distinct. These periods are named in corresponding order, "day," "evening," "night" and "morning." During the first complete rotation of the physical universe,[33] God did two things. (1) God desired light into existence, and (2) He thought to name the pre-existent dark "night" and the created light "day."

In contrast, Nachmanides asserts that during this first twenty-four hour period of the universe, God creates out of nothing a first form and matter from which He produces the space of the physical universe. This space is immediately differentiated into upper and lower regions. The lower region then is differentiated into the four elements. In addition, God creates wisdom, the Throne of Glory, and the element light that fills the upper region. At this stage the universe is a large sphere at whose center is a sphere of earth, that is surrounded in consecutive order by rings of water, air, fire and light.[34]

On Sforno's reading, the text says that at the beginning of time,[35] in no time whatsoever, God, an eternal incorporeal necessary being who is the source of the existence of absolutely every other existent, made, out of absolutely nothing[36] a perfectly spherical, finitely large space. At this stage of creation the universe consisted solely of this space. The sphere is called "heavens."[37] At its core is "the earth" that, at this

---

[28]Which is what "תוהו" means.
[29]Which is what "בוהו" means.
[30]Which is what "חושך" means.
[31]Which is what "רוח" means.
[32]Which is what "תהום" means.
[33]I.e., during day one.
[34]The close similarity of Nachmanides and that of Plato's *Timaeus* cannot be ignored. In this dialogue deity differentiates space into distinct regions through whose essential motion arise the elements.
[35]Which is what "בראשית" means.
[36]Which is what "ברא" means.
[37]From a single point draw two circles, one horizontal and the other vertical, that intersect each at right angles. Now add a second pair of circles from the same point from an infinitesimally different angle from the first pair. Sforno

initial stage, is merely a point at the geometric center of the sphere. It is a compound of prime matter[38] and prime form.[39] Next God creates His celestial intellects[40] and differentiates the earth into a series of rings, each composed of one of three elements of the physical universe – earth, surrounded by water,[41] surrounded by air[42] – by the rotation of the entire sphere on its axis as a vortex. The motion of the particles at the circumference of the ring of air produces a friction that ignites them. Elementary fire consists of these inflamed air particles. The universe as a whole is a rotating sphere whose elements move at a velocity directly proportional to their distance from the earth center of the sphere.

---

imagines a sphere to be composed of an infinite number of such pairs of circles at different inclinations from each other. I.e.,

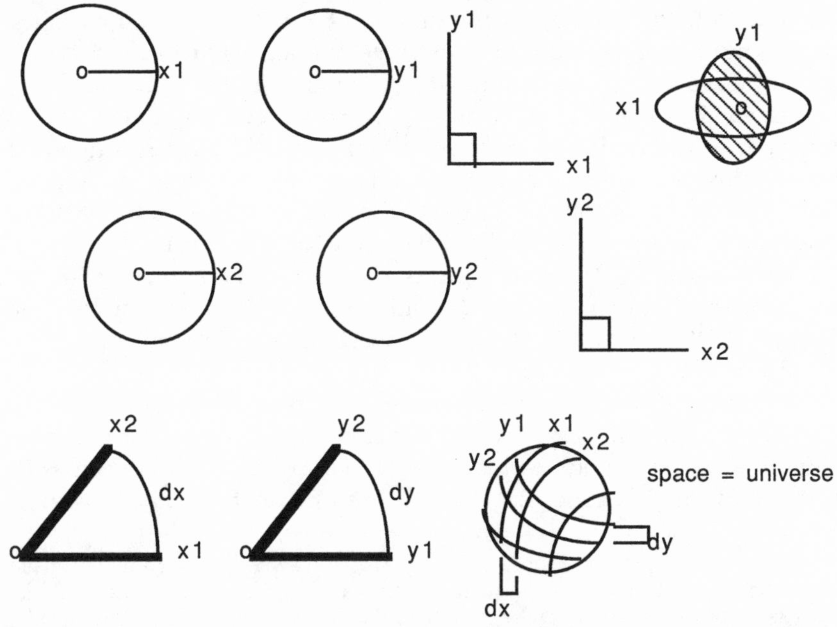

This is one way that Sforno uses the term, שמים, viz. as the space of the universe. Subsequently he uses the term in a more restricted sense as the exterior or upper portions of the universe beyond the central sphere of earth and sky. In every case the term will be translated as "heavens."

[38]Which is what "תוהו" means.

[39]Which is what "בוהו" means.

[40]Which is what "רוח אלהים" means.

[41]Viz., the "תהום."

[42]Viz., the "חושך."

An apparent difference between these philosophical commentators is that Nachmanides takes the term "יום" literally to express the same period of time as an earth day,[43] while Ibn Ezra and Sforno relativize the word. As an earth day marks the time required for the sphere of the planet earth to complete one rotation on its axis, so the term day in the account of creation marks the time required for the sphere of the universe to complete one full rotation cycle. *Prima Facie*, given that the radius of the universe is vastly greater than that of the earth and that Scripture itself says nothing about this question, there is no reason to believe that these two time periods are the same. However, this difference may only be apparent. There is no reason to assume that the velocity of these two spheres is the same. Nachmanides may accept Ibn Ezra's definition of a day and still assert that the two time periods are identical. In fact this is what Plato reports in his *Timaeus*, viz., that the length of the rotation of the motion of the Same, which rules the natural motion of the universe as a whole, is twenty-four hours.[44]

In this respect Sforno's commentary is more radical than that of any of his predecessors. It is clear on his interpretation that the time referred to in the biblical creation story is not our own. His universe rotates through regions of light and dark, but the "light" is not our light, and the "dark" is not our dark. They have nothing to do with the presence or absence of the light of the sun and stars. Rather, the dark is the pure element, air, and the light is an element that existed when our world began that will return at the end of days, but is found nowhere in This World. Consequently, while creation takes place in time, it is in no sense our time.

Nachmanides' commentary does take issue with Ibn Ezra in a number of critical respects. (1) Nachmanides' claim that "אלהים" expresses the power of the powers of everything can itself be read as an elaboration of the sense that Ibn Ezra assigns to the term. However,

---

[43]In his commentary on Gen 2:3 Nachmanides seems to contradict himself when he suggests that each day represents 1,000 years. The context of his discussion of the meaning of the term "day" in Genesis 1:3 is to give the simple, linguistic meaning of the term. In contrast, the context in Gen 2:3 is a discussion of messianism. There the interpretation is presented within the framework of Jewish mysticism, and, as we noted above, linguistic/ philosophical commentaries cannot be compared with kabbalistic ones. As noted in the introduction, there is no incoherency in the fact that a statement within one context literally contradicts a statement confined to the other context.

[44]This is not the only parallel between Nachmanides' commentary and Plato's *Timaeus*. For example, in both cases what deity initially does is demarcate undifferentiated regions of empty space into separate regions from which arise the elements of the physical world of generation and corruption.

there is one significant difference. The "powers" of which Ibn Ezra speaks are the angels. For Nachmanides they are the first form and matter whose combination produces the four primary elements of earth, water, air and fire. In this respect Sforno's commentary is closer to Ibn Ezra's. For Sforno the term "אלהים" is a general term for the species of all immortal, immaterial intellects, which includes both angels and God.

(2) According to both Nachmanides and Sforno, first form and matter respectively are "בוהו" and "תוהו." The entire physical universe is composed of a single uniform stuff that has a single essential nature. תוהו is that stuff and בוהו is its nature. Its creation begins the universe. In contrast, for Ibn Ezra "בוהו" and "תוהו" are synonyms. However, all three agree that these terms name the pre-existent material out of which the material universe is actualized.

(3) All of the commentators read the biblical text as saying that God created elements from which the universe was formed. However, they differ in how the Bible expresses it. According to Ibn Ezra, the text implies the existence of fire and explicitly mentions the other three classic elements. ארץ is earth, מים is water, and רוח is air. Furthermore, he notes that the light is an additional element that is generated on the first day.

Nachmanides has a number of problems with this interpretation. First, he considers it to be an unnecessary confusion to have the same Hebrew term, "ארץ" function in different contexts to mean both an element and a region of physical space. In his commentary this term and the word "שמים" combine to name the undifferentiated space that subsequently is distinguished into the lower and upper physical realms. He introduces the term "עפר" for the element earth. Second, he objects to Ibn Ezra's inclusion of אור on the same level with the pre-existent elements. It is clear that light is something formed out of the created first matter and not itself one of the elements. Third, he notices Ibn Ezra's failure to account for the terms "תהום" and "חושך" in the text. Nachmanides identifies the former with elementary water and the latter with elementary fire.

Sforno's commentary once again is more radical than both of his predecessors. In agreement with Ibn Ezra and in opposition to Nachmanides, "מים" names the element water and "ארץ" names the element earth. In other words, given a choice between the two interpretations, Sforno chooses the more literal account. "תהום" is the name of the ring of water that at the initiation of the universe encircles the earth. However, since he identified "רוח" with the angels, instead of associating "חושך" with fire, he identifies it with air, the object to which Nachmanides referred the term "רוח." Whereas Ibn Ezra and

Nachmanides follow the accepted scientific Aristotelian tradition of their day in listing four primary elements as the building blocks of the terrestial world, Sforno lists three. On his analysis fire is itself something generated from the elements, viz., from the natural motion of the air. Hence, in spite of their difference in terminology, neither Ibn Ezra nor Nachmanides in this case add anything to the accepted Aristotelian cosmology of their day, whereas Sforno makes a radical departure. Sforno's physics is closer to the Stoics, whose active principle of the universe was *pneuma*, a mixture of fire and water, than it resembles the Aristotelians. Also in this respect, Sforno's commentary comes closer to the implicit physics of the biblical text than any of his predecessors.[45]

(4) According to both Nachmanides and Sforno, "בראשית" clearly expresses the beginning of the time of the universe. It is not a mere grammatical formalism for initiating the account as it is for Ibn Ezra.

This issue points to the main substantive difference between their interpretations of the first day of creation. Ibn Ezra's explanation that the verb "ברא" means to ordain limits on materials presupposes that those materials already exist, and, as we already have noted, he is aware that this interpretation is controversial. While Ibn Ezra believes that the "out of nothing" modification of "to create" is not essential, Nachmanides and Sforno see this characteristic as the essential feature of what creating is. In terms of the language of the biblical text, the issue expresses itself in how these commentators differentiate "ברא" from "עשה." They agree that the first verb applies to God's action on day one, and the second verb expresses what occurred during the next five days in consequence of God's act. For Ibn Ezra, what God ordained as an indefinite potentiality at first subsequently was made into a definite actuality by the angels. For Nachmanides and Sforno, God first brings forth matter out of absolutely nothing at all solely through His desire or thought.[46] Hence, while Ibn Ezra tells us that for God to "say" something means that God wills the angels to make something potential actual, in the case of Nachmanides and Sforno, it is God Himself who brings forth what is potential to actuality. In other words, for Nachmanides and Sforno "to say" and "to create" are synonyms. On their account, with respect to the first day, God's one creative act produces (a) the first form and matter that constitute the undifferentiated sky and earth, as well as (b) the potentialities within space from which subsequently actual different

---

[45]See my "Creation in Genesis in the Hebrew Scriptures" (forthcoming).

[46]Desire and thought, in God's case, in consequence of His oneness, is the same thing.

objects arise. The earth at its inception contains the elements from which the different species of entities in the sublunar world are generated, and the sky contains the light from which the different heavenly objects emerge.

It is of interest to note that, whereas Nachmanides introduces some products of the first day solely on the authority of the midrash[47] and Ibn Ezra does not, in fact angels play a dominate role in Ibn Ezra's cosmology that is lacking in Nachmanides' counterpart. In this respect, in spite of Nachmanides' commitment to both rabbinic homily and mysticism, his account ultimately is more naturalistic than Ibn Ezra's. Beyond the origin of the universe on the first day, whereas the latter's scientific cosmology is dominated by the causal influence of non-material entities from the heavens, the former's cosmology sees all subsequent causal explanation strictly in terms of the inherent nature and stuff of the fundamental matter of the universe itself. In this respect the astronomy of the mystic Nachmanides is closer to modern astrophysics than the counterpart of the rationalist Ibn Ezra. For this reason it is not surprising that the commentary of the Renaissance rabbi Sforno more resembles Nachmanides than Ibn Ezra. First, Nachmanides, unlike Ibn Ezra, can differentiate between heavenly bodies that reflect rather than emit light.[48] Second, what is far more important, Ibn Ezra's stars are created by angels on the fourth day, while Nachmanides' celestial objects arise naturally on that day as solidified forms out of their uniform material of elementary light. Like Ibn Ezra's universe, Sforno's contains angels, which are identified with the celestial intellects. However, like Nachmanides' angels, they play little role in the origin of the physical universe.

Day Two (1:6-8)

According to Ibn Ezra, on the second day, in a single unit of time, the sky is produced, the waters are separated from the earth, the sky is named heaven and the earth is named earth. In other words, it is not the case that the heavens are created on the second day while the dry land and the seas are distinguished on the first. These seemingly distinct events are the product of a single act. This is what Scripture means by saying "it was so" and "it was good," i.e., they express distinct, single units within creation. In this case, the air[49] is stretched out between the water and the earth, transforming them into three distinct regions of dry land, bodies of water, and sky. It is not that these

---

[47]Viz., wisdom and the Throne of Glory.

[48]See Days Three and Four below.

[49]I.e., God's wind (רוח אלוהים).

regions did not already exist. As noted above, everything that will be already is created on the first day. Rather, on the second day these regions are confined within their proper limits. What happens is what had been indefinite now becomes definite.

According to Nachmanides, on the second day two events occur simultaneously. The upper region of space becomes filled with a primary material, called "sky,"[50] from which the heavens[51] are formed. The occupying sky itself is a ring of congealed water stretched out from the exact center of the region of elementary water formed on the first day. The space occupied is the heavens. On the first day it was a mere geometric point that contains a specific potentiality that now, through the filling motion of the sky, is actualized as the distinct location for all heavenly objects.

Sforno's explanation closely parallels that of Nachmanides with the following differences. The sky is composed from a combination of elementary air and water called "mist." God stretches it out between the ring of water and its ignited circumference at the world's periphery. Then He compresses some of this air within the mist into a separate ring that He forces between the sphere of earth and water encircling it at the center of the physical universe.[52]

---

[50]"רקיע."

[51]"שמים."

[52]*Prima facie* what Sforno says means that the רקיע is some of the portion of the ring of water below the central sphere of the earth, viz.,

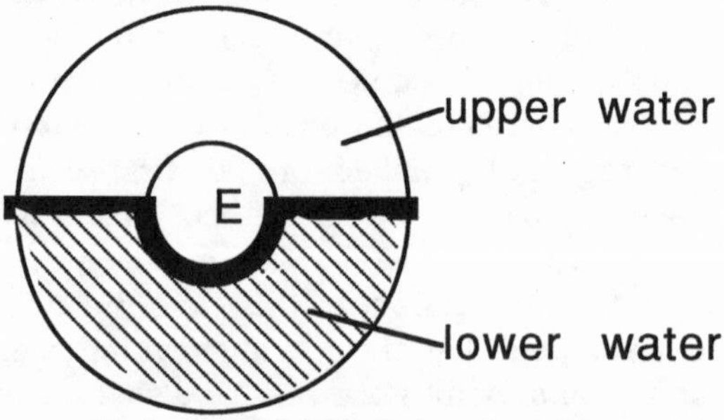

However, it is more likely that he intended to describe some water at the lower or interior surface of the ring of water surrounding the earth core. In either case, the רקיע becomes a strip of mist stretched out along the lower as well as the upper surface of the water ring, viz.,

Except with respect to the differences noted in their commentaries on the first day, the descriptions of Ibn Ezra, Nachmanides, and Sforno substantially differ in only three respects. First, Nachmanides and Sforno reject Ibn Ezra's judgment that the differentiation of the earth into regions of dry land and seas takes place on the second day. Following the literal order of Scripture, these events occur on the third day. The element water[53] is separated from the element earth,[54] the space occupied by the former is called "seas," and the dry land occupied by the latter is called "earth."

Second, the ontology of Nachmanides and Sforno includes five rather than four elements. Although all of them include the four classical elements under different names – fire,[55] air,[56] water[57] and earth[58] – Nachmanides and Sforno add a fifth celestial element[59] for the heavenly objects.

Third, all three disagree about the meaning of the terms "כן" and "טוב." Ibn Ezra and Nachmanides agree that "כן" signifies that what preceeded is a single unit, but they disagree about "טוב." Ibn Ezra treats the term as a synonym for "כן." According to Nachmanides, "טוב" means that the created unit will persist forever. Similarly, while Ibn Ezra says that when God "sees," He sees with His mind, according to Nachmanides, the verb signifies that God makes His object permanent. In contrast, Sforno asserts that the term that expresses permanence is "כן." Furthermore, "to see" means "to desire," and "טוב" indicates a yet

---

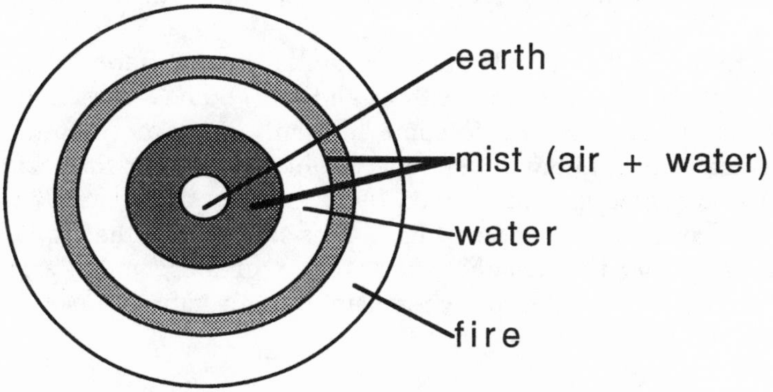

[53]"תהום."
[54]"עפר."
[55]"אור" for Ibn Ezra and "חושך" for Nachmanides.
[56]"רוח" for both Ibn Ezra and Nachmanides, and "חושך" for Sforno.
[57]"מים" for Ibn Ezra and Sforno, and "תהום" for Nachmanides.
[58]"ארץ" for Ibn Ezra and Sforno, and "עפר" for Nachmanides.
[59]Viz., "אור."

unrealized end that is expressible in terms of theoretical, moral knowledge.

Nachmanides and Sforno endow the elementary structure of the universe with a permanence that Ibn Ezra's description lacks. Their optimism is a consequence of the inherent goodness of the Creator. However, Nachmanides did not make clear the sense in which God's product will endure. As Sforno indicates, its goodness does not reside in what the physical world *is*. Rather, it lies in what the universe through natural knowledge must and/or ought to and/or will *become*. It also is true that Sforno makes it clear that while species cannot become extinct, neither can they evolve. Still, his biblical cosmogony is a moral physics.[60] The absolute goodness of the universe lies in its operation as a whole from its beginning to its end, and not in any part of the universe at any separate period of time. On his view to reshape what was created in order to benefit human civilization is superior to merely preserving the given state of nature. That nature can be improved through human intellect is itself a law of his physics.

Days Three and Four (1:9-19)

According to Ibn Ezra and Nachmanides, the vegetation arises naturally from a power[61] placed into the earth on the first day. In the same way water generates the things that swarm and fire generates the stars. According to Nachmanides, the heavenly objects are generated through the interaction of light and the רקיע. As such these objects are composites of the distinct celestial element[62] set in a region of solidified water.

There seems to be only one substantial new difference in their descriptions of the work of days three and four. Both Nachmanides and Sforno are aware that while some heavenly substances emit light, others receive the light and then reflect it. In contrast, Ibn Ezra does not seem to recognize any distinction between stars and other kinds of celestial objects that do not emit light. This seems to be the implication of his claim that the designations "great," "greater," and "lesser" of the heavenly bodies refer to the intensity of their light and not to their relative size.

---

[60] I.e., the laws of the universe are not morally neutral.

[61] כוח.

[62] Viz., אור.

Days Five and Six (1:20-31)

Ibn Ezra says that the souls of the living things[63] are created on days five and six. Nachmanides and Sforno say that it is the things themselves.[64] The life created is formed either out of elementary water or earth. The former are created on the fifth day and the latter on the sixth. The products of the fifth day are שרץ,[65] רמש,[66] things that fly, and תנינים.[67] The products of the sixth day are בהמה,[68] חיתו ארץ,[69] other kinds of רמש, and man.

All of the commentaries agree that the charge to be fruitful and multiply is a statement of what will happen and not a command, since every material life form, excluding man, has no choice in this matter. They copulate through instinct rather than through reason.

Ibn Ezra and Sforno interpret the "us" in "let us make man" to refer to the angels, and they follow Saadia[70] in claiming that "in His image" means in the image of God, and that God and man are similar with respect to possessing and using theoretical wisdom to govern themselves as well as others. This capacity is taken by Ibn Ezra to be the referent of the term "glory"[71] as it modifies both God and man. Hence, near the end of the sixth day God commands His angels to form one more land animal whose soul is unique in comparison with other physical creatures in that it resembles God with respect to being able to rule through the use of abstract reason in determining judgments. The biblical term that expresses this point of identity between God and man is "glory."

Ibn Ezra also mentions the homiletic interpretation of "He created them[72] male and female" to mean that the first human being had two

---

[63]I.e., those physical objects that have souls.

[64]The issue between them is the meaning of "נפש חיה." Ibn Ezra says it means the soul of something that is alive, whereas Nachmanides and Sforno say that it means a thing that lives in virtue of having a soul.

[65]According to Nachmanides, these are things that have constant motion.

[66]According to Nachmanides, these are things that creep upon the earth. Ibn Ezra calls them tiny things that live on the land.

[67]According to Nachmanides, these are the great sea-monsters.

[68]According to Nachmanides, these are animals that eat plants. Ibn Ezra says that they are domestic animals. Sforno says that they are land animals in general.

[69]According to Nachmanides, these are carnivorous animals. Ibn Ezra says that they are wild life.

[70]Saadia Ben Joseph Al-Fayyumi (@ 855-@ 955 C.E.).

[71]כבוד.

[72]Viz., האדם.

faces set on his (her, its) body back to back.[73] However, this explanation baffles him.[74]

According to Sforno, God created the paradigmatic human being as an actual mortal animal[75] who possesses choice and the potential to become an immortal intellect.[76] It is this potential that uniquely defines the human species. Insofar as the potential is not achieved, the human is a mere animal; insofar as it is achieved the human belongs to the species of deities[77] whose other members are God and the angels. Angels are unique in that they are perfect by nature and not by choice. Humans are unique in that they become perfect by choice but not by nature. Only God by nature chooses His perfection.

There is general agreement between Ibn Ezra and Sforno in interpreting this section on the creation of man. However, since Nachmanides interprets the entire event of creation to be God's single activity, he cannot refer the "us" to angels. On his view, God performs a single act on the first day that sets potentialities into the as yet undifferentiated space. From that point on all differentiation and actualization emerges out of the space itself. That space was identified as heaven and earth. Hence, on Nachmanides' interpretation, the "us" is heaven and earth. What first emerges are the souls of the different life forms. Then their bodies arise. Next, the human soul is distinguished from the others by receiving special powers,[78] and only then is the human body made definite for this special human soul.

Of all these rabbinic commentators, Nachmanides' interpretation of creation comes closest to the cosmogony of Plato's *Timaeus*. This is especially true in this case, where both writers picture the culmination of creation in the souls of living things and not their bodies. However,

---

[73]For a hellenistic parallel to this homily, see Aristophanes' speech in Plato's *Symposium* (189a-194a).

[74]Cf. his commentary on נעשה אדם in Gen 1:26.

[75]"בהמה."

[76]I.e., to become a "צלם אלהים."

[77]"אלהים."

[78]From Nachmanides' statement that "the souls of men as well as angels are included in the host of heaven" [*Ramban (Nachmanides): Commentary on the Torah. Genesis*, translated into English by Charles B. Chavel, New York, Shilo, 1971. pg. 59, n. 240], Chavel comments that human souls were created at the beginning of creation, and he refers readers to Nachmanides' correspondence in support of this interpretation. However, this explanation does not follow from Nachmanides' actual words in this passage, and in fact directly contradicts what he says in his commentary on Gen 1:26. Furthermore, even if it is the case that Nachmanides says one thing in his correspondence, it does not automatically follow that that statement can legitimately be used to interpret his published commentaries.

this is not to say that Nachmanides' doctrine of creation is identical with that of *The Timaeus*. There are notable differences, not least of which is that on Plato's account the first soul is that of a male member of the human species, and only in consequence of its imperfection do other forms of life emerge. In contrast, according to Nachmanides, the souls of the other life forms are created first, and the human soul is not differentiated by gender.

Day Seven (2:1-3)

"To bless" means to note that a subclass of a species possesses a capacity for its benefit not shared by the other members of the species. Living things are unique among physical objects in possessing the ability to procreate; man is unique among living things in possessing the ability to be rational; and the seventh day is unique among days in that on it all forms of labor are prohibited.

Both Ibn Ezra and Nachmanides reject the inference that God finishing His work on the seventh day means that God labored on this day. Ibn Ezra emphatically says that to conclude an action is not itself an action.

According to Sforno no time passes between the first and the sixth days. In effect they are a single moment. The "rest" of the seventh day refers to the realization of God's end for the universe. However, with respect to God's role, creation ceases, because His end is accomplished. From this point on creation becomes a human activity. Humans are now to begin the process of civilizing nature towards the end of actualizing all of God's knowledge. As such the Sabbath at one and the same time is a remembrance of God's completion of His end at the beginning of This World with the creation of physical nature, and an expectation of man's completion of his end with the actualization of spiritual nature at the beginning of the World To Come.

Critical Terms

אדם: Human. Living things in the lower world formed from the element earth (n) who possess the ability to make rational judgments (i), and/or to voluntarily choose the good (s)

אור: Light. The created element light, made definite on day one (i, s); [1] fire (i) [2] the material from which the heavenly objects were formed (n, s)

The first actual thing formed out of first matter; located above the heavens (n)

אותות: Moments (i)

אלהים: God. A general term of respect and veneration for the one deity of the universe with reference to His authority over the angels in administering nature. (i)

The power of the powers of everything (n)

Deity. The species of immaterial entities; immortal, learned intellects, viz., God, angels, and souls *qua* actualized human intellect (s)

אמר: Says. When God is the subject it expresses the fact that God makes physical objects by willing them through the mediation of the angels. (i)

Brings forth into actual existence (n)

ארץ: Earth. [1] The primordial element earth (i, s)

[2] The lower region of the physical universe (i); the geometric center of the universe at its beginning (s).

A primordial space created on day one; something not as yet real (ממש) that contains within itself the power or potentiality (כוח) to bring something forth into actuality; one of two materials from which the entire universe is formed; the stuff from which are formed the four elements (n)

[3] The planet earth created on day three ; that sphere within the universe which life inhabits (n, s)

את: What is like the essence of a thing (n)

בהמה: Domesticated animals (i)

Living things in the lower world formed from the elementary earth that eat עשב (n)

Animal life with a soul that inhabits the earth (s)

בוהו: A synonm for תוהו (i)

First form; the essential nature of all of the material universe (n, s)

בקר: Morning. The period of the physical universe's rotation cycle in which light and dark are mixed and distinguishable (i)

A non-temporal period of transition from night to day (s)

ברא: Creates. To ordain limits on materials in order to appoint the existence of something new (i, s); a non-temporal act by God (s)

To bring forth matter from absolutely nothing at all solely through desire; God's first action on the first day of creation (n)

בראשית: When (i) At the first moment of time (n)

ברך: Blesses. To note that a subclass of a species has been granted a capacity for its benefit not shared by the other members of the species. (i)

דמות: Likeness. A similarity between two things [true likeness = an identity between two things] (s)

דשא: Vegetation. A created entity made definite on day three. (i) A collective term for individual species of עשב. (n) Grass for animal food (s)

זרע: Procreation (s)

חושך: Dark. The primary element fire (n)

The primary element air; encircles the ring of water at the beginning of the universe (s)

חיתו ארץ: wild animals (i); animal life (s)

Living things in the lower world, formed from the element earth, that eat meat (n)

טוב: It was good. What preceded was a single unit. (i)

It will persist forever (n)

The end (τέλοσ) of the universe as a whole, expressible as all knowledge (s)

יום: Day. [1] A complete cycle of the physical universe's rotation on its axis. (i)

The period of the cycle in which light dominates in the absence of dark. (i) A non-temporal period when the influence of light is dominant (s)

[2] A twenty-four hour period of time {פשט} (n).

[3] The unit of what is brought forth into actual existence through a single divine decree; a period of 1,000 years {פנימיה} (n)

כן: It was so. What preceded was a single unit (i)

What preceded is established (s)

What preceded will exist continually through the history of the universe (n)

לילה: Night. The name of the dark

The period of the physical universe's rotation cycle in which dark dominates in the absence of light (i) A non-temporal period when the influence of dark is dominant (s)

מאורות: Stars. A created entity made definite on day four. (i)

Lights made from light, located in the upper ring of the sky (s)

Heavenly objects. A general term for the sun, the moon and the stars; solidified bodies formed from light that receive and then reflect light on the lower world (n)

המאור הגדול: The sun. The large light that causes the warm and dry things in the lower world to grow and reproduce (n)

המאור הקטן: The moon. The small light that causes the cool and wet things in the lower world to bear fruit (n)

משל: Governs. To cause change; to make to come to be and/or pass away (n)

מועדים: [1] Hours (i)]2] Signs of irregular events in the heaven (i).

מים: Water. The primordial element water (i, s); naturally located between the elements earth and air. (i) The lower waters are the pools and the seas; the upper waters are a ring of water above the sky (s)

נפש חיה: Animal soul.

A general term for created entities made definite on day five (for sea-life) and day six (for land life) (i)

Living things in the lower world. A general term for things formed either from the elementary waters or from the elementary earth (n)

Life with a soul; the general species of animals, fish, birds and humans (s)

עוף: Flying living things in the lower world formed from the elementary waters (n)

ערב: Evening. The period of the physical universe's rotation cycle in which light and dark are mixed but indistinguishable. (i) A non-temporal period of transition from day to night (s)

עשב: Plants. Any species of עשב; actualized out of the potency of the primordial earth (n); Grass for human food (s)

עשה: Makes. The acts performed on days two through six of creation to bring about something new as a definite actuality. (i) To set something in order (תקון) according to its proportion (על מתכונתו) (n)

צבא השמים: The hosts of the heavens. The corporeal and incorporeal objects that are located in the heavens, viz. the sun, the moon, the stars (הכוכבים), the separate intellects (השכלים הנבדלים), the angels (המלאכים), and human souls (נפשות האדם) (n)

צלם: Image. An eternal intellectual essence whose content is the good (s)

צלם אלוהים: Divine image. Life with soul with the potential to become a deity; a human *qua* his potential to realize the image (s)

ראה : Sees. To see in thought (i)

To make permanent (n)

To desire (s)

רוח: Wind. The element air. (i, n)

Intellect (s)

רוח אלוהים: The wind of God.

God's desire (חפץ) expressed through His decree of creation (i)

Angels (s)

רמש: Tiny land-life (i)

Living things in the lower world formed from the element earth that creep upon the earth (n)

רקיע: Sky. Another term for שמים. A created element made definite on day two. (i)

A primary material (חומר ראשון) made out of the combination of first matter (חומר ראשון) and first form (צורה ראשונה) from which the heavens are constructed; a ring of congealed water, stretched out from the exact center of the primordial sphere of water (n)

A ring of mist formed from the mixture of water and dark at the upper surface with condensed wet air at the lower surface of the ring of water surrounding the earth (s)

שבת: Rest. Realizing an end (s)

השבת: Sabbath. God's end (s)

שמים: Heaven. The upper region of the physical universe. (i)

[1] A primordial space created on day one. (n, s) Something not (yet) real (ממש) that contains within itself the power or potentiality to bring something forth into actuality; one of two materials from which the entire universe is formed; a geometric point that contains the potency (כוח) to realize everything in the upper, incorporeal world (n)

[2] The upper world created on day two. (n, s) The space in which reside all of the heavenly objects (n, s); that upper portion of the corporeal universe composed of the רקיע. (n)

שרץ: Living things in the lower world formed from the elementary waters who have constant motion (n)

תהום: Deep. The primary element, water (n)

A primordial ring of water encircling the earth at the beginning of the universe (s)

תוהו: The pre-existent material from which the universe was created (i, n, s); a capacity (כוח) for reproduction in the earth (i)

First matter (חומר ראשון); the stuff of all of the material universe. (n, s)

תנינים: The living things in the lower world formed from the elementary waters (n)

Abbreviations

(i) Ibn Ezra
(n) Nachmanides
(s) Sforno

Summary: The Elemental Universe

	Ibn Ezra	Nachmanides	Sforno
Pre-elemental material	תוהו ובוהו	תוהו ובוהו ארץ ושמים	תוהו ובוהו
Elements			
fire	אור	חושך	—
air	רוח	רוח	חושך
water	מים	תהום	מים
earth	ארץ	עפר	ארץ
celestial element	—	אור	אור

An English Translation Based on the Commentaries of Ibn Ezra, Nachmanides and Sforno

Hebrew text
English Translation

בראשית א

1. בראשית ברא אלהים את השמים ואת הארץ:

1. At the first moment of time, God, the eternal incorporeal necessary being who is the source/power of the existence of absolutely every other existent, solely through desire, ordains limits on what is absolutely nothing (or, on pre-existent materials [Ibn Ezra]) in order to appoint what is like the essence of two primordial elemental spaces which contain the power (= potency = capacity) to be realized/actualized simultaneously from a geometric center into the lower world and from an encircling spherical region into the upper world.

2. וארץ היתה תהו ובהו וחשך על-פני תהום ורוח אלהים מרחפת על-פני המים:

2. The lower region of the physical universe consists of a primary stuff and form whose combination constitutes the body and essential nature of the material universe. Fire encircles air that encircles water that encircles earth. {(Ibn Ezra and Nachmanides) By means of God's element air, the element fire encircles the element water. (Sforno) By means of God's angels/intellects, the element air encircles the element water. }

3. ויאמר אלהים יהי אור ויהי אור:

3. Through the mediation of the angels, from the primary stuff and form, God wills into actuality the elementary light (which Ibn Ezra identifies with fire) from which the celestial objects are formed.

4. וירא אלהים את-אור כי טוב ויבדל אלהים בין האור ובין החשך:

4. God conceives of the elementary light as a single unit (Ibn Ezra), that persists forever (Nachmanides), that God desires to be a moral end that is expressible through knowledge of the universe as a whole (Sforno). God separates this primary material of celestial objects from the elementary dark [= fire (Nachmanides); = air (Sforno)] of terrestial objects.

5. ויקרא אלהים לאור יום ולחשך קרא לילה ויהי-ערב ויהי בקר יום אחד:

5. God names the period of the rotation of the universe in which the influence of light dominates "day," and the period in which the influence of dark dominates "night." This period is the amount of time required to bring into actual existence what God decrees in a single act as a single unit, be it as little as no time at all or as much as a thousand years. In this first cycle of the rotation of the universe there is evening {viz., the period during which light and dark are mixed and indistinguishable (Ibn Ezra) or the point that marks the transition from day to night (Sforno)} and morning {viz., the period during which light and dark are mixed and distinguishable (Ibn Ezra) or the point that marks the transition from night to day (Sforno)}.

6. ויאמר אלהים יהי רקיע בתוך המים ויהי מבדיל בין מים למים:

6. Through the mediation of the angels God wills into actuality a sky, viz., an elementary material formed from primary stuff and form into something intermediate between water and air, viz., either a ring of congealed water (Nachmanides) or of condensed wet air, stretched out within the region of the elementary water, from either its exact center (Nachmanides) or its lower surface (Sforno), in order to make the different regions of waters distinct.

7. ויעש אלהים את-הרקיע ויבדל בין המים אשר מתחת לרקיע ובין המים אשר מעל לרקיע ויהי כן:

7. God makes the sky an actuality by imposing upon the water a fixed order according to definite proportions that separate the water below the sky from the water above the sky. It is a single unit established to persist throughout the history of the universe.

8. ויקרא אלהים לרקיע שמים ויהי-ערב ויהי בקר יום שני:

8. God names the sky, viz., the spatial region in the upper portion of the sphere of the universe in which all of the celestial objects reside, "heaven." In the second cycle of the rotation of the universe the alternating regions of dominant dark and light are not discrete.

9 ויאמר אלהים יקוו המים מתחת השמים אל-מקום אחד ותראה היבשה ויהי-כן:

9. Through the mediation of the angels God wills that the water beneath the heaven be collected to one place so that dry-land will appear. It is a single unit established to persist throughout the history of the universe.

10. ויקרא אלהים ליבשה ארץ ולמקוה המים קרא ימים וירא אלהים כי-טוב:

10. God names the dry-land (the planet) 'earth', viz., the sphere within the universe which life inhabits, and He names the collection of water 'seas.' God conceives of the earth and seas as a single unit that persists forever that God desires to be a moral end that is expressible through knowledge of the universe as a whole.

11. ויאמר אלהים תדשא הארץ דשא עשב מזריע זרע עץ פרי למינו אשר זרעו-בו על-הארץ ויהי-כן:

11. Through the mediation of the angels God wills that the earth produce vegetation, viz., the different species of plants that are food for animals, that produce its own kind of fruit tree whose inner-seed is on the (planet) earth. It is a single unit established to persist throughout the history of the universe.

12. ותוציא הארץ דשא עשב מזריע זרע למינהו וירא אלהים כי-טוב:

12. God conceives of the vegetation of plants, that produce its own kind of fruit that the (planet) earth brings forth, as a single unit that persists forever that God desires to be a moral end that is expressible through knowledge of the universe as a whole.

13. ויהי-ערב ויהי בקר יום שלישי:

13. In the third cycle of the rotation of the universe the alternating regions of dominant dark and light are not discrete.

14. ויאמר אלהים יהי מארת ברקיע השמים להבדיל בין היום ובין הלילה והיו לאתת
ולמועדים ולימים ושנים:

14. Through the mediation of the angels God wills into actuality the heavenly objects – i.e., bodies solidified from the element light, viz., the sun, the moon and the stars – located in the upper ring of the sky of heaven, in order to distinguish the period of the rotation of the universe when light is dominant from the period when dark is dominant, as well as to differentiate minutes, hours, days and years.

15 והיו למאורת ברקיע השמים להאיר על-הארץ ויהי-כן:

15. The heavenly objects located in the sky of heaven receive and then reflect the element light upon the lower world of the planet earth. It is a single unit established to persist throughout the history of the universe.

16. ויעש אלהים את-שני המארת הגדלים את-המאור הגדל לממשלת היום ואת-המאור הקטן
לממשלת הלילה ואת הכוכבים:

16. God makes two large heavenly objects by imposing upon the light a fixed order according to definite proportions. This order determines the sun to govern what comes to be and passes away when elementary light dominates the period of the physical universe's rotation cycle and determines the moon to govern what comes to be and passes away when elementary dark dominates. In the same way God makes the stars.

17. ויתן אתם אלהים ברקיע השמים להאיר על-הארץ:

17. God places them in the sky of heaven so that the sun causes the warm and dry things on the planet earth to grow and reproduce, and the moon causes the cool and wet things on the planet earth to bear fruit.

18. ולמשל ביום והלילה לוהבדיל בין האור ובין החשד וירא אלהים כי-טוב:

18. God conceives of the heavenly objects governing the day and the night and the separation of the elementary light from the dark as a single unit that persists forever that God desires to be a moral end that is expressible through knowledge of the universe as a whole.

19. ויהי-ערב ויהי-מקר יום רביעי:

19. In the fourth cycle of the rotation of the universe the alternating regions of dominant dark and light are not discrete.

20. ויאמר אלהים ישרצו המים שרץ נפש חיה ועוף יעופף על-הארץ על-פני רקיע השמים:

20. Through the mediation of the angels God wills into actuality that the waters produce living things that have constant motion and living things that fly above the planet earth on the sky of heaven.

21. ויברא אלהים את-התנינם הגדלים ואת כל-נפש החיה הרמשת אשר שרצו המים למינהם
ואת כל-עוף כנף למינהו וירא אלהים כי-טוב:

21. God ordains limits on the elements to appoint into existence in the lower world every kind of large living thing formed from the elementary waters, every kind of tiny living, creeping thing formed from the elementary earth, and every kind of living, winged thing that flies. God conceives of this creation of living things as a single unit that persists forever that God desires to be a moral end that is expressible through knowledge of the universe as a whole.

22. ויברך אתם אלהים לאמר פרו ורבו ומלאו את-המים בימים והעוף ירב בארץ:

22. God notes these kinds of living things are uniquely granted a beneficial capacity to reproduce, multiply, and fill their designated regions of space.

23. ויהי-ערב ויהי בקר יום חמישי:

23. In the fifth cycle of the rotation of the universe there is evening and morning.

24. ויאמר אלהים תוצא הארץ נפש חיה למינה בהמה ורמש חיתו-ארץ למינה ויהי-כן:

24. Through the mediation of the angels God wills that the planet earth bring forth into actuality every kind of living thing that creeps upon the earth, or that is domesticated or wild (Ibn Ezra), or that eats plants or meat (Nachmanides). It is a single unit established to persist throughout the history of the universe.

25. ויעש אלהים את-חית הארץ למינה ואת-הבהמה למינה ואת כל-רמש האדמה למינהו
וירא אלהים כי-טוב:

25. God conceives of His making of every kind of living thing in the lower world formed from the element earth – what creeps upon the ground, what is domesticated or wild, and what eats plants or meat – as a single unit that persists forever that God desires to be a moral end that is expressible through knowledge of the universe as a whole.

26. ויאמר אלהים נעשה אדם בצלמנו כדמותנו וירדו בדגת הים ובעוף השמים ובבהמה
ובכל-הארץ ובכל-הרמש הרמש על-הארץ:

26. Through the mediation of the angels God wills into actuality by setting in order, according to its proportions, humans, viz., living things in the lower world formed from the element earth who possess the ability to make rational judgments (Ibn Ezra) and voluntarily to choose the good (Sforno), who in this respect are similar to God and the angels. They subdue the fish of the sea, the flying-life of the sky, the domesticated/plant-eating land-life, all (wild/meat-eating life of) the land, and all creeping (life) that creeps upon the land.

27 ויברא אלהים את-האדם בצלמו בצלם אלהים ברא אתו זכר ונקבה ברא אתם:

27. God ordains limits on the element earth in order to appoint into existence the male and female human with the potential to become

a deity by realizing the eternal intellectual essence that is the good.

ויברך אתם אלהים ויאמר להם אלהים פרו ורבו ומלאו את-הארץ וכבשה ורדו בדגת הים 28.
ובעוף השמים ובכל-חיה הרמשת על-הארץ:

28. God notes that these two kinds of humans are uniquely granted a beneficial capacity to reproduce, multiply, fill and conquer the planet earth, as well as to subdue the fish of the sea, the flying-life of the sky, and all the domesticated/plant-eating life that creeps upon the planet earth.

ויאמר אלהים הנה נתתי לכם את-כל-עשב זרע זרע אשר על-פני-כל-הארץ 29.
ואת-כל-העץ אשר-בו פרי-עץ זרע זרע לכם יהיה לאכלה:

29. Through the mediation of the angels God wills into actuality as food for all of the animals every plant that produces seed all over the planet earth as well as every kind of fruit tree.

ולכל-חית הארץ ולכל-עוף השמים ולכל רומש על-הארץ אשר-בו נפש חיה 30.
את-כל-ירק עשב לאכלה ויהי-כן:

30. For all animal and creeping life of the planet earth as well as for all flying life of heaven will all green plants be food. It is a single unit established to persist throughout the history of the universe.

וירא אלהים את-כל-אשר עשה והנה-טוב מאד ויהי-ערב ויהי בקר יום הששי: 31.

31. God conceives of everything He made as the single unit that persists forever that God most desires to be the moral end that is expressible through knowledge. In the sixth cycle of the rotation of the universe the alternating regions of dominant dark and light are not discrete.

בראשית ב

ויכלו השמים והארץ וכל-צבאם: 1.

1. The upper world, the lower world, and all the corporeal and incorporeal objects located in the upper world – viz., the sun, the moon, the stars, the separate intellects, the angels and human souls – are finished.

ויכל אלהים ביום השביעי מלאכתו אשר עשה וישבת ביום השביעי מכל-מלאכתו אשר עשה: 2

2. On the seventh complete cycle of the physical universe's rotation on its axis God finishes the acts that he performs on cycles two

through six to realize the end of setting in order according to their proportions as a definite actuality the materials appointed into existence on the first complete cycle.

3. ויברך אלהים את-יום השביעי ויקדש אתו כי בו שבת מכל-מלאכתו אשר-ברא אלהים לעשות:

3. God notes that the seventh complete cycle of the rotation of the universe on its axis is unique in being sanctified as God's end, because on it God realizes the end of the acts he performs to set the universe in order according to its proportions as a definite actuality.

Works Consulted

Primary

מקראות גדולות. Part I. New York, Pardes Publishing House, 1951.

פירושי התורה לרבינו משה בן נחמן (רמבן). משה בן נחמן. Edited by Charles B. Chavel. Jerusalem, מוסד הרב קוק, 1959. Translated into English by Charles B. Chavel. *Rambam (Nachmanides): Commentary on the Torah*. New York, Shilo, 1971.

Oles, M. Arthur. "A Translation of the Commentary of Abraham Ibn Ezra on Genesis with a Critical Introduction." Unpublished Ph.D. dissertation. Cincinnati, Hebrew Union College-Jewish Institute of Religion, 1958.

Secondary

Altmann, Alexander. "A Note on the Rabbinic Doctrine of Creation." *Journal of Jewish Studies* VII (1956) pp. 195-206.

Baron, Salo Wittmayer. *A Social and Religious History of the Jews*. Philadelphia, Jewish Publication Society of America, 1942.

Braude, William G. "Maimonides' Attitude to Midrash." *Studies in Jewish Bibliography, History and Literature in Honor of I. Edward Kiev*. New York, Ktav, 1971. pp. 75-82.

Casper, Bernard. *Introduction to Jewish Bible Commentary*. New York, Thomas Yoseloff, 1960.

Feldman, William M. *Rabbinical Mathematics and Astronomy*. London, M.L. Cailingold, 1931.

Greenstein, Edward L. "Medieval Bible Commentaries." In Barry W. Holtz (ed.). *Back to the Sources: Reading the Classic Jewish Texts*. New York, Summit Books, 1984. pp. 213-259.

Jacobs, Louis. *Jewish Biblical Exegesis*. New York, Behrman House, 1973.

Jacobs, Louis. *Studies in Talmudic Logic and Method*. London, Vallentine Mitchell, 1951.

Kasowsky, Chaim. אוצר לשון התלמוד. Jerusalem, מדרש תחינוך והתרבות של ממשלת ישראל, 1954-1982.

Kasher, M.M. תורה שלמה. Jerusalem, 1927.

Kasher, M.M. *Encyclopedia of Biblical Interpretation*. Vol. 1. English translation by H. Freedman. New York, American Biblical Encyclopedia Society, 1953.

Rabinovitch, Nachum L. *Probability and Statistical Inference in Ancient and Medieval Jewish Literature*. Toronto, University of Toronto Press, 1973.

Rosenthal, Erwin I.J. "Medieval Jewish Exegesis: Its Character and Significance" *Journal of Jewish Studies* 9 (1964), pp. 265-81.

Saperstein, Marc. *Decoding the Rabbis: A Thirteenth-Century Commentary on the Aggadah*. Cambridge, Harvard University Press, 1980.

Seltzer, Robert M. *Jewish People, Jewish Thought: The Jewish Experience in History*. New York, Macmillan, 1980.

Silver, Daniel J. *Maimonidean Criticism and the Maimonidean Controversy, 1180-1240* . Leiden, E.J. Brill, 1965.

29

Some Forms of Divine Appearance In Ancient Jewish Thought

Michael Fishbane
Brandeis University

In the course of his philosophical reinterpretation of biblical anthropomorphisms, Maimonides (*Guide*, I.46) refers to a "comprehensive dictum" whereby the ancient Sages rejected "everything that is suggested to the estimative faculty by any of the attributive qualifications mentioned by the prophets."[1] This dictum is the well-known epigram of Rabbi Yudan found in midrash *Genesis Rabbā* (XXVII. 1): "Great is the power of the prophets, for they liken a form to its creator *(gādōl kōḥan shel nevī'īm she-medammīn sūrāh le-yōṣerāh)*." Maimonides goes on to state that by this formulation the Sages have made it "clear and manifest that all the forms apprehended by all the prophets 'in the vision of prophecy' are created forms of which God is the creator."[2] In the Arabic original, the word used to render "the forms" is *al-ṣūwar*.[3] Since ibn Tibbon, this latter has been translated into Hebrew by *ha-ṣūrōt*.

Since Maimonides cites his midrashic source in the original Hebrew, it is obvious that his own use of *al-ṣūwar* is intended to refer back to Rabbi Yudan's use of *ṣūrāh* – even as he has considerably expanded and transformed its meaning. In its primary context, the word *ṣūrāh* simply refers to a human form. It is adduced in the epigram in order to explain the opening lemma from Eccles. 2:21 ("There is a *man*

[1] *The Guide of the Perplexed*, trans. by Sh. Pines (Chicago: University of Chicago Press, 1963), 102 (=55a).
[2] *Ib.*, 103.
[3] See the edition of S. Munk (Jerusalem: Azriel, 1929), 69 l. 22 (also ll. 23-24).

who works with wisdom...") with reference to God himself. A bit more puzzling is the sage's choice of Dan. 8:16 to support his anthropomorphic point. On the surface, this text was presumably adduced here because in this citation a divine form with a human appearance is said to have the voice of a "man." The even "better" prooftext next brought by another Rabbi Yudan (probably R. Yehudah b. Simon)[4] from Ezek. 1:26 was apparently due to a parallel consideration; since once again a prophet has a vision of God in human form. In this case, it is no less than a vision of the supernal Glory *(kāvōd)* seated on the heavenly Throne, looking "like the image of a man." This may be why it is called "better" that the passage from Dan. 8:16; but one is still perplexed why angelic and archangelic revelations were adduced to prove the anthropomorphic reading of Eccles. 2:21. I shall return to the matter further on.

By comparison with his source, Maimonides only cites the prooftext from Ezekiel and goes on to interpret the epigram as pertaining to "all the forms apprehended by all the prophets." In this "comprehensive" rereading of Rabbi Yudan's use of *ṣūrāh* Maimonides finds ancient rabbinical support for his own view that all the anthropomorphisms of Scripture (both of God and the angels) must not be taken literally. Granted, the medieval commentators of the *Guide* (like Ephodi and Abarbanel) explained these divine "forms" as creations in the imaginative faculty by God, the Active Intellect. But one may nevertheless wonder whether there is more to Maimonides' decision to refer to the appearance of "divine forms" by the term *al-ṣūwar (ha-ṣūrōt)*, and to speak of them as "created" entities. An examination of two other passages in his writings suggests that this vocabulary was actually part and parcel of quite another tradition of Jewish metaphysical speculation.

The first passage occurs in the *Mishneh Tōrāh, Hilkhōt Yesōdei ha-Tōrāh* (VII. 1). Maimonides speaks here of those who enter the mystical meditations of *'pardēs'* as persons "whose knowledge is ever turned upward, bound beneath the Throne (in order) to understand the various *holy and pure forms (ha-ṣūrōt ha-qedōshōt veha-ṭehōrōt).*" The striking similarity between this language and the expression *ha-ṣūrōt ha-qedōshōt* in *Sēfer ha-Bahīr,* where it is also used to describe the hypostatic divine forms supporting the heavenly throne, was first

[4]See the variants of this homily collected in the critical edition of Theodor-Albeck, *Midrash Bereshīt Rabbā* (Jerusalem: Wahrmann Books, 1965), 255 f. In consideration of these, Theodor glosses "R. Yudan" in his ms. with "(b. R. Simon)."

observed by G. Scholem.[5] Quite clearly, one of the technical terms for the angelic "forms" in medieval Jewish speculations on the divine Chariot *(Ma'aśeh Merkāvāh)* was the word *ṣūrōt*. But this usage was no late invention. It rather derives from a millenium old tradition of thought, fragmentarily preserved in a variety of ancient sources – magical, Gnostic and Jewish. For example, the antiquity of the phrase *ṣūrōt qedōshōt* can be shown from an invocation to Thoth-Hermes found among the Greek magical papyri. Here "holy Thauth," whose true visage is hidden, is said to appear in various *morphais hagiais* ("holy forms").[6] As for the larger complex of ideas expressed, Moshe Idel has recently called attention to a precise correspondence between the speculation on 71 *ṣūrōt* supporting the divine Throne (i.e., 71+1) found in *Sēfēr ha-Bāhīr*[7] and the 72 divine *morphē* (forms) of the heavenly Chariot mentioned in the Gnostic treatise known as *On the Origin of the World.*[8] As compared with the relatively clear computation in the Jewish mystical source (which speculates that the divine Throne was comprised of 64+7+1 components), the presentation in the Gnostic text is arguably derivative.[9] If this be so, the Gnostic tradition at hand would remain a precious witness to the considerable antiquity of such theosophical speculations (preserved here in a Jewishly-oriented Christian milieux);[10] but it would not express their earliest forms. At the present time, the exact nature of such older Jewish traditions is not known. However, the occurance of such locutions as *ṣūrōt elohim hayyim* ("forms of the living God") and *ṣūrōt kavod* ("forms of glory") among various *Merkāvāh* speculations preserved among the Dead Sea Scrolls clearly pushes back the existence of native speculative

---

[5]*Les origines de la Kabbale* (Paris: Aubier, 1966), 64 n. 10. See *Sēfēr ha-Bāhīr*, ed. R. Margulies (Jerusalem: Mossad Ha-Rav Kook, 1978), par. 98; and G. Scholem, *Das Buch Bahir* (Leipzig: W. Drugulin, 1923; Darmstadt: Wissenschaftliche Buchgesellschaft, 1970), 70 (par. 67).

[6]See *Papyri Graecae Magicae. Die Griechichen Zauberpapyri*, K. Preisendanz, ed. (Leipzig-Berlin: B. Teubner, 1931), II; xiii. 270-77 (esp. l. 272). The text also appears in *Poimandres. Studien zur Griechisch-Ägyptischen und Früchristlichen Literatur*, R. Reitzenstein (Leipzig: B. Teubner, 1904), 22.

[7]Margulies, *Sēfēr ha-Bāhīr*, par. 95; Scholem, *Das Buch Bahir*, 65 (par. 63).

[8]II, 5, 104f. See J. M. Robinson, ed., *The Nag Hammadi Library* (San Francisco: Harper & Row, 1977), 166.

[9]See the full discussion in M. Idel, *"Le-Ba'ayat Ḥēqer Mesōrōt shel Sēfēr ha-Bāhīr," Rēshīt ha-Mīsṭiqāh ha-Yehūdīt ba-Eirōpāh, Meḥqārei Yerūshālayīm be-Maḥshevet Yisra'el* 7.3-4 (1987), 57-63.

[10]Cf. the observation of W. Schoedel, "Scripture and the Seventy-Two Heavens of the First Apocalypse of James," *Novum Testamentum* 12 (1970), 128 f. I plan to return to a number of the issues in this apocalypse in a separate study.

traditions (with a precise vocabulary) to the turn of the millenium.[11] M. Idel has correctly stressed the importance of this evidence for reconstructing the ancient Jewish mystical tradition.[12]

A second passage in Maimonides' legal writings allows us to corroborate this line of argument, and to perceive even more of the mystical tradition to which the philosopher was heir. Indeed, it is quite clear from the Introduction to *Sanhedrīn* XI *(Pereq Ḥeleq)* of his *Commentary to the Mishnah* that Maimonides was effected in his youth by the ancient Jewish speculations on the awesome extension of the divine Form known as *Shi'ūr Qōmāh*. Speaking of the difficulty in this (legal) context to do justice to the theme of Moses' prophecy, to the existence and hierarchical order of the angels, and to other matters, Maimonides notes:

> The circle would have to be extended to include a discourse on the forms *(fi al-ṣūwar; ba-ṣūrōt)* which the prophets mentioned in connection with the creator and the angels; into this enters the *Shi'ūr Qōmāh* and its subject matter. For (a treatment of) this subject alone, even if shortened to the utmost degree, a hundred pages would not suffice....[13]

While the authenticity of this passage cannot be doubted,[14] the sentence dealing with the *Shi'ūr Qōmāh* speculations has been boldly crossed out in Maimonides' own autograph of his commentary on *Nezīkīn* (Ms. 295 of the Edward Pococke Collection of the Bodleian Library).[15] The reasons for this suppression are not entirely clear. Given his clear reverence for other esoteric subjects in his major works,[16] one may wonder whether Maimonides' public *responsum* on the subject (in which he attributed the *Shi'ūr Qōmāh* speculations to a Byzantine preacher)[17] reflects his full view of the matter. In any case, Maimonides understood such speculations as part of "a discourse on the forms *(al-ṣūwar)* which the prophets used in connection with the

---

[11]See C. Newsome, *Songs of the Sabbath Sacrifice – A Critical Edition* (Atlanta: Scholar's Press, 1985), 293.

[12]See *op. cit.*, 61-63.

[13]*Māvō' le-Pereq Ḥēleq mi-Pērūsh ha-Mishnāh le-Rabbēnū Mōshe ben Maimōn* (Berlin, 1901), 24 (Arabic-Hebrew section).

[14]S. Lieberman, in his Appendix (D) to G. Scholem, *Jewish Gnosticism, Merkabah Mysticism and Talmudic Tradition* (New York: The Jewish Theological Seminary of America, 1965), 124 n. 32, lists 4 mss.

[15]See Solomon Sasson's introduction to *Maimonides Commentarius in Mischnam* (Copenhagen: E. Munksgaard, 1956), I, Chaps. ii-vi.

[16]Cf. M. Idel, "*Sitre 'Arayot* in Maimonides' Thought," in *Maimonides and Philosophy*, S. Pines and Y. Yovel, eds. (Dordrecht: M. Nijhoff, 1986), 79-91 (esp. 84 f).

[17]See *R. Mōshe b. Maimōn. Teshūvōt*, Y. Blau, ed. (Jerusalem, 1957), I, 200 f.

creator and the angels." The similarity of this formulation (in content and terminology) with that found in the *Guide* (I. 46) is evident. It remains to add that this use of *ṣūrāh* with respect to God himself (and not just to angelic forms) is also derived from an earlier tradition.

Two complementary lines of testimony may be adduced. The first cluster of evidence derives from 4th century Patristic sources. As G. Stroumsa has noted, both Basil the Great (cf. *Homilies on the Origin of Man*, I. 13) and Arnobius (cf. *Against the Nations*, III.12) speak of the "forms" of God in their vigorous attacks on ancient Jewish anthropomorphisms.[18] The first Father uses the Greek term *morphē*; the other employs the Latin *formae*. Given the technical nature of these terms, in polemical reactions to Jewish ways of thinking *(ioudaikōs)*, there are strong reasons to suppose that we have here an echo of older Jewish anthropomorphic formulations – somewhat parallel to the Christian-Gnostic use of *morphē* to render angelic "forms" in *On the Origin of the World*. The even more precise reference to the "*morphē* of God" in the old christological hymn found in Phil. 2:6-11 would further seem to suggest that the word *morphē* in these contexts reflects an earlier Jewish speculative tradition on the visible God.[19] Indeed, one might even suspect that this term reflects old Jewish discussions using the Hebrew word *ṣūrāh* (or its Aramaic cognate) in the sense of a divine "form." This possibility is strengthened by the striking reference in the *Odes of Solomon* to the *demūtā* (likeness) and *ṣūrtā* (form) of God (7:4, 6).[20] In turn, these two Syriac terms allow us to retrieve a parallel cluster of evidence in native Jewish sources.

Let us start with an important variant of Rabbi Yudan's epigram found in the *Pesīqtā de-Rav Kahanā, Pārāh* 4. In this formulation we read: "Great is the power of the prophets who compare the likeness (*demūt*) of the Power *(gevūrāh)* on High to the likeness *(demūt)* of man."[21] Several points are striking here, the first being the very term *gevūrāh*. In his wide-ranging discussion on the subject, E. Urbach has

---

[18]See G. Stroumsa, "Form(s) of God: Some Notes on Metatron and Christ," *Harvard Theological Review* 76 (1983) 271 f.

[19]Following Stroumsa, *id.*, 282 f. He further argues that the hymn speaks of a *kenōsis* whereby Christ divested himself of the "form of God" and took on the "form of the servant." By contrast, D. Georgi has argued that the latter phrase points to Isaiah's suffering servant and a "speculative wisdom mysticism" in Hellenistic Judaism. See "Der vorpaulinische Hymnus Phil. 2:6-11, in E. Dinkler, ed., *Zeit und Geschichte, Danksgabe an Rudolf Bultmann* (Tübingen: Mohr, 1964), 263-93 (esp. 291).

[20]See J. H. Charlesworth, *The Odes of Solomon* (SBLTT 13, Pseudepigrapha Series 7; Missoula: Scholar's Press, 1977), 36.

[21]*Pesīqtā de-Rav Kahanā*, B. Mandelbaum, ed. (New York: Jewish Theological Seminary, 1963), I, 65.

shown how this term is used in rabbinic literature as a divine epithet for the power and might of God.[22] He also correctly observes that this term is the equivalent of Greek *dynamis,* which is used in contemporary Hellenistic sources to indicate the 'power' or 'force' manifested by the gods.[23] What is missing, however, is a consideration of the phrase of "the likeness of the *gevūrāh* on High." What might this notion mean? Simply on the basis of the words themselves, it seems that what is mentioned here is the hypostatic "likeness" (or manifest form) of God himself (i.e., the "*gevūrāh*"). Accordingly, the force of the epigram in the *Pesīqtā* passage is to highlight the power of the prophets who dare compare this heavenly "likeness" to the human form of man.

In the context of the homily as a whole, this formulation of the epigram helps explain why prooftexts are adduced from Dan. 8:16 and Ezek. 1:26. For just as Rabbi Yudan's saying refers to the portrayal of a divine hypostasis in the likeness of man, so do the two prooftexts – and the citation adduced from Ezekiel is "better" than the one drawn from Daniel because it portrays a hypostatic figure of God on high (on the Throne of Glory) "in the likeness *(demūt)* of man." But what bearing does all this have on the primary lemma of the homily and its subsequent exegesis? Since the lemma is taken from Eccles. 8:1 ("Who is like the wise one, and who knows the meaning of the matter? The wisdom of a *man* will enlighten his face..."), one must minimally conclude that the "man" mentioned here is to be understood (*via* Rabbi Yudan's epigram) as the hypostatic likeness of God, which is itself in the likeness of man. But since the first part of the lemma (mentioning the work of "the wise one") is also specifically interpreted by the preacher with respect to God as creator (citing Prov. 3:9), one must conclude that this interpretation also applies to the "man" mentioned in the latter part. The result of these various exegetical transformations is that "the likeness of the *gevūrāh*" is presented as the creator in the visible form of a man.

It would thus seem that the epigram and homily in *Pesīqtā de-Rav Kahanā, Pārāh* 4 preserve a valuable fragment of ancient rabbinic theology. Beyond the purely contextual argument just advanced, several external considerations may be added. For example, a close look at the ancient christological hymn found in Col. 1:15-20 shows an liturgical formulation of the distinction between an invisible God and his visible likeness. Indeed in this old prayer Christ is referred to as *eikōn tou theou aoratou,* "a likeness of the invisible God" (v. 15). Since

---

[22]See *Ḥazal; Pirqei Emūnōt ve-Dē'ōt* (Jerusalem: Magnes Press, 1975; 3rd ed.), ch. 5.
[23]*Id.*, 73 f., and notes.

this use of *eikōn* undoubtedly reflects the Hebrew word *demūt* (or Aramaic *demūta*),[24] one must suspect that older Jewish speculations on a primordial divine being informs this theologoumenon. The succeeding references in the hymn to Christ as "the head of the Body" (v. 18) through whom "all things have been created" (v. 16) further points to theosophical speculations on a divine Anthropos who was involved in the creation.[25] The wide variety of such ancient Jewish theology is further indicated by the (later) tradition of Shahrastānī that, "four hundred years" before Arius (i.e., in the 1st century, C.E.), the sect of Magharians held the view that God's anthropomorphic appearances in the Bible were those of an angelic hypostasis, believed to be the creator of the world.[26]

The teaching in the *Pesīqtā* homily that the divine hypostasis was also the creator of heaven and earth is also confirmed by a passage in a rabbinic source, where the point is made directly and not by a round-about-exegesis. In the *Avōt de-Rabbī Nāthān* (A, 39) we read the following: "Because of sin, it is not given to man to know *(lēyda')* what is the 'likeness *(demūt)* on High;' for were it not for this (viz., sin), all the keys would be given to him, and he would know *(yōdē'a)* how the heavens and the earth were created."[27] According to S. Lieberman, this striking passage points to an old Jewish doctrine of a divine Demiurge involved in the creation, much like notions developed at length in Gnostic sources.[28] Moreover, this particular background invites closer attention to the reference made to a secret knowledge *(da'at)* lost through sin – specifically, a knowledge of the "*demūt* on High" and the mysteries of creation. The existence of an esoteric knowledge of divine and cosmological secrets was already developed among the Qumran

---

[24]So also R. P. Martin, "*morphē* in Philippians II.6," *Expository Times* 70 (1958-59), 183 f., followed by Stroumsa, *op. cit.*, 284 n. 73.

[25]Cf. Stroumsa, *id.*, 284. I am also persuaded by his suggestion (n. 74) that "the apposition" of *tēs ekklēsias* ("of the Church") after the reference to Christ as "the head of the Body" is "most probably an interpolation of the writer of the letter."

[26]See N. Golb, "Who Were the Magariya?," *Journal of the American Oriental Society* 80 (1960), 347-59. Shahrastānī's work, *Kitāb al-Milal wa'al Niḥal* is discussed by H. A. Wolfson, "The Pre-Existent Angel of the Magharians and Al-Nahawandi," *Jewish Quarterly Review* 51 (1960-61), 89-106. The tradition of "an angel who created the world" is not mentioned by Shahrastānī, but is reported by Qirqisānī and al-Nahāwandī. See Wolfson, 90-91, 102. In this context (pp. 96, 100), Wolfson also refers to the Collosian passage mentioned above, but he arrives at a different solution.

[27]In the ed. of S. Schechter, p. 116.

[28]See "How Much Greek in Jewish Palestine," in A. Altmann, ed., *Biblical and Other Studies* (Brandeis Texts and Studies, 1; Cambridge: Harvard University Press, 1963), 141.

sectarians. Note in particular the propaedeutic comment found in the *Manual of Discipline:* "to make known to the upright the knowledge *(da'at)* of the Most High, and to instruct the wisdom *(ḥokhmāh)* of the sons of heaven (viz., the angelic host) to the perfect of way" (1 *QS* IV.22).[29] It thus stands to reason that the teaching in our *Pesīqtā* homily, of a creation performed with "wisdom *(ḥokhmāh)*" by a divine hypostasis, also refers to such a complex of esoteric speculations. If we would therefore find any significant difference between this passage and that found in the *Avōt de-Rabbī Nāthān,* it would seem to rest in the fact that the particular form of the "likeness on High" is not specified here, whereas the whole burden of the *Pesīqtā* homily is to indicate that just this heavenly hypostasis had the "likeness" of a man. R. Yudan perhaps preserves a more esoteric distinction between the invisible God and his visible "likeness" when he exclaims that the representation of manifestations of God in human form is the daring deed of the prophets.

Let us return to the formulation of the epigram in *Genesis Rabbā* XXVII.1. How is it to be understood? In the light of the *Pesīqtā* text, where there is a clear exegetical progression from the initial lemma and prooftexts (connecting the "man" to the divine creator) to R. Yudan's epigram (connecting this "man" to a divine hypostasis between the invisible *gevūrāh* and human beings) and thence to the supporting prooftexts (connecting this hypostasis to other angelic or archangelic hypostases), this first text is doubly puzzling. Because in this case the epigram (comparing a human form, *ṣūrāh,* to its creator) immediately follows the inaugural lemma (from Eccles. 2:21; refering to a "man who works with *ḥokhmāh*"), one is inclined to understand the epigram as an exegetical means of identifying the "man" of the lemma with God. But then one wonders, first, what purpose is served by following the epigram with a text dealing with the creation; and further, what purpose is served by following the epigram with proofs dealing with angelic hypostases (and not God himself) in the image of man (and not vice versa).

On the basis of these various considerations, one might conclude that Rabbi Yudan's epigram in *Genesis Rabbā* XXVII.1 is a secondary softening of the formulation found in the *Pesīqtā de-Rav Kahanā, Pārāh* 4. But if we take into account the various ancient evidence on the use of *ṣūrāh* as a divine hypostasis (and also the parallelism between *ṣūrtā* and

---

[29]For a valuable consideration of the relationship between such knowledge a gnostic knowledge in the strict sense, see I. Gruenwald, "Knowledge and Vision," *Israel Oriental Studies* 3 (1973), esp. 63-87.

demūta in the *Odes of Solomon*), a different possibility arises; namely, that in addition to the manifest meaning of *ṣūrāh* as "human form" (in contrast to the creator) it also refers to a hypostatic "form" created by God. Presumably, Rabbi Yudan chose this word (rather than *yeṣūr*, for example) with just this purpose in mind. And once we conclude that *ṣūrāh* serves the double purpose of referring to a divine hypostasis in human form, we can easily understand the exegetical function of the epigram between a lemma on a "man" who "works with wisdom" and biblical texts referring to the creation. As in the *Pesīqtā* passage, the creation is performed by a divine hypostasis in the form of a man. Moreover, on this explanation of the evidence we can also best understand the role of the prooftexts. For if the epigram itself refers to a divine hypostasis in human form, it makes sense that the proofs should do so as well. The purpose of Rabbi Yudan's epigram in *Genesis Rabbā* must therefore be to underscore the daring of the prophets who compare the divine hypostasis in the form of a man (the *ṣūrāh*) to its creator, the invisible God beyond. Presumably the somewhat esoteric nature of this teaching accounts for its compressed and opaque formulation.

If the preceding interpretation of the word *ṣūrāh* is correct, there are further consequences for Jewish thought. For the notion of a created Anthropos in *Genesis Rabbā* XXVII.1 dovetails in a most interesting way with the view of some Jews mentioned by Justin Martyr in his *Dialogue with Trypho the Jew*. In chapter 128 of this work, Justin attributes to his polemical opponents *(houtoi)* the view that the Power *(dynamis)* manifested by God ("the Father of All") is sometimes "called an angel *(angelos)*," at othertimes "the Glory *(doxa)*," and "he is called a man or son of man when he appears in such forms as these *(en morphais toiautais)*." Justin even says that these people believe that the Father "creates *(poiei)*" these angels repeatedly. In a recent study, Sh. Pines has thoroughly analyzed this passage and particularly succeeded in putting the latter notion in the wider context of early christology.[30] It now seem that our previous discussion of angelic manifestations of the *gevūrāh*, and the idea that these are created forms, can reciprocally place Justin's interlocutors within the context of early Jewish theosophical speculations. Moreover, not only can we now specifically correlate the Greek vocabulary with its ancient Hebrew equivalents. The particular reference to divine appearances in human

---

[30] *"Hā-El, Ha-Kāvōd, Veha-Melākhīm lefī Shīṭāh Teolōgīt shel Ha-Mē'āh Ha-Shenīyāh La-Sefīrāh,"* in *Meḥqārei Yerūshālāyīm Be-Maḥshevet Yiśrā'ēl* 6.3-4 (1987), 1-12, esp. 4 f.

shape as *en morphais* is also especially supportive of the proposal advanced above regarding the created *ṣûrāh* in Rabbi Yudan's epigram.

The correspondence between Justin's text and *Genesis Rabbā* XXVII. 1 yields further fruits: for it suggests that when R. Saadya Gaon spoke centuries later of the earthly revelations of God as manifestations of the "Created Glory *(ha-kāvōd ha-nivrā')*," he was heir to a strand of ancient theosophical speculation.[31] The precise channels whereby Saadya received this tradition are not known; but one cannot exclude the fact that he continues an old midrashic line of thought.[32] It is most significant in this regard that Saadya spoke of this supernal figure through reference to Ezek. 1:26, and that he called it a *ṣûrāh*.[33] It is therefore not the least of the paradoxes of the history of ideas that the language of religious philosophy, so keen to purify anthropomorphic thought, should also derive from mystical theosophy – in which knowledge of the 'Form(s) of God' is the highest wisdom. Any chapter on the historical relationships between the philosophers and their sources must bear this in mind. Maimonides' remark in *Guide* I.46 that all divine manifestations are "created forms" *(ṣûrōt nivrā'ōt)* should therefore be viewed in this light. And this is also the context in which we should understand his statement that the angels are "created of form" *(berū'îm ṣûrāh)*, but without any substance or body (cf. *Sēfēr Ha-Madā'*, Ch. II, hal. 3).

[31]See further the remarks of A. Altmann on the "Created Glory" and the ancient mystical traditions involved, in his "Saadya's Theory of Revelation: its Origin and Background," *Studies in Religious Philosophy* (Ithaca, N.Y.: Cornell University Press, 1969), 140-60, esp. 152, 157.

[32]Pines, *op. cit.*, 10, connects Saadya's notion to the 'Jewish' tradition reflected in Justin's text.

[33]*Sēfēr Ha-Nivḥār Bā-Emūnōt Ve-Dē'ōt*, II; see the Arabic text in the edition of Y. D. Kafaḥ (New York: Sura – Yeshivah University, 1970), 103. Kafaḥ translates *demūt* here; but cp. D. Slutzki, *Sēfēr Ha-Emūnōt Veha-Dē'ōt* (Leipzig, 1864), 51.

30

Female Imaging of the Torah: From Literary Metaphor to Religious Symbol

Elliot Wolfson
New York University

I

It is widely acknowledged that one of the more overtly innovative features of kabbalistic symbolism is its ready utilization of masculine and feminine images to depict aspects of the divine reality. It is the purpose of this paper to trace the trajectory of one of the central motifs, the feminine personification of the Torah, from classical midrashic sources to kabbalistic texts. At the outset it will be noted that we are dealing not with one image but rather a cluster of images whose formation spans a wide historical range. While it is undeniably true that literary images in religious texts often reflect the social and cultural milieu that, at least in part, helped foster these images, it is also equally true that the evolution of ideas within "traditional" Jewish sources proceeds along an internal axis, with older texts influencing subsequent formulations and generating significant, though at times subtle, semantic transformations.

One may reasonably conjecture that the rabbinic depiction of the Torah in images related to a female personification reflects an older idea found in Jewish sources, of both Palestinian and Alexandrian provenance, concerning the feminine Sophia or Wisdom.[1] Insofar as the

[1]The point was already made by A. Green, "Bride, Spouse, Daughter: Images of the Feminine in Classical Jewish Sources," in S. Heschel, ed., *On Being a Jewish*

identification of Torah as *Ḥokhmah*, or Sophia, first made explicitly in literary form in the books of Baruch and Ben Sira,[2] became widespread in the classical rabbinic sources,[3] it seems reasonable to suggest that such a conception may underlie the feminine characterization of the Torah. Yet, it seems to me that there is an essential difference between the older speculation on Sophia in the Wisdom and apocalyptic literature and the feminine characterization of Torah in the rabbinic texts. In the latter, unlike the former, it is clear that the feminine images were originally meant figuratively and are thus almost always expressed within a parabolic context as literary metaphors. I do not mean to suggest that the Torah was not personified by the rabbis; indeed, for the rabbis the Torah did assume a personality of its own, culminating in the conception of the Torah as the pre-existent entity that served as the instrument with which God created

---

Feminist (New York, 1983), p. 253. The scholarly literature on the Jewish conception of Wisdom is vast. I will mention here only several studies that emphasize the view that the figure of Wisdom in Israel is derived from or represents a revision of an authentic mythic goddess. See U. Wilckens, *Weisheit und Torheit* (Tübingen, 1959), pp. 193-195; H. Conzelmann, "The Mother of Wisdom," in J. M. Robinson, ed., *The Future of Our Religious Past* (New York, 1971), pp. 230-243; B. L. Mack, *Logos und Sophia* (Göttingen, 1977), pp. 34-62; E. S. Fiorenza, "Wisdom Mythology and Christological Hymns," in R. Wilkens, *Aspects of Wisdom in Judaism and Early Christianity* (Notre Dame, 1975), pp. 29-33; B. Lang, *Wisdom and the Book of Proverbs: An Israelite Goddess Redefined* (New York, 1986), pp. 126-136; M. Hengel, *Judaism and Hellenism* (Philadelphia, 1974), 1: 154-155. For the feminine characterization of Sophia in Philo of Alexandria, especially as the "daughter of God," see H. Wolfson, *Philo, Foundations of Religious Philosophy in Judaism, Christianity and Islam* (Cambridge, 1947), 1: 256; J. Laporte, "Philo in the Tradition of Biblical Wisdom Literature," in Wilkens, pp. 116-118. In the case of Philo there is some evidence for an interchange between the feminine figure of Wisdom and the masculine Logos; see Mack, *op. cit.*, pp. 153-158; Hengel, *op. cit.*, 2: 111, n. 418. Such a process is clear as well in the case of early Christian doctrine where the Jewish conception of the incarnation of Wisdom in Torah served as the basis for the eventual Christological identification of Jesus with Sophia, as expressed, for instance, in Matthew 11: 28-30. Cf. J. Robinson, "Jesus as Sophos and Sophia," in Wilkens, pp. 1-16; V. R. Mollenkott, *The Divine Feminine* (New York, 1983), pp. 100-101. On the possible influence of Jewish-Wisdom speculation on the Gnostic conception of Sophia, see the review of the problem by G. MacRae, "The Jewish Background of the Gnostic Sophia Myth," *Novum Testamentum* 12 (1970): 86-101.

[2]See M. Hengel, *Judaism and Hellenism*, 1: 161.

[3]Cf. H. A. Fischel, "The Transformation of Wisdom in the World of Midrash," in Wilkens, pp. 70-71, 82; J. Neusner, *Torah: From Scroll to Symbol in Formative Judaism* (Philadelphia, 1985), pp. 118-19.

the world.[4] Nevertheless in the rabbinic writings the female images of the Torah are for the most part metaphorical in their nuance. To cite one striking example at the outset. In the Palestinian Talmud the following tradition is recorded:

> What is [the practice] regarding standing before the Torah-scroll? R. Ḥilqiah [in the name of] R. Simon said in the name of R. Eleazar: Before her son you stand, how much more so before the Torah herself![5]

Insofar as the sage is here referred to as "her son,"[6] it is reasonable to assume that the Torah is being characterized metaphorically as a female, specifically, a mother figure. In the parallel version of this passage in the Babylonian Talmud the feminine image is removed, although the basic meaning is left intact:

> What is [the practice] regarding standing before the Torah-scroll? R. Ḥilqiah and R. Simon and R. Eleazar said: It is an argument *a fortiori*, if we stand before those who study it, how much more so [is it required to stand] before it![7]

The figurative characterization of the sage as the son of Torah gives way in the second passage to the more straightforward characterization "those who study it." The second passage in no way alters the meaning of the first passage, but simply renders it in a less metaphorical way. The implied image of the Torah as the mother is obviated by the fact that the one who studies the Torah is not described as the son of Torah. Although other examples could be adduced, suffice it here to conclude from the example that I have given that the figurative depiction of the Torah in feminine terms in no way implies some mythical entity. Indeed, it is correct, following the locution of R. Meyer, to speak of a suppression in classical rabbinic thought of the mythological character of the hypostatized *Ḥokhmah* in favor of a "nomistic rationalism."[8] In the course of time, however, the literary tropes did yield in Jewish texts a decidedly mystical and mythical concept of Torah as the divine feminine. One can speak, therefore, of a remythologization of the Torah that results from a

---

[4]This theme has been discussed by many scholars. See M. Hengel, *Judaism and Hellenism*, 1: 171, and other sources cited in 2: 111-112, n. 420.

[5]J. Megillah 4:1 (ed. Venice, 74d).

[6]The phrase "son of the Torah" is a common designation in the rabbinic corpus for one who studies Torah. See the examples adduced by Neusner, *Torah: From Scroll to Symbol in Formative Judaism*, p. 143.

[7]B. Qiddushin 33b.

[8]R. Meyer, *Tradition und Neuschöpfung im antiken Judentum*, BAL 110, 2 (1965), p. 84. Cf. Hengel, *Judaism and Hellenism*, pp. 170-171.

literary transference of the images from the realm of metaphor to that of symbol.[9]

II

There are several distinct feminine images of the Torah in the body of classical rabbinic literature. I would like to mention here three of the more salient images: daughter of God, or sometimes expressed as the daughter of the king, the bride, and the mother.[10] With respect to all three the relevant talmudic and midrashic contexts make it clear that we are dealing with figurative expressions, i.e., metaphorical characterizations of the Torah, rather than any hypostatic element. In the case of the former, the daughter of God or the king, it is necessary to make a further distinction: this image occurs either in the context of a wedding motif[11] (to be discussed more fully below) or outside that specific context.[12] Moreover, in the case of the bride, it is also possible to make several distinctions: the Torah is characterized respectively as the bride of Israel, God or even Moses.

The feminine characterization of the Torah as a bride of Israel is connected in several sources, both in the Babylonian Talmud and other collections of scriptural exegeses, with the midrashic reading of the word heritage, *morashah,* in the expression describing the Torah, "heritage of the congregation of Jacob" (Deut. 33:4), as *me'orasah,* i.e., betrothal.[13] In *Sifre Deuteronomy,* for example, one reads as follows:

> Another interpretation [of "a heritage of the congregation of Jacob," *morashah qehillat Ya'aqov*]: Do not read heritage *(morashah)* but betrothal *(me'orasah).* This teaches that the Torah is betrothed to

---

[9]In treating the genesis and emergence of the feminine conception of Torah in kabbalistic sources as primarily an internal literary development rather than a transformation of ancient terms and ideas by means of an external, essentially non-Jewish system of belief, my approach differs fundamentally from that of Scholem who saw this development as a "gnostic transfiguration" of aggadic modes of discourse. See, in particular, *Origins of the Kabbalah* (Princeton, 1987), pp. 92-93.

[10]Cf. *Exodus Rabbah,* 30:6 where the father is identified as the Holy One, blessed be He, and the mother with the Torah. The passage there seems to be based on B. Berakhot 35b where the father is likewise identified with the Holy One, blessed be He, but the mother with *Keneset Yisra'el.*

[11]See, e.g., *Pesiqta' Rabbati,* ed. M. Friedman (Tel Aviv, 1963), 20, 95a, where the Torah is parabolically characterized as the king's daughter and a bride. In that context, however, no mention is made of who the groom is, though one may reasonably conjecture that it is Israel. See *ibid.,* 96b. Cf. *Leviticus Rabbah,* 20:10; *Numbers Rabbah,* 12:4; *Deuteronomy Rabbah,* 8:7; *Canticles Rabbah,* 8:11, § 2.

[12]Cf. B. Sanhedrin 101a; *Exodus Rabbah,* 33:1.

[13]See B. Berakhot 57a; Pesaḥim 59b. And cf. references in the following notes.

> Israel and [is to be considered] a married woman [i.e., that is forbidden] in relation to the nations of the world.[14]

The above aggadic notion is even applied in one talmudic context to a legal discussion concerning the position enunciated by R. Yoḥanan that a non-Jew engaged in Torah is deserving of corporeal punishment. According to the one who reads the expression *morashah,* heritage, as *me'orasah,* bethrothal, the non-Jew who is involved with Torah is to be treated like the individual who has relạtions with a woman who is betrothed to another man, and such an individual receives the punishment of stoning.[15] In still another talmudic context this midrashic reading of Deut. 33:4 serves as a basis for the following homiletical interpretation:

> R. Ḥiyya taught: Whoever is involved in Torah before an ignoramus it is as if he had sexual relations with his [i.e., the ignoramus'] betrothed right in front of him, as it says, 'Moses commanded the Torah to us, as the heritage of the congregation of Jacob.' Do not read heritage *(morashah)* but rather betrothal' *(me'orasah).*"[16]

Whatever the subsequent usages made of this older midrashic reading, the root-idea here is the aggadic notion that the Torah is compared to a woman betrothed to the congregation of Jacob, the Jewish people.[17]

This feminine characterization of the Torah is also connected in some texts to the metaphorical depiction of the Sinaitic theophany as a wedding-day.[18] In one of the earliest collections of homiletical

---

[14]*Sifre Deuteronomy,* 345, ed. L. Finkelstein (New York, 1969), p. 402. Cf. parallel in *Midrash Tanna'im on Deuteronomy,* ed. D. Hoffmann (Berlin, 1909), p. 212.

[15]B. Sanhedrin 59a. Cf. R. Judah Loew of Prague, *Ḥiddushe 'Aggadot* (Jerusalem, 1972), Sanhedrin, p. 163; *idem, Tif'eret Yisra'el,* ed. by H. Pardes (Jerusalem, 1979), chap. 68, p. 533; *idem, Gur 'Aryeh* (Jerusalem, 1972), vol. 1, p. 57.

[16]B. Pesaḥim 49b.

[17]Cf. *Exodus Rabbah,* 33:6.

[18]According to some midrashic sources, God's coming to Sinai to give the Torah to Israel is described parabolically as a bridegroom coming to meet his bride. In such cases, then, Israel, and not the Torah, is the bride. Cf. *Mekhilta' de-Rabbi Ishmael,* B aḥodesh, 3 (ed. by H. S. Horovitz and I. A. Rabin, [Jerusalem, 1970] p. 214); *Mekhilta' de-RaSHBi,* ed. by J. N. Epstein and E. Z. Melamed (Jerusalem, 1955) pp. 142-43; *Tanḥuma',* Qedoshim, 2; *Deuteronomy Rabbah,* 3:12 (God is compared to the groom, Israel to the bride, the Torah to the marriage contract, and Moses to the scribe who writes that contract); cf. *Yalqut Shim'oni,* Yitro, § 279. The passage is cited in the name of *Bereshit Rabbah* in Judah ben Yaqar, *Perush ha-Tefillot we-ha-Berakhot,* ed. by S. Yerushalmi (Jerusalem, 1979), pt. 1, p. 90; cf., however, p. 104, where another part of the same source is correctly given as *Deuteronomy Rabbah.* For an alternative use of the same theme, see *ibid.,* pt. 2, p. 37: "There are some who explain that [in the second of the seven wedding blessings] the canopy *(ḥupah)*

midrashim, *Pesiqta' de-Rav Kahana'*, assumed to be of Palestinian provenance from the fifth-century, the image is clearly stated:

> 'In the third month' (Exod. 19:1). The third month came. [This may be compared] to a king who betrothed a woman, and set a time [for the marriage]. When the time arrived they said: 'It is time to enter the [marriage] canopy.' Similarly, when the time arrived for the Torah to be given, they said, 'It is time for the Torah to be given to Israel.'[19]

In this midrashic comment the event at Sinai is again compared to a wedding; the giving of the Torah is thus likened to entering the marriage canopy. But here, unlike some other early sources,[20] the bridegroom is not God but Israel, and correspondingly the bride is not Israel but the Torah itself. The Sinaitic revelation is thus the wedding of the Jewish people, the groom, to the Torah, the bride. That this interpretation is correct is borne out by a later version of this passage in the thirteenth-century Yemenite collection, *Midrash ha-Gadol*, which reads as follows:

> 'In the third month' (Exod. 19:1). The third month came. [This may be compared] to a king who betrothed a woman, and set a time [for the marriage]. When the time arrived they said: 'It is time for the woman (!) to enter the [marriage] canopy.' Similarly, when the time arrived for the Torah to be given, they said, 'It is time for the Torah to be given to Israel.'[21]

This view of Torah as the bride informed the midrashic reading attested in several sources of another key verse, Exod. 31:18, 'When He

---

is mentioned and afterward the marriage (*qiddushin*) so as to allude to the fact that before God gave the Torah to Israel He placed them in a canopy *(ḥupah)*, i.e., the clouds of glory [see below nn. 41 and 43], and afterward gave them the Torah, which is like a [document of] marriage *(ke-qiddushin)*, for His name was sanctified upon His people, Israel." See *ibid.*, p. 38, where Judah ben Yaqar repeats this explanation, but adds at the end: "Therefore the blessing of *'erusin* is made first because the giving of the Torah and the commandments is the essence." See also commentary of Rashi to Exod. 19: 17 and Deut. 33:2; M. Ta'anit 4:8 and parallel in *Numbers Rabbah*, 12:8. Cf. *Pirqe Rabbi 'Eli'ezer*, chap. 41 where the image of Moses as the best-man is added to that of God as the groom and Israel as the bride. The kabbalisic transformation of this aggadic motif provides yet a third way to construe this relationship: the event at Sinai is the wedding of the Holy One, blessed be He, the masculine potency of the divine which corresponds to the Written Torah, and the *Shekhinah*, the feminine potency which corresponds to the Oral Torah. See *Zohar* 1: 8a; 3: 98a-b.

[19]*Pesiqta' de Rav Kahana'*, ed. by B. Mandelbaum (New York, 1962), 12, pp. 210-11.

[20]See above, n. 18.

[21]*Midrash ha-Gadol on Exodus*, ed. by M. Margulies (Jerusalem, 1983), p. 384.

finished speaking with him on Mt. Sinai, He gave Moses the two tablets of the pact, stone tablets inscribed with the finger of God.' The word *ke-khalloto,* "when he finished," was read in accord with its masorertic defective spelling (without the *waw*) as *ke-khallato,* i.e., "as his bride."[22] This reading, then, confirmed the idea that the Torah was given to Israel – through Moses – as a bride. From this were generated, in turn, several homiletical interpretations that compare the scholar himself, or the words of Torah that proceed from his mouth, to a bride.[23] This reading, moreover, served as the basis for the following passage in the medieval collection of moral precepts, *'Orḥot Ḥayyim,* spuriously attributed to R. Eliezer ben Hyrcanus[24]: "Whoever rejoices with the groom it is as if he received the Torah from Sinai, as it says, 'When He finished *(ke-khalloto)* [speaking with him on Mt. Sinai], He gave Moses etc.' It is written, 'as his bride' *(ke-khallato).* The day in which the Torah was given was certainly like the day when the bride enters her bridal canopy."[25] To be sure, the connection

---

[22]Similarly, there was a widely accepted midrashic tradition – attributed in some sources to R. Joshua of Sikhnin in the name of R. Levi – to read the words *kallot Moshe* in Num. 7:1, "On the day that Moses finished setting up the Tabernacle," as *kallat Moshe,* i.e., the bride of Moses. Cf. *Pesiqta' Rabbati,* 5, 18a; *Pesiqta' de-Rav Kahana',* 1, p. 9; *Tanḥuma',* Naso', 20; *Tanḥuma',* ed. Buber, Naso', 28; *Numbers Rabbah,* 12:8; *Midrash 'Aggadah,* ed. S. Buber, to Num. 7:1, p. 89; commentary of Rashi *ad loc.*; *Midrash Ha-Gadol on Numbers,* ed. Z. M. Rabinowitz (Jerusalem, 1983), p. 104; *Zohar* 1:236b; 2:5b, 140b; 3:4b, 148a, 226b *(Ra'aya' Mehemna').* It must be pointed out, however, that in the case of Num. 7:1, unlike Exod. 31:18, the spelling of the word *kallot* according to the masoretic text is in the plene form and not the defective; hence the rabbinic exegesis creatively changes the accepted orthography. This was already noted by the author of the *Ra'aya' Mehemna'*; see *Zohar* 3:254a. Cf. also the commentary of *Minḥat Shai* to Num. 7:1, R. Judah Loew of Prague, *Gur 'Aryeh* (Jerusalem, 1972), vol. 4, fols. 28a-b; and Buber's note to his edition of *Pesiqta' de-Rav Kahana',* fol. 6a, n. 104.

[23]Cf. *Exodus Rabbah,* 41:5 and parallels in *Tanḥuma',* Ki Tissa', 16 and *Tanḥuma',* ed. Buber, Ki Tissa', 11 (fols. 56a-b); *Bereshit Rabbati,* ed. Ch. Albeck, p. 111.

[24]On the possibility that Moses de León authored this text, see G. Scholem, "Meqorotaw shel ma'aseh R. Gadi'el ha-Tinoq be-Sifrut ha-Qabbalah," *Le-'Agnon Shai,* ed. by D. Sadan and E. E. Urbach (Jerusalem, 1959), pp. 294-95; *idem, Major Trends in Jewish Mysticism* (New York, 1961), pp. 183, 200; *idem, Kabbalah* (Jerusalem, 1974), p. 432. Other scholars, however, beginning with Menaḥem ben Judah de Lonzano (1550-c. 1624), attribute the work to R. Eliezer ben Isaac of Worms, also known as Eliezer ha-Gadol, an eleventh-century German talmudist. Cf. I. Abrahams, *Hebrew Ethical Wills,* 1 (Philadelphia, 1926), pp. 31-49; J. Dan, *Hebrew Ethical and Homiletical Literature* (Jerusalem, 1975), pp. 93-94 (in Hebrew).

[25]*'Orḥot Ḥayyim,* § 25.

between the Sinaitic revelation and an actual wedding underlies earlier teachings, such as the view attributed to R. Joshua ben Levi that one who gladdens the groom with the five voices of joy merits the Torah that was given in five voices.[26] But in the passage from *'Orḥot Ḥayyim* this connection is predicated specifically on the notion that the event at Sinai was itself a wedding between Israel, the groom, and Torah, the bride.

A still further stage in this metaphorical depiction may be gathered from those midrashic passages in which the Torah is parabolically compared to the king's daughter who is given over in marriage to Israel. Thus in *Deuteronomy Rabbah,* whose final stage of redaction is set in the ninth-century but which undoubtedly contains earlier material, we find the following parable:

> Another explanation: 'The thing is very close to you' (Deut. 30:14). R. Samuel ben Naḥman said, To what may this be compared? To a princess whom no one knew. The king had a friend who would come to the king all the time, and the princess stood before him. The king said to him: See how much I cherish you, for no one knows my daughter, and she stands before you. Similarly, the Holy One, blessed be He, said to Israel: See how much I cherish you, for no creature in My [celestial] palace knows the Torah, and I have given it to you.[27]

The metaphorical depiction of the Sinaitic revelation as a marriage and the Torah as the king's daughter is highlighted even more in a passage in *Numbers Rabbah.* The relevant remark occurs in that part of the midrash which, although based on much earlier materials, was apparently compiled in the twelfth-century in the school of Moses ha-Darhsan, an eleventh-century scholar and aggadist of Narbonne:

> To what may this be compared? To a king who married off his daughter and gave her a great wedding celebration....Thus did the Holy One, blessed be He, do when He gave the Torah to Israel....This was naught but a wedding celebration.[28]

In this text we see again that the event at Sinai is compared to a wedding, *qiddushin;* the bride is the Torah, which is characterized as well as the daughter of the king, i.e., God, and the groom is Israel.

A crucial stage in the literary process occurs when the parabolic image of the Torah as bride is subsumed under the image of the king's daughter without any obvious link to the wedding motif. Such a description of the Torah as the king's daughter, *bat melekh,* is to be

---

[26]B. Berakhot 6a.

[27]*Deuteronomy Rabbah,* 8:7 (ed. by S. Lieberman [Jerusalem, 1964], p. 121).

[28]*Numbers Rabbah,* 12:4.

found in R. Eleazar Kallir's *silluq* for the Torah reading of the pericope *Sheqalim*. The entire *silluq* is a hymn for the measurements or dimensions of the Torah, indeed in terms often characteristic of the *shi'ur qomah* speculation,[29] but in one place in particular it states that "the measure of the king's daughter *(middat bat melekh)*[30] is superior in all, elevated in length, width, depth and height, for there is a limit to every end, but her word expands forever without end."[31] It is fairly obvious that the king's daughter is the Torah whose infinite worth and meaning is here depicted in spatial terms. While it is clear that the image of the king's daughter here has no explicit connection to the metaphorical or parabolic description of the Sinaitic revelation as a wedding, it is not yet obvious that the Torah has assumed an hypostatic status.

Another example of the feminine characterization of the Torah removed from the nupital context may be gathered from the well-known passage attributed to the second century Tanna, R. Shim'on bar Yoḥai, in the *Tanḥuma'*, a Babylonian-Geonic recension of the Yelammedenu midrash stemming from the seventh-century, in which the Torah is compared parabolically to a king's daughter who is set within seven palaces. The king reportedly says: "Whoever enters against[32] My daughter, it is as if he enters against Me." The meaning of

---

[29]This fact has been pointed out by several scholars. See M. Idel, "Tefisat ha-Torah be-sifrut ha-hekhalot we-gilguleha ba-qabbalah," *Jerusalem Studies in Jewish Thought* 1 (1981): 40 and references to other scholarly literature given there in n. 49.

[30]See, however, the reading established in E. E. Urbach, "Perush le-silluq ha-qalliri le-farashat sheqalim 'az ra'ita we-safarta," *Sefer Ḥayyim Shirman*, ed. S. Abramson and A. Mirski (Jerusalem, 1970), p. 20: "the measure of the king *(middat melekh)* is superior in all."

[31]I have utilized the text printed in *Seder 'Avodat Yisra'el* (Berlin, 1937), p. 57. Cf. L. Zunz, *Literaturgeschichte der synagogalen Poesie* (Berlin, 1865), p. 43; L. Landshuth, *'Amude ha-'Avodah Reshimat Roshe ha-Payyṭanim u-Me'aṭ mi-Toldotehem 'al Seder 'Alfa' Beta 'im Mispar Piyyuṭehem ha-Nimṣa'im be-Sifre Tefillot* (Berlin, 1857), p. 27.

[32]The Hebrew reads: *she-yikanes 'al*, which I take to mean the negative connotation of entering against someone. See, however, Scholem, *Origins*, p. 170, who translates: "Whoever enters my daughter's presence is as one who enters my presence," and cf. the translation in F. Talmage, "Apples of Gold: The Inner Meaning of Sacred Texts in Medieval Judaism," in *Jewish Spirituality From the Bible Through the Middle Ages*, ed. by A. Green (New York, 1986), p. 347, n. 21: "If any one reaches my daughter, it is as if he reaches me." It strikes me that these rather neutral translations miss the point of the midrashic parable. Support for my rendering may be gathered from the continuation of the text (for reference, see following note) where the word *bizah*, i.e., to desecrate, is used in place of *nikhnas 'al*, to enter upon.

the parable is immediately rendered in the continuation of the midrash:

> The Holy One, blessed be He, says: 'If a man desecrates My daughter, it is as if he desecrates Me. If a person enters the synagogue and desecrates My Torah, it is as if he rose and desecrated My Glory.'[33]

It is clear that this statement is drawing upon the language of ancient Jewish mystical speculation as is evident from the description of the Torah as the princess hidden within seven palaces or *hekhalot.* I am also inclined to believe that the reference to the divine glory at the end of the passage is related to the use of this *terminus technicus* in *merkavah* literature to refer to the anthropomorphic manifestation of the divine. It is thus significant that a link is made between the glory and the Torah.[34] That is, the Torah in the synagogue hid within the ark is meant to conjure up the image of the *kavod* hid behind the various palaces in the celestial realm. Hence, the one who rises against the Torah is comparable to one who rises against the *kavod.*[35] Be that as it may, the essential point for the purposes of this analysis is that here the feminine characterization of Torah as God's daughter is affirmed without any conspicuous connection to the Sinaitic theophany or to the wedding imagery.

In still another passage from a work entitled *Midrash 'Alfa' Betot,* one finds an alternative depiction of the wedding motif. Before proceeding to an analysis of the relevant passage, it is necessary to make a preliminary observation about this source. The provenance and subsequent literary history of this text is somewhat obscure. S. Wertheimer, who published the text on the basis of only one manuscript, conjectured that this text presumably was a part of the eighth-century mystically-oriented midrash *'Otiyyot de-Rabbi 'Aqiva'.*[36] Admittedly, the lack of a fuller picture regarding the history of this text makes citation from it somewhat suspect, especially in the context of trying to present the development of a motif. Still, it can be argued from the language of the text that it indeed draws

---

[33]*Tanḥuma',* Pequde, 4.

[34]See the anonymous commentary on the seventy names of God, apparently deriving from the circle of the German Pietists, cited by Idel, "Tefisat ha-Torah," p. 42, n. 53: "The Torah [is] the glory of the Holy One, blessed be He."

[35]Cf. *Canticles Rabbah,* 8:11, § 2, the view of R. Joshua ben Levi cited by R. Simon: "in every place that the Holy One, blessed be He, placed His Torah, He placed His *Shekhinah.*" This view opposes the previous one, attributed to the "rabbis" generally, which maintained that God calmed the angels by assuring them that while He would give His daughter, i.e., the Torah, to the people of Israel who inhabit the earth, He would not place His *Shekhinah* below.

[36]Cf. *Batte Midrashot* (Jerusalem, 1980), 2: 419.

heavily from the *merkavah* sources and thus represents an important stage in the literary transmission of Jewish mysticism. Even if it cannot be shown conclusively which medieval mystic in particular had this text and was influenced by it, the text itself stands as testimony to a link in the chain of Jewish mystical speculation. At some point some Jewish mystics conceived the Torah in this way, and the conceptual and phenomenological relationship that this view has to other ideas in kabbalistic documents can easily be demonstrated.

In the text of *Midrash 'Alfa' Betot* one finds that the Torah, personified as the daughter of God, is characterized as the bride of Moses:

> Another explanation: 'Behold it was very good' (Gen. 1:21). The word good refers to Moses, as it says, 'and she saw how good he was' (Exod. 2:2). This teaches that in that very time the Holy One, blessed be He, revealed to the Torah the throne of glory, and He brought forth all the souls of the righteous[37]....And He brought forth the souls of Israel....And afterwards He brought forth the soul of Moses from underneath His throne for he would in the future explain the Torah in seventy languages.[38] God showed him to the Torah and said, 'My daughter, take joy and be gladden by this Moses, My servant, for he will be your groom and husband. He will be the one to receive you in the future and to explicate your words to the sixty myriad Israelites.[39]

This comment is an elucidation of a verse in Genesis, suggesting therefore that the setting here is the event of creation. The Sinaitic revelation is only alluded to as a future reference. Significantly, Moses is called the groom of the Torah for he will be the one to receive the Torah at Sinai and explicate it to the Israelite people. Unlike earlier sources the wedding at Sinai is not between God and Israel, or Israel and the Torah, but rather Moses and the Torah. The same aggadic tradition is preserved in a comment of Judah ben Barzilai, citing some older source *(nusḥa' de-rishonim).* According to the legend mentioned by this authority, at the birth of Abraham God was said to have had the following conversation with the Torah:

---

[37]The notion that the souls of the righteous are hidden beneath the throne of glory is a much older motif in Jewish sources. See B. Shabbat 152b and parallels.

[38]On Moses' posture as the official translator of the biblical text, see *ibid.*, p. 447.

[39]*Ibid.*, p. 424. The passage from this relatively late text draws upon much earlier ideas regarding the pre-existence of the Torah and other elements, including the throne and the souls of Israel, to the creation of the world. See, e.g., *Genesis Rabbah* 1:4 (ed. Theodor and Albeck, p. 6); *Pirqe R. 'Eli'ezer*, chap. 3.

He said to her, 'My daughter, come and we will marry you to Abraham, My beloved.' She said to Him: 'No, [I will not marry] until the humble one [i.e., Moses] comes.'[40]

In the continuation of the text we read that God then requested of the *Sefer Yeṣirah* to wed Abraham and, unlike the Torah, it agreed. The purpose of the legend is thus to explain the special connection of *Sefer Yeṣirah* to Abraham as established in the traditional attribution. What is of immediate interest for us is the view that Moses would be the one to marry the Torah, the latter personified specifically as the daughter of God. As will be seen at a later point in this analysis, the motif of Moses' being wed to the Torah plays a significant role in the more developed kabbalistic symbolism.

In the same collection, moreover, there is another striking passage which offers a graphic description of the Torah as the royal bride, again without any overt connection to the Sinaitic revelation:

Another explanation: 'Behold it was very good' (Gen. 1:21). The meaning of good is Torah, as it says, 'For I give you good instruction, do not forsake My Torah' (Prov. 4:2). This teaches that in that very moment the Torah came from her bridal chamber *(me-ḥadre ḥupatah),*[41] adorned *(mitqashetet)* in all kinds of jewels and in all kinds of royal ornaments. And she stands and dances before the Holy One, blessed be He, and gladdens the heart of the *Shekhinah.* She opens her mouth in wisdom and her tongue with understanding, and praises the name of God with all kinds of praise and all kinds of song.[42]

---

[40]Judah ben Barzilai, *Perush Sefer Yeṣirah,* ed. S. J. Halberstam (Berlin, 1885), p. 268. Cf. Scholem, *Origins,* p. 92, who refers to this text in a different context. From Scholem's comments it would appear that he did not fully grasp the import of the legend.

[41]See *Batte Midrashot,* p. 445 where the Holy One, blessed be He, is said to be answered "from within the chamber [or sanctuary] of his glory *(ḥupat kevodo).*" For this usage of the word *ḥupah,* see, e.g., J. Megillah 1:14 (72c-d). As is well known, the image of the bridal chamber (symbolizing the divine Pleroma) is a central motif in certain Gnostic writings, including the wedding hymn in the *Acts of Thomas* and in other Valentinian texts such as the *Gospel of Philip* (Nag Hammadi II.3: 65, 10-12; 67, 15, 30; 69, 1ff.; 70, 17-22, *passim*) and the *Exegesis on the Soul* (Nag Hammadi II.6: 132, 13, 25). See also Irenaeus, *Against Heresies* 1.7.1. cited in B. Layton, *The Gnostic Scriptures* (New York, 1987), pp. 294-95. Cf. R. M. Grant, "The Mystery of Marriage in the Gospel of Philip," *Vigiliae Christianae* 15 (1961): 129-40; M. Marcovich, "The Wedding Hymn of Acta Thomae," *Illinois Classical Studies* 6 (1981): 367-85, reprinted in *Studies in Graeco-Roman Religions and Gnosticism* (Leiden, 1988), pp. 156-73. The striking correspondence of the Bahiric description of the lower Sophia with the "daughter of light" in the gnostic bridal hymn in the *Acts of Thomas* has already been noted by Scholem, *Origins,* pp. 94-95.

[42]*Ibid.,* p. 424.

In this passage we come across two significant elements: first, the Torah is said to emerge from her bridal chamber adorned with jewels and royal ornaments. The only other reference that I am familiar with in the *hekhalot* corpus to such a motif is to be found in the *Re'uyot Yeḥezqel* where it is stated that within the fourth of the seven heavens, *'arafel*, is found the "[bridal] canopy of the Torah," *ḥupatah shel Torah.*[43] The assumption of an actual *ḥupah* for the Torah, albeit in the celestial realm, is based on an earlier figurative description of the Torah as the bride in her bridal canopy. Thus, for example, the following exegetical comment is found in the Palestinian Talmud: "It is written, 'Let the bridegroom come out of his chamber, the bride from her canopy' (Joel 2:16). 'Let the bridegroom come out of his chamber' refers to the ark, 'the bride from her canopy' refers to the Torah."[44] In the *Midrash 'Alfa' Betot,* as in the *Re'uyot Yeḥezqel,* the *ḥupah* is not merely a figure of speech; it refers to an actually existing entity in the cosmological scheme.

The second point of especial interest in the above passage is that the Torah is depicted as dancing before the Holy One, blessed be He, and gladdening the heart of the divine Presence – significantly, *Shekhinah* is not used interchangeably with the Holy One, blessed be He, but is rather an independent entity, though its exact gender is difficult to ascertain. In several other places in this text the *Shekhinah* is described, together with the throne itself, the glory, and

---

[43]Cf. *Re'uyot Yeḥezqel,* ed. I. Gruenwald, in *Temirin,* ed. I. Weinstock (Jerusalem, 1972), 1: 131. The relationship between this text and that of *Midrash 'Alfa' Betot* was already noted by Gruenwald in his comment to line 82, *ad loc.* It is of interest to note that in several other contexts in the *hekhalot* texts God's sitting on the throne is compared to a groom entering the bridal chamber; the throne, also referred to as the "beautiful vessel," is thus given a definite feminine quality. See P. Schäfer, *Synopse, Zur Hekhalot-Literatur* (Tübingen, 1981) §§ 94, 154, 687; *Geniza-Fragmente zur Hekhalot-Literatur* (Tübingen, 1984), p. 185. See also *Geniza-Fragmente,* p. 105 where it says of the angel MYHShGH that he "beautifies the Ḥashmal, adorns TRPZWHYW the king, and all the attributes of his throne like a bride for her bridal chamber *(we-khol middot kiss'o ke-khallah le-ḥupatah)."* In the last passage it is again clear that the throne is considered to be feminine in nature. Such a tradition is also found in other *merkavah* texts and had an influence on the German Pietists. See E. Wolfson, "Circumcision and the Divine Name: A Study in the Transmission of Esoteric Doctrine," *JQR* 78 (1987): 95, n. 53. For a latter use of this theme, see the text on Metatron discussed by M. Idel, "Seridim nosafim mi-kitve R. Yosef ha-ba' mi-shushan ha-birah," *Da'at* 21 (1988): 49, n. 16.

[44]J. Ta'anit 2:1 (65a). Cf. the reading in *Yalqut Shim'oni,* pt. 2, § 535: "'Let the bridegroom come out of his chamber' refers to the ark, 'the bride from her canopy' refers to the Torah-scroll."

the angels, as standing before God,[45] thereby substantiating the impression that the Presence is not identical with the Holy One, blessed be He. One text, in particular, is noteworthy, for it says that the *Shekhinah* was on the throne of glory from the right side and Moses from the left.[46] Again, it is not clear if this implies an apotheosis of the figure of Moses. In any event, the role of the Torah in the passage cited above is similar to that of the celestial beasts in the *merkavah* texts, i.e., the Torah is described as uttering praise and song before God. Even the image of dancing before God has a parallel in the *merkavah* corpus.[47] Hence, the feminine characterization of the Torah

---

[45]See *Batte Midrashot*, pp. 423, 427, 445.

[46]*Ibid.*, p. 447.

[47]See, e.g., P. Schäfer, *Synopse zur Hekhalot-Literatur*, § 411 where the *nogah* is said to have danced before the divine king. The image of the Torah as the adorned bride dancing before the divine Presence may reflect an existent practice in which the Torah-scroll was dressed up as a bride on her wedding-day. Indeed, one is reminded by this image of the *Simḥat Torah* celebration in which dancing with the Torah figures as a prominent feature. Interestingly enough, both the custom to dance with the Torah and that of crowning the Torah (to be sure, already in the *mishnah* [cf. 'Avot 4:13] one finds the expression *keter Torah*, the crown of Torah, but in that context this image has a purely figurative connotation without any objective correlate) – a practice which eventually became the normative course of action for all year round and not specifically on this one festival – originated apparently in the Babylonian academies during the Geonic period in connection with *Simḥat Torah*. See A. Yaari, *Toledot Ḥag Simḥat Torah* (Jerusalem, 1964), pp. 24-25. Underlying both these ritualisitc performances, but especially the former, is the aggadic image of the Torah as the bride. On the day when the cycle of Torah-reading is completed, the scroll is crowned like a bride, thus recalling the day of revelation at Sinai which itself was likened to a wedding celebration. That the crown placed on the Torah is to bring to mind the bridal crown is obvious from the fact that in the original Geonic responsum the halakhic question to be examined is whether or not a groom could place on his head during his own wedding the crown that was used to crown the Torah during the festival. The wedding motif is even stronger in a later version of this responsum in the fourteenth-century halakhic compedium, *'Orhot Ḥayyim* by R. Aaron ha-Kohen of Lunel, where a noticable change in language is easily detected: "The Ga'on wrote: 'It is forbidden to place the crown that has been placed on the Torah-scroll on the head of the one who completes [the reading] on the day of *Simḥat Torah*." That is, the original prohibition of placing the crown on the head of a groom has been understood as the specific prohibition of placing the crown on the head of the last one called up to the Torah. This reflects the institution of the *ḥatan Torah*, i.e., the groom of the Torah, a particular name applied already in the school of R. Solomon ben Isaac of Troyes in the eleventh-century to the one who was called up to the Torah for the concluding section of Deuteronomy. The name *ḥatan Torah*, as Avraham Yaari has shown, represents a subtle change from what appears to have been the original title, *ḥatam Torah*, i.e., the one who seals or concludes the Torah (cf. M. Megillah

is here abstracted from the particular setting of the Sinaitic theophany. That is, the methaphorical depiction of Torah as the bride is removed from the specific context of a parabolic description of the historical revelation. Moreover, it seems to me that in this text the Torah has already assumed an hypostatic character. We are not simply dealing with the figurative expression of a personified Torah, but with an actual hypostasis of the Torah as a feminine person who emerges from her bridal chamber. This is consistent with the decidedly hypostatic characterization of the *kavod, Shekhinah,* and the *kisse' ha-kavod* found in other parts of this text.

The image of the hypostatic crowned Torah served as a basis for the development of one of the key symbols in the incipient kabbalah. Thus, in a critical passage in *Sefer ha-Bahir,* a foundational text in medieval Jewish mysticism, one reads the following depiction of Torah as the king's daughter:

> Whenever a person studies Torah for its own sake, the Torah above (*ha-Torah shel ma'alah*) unites with the Holy One, blessed be He....And what is the Torah of which you speak? It is the bride that is adorned and crowned *(she-mequshetet u-me'uteret),* and is comprised within[48] all the commandments *(u-mukhlelet be-khol ha-*

4:1). *Ḥatan Torah,* by contrast, means the groom of the Torah, thus complementing the feminine image of the Torah as the bride. In the version of the Geonic responsa of R. Aaron it is assumed that the one reading the Torah is the groom of the wedding celebration and the Torah is the bride. Indeed, in the course of the generations from medieval times through modernity many customs have arisen in connection with the Torah and *ḥatan Torah* which are reminiscent of things done at actual weddings.

[48]In the printed editions of the *Bahir* the reading is *mukhlelet* which I have rendered as is comprised. Cf. Scholem, *Das Buch Bahir* (Darmstadt, 1980), p. 151, who translates the word *mukhlelet* as *enthalten.* See the parallel, in slightly different imagery, in *Sefer ha-Bahir,* ed. R. Margaliot (Jerusalem, 1978), § 190 where it says that God took one thousandth from the splendor of the hidden light and "built from it a beautiful and adorned precious stone *('even yeqarah na'ah u-mequshetet)* and comprised within it all the commandments *(we-khillel bah kol ha-miṣwot).*" It is not impossible that there is a play in § 196 between the word *mukhlelet* and *mekhullelet,* the latter meaning to be crowned. If the latter meaning is implied, then it would fit nicely with the two verbs that preceded it, viz., *mequsheṭet* and *me'uṭeret,* conjuring up further the image of the bride arrayed on her wedding day. Cf. *Bahir* § 91 where the crown (i.e., the *Shekhinah*) is identified as the precious stone that is *mekhullelet u-me'uṭeret.* See the manuscript reading used by Scholem, *op. cit.,* p. 62, n. 9, *me'uṭeret u-mukhlelet,* which he translated as *der gekrönte Edelstein, in dem* [*Alles*] *zusammengefaßt ist* (p. 61). See also *Bahir* § 146 where the sixth of the ten logoi is described as the *kisse' ha-kavod ha-me'u ṭar ha-mukhlal,* rendered by Scholem, p. 104, as *Der Thron der Herrlichkeit, der gekrönt ist, eingefaßt.* For a similar usage of the root *kll* in an 11th century *piyyuṭ* deriving from

> *miṣwot),* and it is the treasure of the Torah *('oṣar ha-Torah).* And she is the one engaged to the Holy One, blessed be He, as it is written, 'Moses commanded the Torah to us, as the heritage of the congregation of Jacob' (Deut. 33:4). Do not read heritage *(morashah)* but rather betrothal' *(me'orasah).* How is this possible? When Israel are involved with the Torah for its own sake she is the one engaged to the Holy One, blessed be He, and when she is the one engaged to the Holy One, blessed be He, she is the heritage of Israel.[49]

Here the midrashic image of the Torah as the betrothed of Israel has been transposed into the divine sphere. That is, the Torah below has its reflection in the Torah above which is joined to the masculine potency of the divine, the Holy One, blessed be He, by means of the study of Torah in the mundane sphere.[50] Furthermore, this supernal Torah, the feminine potency of the divine, is described as the bride that is adorned and crowned and which is comprised within all the commandments. It is on account of the latter that the supernal Torah is called the *'oṣar ha-Torah.*[51] A similar expression is employed in yet another passage, wherein the treasure of the Torah, *'oṣarah shel Torah,* is identified as the fear of God, *yir'at YHWH,* based on the

---

Southern Italy, see *The Poems of Elya bar Schemaya,* ed. Yonah David (Jerusalem, 1977), p. 128, where *hukhlelah* is used synonymously with *hukhtarah.* Tracing the particular usage of such key words as this may prove helpful in determining the literary origin of parts of the *Bahir.* On the merging of the images of the crown and the throne, cf. the following passage describing the bride (Sophia) in the wedding hymn in the *Acts of Thomas* (cf. n. 41, above): "On the crown of her head sits the king" (translated in Marcovich, "The Wedding Hymn," p. 160).

[49]*Sefer ha-Bahir,* § 196. Cf. Scholem, *Origins,* p. 174.

[50]The theurgical dimension of Torah-study is repeated in the *Bahir* § 185 where it is stated that "whoever studies Torah bestows love *(gomel ḥesed)* upon his Creator, as it is written, '[O Jeshurun, there is none like God], riding the heavens with your help' (Deut. 33:26), that is to say, when you study Torah for its own sake *(Torah lishmah)* then you help Me [i.e., God], and I ride the heavens."

[51]The connection between *'oṣar* and Torah is based on earlier midrashic sources. See, e.g., *Midrash Tehillim,* 119:9, ed. Buber (Jerusalem, 1977), p. 493: "'*Oṣarot* refers to the Torah, as it is written, 'A precious treasure (*'oṣar neḥmad*) etc.' (Prov. 21:20)." And see *Midrash 'Otiyyot de-R. 'Aqiva',* ed. Wertheimer, *Batte Midrashot,* 2: 348: "'*Oṣar* is the Torah, as it is said, 'The fear of the Lord is his treasure *('oṣaro)'* (Isa. 33:6), and Torah is fear, as it is said, 'And all the peoples of the earth shall see that the Lord's name is proclaimed over you, and they stand in fear of you' (Deut. 28:10)." Besides the nexus established between fear and Torah (repeated in the *Sefer ha-Bahir;* see following note), from the last citation it is clear that in this text Torah is already identified with the name of God, a theme more fully exploited in medieval kabbalah.

verse, 'the fear of God was his treasure' (Isa. 33:6).[52] From that context, moreover, it is clear that the fear of God, or the treasure of Torah, refers to the last of the divine potencies as it is presented as the last item in a series of cognitive-emotive states that are symbolic referents of God's attributes, i.e., Wisdom *(Ḥokhmah)*, Understanding *(Binah)*, Counsel *('Eṣah)* which corresponds to the attribute of bestowing kindness *(gemilat ḥasadim)*, Strength *(Gevurah)*[53] identifed also as the attribute of Judgment *(Middat ha-Din)*, Knowledge *(Da'at)* or the attribute of truth *('Emet)*, and the Fear of God *(Yir'at YHWH)* which is described as the treasure of Torah *('oṣarah shel Torah)*.[54] It is fairly obvious, then, that the treasure of the Torah is a technical reference to one of the divine attributes in the same way that the other items in the list are; in particular, the attribute to which this phrase refers is the *Shekhinah*.[55] In the case of the *Bahir*, therefore, one is transferred from the realm of metaphor to that of symbol. That is, the king's daughter in the *Bahir* is no longer merely a literary expression used in a metaphorical context; it is rather a living symbol that names one of the divine potencies.[56]

---

[52]See the passage from *Midrash 'Otiyyot de-R. 'Aqiva'* cited in the previous note.

[53]In the standard Hebrew editions of the *Bahir* the reading is "and *Binah* which is the attribute of Judgment." This reading is obviously corrupt as *Binah* was mentioned already at an earlier stage in the sequence in between *Ḥokhmah* and *'Eṣah* (i.e., *Ḥesed*). See the more accurate reading preserved in Menaḥem Recanati, *Perush 'al ha-Torah* (Jerusalem, 1961), 39d: "In the *Sefer ha-Bahir* [it is written]: Counsel *('Eṣah)* is the bestowing of kindness *(gemilut ḥasadim)*, strength *(Gevurah)* is the attribute of Judgment." This reading is reflected as well in Scholem's translation, *Das Buch Bahir*, § 129, p. 140: 'Rat' – das sei das Wohltun, 'Starke' – das sei Prinzip der Strenge."

[54]*Sefer ha-Bahir*, § 186.

[55]Cf. the commentary of *'Or ha-Ganuz, ad loc.* For a different explanation, see *Ma'arekhet ha-'Elohut* (Jerusalem, 1963), 66a, where the Bahiric symbolism is interpreted as a reference to the ninth *sefirah* or *Yesod*. See Scholem, *Das Buch Bahir*, § 129, p. 141, n. 2, who suggests that the "fear of God" in the *Bahir* has a double meaning; it can refer either to *Binah* or to the last *sefirah*, i.e., the *Shekhinah*. See, however, idem, *Origins*, p. 136, where Scholem unequivocally states that in the *Bahir* the "fear of God" refers symbolically to the third *sefirah* or *Binah*. This interpretation indeed fits several other passages in the *Bahir*, most notably §§ 103 (Scholem: § 72) and 190 (§ 131). In the latter case, however, it is clear that an intrinsic connection is established between the primordial light, which is identified as the "fear of God," and the *Shekhinah*.

[56]The use of the expression *bat melekh* to refer to the *Shekhinah*, which is also identified as prayer, the tenth kingdom, and the angel of the Lord, is found in a passage from Eleazar of Worms, *Sefer ha-Ḥokhmah;* see MS. Oxford 1812, fols. 60b-61a. Cf. Scholem, *Origins*, pp. 184-86; J. Dan, *The Esoteric Theology of Ashkenazi Ḥasidism* (Jerusalem, 1968), pp. 118-24 (in Hebrew). It is not clear

From still other passages in the *Bahir* it can be shown that the Torah is characterized as a feminine personification. Thus, in one of the opening passages one finds the following complicated sequence: the Torah begins with the letter *bet (be-reshit)* which stands for blessing *(berakhah)* for the Torah is called blessing, but blessing in turn is identified as the beginning (*reshit*) which is nothing but wisdom (*ḥokhmah*).[57] It is further specified there that this is, employing the imagery of 1 Kings 5:26, the wisdom which God gave to Solomon,[58] an event parabolically depicted as the king giving over his daughter[59] in marriage to his son.[60] In another passage, which ostensibly sets out to explain the function of the *bet* at the end of the word *zahav*, i.e., gold, a similar parable is offered:

> This may be compared to a king who had a good, pleasant, beautiful and perfect daughter. He married her to a prince, and he dressed her, crowned (*'iṭṭrah*) and adorned (*qishṭah*) her, and gave her to him for much money. Is it possible for the king to sit outside his house [i.e, without being *with* his daughter]? No! But can he sit all day and be with her constantly? No! What does he do? He places a window between himself and her, and whenever the daughter needs the father or the father the daughter, they join together by means of the window.[61]

In the next paragraph we are given additional information to help us identify the *bet* at the end of the word *zahav:* it is the wisdom with which God will build the house.[62] Hence, the king's daughter, all dressed, adorned and crowned for her wedding to the prince, is divine wisdom. That the further identification with Torah is here implied may be gathered from the fact that the parable is largely based on a midrashic passage in *Exodus Rabbah*[63] which deals specifically with the Torah:

---

from the passage in question if one is justified to go further and identify the *bat melekh* with the Torah as is clearly the case in the Bahiric material. See, however, A. Farber, "The Concept of the Merkabah in Thirteenth-Century Jewish Esotericism – 'Sod ha-'Egoz' and Its Development" (Ph.D. thesis, Hebrew University, 1986), p. 242, n. 40 (in Hebrew).

[57]The sequence of images in the *Bahir* is close to that which is found in Judah ben Barzilai's *Perush Sefer Yeṣirah*, p. 57. Cf. Scholem, *Origins*, p. 93.

[58]Cf. *Sefer ha-Bahir*, § 77, where this wisdom is identified as the *Shekhinah.*

[59]The image of the king's daughter also appears in *Sefer ha-Bahir*, §§ 54, 63, 93.

[60]*Ibid.* § 2. Cf. § 65; Scholem, *Origins*, pp. 92-93.

[61]*Ibid.* § 54.

[62]*Ibid.* § 55. The scriptural reference is to Prov. 24:3.

[63]This has already been recognized by Scholem; see *Das Buch Bahir*, p. 40, n. 2; *Origins*, p. 170. See also in the edition of Margaliot, § 54, n. 3.

> The Holy One, blessed be He, said to Israel: 'I sold you My Torah, I was sold with it, as it were....This may be compared to a king who had an only daughter. One of the kings came and took her; he desired to go to his land and to take her as a wife. The king said to him: 'My daughter whom I have given you is an only child; I cannot separate from her, yet I also cannot tell you not to take her for she is your wife. But do me this favor: in whatever place that you go, make a bed-chamber for me so that I may live near you for I cannot leave my daughter.' Thus the Holy One, blessed be He, said to Israel: 'I gave you My Torah. I cannot separate from it, yet I cannot tell you not to take it. In every place that you go make for Me a house so that I may dwell within it, as it says, 'And make for Me a tabernacle.'[64]

The Bahiric parable is thus clearly based on the midrashic one, with some significant differences. In the case of the standard midrash, the king's daughter is identified as the Torah given by God to Israel. God's request of Israel to build a tabernacle is understood midrashically in terms of His need to be close to the Torah which is now in the possession of the Jews. In the *Bahir*, by contrast, the Torah is not mentioned explicitly, though it is implied by the identification of the king's daughter with *ḥokhmah*. In this case, moreover, there is mention of an actual joining of father and daughter, and not merely the desire to be in proximity to one another.

To be sure, this feminine personification of the Torah is not the only one to be found in the *Bahir*. In one passage Torah is identified with the divine attribute of *Ḥesed*, lovingkindness,[65] though in this case, as some of the passages where Torah is linked with the feminine *Ḥokhmah*, the image of water plays a central role.[66] In still another passage mention is made of the "true Torah," *Torat 'emet*, which is said to be within the [divine] attribute of Israel.[67] From the next paragraph we learn that the activity of this *Torat 'emet* is within the *Maḥshavah*, i.e., the divine thought; moreover, it is itself one of the ten logoi which establishes all the rest.[68] Although the meaning of this passage is not altogether clear, it strikes me that the *Torat 'emet* is another name for divine thought, the uppermost attribute which establishes the other nine, and which is particularly evident within the attribute of Israel, i.e., the attribute which in subsequent kabbalah was most frequently identified with the sixth emanation, *Tif'eret*. In the list of the ten logoi one reads that the third of these is identified

---

[64]*Exodus Rabbah*, 33:1.
[65]*Sefer ha-Bahir*, § 136.
[66]Cf. Scholem, *Origins*, p. 132.
[67]*Sefer ha-Bahir*, § 137. Cf. Scholem, *Origins*, pp. 144-45.
[68]*Ibid.*, § 138.

as the quarry of Torah, *meḥaṣev ha-Torah,* or the treasure of wisdom, *'oṣar ha-ḥokhmah* (reminiscent of the expression *'oṣar ha-Torah* used in a previous context), for God is said to have hewn the letters of the Torah and carved them within this attribute.[69] Finally, the most important alternative conception of the Torah is offered in an elaborate reworking of an earlier aggadic idea concerning the primordial light which was hidden by God for the benefit of the righteous in the world-to-come.[70] According to the *Bahir,* God took a portion from that primordial light, comprised within it the thirty-two paths of wisdom, and then gave it to people of this world. This light is named the "treasure of the Oral Torah," *'oṣarah shel Torah she-be'al peh.* "The Holy One, blessed be He, said: If they observe this attribute in this world, for this attribute is considered as part of this world, and it is the Oral Torah, they will merit life in the world-to-come, which is the good hidden for the righteous."[71] From this it follows that the Oral Torah represents a fragment from the primordial divine light that is operative in the mundane realm. The means to attain the full light in the spiritual realm is to observe the commandments of the Torah as mediated through the rabbinic oral tradition. The precise relationship between the Written Torah and the Oral Torah is addressed in a subsequent passage. Interpreting Prov. 6:23, "For the commandment *(miṣwah)* is a lamp, the Torah a light," the *Bahir* establishes that "commandment" corresponds to the Oral Torah and "Torah" to Scripture.[72] Admittedly, the Written Torah is a much greater light, but the candle of the Oral Torah is necessary to elucidate the meaning of Scripture. This relationship is illuminated by means of a parable: even though it is broad daylight outside, it is sometimes necessary to use a candle in order to see what is hidden in a room in a house.[73]

---

[69]*Ibid.,* § 143. Cf. Scholem, *Origins,* pp. 134, 145, 175. The language of the *Bahir* is appropriated, without the source being named, already by R. Asher ben David, a thirteenth-century Provençal kabbalist and nephew of the famous R. Isaac the Blind. See *Perush Shem ha-Meforash,* ed. M Ḥasidah, *Ha-Segullah* 1-3 (Jerusalem, 1934-36), p. 6, reprinted in J. Dan, *Qabbalat R. 'Asher ben David* (Jerusalem, 1980), p. 18. For another example of the influence of the *Bahir* on this kabbalist, see Scholem, *Das Buch Bahir,* § 132, p. 145.

[70]Cf. B. Ḥagigah 12a.

[71]*Sefer ha-Bahir* § 147.

[72]Cf. Maimonides' introduction to the *Mishneh Torah:* "'And I will give you tablets of stone and the Torah and the commandments' (Exod. 24:12). 'Torah' refers to the Written Torah, 'and the commandments' refers to that which is called the Oral Torah." The Oral Torah is identified as commandment already in B. Berakhot 5a. Cf. *Zohar* 2: 166b; 3: 40b.

[73]*Sefer ha-Bahir* § 149.

According to the standard kabbalistic interpretation of this critical Bahiric text that evolved in thirteenth-century Spain, the light or the Written Torah was said to symbolize the masculine potency, usually identified as the sixth emanation, *Tif'eret,* whereas the Oral Torah or the lamp was said to symbolize the feminine potency, the *Shekhinah.*[74] To be sure, the depiction of the Oral Torah in terms that are applicable to the feminine Presence has a basis in the *Bahir* itself. Notwithstanding this fact, it is evident that such a conception contradicts the other major image found in the *Bahir* according to which the Torah in a generic sense, and not specifically the Oral Torah, was characterized as the feminine potency of God. It is not impossible that we are dealing with two distinct stages in the literary composition of the *Bahir.* Perhaps at an earlier stage the Torah was simply described in a way that developed organically out of older midrashic sources, whereas at a later stage there developed the unique kabbalistic conception of the dual-Torah as corresponding symbolically to the two attributes of God. Proof of my conjecture may be found in the subtle shift in terminology from *'oṣar ha-Torah,* the treasure of Torah, to *'oṣar shel Torah she-be'al peh,* the treasure of the Oral Torah. That is, in the first passage (§ 196) where Torah is generally described as a feminine potency, it is referred to as the "treasure of Torah," whereas in the second passage (§ 147) where the masculine-feminine duality is introduced, the feminine aspect of Torah is referred to as the "treasure of the Oral Torah." It is, however, difficult to ascertain with any certainty if and when this change may have occurred. What is crucial, however, is that while the correlation of the dual-Torah to the male-female polarity within the divine became the norm in kabbalistic documents in thirteenth-century Spain, it can nevertheless be shown that the older mythical-aggadic image did not entirely disappear.

One finds in subsequent kabbalistic texts traces of the identification of the Torah with the feminine potency, particularly the

---

[74]See, e.g., *Perush ha-'Aggadot le-R. 'Azri'el,* ed. I. Tishby (Jerusalem, 1945), pp. 3, 49, 53; Ṭodros Abulafia, *Sha'ar ha-Razim,* ed. Ch. Erlanger (Bene Beraq, 1986), p. 74.

Shekhinah.[75] There thus may be a kabbalistic reworking of this motif in a relatively early text, Judah ben Yaqar's *Perush ha-Tefillot we-ha-Berakhot*. In the context of commenting upon the Friday evening prayer, 'You shall sanctify the seventh day,' *we-'atah qiddashta 'et yom ha-shevi'i*, which ben Yaqar interprets in terms of *qiddushin*, i.e., a wedding service, he cites the midrashic text from *Deuteronomy Rabbah* mentioned above,[76] in which Moses is described as the scribe who writes the marriage contract (the Torah), Israel is the bride, and God is the groom. Ben Yaqar then cites from the continuation of the same source a comment attributed to Resh Laqish to the effect that the illumination of Moses' face mentioned in Exod. 34:29, could be explained by the fact that in the process of writing the Torah, which was written with black fire on parchment of white fire,[77] Moses wiped the quill with which he was writing in his hair. According to ben Yaqar the import of this statement is "to say that Moses too betrothed the Torah and she was his bride and portion."[78] Do we have here a cryptic reference to the Torah as the feminine persona of the divine, the *Shekhinah*, who is wedded to Moses, the biblical figure who symbolizes the masculine potency of God? Support for this interpretation may be gathered from a second comment of ben Yaqar on this midrashic passage. "A crown of splendor *(kelil tif'eret)* You placed on his [Moses'] head'...a crown of splendor, as it says in *Deuteronomy Rabbah*, he was writing when he was above [i.e., on Mount Sinai], and he would wipe the quill in his hair and illuminate his face."[79] In the

[75]This is to be distinguished from another idea expressed in thirteenth-century kabbalah concerning the revelation of the Written Torah, the masculine potency, through the mediation of the Oral Torah, the feminine potency. See, e.g., R. Ezra of Gerona, *Perush 'al Shir ha-Shirim*, in *Kitve Ramban*, ed. by C. B. Chavel (Jerusalem, 1978), 2: 487. See also the text cited and discussed by G. Scholem, *On the Kabbalah and Its Symbolism* (New York, 1969), pp. 49-50. According to the author of that text, the Written Torah that we have on this earth has already passed through the medium of the Oral Torah; the Written Torah in and of itself is a purely mystical construct. Scholem assumed that the aforementioned text was written by R. Isaac the Blind. See, by contrast, M. Idel, "Ḥomer qabbali mi-bet midrasho shel R. David ben Yehudah he-Ḥasid," *Jerusalem Studies in Jewish Thought* 2 (1982/3): 170, n. 9.

[76]In this context, however, ben Yaqar cites the source as part of *Bereshit Rabbah*; see above, n. 18.

[77]This characterization was originally used to describe the status of the primordial Torah, or the Torah in a state before the world existed. See J. Sheqalim 6:1; *Tanḥuma'*, Bereshit, 1. The usage in this context is clearly secondary.

[78]*Perush ha-Tefillot we-ha-Berakhot*, pt. 1, p. 90.

[79]*Ibid.*, p. 104.

first passage this state of illumination was explained by reference to the idea that Moses was betrothed to the Torah; in the second passage the same notion is expressed by the idea that Moses is crowned by a crown of splendor. The image of Moses' being crowned is equivalent to that of his being wedded to Torah.[80] Moreover, as it can be ascertained from another passage in ben Yaqar, the *Shekhinah* is characterized as the "crown on the head of the king" *(ke-'aṭarah be-rosh ha-melekh)*,[81] i.e., the crown on the head of *Tif'eret*. It seems to me, therefore, that Moses stands symbolically for *Tif'eret*, and the crown on his head, as well as the Torah to which he is wedded, for the *Shekhinah*.

A similar kabbalistic usage of this aggadic motif may be found in the writings of one of ben Yaqar's more celebrated students, Naḥmanides (1194-1270). Thus, for example, Naḥmanides returns to this theme in his comments on the very first word of the Pentateuch. After establishing that the opening word of Scripture, *bereshit*, refers simultaneously[82] to the emanation of the upper Wisdom, or the "Wisdom of Elohim," symbolized by the heave-offering *(terumah)* which is utterly beyond human comprehension, and to the last of the ten emanations, the lower Wisdom, the "Wisdom of Solomon," i.e., the *Shekhinah*, symbolized by the *ma'aser* which is a measure that can be comprehended, Naḥmanides turns his attention to the rabbinic reading of the key word which interprets *reshit* as a reference to Israel:

> And Israel, who are called the 'beginning' *(reshit)*, refers to the Community of Israel *(Keneset Yisra'el)*, who is compared in the Song of Songs to the bride, and which Scripture calls [by the names] daughter, sister and mother[83]....And thus [is the meaning of] 'he saw the beginning for himself' (Deut. 33:21)[84] spoken with reference to Moses. It is held [by the rabbis][85] that Moses contemplated [the divine] within a speculum that shines *(be-'ispaqlarya' ha-me'irah)*, 'and he saw the beginning for himself,' and thus he merited the Torah. It is all one intention.[86]

---

[80]Indeed the crown for ben Yaqar, as for other kabbalists, is a symbol for sexual unification.

[81]See *Perush ha-Tefillot we-ha-Berakhot*, "Addenda," p. 27.

[82]I have followed the explanation of this difficult passage offered by several of the standard commentaries on Naḥmanides' commentary. Cf. in particular Shem Tob ibn Ga'on, *Keter Shem Tov*, in *Ma'or wa-Shemesh*, ed. J. Koriat (Livorno, 1839), 27a.

[83]See Naḥmanides' commentary to Gen. 24:1.

[84]It should be noted that I have rendered the biblical expression literally which accords with the kabbalistic interpretation proferred by Naḥmanides.

[85]Cf. B. Yevamot 49b.

[86]Naḥmanides, *Perush 'al ha-Torah*, to Gen. 1:1, ed. C. B. Chavel (Jerusalem, 1969), 1: 11.

For Naḥmanides, then, Moses beheld the vision of the *Shekhinah* – the "beginning" *(reshit)* alluded to in Deut. 33:21 – through the upper masculine attribute, the speculum that shines, and as a result he merited the Torah.

That the Torah corresponds symbolically to the *Shekhinah* may be gathered from a second comment of Naḥmanides:

> 'And this is the offering,' *we-zot ha-terumah* (Exod. 25:3). By way of [kabbalistic] truth this is like [the verse] 'And the Lord gave wisdom to Solomon' (1 Kings 5: 26)....And in *Exodus Rabbah* [it says]: 'And this is the offering that you shall take from them' [this refers to] the Community of Israel *(Keneset Yisra'el)*, which is the offering *(terumah)*....The Holy One, blessed be He, said to Israel: 'I have sold you My Torah and, as it were, I have been sold with her, as it says, 'Bring Me an offering' (Exod. 25: 2), for the offering is to Me and I am with her.[87]

In this case, in contrast to the one mentioned above, the word *terumah* itself is given the same symbolic valence as *zot*. Now, insofar as it is clear from other contexts in Naḥmanides that the word *zot*, the feminine form of the demonstrative pronoun, refers to the *Shekhinah*,[88] we may further infer that in this case *terumah* refers to *Shekhinah*. Moreover, utilizing the midrashic comment from *Exodus Rabbah*, Naḥmanides is able to equate *terumah* and Torah; yet, inasmuch as *terumah* is synonymous with *zot*, and *zot* stands for *Shekhinah*, it follows that Torah likewise stands for the *Shekhinah*. This interpretation is corroborated by another brief comment of Naḥmanides: "The word *zot* (this) alludes to the blessing which is the Torah, and it is the covenant, as it is written, 'This is my covenant' *(zot beriti)* (Isa. 59:21)."[89] Hence, *Shekhinah* equals blessing, which equals the Torah and the covenant.

The symbolic nexus that I have described above is preserved as well in the following kabbalistic interpretation of Baḥya ben Asher on the midrashic reading of Deut. 33:4, "do not read heritage *(morashah)* but betrothal *(me'orasah)*":

> By way of the kabbalistic explanation *('al derekh ha-qabbalah)* they had to interpret in this way, for this Torah *(zot ha-Torah)* is betrothed to Jacob, and she is called Rachel. In a time of anger the *Shekhinah* disappears, 'Rachel cries over her children, she refuses to be

---

[87]*Ibid.*, Exod. 25:3 (p. 1:454).
[88]Cf. *ibid.*, Gen. 2: 20 (1:39), 9: 12 (1: 64-65).
[89]*Ibid.*, Deut. 33:1 (2: 491).

> comforted for her children, who are gone' (Jer. 31:15). And in a time of favor Rachel is the wife of Jacob, and this is clear.[90]

According to the kabbalistic interpretation of the midrashic passage, Torah is the *Shekhinah* or Rachel who is betrothed to *Tif'eret* symbolized by the figure of Jacob. In times of distress the two are separated and Rachel weeps over her children, but in times of mercy they are united in matrimony. Following the tradition of Judah ben Yaqar and Naḥmanides, Baḥya likewise affirms that the Torah is the feminine Presence.

It is, however, in the classical kabbalistic text of this period, the *Zohar,* that the image of the Torah as a woman not only resurfaces but is again elevated to a position of supreme importance. Indeed, one finds that some of the more powerful passages describing Torah in a mystical vein in the *Zohar* draw heavily from the feminine image of the Torah. Specifically, the feminine personification of the Torah is utilized by the author of the *Zohar* to describe the hermeneutical relationship between mystic exegete and Scripture. Thus, for example, in one passage we read the following explanation attributed to R. Isaac for why the Torah begins with the letter *bet* which is opened on one side and closed on the three other sides:

> When a person comes to be united with the Torah, she (!) is open to receive him and to join him. But when a person closes his eyes from her and goes another way, she is closed from another side.[91]

In this context, then, it is clear that the author of the *Zohar* upholds the possibility of an individual's uniting with the Torah; indeed, in the continuation of the text, this unification is referred to as joining the Torah face-to-face *(le-'itḥaber bah be-'oraita' 'anpin be-'anpin).* The Torah is open and closed, depending on the actions and efforts of the given person. Underlying this suggestive remark is the older feminine personification of the Torah. What is implied in this passage is elaborated upon in greater detail in the famous Zoharic parable[92] in which the Torah is likened to a beautiful princess secluded in her palace. From a small opening within her palace the princess hints to her lover, the mystic exegete, revealing her face only to him and then immediately concealing it from the view of others. These stages of disclosure correspond metaphorically to the various layers of meaning

---

[90]*Rabbenu Baḥya 'al ha-Torah*, ed. C. B. Chavel (Jerusalem, 1981), Deut. 33:4, p. 478. On the Zoharic influence in this passage of Baḥya, see E. Gottlieb, *The Kabbalah in the Writings of R. Baḥya ben Asher ibn Ḥalawa* (Jerusalem, 1970), p. 20 (in Hebrew).

[91]*Zohar* 3:35b-36a.

[92]*Zohar* 2: 99a-b.

embedded in the scriptural text. In the final stage, the Torah reveals itself face-to-face to the mystic (*'itgali'at le-gabe 'anpin be-'anpin*) and communicates to him all of its inner secrets and esoteric truths. In the moment that the Torah reveals all its secrets to the mystic, the latter is called *ba'al Torah*[93] or *ma'are de-veta'* ("master of the house"),[94] two expressions that allude to the fact that the mystic has united with the Torah or *Shekhinah* in a sexual embrace. I have elsewhere dealt at length with the erotic nature of reading that is here suggested.[95] What is critical for this analysis is the obvious characterization of the Torah as a feminine persona. Kabbalistic exegesis is a process of denuding the Torah akin to the disrobing of the princess by her lover. This is stated explicitly by R. Moses de León (c. 1240-1305), assumed by most modern scholars to be the author of the bulk of the *Zohar*, in his *Mishkan ha-'Edut* (1293):

> Our holy Torah is a perfect Torah, 'all the glory of the royal princess is inward' (Ps. 45:14). But because of our great and evil sins today, 'her dress is embroidered with golden mountings' *(ibid.)*....Thus God, blessed be He, laid a 'covering of dolphin skin over it' (Num. 4:6) with the visible things [of this world]. And who can see and contemplate the great and awesome light hidden in the Torah except for the supernal and holy ancient ones. They entered her sanctuary, and the great light was revealed to them....They removed the mask from her.[96]

It seems reasonable to suggest, moreover, that this feminine personification of the Torah underlies an oft-repeated theme in the Zoharic corpus to the effect that the *Shekhinah*, the feminine presence of God, is immanent in a place where a mystic sage is studying or interpreting the Torah.[97] While the link between Torah-study and the dwelling of the *Shekhinah* is clearly affirmed in earlier rabbinic sources,[98] there are two significant differences between the claims of

---

[93]For the Aramaic equivalent to this expression, see *Zohar* 1: 242b.

[94]Cf. *Zohar* 1: 21b, 236b, 239a.

[95]See E. Wolfson, "The Hermeneutics of Visionary Experience: Revelation and Interpretation in the *Zohar*," *Religion* 18 (1988): 321-24. See also M. Idel, *Kabbalah: New Perspectives* (New Haven, 1988), pp. 227-28.

[96]*Mishkan ha-'Edut*, MS Berlin Or. Quat. 833, fol. 1b. For a discussion of this text and its conceptual background, see D. Cohen-Alloro, *The Secret of the Garment in the Zohar* (Jerusalem, 1987), p. 43 (in Hebrew).

[97]Cf. *Zohar* 1: 9a, 135b, 164a, 245a; 2: 94b, 134b *(Ra'aya' Mehemna')*, 149a, 155b, 188b, 209a; 3: 22a, 35a, 58b, 60b, 61a, 213a, 268a-b, 298a; *Zohar Ḥadash*, 28b, 29a, 95a *(Midrash ha-Ne'elam)*.

[98]M. 'Avot 3:2, 3:6; B. Berakhot 6a; Sanhedrin 39b; Targum to Ps. 82:1; *Midrash Tehillim* on Ps. 105:1 (ed. Buber, p. 448); *Deuteronomy Rabbah* 7:2. See E. E. Urbach, *The Sages Their Concepts and Beliefs* (Jerusalem, 1978), p. 33 (in Hebrew).

the *Zohar* and the classical texts. First, the position of the rabbis is not that study of Torah is a means to bring the divine Presence, but rather that as a natural consequence of fulfilling God's will the *Shekhinah* will be present. In the case of the *Zohar,* by contrast, it is evident that Torah-study becomes one of several means to attain the desired result of *devequt,* i.e., cleaving to the divine; consequently, Torah-study is transformed into a decidedly mystical praxis. Second, in the *Zohar* the erotic nature of the unification between the sage and the *Shekhinah* as a result of Torah-study is stressed in a way entirely foreign to the classical literature. Of the many examples that could be cited to demonstrate the point, I will mention but one: "Come and see: All those engaged in the [study of] Torah cleave to Holy One, blessed be He and are crowned in the crowns of Torah...how much more so those who are engaged in the [study of] Torah also during the night...for they are joined to the *Shekhinah* and they are united as one."[99] While Torah-study is here upheld as a means for anyone to cleave to God, the mystics who study Torah during the night are singled out as the ones who are actually united with the *Shekhinah,* a position well-attested in many passages in the voluminous corpus of the *Zohar.* That the cleaving to *Shekhinah* as a result of studying Torah is indeed based on a feminine characterization of Torah, as I have suggested, can be supported by the following Zoharic passage: "Whoever is engaged in the [study of] Torah it is as if he were engaged in the palace of the Holy One, blessed be He, for the supernal palace of the Holy One, blessed be He, is the Torah."[100] Now, the meaning of this statement can only be ascertained by noting that the palace of the Holy One, blessed be He, is a standard symbol in the Zoharic kabbalah for the *Shekhinah.* Hence, to be occupied with the study of Torah is to be occupied with the *Shekhinah,* for the *Shekhinah,* the supernal palace, is the Torah.

It is of interest to note in passing the following comment on this passage by the kabbalist, R. Ḥayyim Joseph David Azulai (1724-1806):

> It is possible that the [intent here is that the] Oral Torah corresponds to *Malkhut* [i.e., the *Shekhinah*] which is called *hekhal* (palace)....And this is [the meaning of] what is written, 'Whoever is engaged in Torah,' for the word engaged *('ishtaddel)* for the most part connotes that one is occupied in detailed study *(she-'oseq be-'iyyun)* of the Oral Torah, and by means of this study one causes the unity of the Holy One, blessed be He, and the *Shekhinah.* Therefore one is 'engaged in the palace of the Holy One, blessed be He,' to unify her with her beloved.[101]

---

[99] *Zohar* 3: 36a.
[100] *Zohar* 2: 200a.
[101] See commentary of *Niṣoṣe 'Orot, ad loc.*

This eighteenth-century kabbalist is compelled to explain the Zoharic identification of the palace with the Torah as a reference to the Oral Torah for, on the one hand, it is clear that palace refers to *Shekhinah* and, on the other hand, the accepted kabbalistic symbolism is such that *Shekhinah* is the Oral Torah. I have cited Azulai's comment for it is instructive of the way that a traditional commentator on the *Zohar* is forced to interpret a given text in light of the standard symbolic reference, thereby obscuring the original meaning of the text. In fact, it seems to me that the intent of the author of the *Zohar* is to stress that by means of the kabbalistic study of Torah, i.e., the Written Torah, one is intimately engaged with the *Shekhinah,* for indeed the *Shekhinah,* or the supernal palace, is the Torah. In this passage, then, the *Zohar* is reverting to the older kabbalistic symbolism that is found in *Sefer ha-Bahir*.

From still other kabbalistic texts it can be shown that the feminine characterization of Torah played a critical role. Thus, for example, the anonymous author of *Tiqqune Zohar* on several occasions employs this imagery in his kabbalistic discourses. I cite here one striking example of this phenomenon:

> The word *bereshit,* this is the Torah *('oraita'),* concerning which it says, 'The Lord created me at the beginning *(reshit)* of His course' (Prov. 8: 22). And this is the lower *Shekhinah* [i.e., the tenth *sefirah*] which is the beginning for the created entities [below the divine realm]....When she takes from *Keter* [the first *sefirah*] she is called 'crown of splendor' *('aṭeret tif'eret),* a crown *('a ṭarah)* on the head of every righteous person *(ṣaddiq),*[102] the crown of the Torah scroll (*taga' de-sefer Torah*), and on account of her it is written, 'He who makes [theurgic] use of the crown *(we-dishtammash be-taga')* perishes.'[103] When she takes from *Ḥokhmah,* which is the beginning *(reshit),* she is called by his name. When she takes from *Binah* she is called by the name *Tevunah*. When she takes from *Ḥesed* she is called the Written Torah, which was given from the right...and when she takes from *Gevurah* she is called Oral Torah....And the *Shekhinah* is the Torah of truth *(Torat 'emet),* as it is written, 'A proper teaching (literally, a Torah of truth) was in his mouth' (Mal. 2:6).[104]

The author of this text, in conformity with what was by-then standard kabbalistic symbolism, depicts the last of the divine emanations, the *Shekhinah,* in multiple ways, depending ultimately on the attribute from which she is said to receive the divine flux. In the moment she

---

[102]Based on a standard rabbinic eschatological image; see, e.g., B. Berakhot 17a.

[103]M. 'Avot 1:13, 4: 5.

[104]*Tiqqune Zohar*, ed. R. Margaliot (Jerusalem, 1978), Haqdamah, 11b.

receives this flux from the right side, or the attribute of Lovingkindness, the *Shekhinah* is identified as the Written Torah, whereas in the moment she receives from the left side, or the attribute of Judgment, she is identified as the Oral Torah.[105] Hence, in this context, the dual-Torah represents two aspects of the *Shekhinah*. Yet, in the beginning and in the end of the passage it is emphasized in a more generic way that the *Shekhinah* is the Torah, or the Torah of truth. Moreover, it is stated that *Shekhinah* is the crown of the Torah, a symbolic image repeated frequently in this book.[106] Utilizing an older kabbalistic symbol, *'aṭarah* (crown), for the *Shekhinah*,[107] the author of *Tiqqune Zohar* identifies this crown by several well-established images from the normative Jewish world. That is, the *Shekhinah* is the crown of the Torah which is also identified with the eschatological crown on the head of the righteous, and, in still other contexts, the crown of Torah is identified with the corona of the *membrum virile* disclosed as part of the circumcision ritual.[108] In one passage in the *Ra'aya' Mehemna'* section of the *Zohar*, assumed to have been written by the author of the *Tiqqunim*, the symbolism of the Torah crown is linked specifically to an existing ritual on *Simḥat Torah:* the Jews crown the Torah, for the Torah "alludes to *Tif'eret*" while the "crown of splendor" on the scroll symbolizes the *Shekhinah*.[109] This clearly represents an effort to preserve something of the older symbolism while still affirming the more widely accepted position. That is, the scroll now symbolizes the masculine potency except for the crown which symbolizes the feminine. Whereas underlying the origin of the crowning ritual was a decidedly feminine characterization of the Torah-scroll, in the case of the kabbalistic explanation the gender of the symbolisim has indeed shifted in accord with a new theosophic system.

---

[105]Elsewhere in *Tiqqune Zohar* the aspect of *halakhah* is identified with the left side of *Shekhinah* and that of *qabbalah* with the right side. Alternatively expressed, *Shekhinah* is called *halakhah* when she goes to receive from her husband, and *qabbalah* after she has already recevied. See I. Tishby, *Mishnat ha-Zohar* (Jerusalem, 1971), 2: 380 and n. 29 for references.

[106]*Tiqqune Zohar*, 10, 25b; 21, 61b; 30, 73a; 36, 78a.

[107]See, in particular, the following comment of R. Isaac the Blind reported by R. Jacob ben Sheshet in *Ha-'Emunah we-ha-Biṭṭaḥon*, printed in *Kitve Ramban*, 2: 401: "And strength alludes to the Oral Torah [i.e., the *Shekhinah*] which is the strength and the crown (*'aṭarah)* of the Torah."

[108]See, e.g., *Tiqqune Zohar*, 30, 73a; 36, 78a.

[109]*Zohar* 3: 256b. Cf Yaari, *Toledot Ḥag Simḥat Torah*, p. 30, who cites this passage in the name of the *Zohar*, without qualifying that it belongs to a later stratum, not authored by the same hand that composed the bulk of the *Zohar*.

There can be no question that in post-Zoharic kabbalistic literature the dominant symbolic association was that of the Written Torah with *Tif'eret* and the Oral Torah with *Shekhinah*. In that sense, the Torah-scroll, the mundane correlate to the supernal Written Torah, was understood in decidedly masculine terminology. Thus, for example, Moses Cordovero (1522-70) explains the rituals surrounding the taking out of the Torah from the ark in the synagogue in terms of the following symbolism:

> The [mystical] intention in the taking out of the Torah-scroll. The reason for this commandment is that the cantor, who corresponds to *Yesod*, goes up from the table, the aspect of *Malkhut*, in the center point of the synagogue, and he goes up to *Binah*...to draw forth the secret of the Torah-scroll from the supernal Ark, i.e., *Tif'eret* [the scroll] from *Binah* in the secret of the ark wherein the Torah is. *Yesod*, the cantor, goes up from the central aspect in *Malkhut* to *Binah*, the ark, to take out from there the Torah-scroll, which is *Tif'eret*, to draw it forth to *Malkhut*, the center point.[110]

According to Cordovero, then, the taking out of the Torah from the ark symbolically reenacts the dynamic process in the sefirotic realm whereby the masculine potency of *Tif'eret* emerges from the supernal palace, *Binah*, in order to unite with the lower, feminine potency, *Shekhinah*. The Torah-scroll therefore corresponds to the masculine rather than the feminine aspect of God.

In the more complicated symbolism of the Lurianic kabbalah one can still see very clearly that the Torah-scroll is a symbol for a masculine attribute of the divine. Ḥayyim Vital (1543-1620) thus writes that the "Torah-scroll is the *Yesod de-'Abba'* which is called the Written Torah, the form of the scroll is like an extended *waw*."[111]

---

[110]*Tefillah le-Moshe* (Prezmysl, 1932), 134b-135a. Cf the comments of R. Meir Poppers, in his commentary *'Or ha-Yashar, ad loc.*: "The reason for [reading] the Torah during the prayer [service] is to unify the prayer, *Malkhut*, with the Torah, *Tif'eret*....Know that the secret of *Tif'eret* is above, concealed within *Binah*, i.e., the Torah scroll is in the supernal Ark, and we take it out from there. We carry the Torah scroll to the table, which is [symbolically] *Malkhut*. The cantor, who represents *Yesod*, carries *Tif'eret* [i.e., the scroll] below to *Malkhut*, which is the table." And cf. Isaiah Horowitz, *Siddur Sha'ar ha-Shamayim* (Jerusalem, n.d.), p. 231.

[111]*Sha'ar ha-Kawwanot* (Jerusalem, n.d.), 109b. Cf. Vital, *'E ṣ Ḥayyim* (Jerusalem, n.d. 1930), Gate 8, chap. 6, fol. 39c; *Mavo' She'arim* (Jerusalem, 1978), p. 49. In the latter context Vital also mentions another tradition according to which the Torah-scroll alludes to (or symbolizes) *Ze'eir 'Anpin*, the written Torah. Concerning this latter symbolism, see also *'Eṣ Ḥayyim*, Gate 20, chap. 3, 96d. And cf. *Sha'ar ha-Miṣwot* (Jerusalem, 1978), p. 79, where Vital identifies the Torah as the "Foundation of the Father," *Yesod de-'Abba'*, which is within *Ze'eir 'Anpin*. See also *Sha'ar Ma'amare RaZa"L* (Jerusalem, 1898), fol. 6d. There is no

Utilizing this symbolism the eminent disciple of Isaac Luria (1534-72) thus explained the taking out of the Torah from the ark and the subsequent opening of the scroll as follows:

> The opening of the ark is performed at first, and this is the matter of *Ze'eir 'Anpin* itself, which breaks forth to emit the *Yesod de-'Abba'* which is within it, to go out from its body. And the opening of the Torah-scroll itself is done afterwards, and this is the secret of the breaking forth of *Yesod de-'Abba'*, which is called the Torah-scroll, and the [forces of] mercy and judgment that are within it are revealed, and they are called the Written Torah.[112]

Alternatively, Vital offers the following explanation which he also heard from his teacher, Isaac Luria, and which he considers to be the better one:

> The first breaking forth is that of *Yesod de-'Imma'* and all the [forces of] mercy within it, which spread forth in *Ze'eir 'Anpin,* and they clothe and surround the *Yesod de-'Abba'* which is within them. By means of this breaking forth of *Yesod de-'Imma'*, the light of *Yesod de-'Abba'* goes forth, from outside *Yesod de-'Imma'*, to the the body of *Ze'eir 'Anpin.* And this breaking forth is the matter of the opening of the ark to take out the Torah-scroll, for the ark is the *Yesod de-'Imma'*, within which is the Torah-scroll, which is the *Yesod de-'Abba'*. Afterwards comes a second breaking forth, which is that of the *Yesod di-Ze'eir 'Anpin* itself, for the light of the *Yesod de-'Abba'* goes out....And this breaking forth is the matter of opening the case of the Torah-scroll itself, so that the illumination of the Torah, and all that is written within it, will be revealed on the outside to the congregation. Afterwards, when the Torah is read, then the light that is within it goes outside, for this is the Torah itself, which is called light.[113]

The Torah-scroll thus symbolizes the aspect of God referred to by the technical expression *Yesod de-'Abba'*, i.e., the foundation of the divine countenance *(parṣuf)* called by the name Father. The ark in which the scroll is kept symbolizes the aspect of divinity referred to as the *Yesod de-'Imma'*, i.e., the foundation of the divine Mother. When the ark is opened, then the light of *Yesod de-'Imma'* emerges and shines upon the

---

contradiction between these two symbolic correspondences for Torah insofar as, according to the Lurianic system as transmitted by Vital, *Yesod de-'Abba'* is revealed or clothed within the mind (literally, knowledge, *da'at*) or *Tif'eret* of *Ze'eir 'Anpin;* cf. *'Eṣ Ḥayyim,* Gate 37, chap. 3, fol. 59a.

[112]*Ibid.,* 48d.

[113]*Ibid.* Cf. *Peri 'E ṣ Ḥayyim,* ed. by Meir Poppers, (Jerusalem, 1980), p. 302: "The secret of the Torah is the secret of *Yesod de-'Abba'* which is within *Ze'eir 'Anpin.* The unification that we perform is that the *Yesod de-'Imma'* is opened, and the lights of mercy and judgment go out from there....The *Yesod* [of] *'Imma'* opens and the consciousness *(moḥin)* within it shine upon Jacob and Rachel [i.e., the lower two countenances, *Ze'eir 'Anpin* and *Nuqba'*]."

body of *Ze'eir 'Anpin,* the divine son. With the opening of the case of the Torah-scroll the light of *Yesod de-'Abba'* breaks forth and shines upon the whole congregation. The process of illumination is completed when the portion of the Torah is read, for it is through the public reading that the light that is hidden within the letters of the scroll is released.[114] It should be noted that Vital similarly explains the theurgical significance of "Torah-study for its own sake" in terms of a process of illumination of the masculine upon the feminine, i.e., *Torah lishmah* is rendered as *Torah le-shem heh,* which means that through study of Torah the light is released from *Yesod de-'Abba',* the Torah, and shines upon *Binah,* symbolized by the letter *heh.*[115] Although the Lurianic symbolism is significantly more complex than that of Cordovero, both sixteenth-century Safedian kabbalists share the view that the Torah-scroll itself symbolizes a masculine aspect of divinity. This, I submit, can be taken as a standard viewpoint in the vast majority of kabbalistic writings.

Only in one very important body of mystical literature does the feminine personification of the Torah reappear to play an instrumental role. I have in mind some of the texts that emerged from the disciples of Israel ben Eliezer, the Ba'al Shem Tov (c. 1700-60), so-called founder of modern Hasidism in eighteenth-century Poland. In a striking passage from the very first published Hasidic text, the *Toledot Ya'aqov Yosef* of Jacob Joseph of Polonnoye (d. 1782), we again encounter the feminine image of Torah. In this case the main concern is the presentation of the Hasidic idea of the study of Torah as a vehicle for mystical union, *devequt,* between the individual and God.[116]

> A person cleaves to the form of the letters of the Torah, which is the bride, and the cleaving of his essence to the inner essence of the letters of the Torah is the true mating *(ha-ziwwug ha-'amiti),* 'naked without garment'[117] or [any] face, [without] advantage or reward, but rather for its own sake, to love her so as to cleave to her. This is the essence and purpose of everything.[118]

---

[114]The connection between the letters of Torah and light is a motif developed in much older kabbalistic sources. For references, see Wolfson, "The Hermeneutics of Visionary Experience," p. 337, n. 61.

[115]Cf. *Sha'ar ha-Miṣwot,* p. 79; *Sha'ar Ma'amare RaZa"L,* fol. 6d; *Peri 'E ṣ Ḥayyim,* p. 352. As is known, in subsequent Hasidic thought the kabbalistic interpretation of *Torah lishmah* as *Torah le-shem heh* took on an entirely different connotation; see the study of Weiss referred to in the following note.

[116]For a study of this pivotal idea in the Beshtian system, see J. Weiss, *Studies in Eastern European Jewish Mysticism* (Oxford, 1985), pp. 56-68.

[117]See Job 24:7, 10.

[118]*Toledot Ya'aqov Yosef* (Jerusalem, 1966, reprint of Koretz ed., 1780), fol. 131b.

Study of Torah thus involves a technique of cleaving to the letters of the Torah which serves, in turn, as a means for one to unite with the divine, for, according to the standard kabbalistic symbolism adopted by the Hasidic writers as well, the Torah is identical with God in His manifest form.[119] The person who studies Torah for its own sake – which here assumes the meaning of studying Torah for the sake of cleaving to its letters[120] – acquires knowledge, *yedi'ah,* which, as Jacob Joseph further explains, has a decidedly sexual nuance: "The expression knowledge here is like the [usage in the verse] 'And Adam knew *(wa-yeda')* Eve' for he cleaves to God and to His Torah, [a state] which is called knowledge, like the knowledge and communion of physical unification *(ziwwug ha-gashmi).*" Torah-study is therefore a form of sexual unification with the divine feminine or the Torah which is the bride.[121]

The view espoused by Jacob Joseph is reiterated in the *Degel Maḥaneh 'Efrayim* of Moses Ḥayyim Ephraim of Sudlikov (c. 1737-1800), the gransdon of the Ba'al Shem Tov. In the case of this author, the Zoharic parable of the Torah as a maiden is used as a basis to characterize the intellectual study and practical fulfillment of Torah as a moment of unification between man and God akin to the sexual unification between husband and wife:

> The Torah and the Holy One, blessed be He, and Israel are all one.[122] For the human person *('adam)* is the Holy One, blessed He, by virtue

---

[119]Cf. G. Scholem, *On the Kabbalah and Its Symbolism,* pp. 43-44. See also Idel, "Tefisat ha-Torah," pp. 23-84; *idem, Kabbalah: New Perspectives,* pp. 244-46. A particularly clear statement of the Hasidic view is to be found in Menaḥem Naḥum of Chernobyl, *Me'or 'Einayim* (Brooklyn, 1984), fol. 37a: "When one cleaves to the letters of the Torah, to behold the splendor of the life-force *(laḥazot be-no'am ziw ha-ḥiyyut)* of the Infinite, blessed be He, which spreads forth in the letters of the Torah, he cleaves to God, blessed be He." On Torah as a means to cleave to the Infinite, see *ibid.,* fols. 13d, 94a.

[120]See Weiss, *Studies,* pp. 58-59.

[121]Elsewhere Jacob Joseph depicts the mystic's cleaving to the Torah in the opposite terms, i.e., the mystic is the female lover and the Torah is the male beloved. Thus he interprets the verse 'I am my beloved's and my beloved is mine' (Song of Songs 6:3) as referring to "one who cleaves to the Torah which is called my beloved' *(dodi)* and then the Torah is [in a state of] 'my beloved is mine.'" See *Ketonet Passim,* ed. G. Nigal (Jerusalem, 1985), pp. 175-76.

[122]On the background of this teaching, see I. Tishby, "Qudsha' berikh hu' 'oraita' we-yisra'el kula' ḥad – maqor ha-'imrah be-ferush 'Idra' Rabba' le-RaMḤaL," *Qiryat Sefer* 50 (1975): 480-92, 668-74; B. Sack, "'Od 'al gilgul ha-ma'amar Qudsha' berikh hu' 'oraita' we-yisra'el kula' ḥad," *Qiryat Sefer* 57 (1982): 179-84. On Moses Ḥayyim Ephraim of Sudlikov's particular use of this expression, see Tishby, *op. cit.,* pp. 482-84.

> of the fact that the Tetragrammaton when written out fully equals forty-five, the numerical equivalence of the [word] *'adam*. The Torah contains 248 positive commandments and 365 negative commandments, and from there is drawn forth the human person below in the aspect of 248 limbs and 365 inner parts. When a person is occupied with Torah for its own sake...he brings his limbs close to their source....He and the Torah become one in unity and perfect oneness *(we-na'aseh hu' we-ha-Torah 'eḥad be-yiḥud we-'aḥdut gamur)* like the unification of a man and his wife, as it is in the *Sabba' Mishpaṭim* [i.e., the section of *Zohar* containing the parable of the princess]....He becomes one unity with the Torah *(we-na'aseh 'im ha-Torah be-yiḥuda' ḥada')*. 'From my flesh I will see God' (Job 19:26) – if with respect to physical unification [it says] 'And they will be of one flesh' (Gen. 2:24), *a fortiori* with respect to spiritual matters he becomes a perfect unity with the Torah *(she-na'aseh 'aḥdut gamur mamash hu' 'im ha-Torah)*.[123]

According to this Hasidic text, then, by being involved in the Torah one merges with or mystically unites with the Torah. This embrace is likened to the sexual embrace of a man with his wife. Just as on the physical level the two become one, so on the spiritual level the individual unites with, actually becomes one with, the feminine Torah.

As a final example of the female characterization of Torah in the voluminous Hasidic corpus, I will cite one comment of Menaḥem Naḥum of Chernobyl (1730-97) in his classic work, *Me'or 'Einayim*, on Exod. 31:18, 'When He finished speaking with him on Mt. Sinai, He gave Moses the two tablets of the pact, stone tablets inscribed with the finger of God.' The rebbe from Chernobyl brought together the midrashic reading of this verse, noted above, and that of Deut. 33:4, "Moses commanded the Torah to us, as the heritage of the congregation of Jacob," also noted above, two of the main loci for the rabbinic notion of the feminine Torah:

> By means of the Torah the groom and bride are united, the Community of Israel *[Shekhinah]* and the Holy One, blessed be He *[Tif'eret]*....The unification of the groom and bride is always something novel for they have never been united before. Thus must a person unite the Holy One, blessed be He [with His *Shekhinah*] every day anew....And this is [the import of the midrashic teaching of Deut. 33:4] 'do not read heritage *(morashah)* but betrothal *(me'orasah)*.' For the Torah is not called heritage but rather betrothal which is the aspect of the bride, so that the unity will always be new like a bride in her wedding.[124]

---

[123] *Degel Maḥaneh 'Efrayim*, 52a. For a discussion of this passage with a slightly different emphasis, see M. Idel, *Kabbalah: New Perspectives*, p. 245.

[124] *Me'or 'Einayim*, fol. 40d.

The midrashic reading of the word *ke-khalloto* in Exod. 31:18 as *ke-khallato* is here transformed by the Hasidic master in terms of the older kabbalistic symbolism. That is, the Torah is the bride and by means of studying Torah one assists in the unification of male and female, the Holy One and the *Shekhinah.*

The Hasidic writers thereby retrieved the older image of the Torah as the bride in their characterization of the ideal of cleaving to God through the Torah. It seems that the ideas and imagery expressed in earlier sources of an aggadic and mystical nature enabled the Hasidic masters to foster once again the feminization of the Torah. This process, in my opinion, attests to the centrality of this motif in Jewish spirituality. Although the alternative kabbalistic model which equated the Written Torah with the masculine potency and the Oral Torah with the feminine is found in the theoretical literature of the Hasidim, it was primarily the image of the Torah as the bride that was revitalized in Hasidic thought.

Let me conclude with a brief analysis of a story by Shmuel Yosef Agnon (1888-1970), *'Aggadat ha-Sofer* ("The Tale of the Scribe"), which highlights the deep sexual implications of the feminine image of Torah in Judaism. Moving in an almost full circle from the Geonic origins of crowning the scroll on *Simḥat Torah* based on the aggadic depiction of Torah as the bride,[125] we arrive at Agnon's description of the scene inside the synagogue on the night of *Simḥat Torah* which likewise draws largely upon this very image. All the people, we are told, were dancing with enthusiasm and were cleaving to the holy Torah; when the young children saw their fathers receive the honor of carrying the Torah they would jump towards them "grasping the scroll, caressing, embracing, kissing it with their pure lips that have not tasted sin."[126] At the seventh, and last, round of the procession around the pulpit the cantor turned to the congregation and summoned all those involved in Torah-study to come forth to carry the scrolls. After several of the youth came forward, the cantor again turned to the congregation to summon the scribe, Raphael, to honor him with carrying the Torah and singing a special melody. Here the narrative continues with the description that is most relevant to our concerns:

> Raphael held the scroll in his arm, walking in the lead with all the other youths following him in the procession around the pulpit. At that moment a young girl pushed her way through the legs of the dancers, leaped toward Raphael, sank her red lips into the white mantle of the

---

[125]See above, n. 47.

[126]I have utilized the translation of Isaac Frank published in S. Y. Agnon, *Twenty-One Stories*, ed. by N. N Glatzer (New York, 1970), p. 22.

> Torah scroll in Raphael's arm, and kept on kissing the scroll and caressing it with her hands.[127]

In the continuation of the story we learn that the young girl described in this passage was Miriam, who later married Raphael. In the context of the tale the description of the celebration on *Simḥat Torah* serves as a flashback, prompted by Raphael's singing the very same melody as he clutched and danced with the Torah he had just written for the memory of Miriam shortly after she had died at a young age. Agnon thus describes the scene of Raphael's celebrating with the Torah-scroll after Miriam's death in terms that are meant to echo the past event of *Simḥat Torah:*

> Raphael came toward Miriam and bowed before her with the Torah scroll in his arm. He could not see her face because she was wrapped in her wedding dress....Raphael is wrapped in his prayer shawl, a Torah scroll in his arm, and the scroll has the mantle of fine silk on which the name of Miriam the wife of Raphael is embroidered. The house becomes filled with many Torah scrolls, and many elders dancing....They dance without motion...and Miriam stands in the center....She approaches Raphael's scroll. She takes off her veil and covers her face with her hands. Suddenly her hands slide down, her face is uncovered, and her lips cling to the mantle of the Torah scroll in Raphael's arms.[128]

The Torah-scroll written for Miriam by Raphael, of course, reflects the scroll carried by Raphael on that *Simḥat Torah* night when they were first brought together. It was through the scroll that the fates of Raphael and Miriam were inextricably linked. Indeed the Torah is the ritualistic object which binds together the scribe and his wife. The scroll is therefore obviously meant to be an erotic symbol, i.e., it functions as the object upon which the sexual passions of both Raphael and Miriam have been displaced. Admittedly, with respect to the gender of the scroll there is here some equivocation for it serves as both a masculine object for Miriam and a feminine one for Raphael. Thus Raphael is described in the *Simḥat Torah* scene as clutching the Torah the way he would his bride, while Miriam keeps kissing the white mantle of the Torah as if it were her groom. Similarly, in the death scene Miriam's lips are said to cling to the mantle of the Torah in Raphael's arms as if she were kissing her husband. Yet, the story ends with a description of Raphael sinking down with his scroll, and "his wife's wedding dress was spread out over him and over his scroll."[129]

---

[127] *Ibid.*, pp. 23-24.
[128] *Ibid.*, pp. 24-25.
[129] *Ibid.*, p. 25.

With the death of Miriam, then, the scroll fully assumes its role as the feminine persona vis-à-vis Raphael the scribe.

Underlying this latter characterization one will readily recognize the mythical motif of the feminine Torah that I have traced in midrashic and kabbalistic sources. For Agnon, however, it is the metaphorical aspect of this motif that again becomes primary, for the Torah, depicted in strikingly effeminate terms, is to be taken in a figurative sense as the object of Raphael's displaced sexual desire. That is, the Torah serves as a substitution for the earthly Miriam, whose own erotic yearnings are symbolized by the fact that her lips are sunk in, or cling to, the mantle of the scroll which is clutched by Raphael. Although Agnon is clearly drawing on the older image of the Torah as a bride, and furthermore reflects actual religious observances that are themselves rooted in that image, it is nevertheless the case that the force of the feminine image of the Torah as a religious symbol is substantially weakened; or, to put the matter in somewhat different terms, in Agnon's story the *Shekhinah,* Miriam and the Torah all fuse into one image. The symbol, which developed in mystical texts out of a literary metaphor in midrashic sources, has become again in the modern work of fiction a literary metaphor, but one which is intended to characterize the mundane by the sacred rather than the sacred by the mundane.

Index

Brown Judaic Studies

140001	*Approaches to Ancient Judaism I*	William S. Green
140002	*The Traditions of Eleazar Ben Azariah*	Tzvee Zahavy
140003	*Persons and Institutions in Early Rabbinic Judaism*	William S. Green
140004	*Claude Goldsmid Montefiore on the Ancient Rabbis*	Joshua B. Stein
140005	*The Ecumenical Perspective and the Modernization of Jewish Religion*	S. Daniel Breslauer
140006	*The Sabbath-Law of Rabbi Meir*	Robert Goldenberg
140007	*Rabbi Tarfon*	Joel Gereboff
140008	*Rabban Gamaliel II*	Shamai Kanter
140009	*Approaches to Ancient Judaism II*	William S. Green
140010	*Method and Meaning in Ancient Judaism*	Jacob Neusner
140011	*Approaches to Ancient Judaism III*	William S. Green
140012	*Turning Point: Zionism and Reform Judaism*	Howard R. Greenstein
140013	*Buber on God and the Perfect Man*	Pamela Vermes
140014	*Scholastic Rabbinism*	Anthony J. Saldarini
140015	*Method and Meaning in Ancient Judaism II*	Jacob Neusner
140016	*Method and Meaning in Ancient Judaism III*	Jacob Neusner
140017	*Post Mishnaic Judaism in Transition*	Baruch M. Bokser
140018	*A History of the Mishnaic Law of Agriculture: Tractate Maaser Sheni*	Peter J. Haas
140019	*Mishnah's Theology of Tithing*	Martin S. Jaffee
140020	*The Priestly Gift in Mishnah: A Study of Tractate Terumot*	Alan. J. Peck
140021	*History of Judaism: The Next Ten Years*	Baruch M. Bokser
140022	*Ancient Synagogues*	Joseph Gutmann
140023	*Warrant for Genocide*	Norman Cohn
140024	*The Creation of the World According to Gersonides*	Jacob J. Staub
140025	*Two Treatises of Philo of Alexandria: A Commentary on De Gigantibus and Quod Deus Sit Immutabilis*	David Winston/John Dillon
140026	*A History of the Mishnaic Law of Agriculture: Kilayim*	Irving Mandelbaum
140027	*Approaches to Ancient Judaism IV*	William S. Green
140028	*Judaism in the American Humanities*	Jacob Neusner
140029	*Handbook of Synagogue Architecture*	Marilyn Chiat
140030	*The Book of Mirrors*	Daniel C. Matt
140031	*Ideas in Fiction: The Works of Hayim Hazaz*	Warren Bargad
140032	*Approaches to Ancient Judaism V*	William S. Green
140033	*Sectarian Law in the Dead Sea Scrolls: Courts, Testimony and the Penal Code*	Lawrence H. Schiffman
140034	*A History of the United Jewish Appeal: 1939-1982*	Marc L. Raphael
140035	*The Academic Study of Judaism*	Jacob Neusner
140036	*Woman Leaders in the Ancient Synagogue*	Bernadette Brooten
140037	*Formative Judaism: Religious, Historical, and Literary Studies*	Jacob Neusner
140038	*Ben Sira's View of Women: A Literary Analysis*	Warren C. Trenchard
140039	*Barukh Kurzweil and Modern Hebrew Literature*	James S. Diamond

140040	*Israeli Childhood Stories of the Sixties: Yizhar, Aloni,Shahar, Kahana-Carmon*	Gideon Telpaz
140041	*Formative Judaism II: Religious, Historical, and Literary Studies*	Jacob Neusner
140042	*Judaism in the American Humanities II: Jewish Learning and the New Humanities*	Jacob Neusner
140043	*Support for the Poor in the Mishnaic Law of Agriculture: Tractate Peah*	Roger Brooks
140044	*The Sanctity of the Seventh Year: A Study of Mishnah Tractate Shebiit*	Louis E. Newman
140045	*Character and Context: Studies in the Fiction of Abramovitsh, Brenner, and Agnon*	Jeffrey Fleck
140046	*Formative Judaism III: Religious, Historical, and Literary Studies*	Jacob Neusner
140047	*Pharaoh's Counsellors: Job, Jethro, and Balaam in Rabbinic and Patristic Tradition*	Judith Baskin
140048	*The Scrolls and Christian Origins: Studies in the Jewish Background of the New Testament*	Matthew Black
140049	*Approaches to Modern Judaism I*	Marc Lee Raphael
140050	*Mysterious Encounters at Mamre and Jabbok*	William T. Miller
140051	*The Mishnah Before 70*	Jacob Neusner
140052	*Sparda by the Bitter Sea: Imperial Interaction in Western Anatolia*	Jack Martin Balcer
140053	*Hermann Cohen: The Challenge of a Religion of Reason*	William Kluback
140054	*Approaches to Judaism in Medieval Times I*	David R. Blumenthal
140055	*In the Margins of the Yerushalmi: Glosses on the English Translation*	Jacob Neusner
140056	*Approaches to Modern Judaism II*	Marc Lee Raphael
140057	*Approaches to Judaism in Medieval Times II*	David R. Blumenthal
140058	*Midrash as Literature: The Primacy of Documentary Discourse*	JacobNeusner
140059	*The Commerce of the Sacred: Mediation of the Divine Among Jews in the Graeco-Roman Diaspora*	Jack N. Lightstone
140060	*Major Trends in Formative Judaism I: Society and Symbol in Political Crisis*	Jacob Neusner
140061	*Major Trends in Formative Judaism II: Texts, Contents, and Contexts*	Jacob Neusner
140062	*A History of the Jews in Babylonia I: The Parthian Period*	Jacob Neusner
140063	*The Talmud of Babylonia: An American Translation. XXXII: Tractate Arakhin*	Jacob Neusner
140064	*Ancient Judaism: Debates and Disputes*	Jacob Neusner
140065	*Prayers Alleged to Be Jewish: An Examination of the Constitutiones Apostolorum*	David Fiensy
140066	*The Legal Methodology of Hai Gaon*	Tsvi Groner
140067	*From Mishnah to Scripture: The Problem of the Unattributed Saying*	Jacob Neusner
140068	*Halakhah in a Theological Dimension*	David Novak

140069 *From Philo to Origen: Middle Platonism in Transition* Robert M. Berchman
140070 *In Search of Talmudic Biography: The Problem of the Attributed Saying* Jacob Neusner
140071 *The Death of the Old and the Birth of the New: The Framework of the Book of Numbers and the Pentateuch* Dennis T. Olson
140072 *The Talmud of Babylonia: An American Translation. XVII: Tractate Sotah* Jacob Neusner
140073 *Understanding Seeking Faith: Essays on the Case of Judaism. Volume Two: Literature, Religion and the Social Study of Judiasm* JacobNeusner
140074 *The Talmud of Babylonia: An American Translation. VI: Tractate Sukkah* Jacob Neusner
140075 *Fear Not Warrior: A Study of 'al tira' Pericopes in the Hebrew Scriptures* Edgar W. Conrad
140076 *Formative Judaism IV: Religious, Historical, and Literary Studies* Jacob Neusner
140077 *Biblical Patterns in Modern Literature* David H. Hirsch/ Nehama Aschkenasy
140078 *The Talmud of Babylonia: An American Translation I: Tractate Berakhot* Jacob Neusner
140079 *Mishnah's Division of Agriculture: A History and Theology of Seder Zeraim* Alan J. Avery-Peck
140080 *From Tradition to Imitation: The Plan and Program of Pesiqta Rabbati and Pesiqta deRab Kahana* Jacob Neusner
140081 *The Talmud of Babylonia: An American Translation. XXIIIA: Tractate Sanhedrin, Chapters 1-3* Jacob Neusner
140082 *Jewish Presence in T. S. Eliot and Franz Kafka* Melvin Wilk
140083 *School, Court, Public Administration: Judaism and its Institutions in Talmudic Babylonia* Jacob Neusner
140084 *The Talmud of Babylonia: An American Translation. XXIIIB: Tractate Sanhedrin, Chapters 4-8* Jacob Neusner
140085 *The Bavli and Its Sources: The Question of Tradition in the Case of Tractate Sukkah* Jacob Neusner
140086 *From Description to Conviction: Essays on the History and Theology of Judaism* Jacob Neusner
140087 *The Talmud of Babylonia: An American Translation. XXIIIC: Tractate Sanhedrin, Chapters 9-11* Jacob Neusner
140088 *Mishnaic Law of Blessings and Prayers: Tractate Berakhot* Tzvee Zahavy
140089 *The Peripatetic Saying: The Problem of the Thrice-Told Tale in Talmudic Literature* Jacob Neusner
140090 *The Talmud of Babylonia: An American Translation. XXVI: Tractate Horayot* Martin S. Jaffee
140091 *Formative Judaism V: Religious, Historical, and Literary Studies* Jacob Neusner
140092 *Essays on Biblical Method and Translation* Edward Greenstein
140093 *The Integrity of Leviticus Rabbah* Jacob Neusner
140094 *Behind the Essenes: History and Ideology of the Dead Sea Scrolls* Philip R. Davies

140095	*Approaches to Judaism in Medieval Times, Volume III*	David R. Blumenthal
140096	*The Memorized Torah: The Mnemonic System of the Mishnah*	Jacob Neusner
140098	*Sifre to Deuteronomy: An Analytical Translation. Volume One: Pisqaot One through One Hundred Forty-Three. Debarim, Waethanan, Eqeb*	Jacob Neusner
140099	*Major Trends in Formative Judaism III: The Three Stages in the Formation of Judaism*	Jacob Neusner
140101	*Sifre to Deuteronomy: An Analytical Translation. Volume Two: Pisqaot One Hundred Forty-Four through Three Hundred Fifty-Seven. Shofetim, Ki Tese, Ki Tabo, Nesabim, Ha'azinu, Zot Habberakhah*	Jacob Neusner
140102	*Sifra: The Rabbinic Commentary on Leviticus*	Jacob Neusner/ Roger Brooks
140103	*The Human Will in Judaism*	Howard Eilberg-Schwartz
140104	*Genesis Rabbah: Volume 1. Genesis 1:1 to 8:14*	Jacob Neusner
140105	*Genesis Rabbah: Volume 2. Genesis 8:15 to 28:9*	Jacob Neusner
140106	*Genesis Rabbah: Volume 3. Genesis 28:10 to 50:26*	Jacob Neusner
140107	*First Principles of Systemic Analysis*	Jacob Neusner
140108	*Genesis and Judaism*	Jacob Neusner
140109	*The Talmud of Babylonia: An American Translation. XXXV: Tractates Meilah and Tamid*	Peter J. Haas
140110	*Studies in Islamic and Judaic Traditions*	William Brinner/Stephen Ricks
140111	*Comparative Midrash: The Plan and Program of Genesis Rabbah and Leviticus Rabbah*	Jacob Neusner
140112	*The Tosefta: Its Structure and its Sources*	Jacob Neusner
140113	*Reading and Believing*	Jacob Neusner
140114	*The Fathers According to Rabbi Nathan*	Jacob Neusner
140115	*Etymology in Early Jewish Interpretation: The Hebrew Names in Philo*	Lester L. Grabbe
140116	*Understanding Seeking Faith: Essays on the Case of Judaism. Volume One: Debates on Method, Reports of Results*	Jacob Neusner
140117	*The Talmud of Babylonia. An American Translation. VII: Tractate Besah*	Alan J. Avery-Peck
140118	*Sifre to Numbers: An American Translation and Explanation, Volume One: Sifre to Numbers 1-58*	Jacob Neusner
140119	*Sifre to Numbers: An American Translation and Explanation, Volume Two: Sifre to Numbers 59-115*	Jacob Neusner
140120	*Cohen and Troeltsch: Ethical Monotheistic Religion and Theory of Culture*	Wendell S. Dietrich
140121	*Goodenough on the History of Religion and on Judaism*	Jacob Neusner/ Ernest Frerichs
140122	*Pesiqta deRab Kahana I: Pisqaot One through Fourteen*	Jacob Neusner
140123	*Pesiqta deRab Kahana II: Pisqaot Fifteen through Twenty-Eight and Introduction to Pesiqta deRab Kahana*	Jacob Neusner
140124	*Sifre to Deuteronomy: Introduction*	Jacob Neusner

140126	*A Conceptual Commentary on Midrash Leviticus Rabbah: Value Concepts in Jewish Thought*	Max Kadushin
140127	*The Other Judaisms of Late Antiquity*	Alan F. Segal
140128	*Josephus as a Historical Source in Patristic Literature through Eusebius*	Michael Hardwick
140129	*Judaism: The Evidence of the Mishnah*	Jacob Neusner
140131	*Philo, John and Paul: New Perspectives on Judaism and Early Christianity*	Peder Borgen
140132	*Babylonian Witchcraft Literature*	Tzvi Abusch
140133	*The Making of the Mind of Judaism: The Formative Age*	Jacob Neusner
140135	*Why No Gospels in Talmudic Judaism?*	Jacob Neusner
140136	*Torah: From Scroll to Symbol Part III: Doctrine*	Jacob Neusner
140137	*The Systemic Analysis of Judaism*	Jacob Neusner
140138	*Sifra: An Analytical Translation Vol. 1*	Jacob Neusner
140139	*Sifra: An Analytical Translation Vol. 2*	Jacob Neusner
140140	*Sifra: An Analytical Translation Vol. 3*	Jacob Neusner
140141	*Midrash in Context: Exegesis in Formative Judaism*	Jacob Neusner
140143	*Oxen, Women or Citizens? Slaves in the System of Mishnah*	Paul V. Flesher
140144	*The Book of the Pomegranate*	Elliot R. Wolfson
140145	*Wrong Ways and Right Ways in the Study of Formative Judaism*	Jacob Neusner
140146	*Sifra in Perspective: The Documentary Comparison of the Midrashim of Ancient Judaism*	Jacob Neusner
140148	*Mekhilta According to Rabbi Ishmael: An Analytical Translation Volume I*	Jacob Neusner
140149	*The Doctrine of the Divine Name: An Introduction to Classical Kabbalistic Theology*	Stephen G. Wald
140150	*Water into Wine and the Beheading of John the Baptist*	Roger Aus
140151	*The Formation of the Jewish Intellect*	Jacob Neusner
140152	*Mekhilta According to Rabbi Ishmael: An Introduction to Judaism's First Scriptural Encyclopaedia*	Jacob Neusner
140153	*Understanding Seeking Faith. Volume Three*	Jacob Neusner
140154	*Mekhilta According to Rabbi Ishmael: An Analytical Translation Volume Two*	Jacob Neusner
140155	*Goyim: Gentiles and Israelites in Mishnah-Tosefta*	Gary P. Porton
140156	*A Religion of Pots and Pans?*	Jacob Neusner
140157	*Claude Montefiore and Christianity*	Maurice Gerald Bowler
140158	*The Philosopical Mishnah Volume III*	Jacob Neusner
140159	*From Ancient Israel to Modern Judaism Volume 1: Intellect in Quest of Understanding*	Neusner/Frerichs/Sarna
140160	*The Social Study of Judaism Volume I*	Jacob Neusner
140161	*Philo's Jewish Identity*	Alan Mendelson
140162	*The Social Study of Judaism Volume II*	Jacob Neusner
140163	*The Philosophical Mishnah Volume I : The Initial Probe*	Jacob Neusner
140164	*The Philosophical Mishnah Volume II : The Tractates Agenda: From Abodah Zarah Through Moed Qatan*	Jacob Neusner
140166	*Women's Earliest Records*	Barbara S. Lesko

140167	*The Legacy of Hermann Cohen*	William Kluback
140168	*Method and Meaning in Ancient Judaism*	Jacob Neusner
140169	*The Role of the Messenger and Message in the Ancient Near East*	John T. Greene
140171	*Abraham Heschel's Idea of Revelation*	Lawerence Perlman
140172	*The Philosophical Mishnah Volume IV: The Repertoire*	Jacob Neusner
140173	*From Ancient Israel to Modern Judaism Volume 2: Intellect in Quest of Understanding*	Neusner/Frerichs/Sarna
140174	*From Ancient Israel to Modern Judaism Volume 3: Intellect in Quest of Understanding*	Neusner/Frerichs/Sarna
140175	*From Ancient Israel to Modern Judaism Volume 4: Intellect in Quest of Understanding*	Neusner/Frerichs/Sarna
140176	*Translating the Classics of Judaism: In Theory and In Practice*	Jacob Neusner
140177	*Profiles of a Rabbi: Synoptic Opportunities in Reading About Jesus*	Bruce Chilton
140178	*Studies in Islamic and Judaic Traditions II*	William Brinner/Stephen Ricks
140179	*Medium and Message in Judaism: First Series*	Jacob Neusner
140180	*Making the Classics of Judaism: The Three Stages of Literary Formation*	Jacob Neusner
140181	*The Law of Jealousy: Anthropology of Sotah*	Adriana Destro
140182	*Esther Rabbah I: An Analytical Translation*	Jacob Neusner

Brown Studies on Jews and Their Societies

145001	*American Jewish Fertility*	Calvin Goldscheider
145003	*The American Jewish Community*	Calvin Goldscheider
145004	*The Naturalized Jews of the Grand Duchy of Posen in 1834 and 1835*	Edward David Luft
145005	*Suburban Communities: The Jewishness of American Reform Jews*	Gerald L. Showstack
145007	*Ethnic Survival in America*	David Schoem

Brown Studies in Religion

147001	*Religious Writings and Religious Systems Volume 1*	Jacob Neusner, et al
147002	*Religious Writings and Religious Systems Volume 2*	Jacob Neusner, et al
147003	*Religion and the Social Sciences*	Robert Segal